INFORMAL SERVICES IN ASIAN CITIES
LESSONS FOR URBAN PLANNING AND MANAGEMENT FROM THE COVID-19 PANDEMIC

Edited by Ashok Das and Bambang Susantono

Asian Development Bank Institute
Kasumigaseki Building 8F
3-2-5, Kasumigaseki, Chiyoda-ku
Tokyo 100-6008, Japan
www.adbi.org

Asian Development Bank
6 ADB Avenue, Mandaluyong City,
1550 Metro Manila, Philippines
Tel +63 2 8632 4444; Fax +63 2 8636 2444
www.adb.org

Some rights reserved. Published in 2022.

ISBN 978-4-89974-261-6 (Print);
ISBN 978-4-89974-262-3 (PDF)
DOI: https://doi.org/10.56506/DYXR6960

ISBN 978-92-9269-716-7 (print);
978-92-9269-717-4 (electronic);
978-92-9269-718-1 (ebook)
Publication Stock No. SPR220359-2
DOI: http://dx.doi.org/10.22617/SPR220359-2

The views in this publication do not necessarily reflect the views and policies of the Asian Development Bank Institute (ADBI), its Advisory Council, ADB's Board or Governors, or the governments of ADB members.

ADBI and ADB do not guarantee the accuracy of the data included in this publication and accepts no responsibility for any consequence of their use. The mention of specific companies or products of manufacturers does not imply that they are endorsed or recommended by ADB in preference to others of a similar nature that are not mentioned.

ADBI and ADB use proper ADB member names and abbreviations throughout and any variation or inaccuracy, including in citations and references, should be read as referring to the correct name. By making any designation of or reference to a particular territory or geographic area, or by using the term "recognize," "country," or other geographical names in this publication, ADBI and ADB do not intend to make any judgments as to the legal or other status of any territory or area.

Please contact pubsmarketing@adb.org if you have questions or comments with respect to content, or if you wish to obtain copyright permission for your intended use that does not fall within these terms, or for permission to use the ADB or ADBI logo.

Notes:
(i)   In this publication, "$" refers to United States dollars.
(ii) ADB recognizes "China" as the People's Republic of China; "Hong Kong" as Hong Kong, China; "Laos" as the Lao People's Democratic Republic; "Vietnam" as Viet Nam; and "Russia" as the Russian Federation.

Contents

Tables, Figures, and Maps

8. Informal Micro, Small, and Medium-Sized Enterprises and Digitalization: Challenges and Policy Actions in Indonesia

9. Fintech, Government Aid, and Informal Household Businesses in ASEAN Economies during the Pandemic

10. Post-Pandemic Employment Recovery: Case Study of Tricycle Drivers in Metro Manila
Table

Figure

Abbreviations

ADB	Asian Development Bank
ADBI	Asian Development Bank Institute
ASEAN	Association of Southeast Asian Nations
BPS	Badan Pusat Statistik, Indonesia
CBO	community-based organization
CIO	community implementation organization
CLP	community-led project
COVID-19	coronavirus disease
CSG	Community Stakeholder Group
CSO	civil society organization
DAK	Special Allocation Fund
DFS	Dhaka Food System
DMC	developing member country
ECQ	enhanced community quarantine
FAO	Food and Agriculture Organization of the United Nations
FGD	focus group discussion
FSM	fecal sludge management
GCQ	general community quarantine
GDP	gross domestic product
GPS	global positioning system
IFC	International Finance Corporation
ILO	International Labour Organization
LPM	linear probability model
LSIP	Livable Settlements Investment Project
MBO	member-based organization
MDP	multidimensional poverty
MPWH	Ministry of Public Works and Housing, Indonesia
MSEs	micro and small enterprises
MSMEs	micro, small, and medium-sized enterprises
NCR	National Capital Region
NGO	nongovernment organization
NIS	National Institute of Statistics of Cambodia
NMES	Nepal Mahila Ekata Samaj
NUA	New Urban Agenda
NUSP	Neighborhood Upgrading and Shelter Project
OECD	Organisation for Economic Co-operation and Development

O&M	operation and maintenance
OMS	Open Market Sales
PRRM	Philippine Rural Reconstruction Movement
PSBB	Pembatasan Sosial Berskala Besar (large-scale social restrictions)
PUV	public utility vehicle
RISE	Revitalising Informal Settlements and Their Environments
SDG	Sustainable Development Goal
SJP	Shobar Jonno Pani
SMEs	small and medium-sized enterprises
TA	technical assistance
TBC	Toilet Board Coalition
TODA	Tricycle Operators and Drivers' Association
TPA	Tubig Pag Asa Inc.
UCCR	Urban Climate Change Resilience
UCCRTF	Urban Climate Change Resilience Trust Fund
UNDP	United Nations Development Programme
UN-Habitat	United Nations Human Settlements Programme
WHO	World Health Organization

Currency Equivalents

(As of 16 August 2022)

Currency unit	–	Bangladeshi taka (Tk)
$1.00	=	95.500
Tk1.00	=	00.010

Currency unit	–	Philippine peso (₱)
$1.00	=	56.020
₱1.00	=	00.018

Acknowledgments

This book aims to contribute to a better understanding of urban informality, shed light on the functioning of informality in key urban sectors, and provide new insights to improve guidelines and policy dialogues for more effective urban planning and infrastructure development.

The Asian Development Bank (ADB) and the Asian Development Bank Institute (ADBI) have jointly published this knowledge product, funded under the regional technical assistance, Asia Infrastructure Insights, being implemented by the Economic Analysis and Operational Support Division (EREA) of ADB's Economic Research and Regional Cooperation Department (ERCD). The book was initiated and co-edited by Bambang Susantono, former ADB Vice-President for Knowledge Management and Sustainable Development (VPKM). Ashok Das, an associate professor in the Urban and Regional Planning Department at the University of Hawaiʻi at Mānoa, was the lead editor, who also guided the conceptualization of the book's structure and foci. Overall project guidance came from Tetsushi Sonobe, dean and chief executive officer of ADBI; Sonoko Suyanama, senior advisor to VPKM; Albert Park, chief economist and director general of ERCD; Joseph Zveglich Jr., deputy chief economist of ERCD; and Lei Lei Song, director of EREA.

This book brings together the knowledge and expertise of 32 authors from around the world (see section on About the Authors). The study and publication process were made possible through the collaboration of staff and teams from ADB, the University of Hawaiʻi, and ADBI. Aimee Hampel-Milagrosa, with assistance from Ashok Das, led the overall publication process, with research and technical support from Jindra Nuella Samson, Lotis Quiao, Orlee Velarde, Joel Temple, and Alice Terry. Fahad Khan guided the implementation of the project's initial phases and organization of the consultation workshops. Gee Ann Burac and Amanda Mamon provided administrative support. The manuscript was copyedited by Cyrel San Gabriel, with inputs from Ashok Das, and proofreading was done by Tuesday Soriano and the ADBI Publication Focal Unit, consisting of Adam Majoe and Oliver Xavier A. Reyes. The book cover and typesetting layout were by Mike Cortes, and the cover design by Ashok Das. Special thanks to Karen Lane, Sarah A. O'Connor, and Duncan McLeod for advice on the ADBI–ADB publication agreements and process; Rodel Bautista, Cynthia Hidalgo, Ma. Katrina M. Fernando, and Melissa dela Torre for the compliance review, events, and web launch support; Ma. Rosario D. Celestino and Razel Gonzaga for printing support; Terje Lange, Lean Alfred Santos, and Maria Angeline B. Garcia for the external and social media outreach.

This book also benefited from external peer review by academics and expert researchers in the field of urban planning and development. We are very grateful for the advice and contributions of Lois M. Takahashi (University of Southern California), Robin King (World Resources Institute, Ross Center for Sustainable Cities), Jiwnath Ghimire (Iowa State University), Subhashni Raj (University of California, Davis), Anjali Mahendra (World Resources Institute, Ross Center for Sustainable Cities), Priyam Das (University of Hawai'i at Mānoa), Steve Commins (UCLA), Ajay Agarwal (Queen's University), and Gregory Randolph (University of Southern California). We also like to thank our ADB internal peer reviewers—ERCD economists Yi Jiang, Minhaj U. Mahmud, Aimee Hampel-Milagrosa, and Jasmin Sibal; and sector specialists from the Sustainable Development and Climate Change Department (SDCC) Arghya Sinha Roy, Navin K. Twarakavi, and Keiko Nowacka; and Chief of Urban Sector Group Manoj Sharma from SDCC. The extensive reviews ensured the quality and content of the book chapters.

This joint publication would not have been possible without the generous support of ADB's Office of the Vice-President for Knowledge Management and Sustainable Development—Woochong Um (managing director, Office of the President, also OIC-VPKM), Rosette Angelica Kapunan-Ong, and Marian Lagmay; the ADBI Publications Committee, chaired by Tetsushi Sonobe, whose members include Peter J. Morgan, David R. Hendrickson, Yohana Kho, Seungju Baek, and Hiroshi Takami; and Hanalei Abbott of the University of Hawai'i at Mānoa.

About the Editors

Ashok Das is an associate professor in the Department of Urban and Regional Planning, University of Hawai'i at Mānoa. Previously, he taught in the Department of Urban Studies and Planning, San Francisco State University. He received his doctor of philosophy (PhD) degree in urban planning from the University of California, Los Angeles (UCLA), and trained as a planner and architect at Kansas State University and at the School of Planning and Architecture, New Delhi. He has worked as an architecture and planning consultant, and was the chief cartoonist for *Architecture+Design*, a leading Indian magazine. His research explores institutional challenges to and innovations in ameliorating urban poverty through the provision of services in developing countries, especially in Southeast and South Asia. Community participation and empowerment, urban informality, slum upgrading, decentralization and local governance, inclusionary housing, and the role of civil society in fostering inclusive urbanization are his key interests. His recent work has explored community-managed integrated microfinance, disaster risk reduction, pro-poor shelter policies, planning education, and the platform economy's impacts on social mobility and economic resilience. A. Das jointly edited a book on the New Urban Agenda and inclusive and sustainable planning in Asia and the Pacific. He serves on the Global Planning Education Committee (GPEC) of the Association of the Collegiate Schools of Planning (ACSP) and has contributed advice and/or research to the Asian Development Bank (ADB), the Ford Foundation, the World Resources Institute, and UN-Habitat.

Bambang Susantono is ADB's former vice-president for knowledge management and sustainable development. As vice-president, B. Susantono was responsible for managing knowledge in ADB and coordinating research and studies on various topics such as energy, transport, water, education, health, finance, digital technology, and urban development; as well as cross-cutting nexus themes such as climate change, environment, governance, gender equality, social development, rural development and food security, and regional cooperation. He also coordinated ADB's annual flagship publications, including *Asian Development Outlook, Key Indicators for Asia and the Pacific,* and *Asian Economic Integration Report.*

In March 2022, B. Susantono was appointed as the Chairman of the Capital City (Ibu Kota Nusantara) Authority, the future capital city of Indonesia, set to be inaugurated in 2024.

B. Susantono has been a distinguished thought leader, author, and active researcher on sustainable development. He has taught at several universities and leading research institutes. He holds a PhD degree in infrastructure planning, and master's degrees in transportation engineering and in city and regional planning from the University of California, Berkeley. Prior to his ADB work, B. Susantono was the vice-minister of Indonesia's Ministry of Transportation and deputy minister for infrastructure and regional development, Ministry of Economic Affairs.

About the Authors

Lara Arjan is an urban planner with over 20 years of experience. She has worked extensively in the Middle East and North Africa region and Canada across a range of projects including urban planning, water resource management, and governance. At the Asian Development Bank (ADB), L. Arjan is an urban development specialist, and manages the Cities Development Initiative for Asia Trust Fund.

Jeetendra Prakash Aryal is a development and resource economist with experience of more than 25 years. He completed school education at Kirtipur Madhyamik Vidhyalaya, Kirtipur, Kathmandu, Nepal. J. P. Aryal earned his master of arts degree in macroeconomics at Tribhuvan University, Nepal, and master of science and doctor of philosophy (PhD) degrees in development and resource economics at the Norwegian University of Life Sciences, Norway.

Joy Amor Bailey is an urban climate change resilience specialist at ADB's Urban Climate Change Resilience Trust Fund (UCCRTF). J. A. Bailey is involved with various international development organizations in Asia and the Pacific implementing projects on climate change, urban governance, and environmental protection. J. A. Bailey is an urban planner and earned an MSc in Environmental Change and Management from the University of Oxford.

Isabel Blackett has recently worked on assignments in Asia with the World Bank, ADB, Bill & Melinda Gates Foundation, WaterAid, and German Agency for International Cooperation (GIZ), among others. Her interests are in increasing equity and working with governments in developing at-scale, poor-inclusive urban sanitation services. From 2005 to 2016, she worked for the World Bank's Water and Sanitation Program and helped develop pro-poor urban sanitation in Indonesia, Viet Nam, the Philippines, Pacific Island countries, and South Asia. Previously, she worked in Southern Africa and East Africa for the United Nations International Children's Emergency Fund (UNICEF), Department for International Development of the United Kingdom (DFID), Credit Institute for Reconstruction (KfW), Danish International Development Agency (Danida), consulting firms, and nongovernment organizations. I. Blackett received a master's degree from the Water, Engineering and Development Centre, Loughborough University.

Panharoth Chhay joined the Asian Development Bank Institute (ADBI) as a research associate in May 2021. She graduated with a PhD degree in development economics from Kobe University. A chapter of her PhD dissertation has been published in a peer-reviewed journal World Development. Her previous research experience is in the field of applied micro-development economics.

Syngjoo Choi is a professor of economics at Seoul National University, Republic of Korea, and is co-director of the Center for Experimental and Behavioral Social Science at Seoul National University. Previously, he worked as an assistant and (tenured) associate professor at University College London, United Kingdom, and served on the Editorial Board of the Review of Economic Studies. He received his PhD in economics from New York University in 2006. His research interests include experimental economics and behavioral economics with particular emphasis on large-scale data collection with experimental methods to measure and identify policy impacts. His research has been published in Science, American Economic Review, Journal of the European Economic Association, and other international journals.

Priyam Das is an associate professor and chair of the Department of Urban and Regional Planning at the University of Hawai'i at Mānoa. She studies urban water governance and access to basic services, focusing on issues of inequality, poverty, and disenfranchisement.

Penny Dutton is an independent consultant with 30 years of experience in social, gender, and community development on water supply, sanitation, and hygiene projects in the Asia and Pacific region. She has worked with the World Bank Water and Sanitation Program, ADB, UNICEF, Department of Foreign Affairs and Trade (DFAT), New Zealand Ministry of Foreign Affairs and Trade (MFAT), WaterAid, Danida, and European Union. P. Dutton has a long-standing interest in improving water supply and sanitation for informal settlements and unserved urban areas.

Joris van Etten is an outposted senior urban development specialist to the ADB Resident Mission in Indonesia. Over the past 20 years, he has worked with cities in more than 40 countries. Currently, J. van Etten oversees the preparation and implementation of ADB urban projects and manages the ASEAN – Australia Smart Cities Trust Fund. Prior to joining ADB, J. van Etten worked for GIZ, UN-HABITAT, the European Commission, and the Institute for Housing and Urban Development Studies.

Hyuncheol Bryant Kim is an associate professor in the Economics Department at Hong Kong University of Science and Technology, and an assistant professor in the Department of Policy Analysis and Management at Cornell University, United States. He is an applied empirical microeconomist focusing on causal impacts of policy interventions in health and education sectors through large-scale data analysis and social experiment. The main goal of his research is to understand the fundamental relationship between human capital investment and individual and societal well-being in Africa and Asia. He received a master's degree from Yonsei University, Republic of Korea, and a PhD degree in economics from Columbia University. His research has been published in leading journals such as Science, Review of Economics and Statistics, Journal of Public Economics, Journal of Health Economics, and other international journals.

Kim Kunhyui is a PhD candidate in international economics at the Graduate School of Asia-Pacific Studies, Waseda University. Before joining ADBI, he worked as a research associate at the Economic Research Institute for ASEAN and East Asia and is currently a learning assistant at Waseda University, teaching econometrics. His research interests include economic development and growth, and regulation.

Saiful Momen teaches at the Department of Environmental Science and Management of the North South University. He is interested in the spatial pattern of economy and demography that is taking shape in the developing world. In addition to studying the political and economic processes that are producing the spatial pattern (often one of polarization), he is interested in nonconventional solutions to environmental problems at the scale of urban areas or smaller units. His recent research includes exploring the potential of rooftops in Dhaka city as quasi-parks, making parts of tertiary neighborhood roads temporary parks, and examining ways to incentivize or induce sorting of household waste at source.

Peter J. Morgan is a senior consulting economist and advisor to the dean of ADBI. Previously, he had 23 years of experience in the financial sector in Asia. His research interests are macroeconomic policy, financial sector regulation and reform, financial development, financial inclusion, fintech, financial literacy, and financial education.

Janet Naco is a community development worker. She has worked with the Food and Agriculture Organization of the United Nations (FAO), International Rescue Committee (IRC), and Helen Keller International (HKI) in Bangladesh over the last 5 years. The focus of her work is on gender, urban food security and nutrition, and protection in humanitarian emergencies. Before embarking on her career in community development, J. Naco was a qualitative researcher at HKI, which is based in Chittagong Hill Tracts, Bangladesh.

Siho Park is a PhD student at University of Illinois at Urbana-Champaign, with an interest in development and behavioral economics. He is currently working as a research assistant in impact evaluation studies in the Philippines and Tonga. S. Park obtained a master's degree in economics from the Chinese University of Hong Kong.

Ellen Pascua worked as a water fund administrator for the Water Financing Partnership Facility. Currently, she provides overall support to the Water Sector Group Secretariat. Before joining ADB in 2003, E. Pascua was a program manager at the Philippine Department of Interior and Local Government's Water Supply and Sanitation Program Management Office where she worked for 17 years, from 1986 to 2003. Her work involved looking after the provision of drinking water supply and sanitation in local government units outside Metro Manila. E. Pascua holds a degree in bachelor of arts in economics.

Neeta Pokhrel is chief of the Water Sector Group. She has over 25 years of experience working with ADB, the private sector, international consulting firms, nongovernment organizations, and water utilities. N. Pokhrel currently leads the strategic development of ADB's water sector and provides knowledge management and implementation support to the operational departments to meet ADB's goal of a resilient and water-secure Asia and the Pacific.

Dil B. Rahut is vice-chair and senior research fellow at ADBI. His research focuses on development microeconomics, agricultural economics, and environmental and natural resource economics. Before joining ADBI, he worked for the International Maize and Wheat Improvement Center, South Asian University, Bank of Bhutan Ltd., Indian Council for Research on International Economic Relations, WorldFish Centre, and Royal Authority of Bhutan. D. B. Rahut received his PhD degree in agricultural economics from Bonn University.

Yasuyuki Sawada is a professor at the Faculty of Economics, University of Tokyo, Japan, and director of the Center for Research and Education in Program Evaluation (CREPE) of the university. From 2017 to 2021, he was ADB's chief economist. His key research areas are development economics, the economics of disasters, and field surveys and experiments. Y. Sawada obtained his PhD degree in economics from Stanford University.

Virinder Sharma is a principal urban development specialist in ADB's Sustainable Development and Climate Change Department. He acts as a program manager of a $150 million multidonor trust fund—the Urban Climate Change Resilience Trust Fund—supported by the Government of the United Kingdom, the Swiss State Secretariat for Economic Affairs, and The Rockefeller Foundation. V. Sharma is a development professional with 30 years of experience with ADB; UK Foreign, Commonwealth and Development Office/ Department for International Development; and the Government of India in designing and implementing multidisciplinary programs.

Lakpa Sherpa is an architect and an urban planner. She received a degree in urban and regional planning and a certificate in disaster management and humanitarian assistance from the University of Hawai'i. L. Sherpa's research interests include inclusive urbanization, participatory planning, and disaster risk reduction. Currently, she is working as an Innovative Partnership Fund expert facilitating the provincial and local government in Nepal to attain functional, sustainable, inclusive, and accountable governance.

Shigehiro Shinozaki is a senior economist at ADB. He supports ADB's developing member countries in improving small and medium-sized enterprise (SME) access to finance through various technical assistance projects. His advisory and research expertise includes policy issues in SME development, inclusive finance, and financial sector development especially in developing Asia. Prior to joining ADB, S. Shinozaki held several expert positions at Japan's Ministry of Finance, the Organisation for Economic Co-operation and Development in France, and as Japan International Cooperation Agency expert in Indonesia. He holds a PhD degree in international studies from Waseda University in Japan.

John Taylor is an urban planner who has worked with both FAO and the United Nations Development Programme in Dhaka, Bangladesh over the last 6 years. His work focuses on issues of urban poverty, food systems, nutrition and food security, and urban governance. Prior to moving to Bangladesh, J. Taylor was director and co-founder of the Indonesian nongovernment organization Kota Kita.

Tiffany M. Tran is a Vietnamese-American architect and urban designer who is passionate about livable cities. She approaches urban development from a people-centric lens that integrates urban planning and development economics. T. M. Tran has a decade of experience partnering with government and private sector clients, including in Indonesia, Ghana, Viet Nam, and the United States. Her policy areas of focus include urban poverty and informality.

Long Q. Trinh joined ADBI as a project consultant in July 2015. His current research interests include financial development (including fintech and financial inclusion in Asia), small and medium-sized enterprise development, international trade, structural change, and economic growth. Before joining ADBI, he had worked as an economist at the Central Institute for Economic Management (CIEM), Viet Nam's leading think-tank, for more than 10 years. L. Q. Trinh received his PhD degree from the National Graduate Institute for Policy Studies in Tokyo, Japan.

Christian Walder is a water supply and sanitation specialist in the Water Sector Group of ADB's Sustainable Development and Climate Change Department. Trained as an environmental engineer, his work focuses on inclusive and sustainable water supply and sanitation solutions. He provides technical expert advice to ADB operations departments and develops knowledge management programs to keep water supply and sanitation high on ADB's development agenda.

Takashi Yamano is a principal economist at ADB's Economic Research and Regional Cooperation Department. His current responsibilities include conducting economic research and reviewing project economic analysis. Prior to joining ADB in 2017, he worked at the International Rice Research Institute, the National Graduate Institute for Policy Studies, Japan, and the World Bank. T. Yamano obtained a joint PhD degree in economics and agricultural economics at Michigan State University in 2000.

Foreword

The global coronavirus disease (COVID-19) pandemic has made policy makers realize that the condition of the informal sector determines how flexibly societies can mitigate the effects of and recover from major health and economic crises. This realization was almost instantaneous. At the onset of global mobility and social interaction restrictions, informal service providers were quick to adapt and carry out important services where formal providers have ceased to operate. Immediately after the crisis, the speed of economic recovery was found to strongly depend on the aggregate systems resilience of societies. This meant that the economy is only as strong as its weakest link—communities at the margins of society, dependent on the informal sector for shelter and livelihoods—and supporting it in a similar fashion as the formal sector is of paramount importance.

The pandemic has shown that inclusive urban planning entails due consideration for the informal sector, whether it is for providing basic water supply and sanitation services, or supporting employment or sustaining livelihoods through small and medium-sized enterprises (SMEs). At the height of the pandemic, government measures to help workers and SMEs cope financially with disruptions brought about by lockdowns proved largely ineffective. In the Asia and Pacific region, where around 70% of employment is informal, governments still found themselves with few mechanisms to mitigate the negative impacts of COVID-19. In 2020, the Asian Development Bank (ADB) called for rethinking social protection measures to target the most vulnerable groups—those hit hardest by the crisis. Interventions such as direct electronic emergency cash transfers to households, coverage for testing and treatment of COVID-19, and financial support for microenterprises are some key policy responses that ADB has identified to support the informal sector.

Initial lessons clearly pointed to the need to abandon a business-as-usual approach toward the informal sector. Traditional methods of policy and planning engagement need to be reconfigured. Innovations in technical project designs, as well as approaches to capacity building and community participation, need to be devised in ways that can transform the informal sector—from mere spectator or recipient of development to cocreator of urban futures. To secure urban futures and remain true to its commitment to a prosperous, inclusive, resilient, and sustainable Asia and the Pacific, ADB cannot ignore informality.

The short-term and long-term impacts of climate change on the informal sector also cannot be ignored; with this in mind, recovery from the COVID-19 pandemic should be used as an opportunity to direct resources for "building back better and greener." The informal sector counts as one of ADB's many partners in steering Asia's growth—whether in innovative investment projects, knowledge sharing activities, or dialogues.

This book presents unique perspectives that illuminate informal urban services provision during the COVID-19 pandemic, as well as lessons that can guide the advancement of inclusive urban planning. It presents the scholarly research of leading experts on urban informality and their latest experience and insights on productive engagement with the informal sector. Bambang Susantono, former ADB Vice-President for Knowledge Management and Sustainable Development, initiated this book project and invited Ashok Das to guide it, given his extensive research experience with urban informality. Prepared jointly by ADB and the Asian Development Bank Institute (ADBI), this publication harnesses the expertise and knowledge of both these and other institutions, to show the breadth of progressive practice in engaging with informality in urban services in the region. The pandemic should be leveraged as a renewed opportunity for urban planners and policy makers to treat the informal sector as the vanguard of socioeconomic resilience. We hope that lessons from this book will not only guide urban planning in Asia and the Pacific but also contribute to a recognition of the informal sector as an indispensable partner in development in the region and beyond.

Bambang Susantono
Former ADB Vice-President for
Knowledge Management and
Sustainable Development (VPKM)

Tetsushi Sonobe
Dean and Chief Executive Officer
ADBI

1

Introduction: Urban Informality and the COVID-19 Pandemic

Ashok Das and Bambang Susantono

1. Urban Informality

Urban informality is now increasingly recognized as a corollary of urbanization. Although it has been variously defined, a common understanding of informality is a lack of conformity to some degree with "formal," such as legally established and recognized institutions, rules and regulations, and practices. The lives and livelihoods of millions in developing Asia and elsewhere in the Global South or developing economies, are deeply linked to the pervasive informal sector.[1] Among them are the urban poor who work in the informal economy and reside in informal settlements, such as squatter settlements and slums—informality's most visible manifestation—and millions more depend on it directly or indirectly (Chen and Beard 2018). The term "informal sector" has a broad ambit, implying the

---

[1] For consistency across chapters, this book uses the term "developing economies" to also allude to what many scholars call the "Global South." According to Dados and Connell (2012), the Global South largely refers to developing regions in Africa, Asia, and Oceania that are at different stages of the development continuum. Using "Global South" in urban planning research is relevant and instrumental for conceptualizing innovative ways to address these cities' unique issues and conditions. These pertain to their institutions and the built form, which still reflect legacies shaped by colonialism, as well as evolving state–society interactions, all of which are significantly different from regions in the so-called developed North, from where today's dominant planning logics and approaches have emerged (Watson 2013). See also Dados and Connell (2012: 13) and Mahler (2017). However, it is important to note that, albeit much less, conditions and challenges like those in the Global South also exist in developed economies.

production and consumption of goods and services through modes and practices of informality, which can be spatial, economic, and/or political. Globally, in developing economies, it is estimated that the informal sector contributes 30% to GDP and 70% of all employment; and the productivity gap between the formal and informal sectors is significant (World Bank 2019a).

In 2002, the International Labour Organization (ILO) was arguably the first multilateral institution to lay out an integrated approach to appreciate informality with its Resolution and Conclusions on Decent Work and Informal Economy. ILO initiated the development of statistical measures to explain the informal sector and officially defined the "informal economy" as all economic activities by workers and economic units that are, *de jure* or *de facto*, not covered or insufficiently covered by formal arrangements. The informal economy was recognized as comprising small or undefined workplaces; unsafe and unhealthy working conditions; low levels of skills and productivity; low or irregular incomes; long working hours; and lack of access to information, markets, finance, training, and technology. Workers in the informal economy were mostly not recognized, registered, regulated, or subject to any form of labor laws or social protection. The lack of development, services, and institutions for promoting and regulating markets were seen as some root causes of informality. In 2015, ILO adopted the *Transition from Informal to the Formal Economy Recommendation* (R.204) to advance the attainment of decent work and economic growth, which is Goal 8 (SDG 8) of the Sustainable Development Goals (SDGs) under the United Nations 2030 Agenda for Sustainable Development.

In October 2016, the New Urban Agenda (NUA) of the United Nations, steered by UN-Habitat, recognized the growing inequality and multiple forms and dimensions of poverty evident in rising urban informality and poverty in both developed and developing countries (United Nations 2017). The NUA is committed to supporting and promoting equally shared opportunities and benefits that urbanization can offer to enable all urban dwellers—whether temporary or permanent, and whether living in formal or informal settlements—to lead decent, dignified, and rewarding lives toward attaining their full human potential. These aim to support the pursuit of SDGs, particularly SDG 11—to make cities and human settlements inclusive, safe, resilient, and sustainable—by providing a comprehensive framework to guide and track urbanization.

Brisk, urbanization-led economic growth in Asia in recent decades has caused unprecedented poverty reduction, but poverty has become more urban and urban inequality has risen. Most poor urban dwellers pursue precarious livelihoods in the informal sector. It is where the debilitating effects of urban inequality are the starkest, but it is also where the poor and the vulnerable become resilient (Cervero 2000; Gulyani and Talukdar 2010). In 2020, cascading exigencies caused by the coronavirus disease (COVID-19) pandemic revealed the urban informal sector's expansiveness and pervasiveness and, in terms of health and otherwise, the vulnerabilities of the poor who depend on it like never before (Corburn et al. 2020; Vijayan 2020). This is why the time is apt for a book of this nature to deepen our understanding of the informal sector in Asia, and how the COVID-19 pandemic has impacted it. This book brings together rich insights on different aspects of urban informality, informal sector services, and the impacts thereon of COVID-19 by presenting the work of researchers at the Asian Development Bank (ADB), the Asian Development Bank Institute (ADBI), other multilateral institutions, as well as academics and independent researchers.

This introductory chapter is organized into five sections. The second section traces a quick epistemological trajectory of how, over the decades, developments in scholarship and practice have influenced how planning and policy making view and engage with the urban informal sector. The third section provides a snapshot of how the efforts of multilateral institutions have helped to illuminate the critical needs of and COVID-19's impacts on the informal sector in Asian cities. The fourth section then presents a brief overview of the history and status of ADB's involvement with urban informality. The fifth section delineates the book's structure and organization and introduces the foci and content of each chapter.

2. Seeing Informality Differently: Historical Trajectories, Epistemic Shifts, and Progressive Influences on Planning and Governance

The practical policy and planning need for earnestly investigating the informal sector is underscored by recent global development consensuses that reflect the accumulated wisdom of long-standing as well as emergent planning scholarship. In the last 15 years or so, much research has demonstrated the inaccuracy and futility of viewing the so-called formal and informal as binaries—legal versus illegal, regular versus irregular, poor versus privileged, desirable versus undesirable, and so forth (Roy and AlSayyad 2004; Banks, Lombard, and Mitlin 2020). For instance, rejecting all state intervention by unequivocally celebrating slums as enterprising (Turner and Fichter 1972; Turner 1977) or simplistically saying that, to resolve the issue of slums, all the state needs to do is unleash dead capital by granting squatters titles (de Soto 2000). Scholars have called for a new epistemology of planning that embraces informality; as a consequence of urbanization, it is inseparable from formality (Roy 2005).

The preponderance of narrow and dichotomous views about informality is exemplified by what was a long-standing debate on whether slums are "spaces of hope" or "spaces of despair" (Chambers 2005; Lloyd 1979). Moreover, the convenience of associating slums and poverty with illegality, vice, and crime also serves to uphold popular disdain for urban informality. Research has traced back the genealogy of prevalent, largely negative, societal notions, and policy attitudes toward informality in developing economies to the efforts of the late 19th and early 20th century urban reformers and chroniclers in Europe and the United States. The genealogy exposed untold destitution and deprivation in fast-industrializing cities of the era (such as Jacob Riis's documentation and photographs of abject poverty and squalid conditions in New York City tenements). This has also fostered and deepened popular myths that slums are hotbeds and nurseries of crime, vice, and immorality (Nuissl and Heinrichs 2013; UN-Habitat 2003). In the post-World War II era, concepts such as Oscar Lewis's "culture of poverty" theory (Lewis 1963)—which argued that sustained poverty generated cultural beliefs, values, attitudes, and practices that prevented people from escaping poverty even if structural barriers gave away—underplayed the debilitating power of structural factors and institutional forces, and propelled the notion of personal and collective responsibility (Small, Harding, and Lamont 2010). Lewis's ideas stemmed from his research on poor communities in Mexico, Puerto Rico, and elsewhere, and, albeit controversial, they influenced strong policy action in the United States, which then likely influenced perceptions and policies pertaining to urban poverty and informality internationally.

The decades following World War II also saw the rise of post-colonial nation states, particularly in Asia and Africa. Emerging from the long shadow of colonialism, these young nation states lacked adequate institutional, human resources, and technical capacities to build systems and approaches to development and planning that are sensitive to the needs and peculiarities of their own societies. Uneven development within countries, limited economic opportunities largely concentrated in cities, and weak agriculture and other primary sector economic activities in rural areas saw urban populations rise rapidly, especially in primate cities, due to rural–urban migration (Chambers 2005). Until the

1990s, policy and planning responses to growing informality in terms of shelter, services, and livelihoods due to rapid urbanization in the post-colonial, developing states reflected an inadequate understanding of migration, slum formation, informal sector dynamics; a narrow application of property rights; and a lack of awareness of the multiple dimensions of poverty. The following paragraphs highlight how, over the decades, our understanding and treatment of informality has gradually progressed due to evolving research and/or pioneering planning practice innovations in areas such as migration, shelter and services provision, property rights, livelihoods, resilience thinking, and the enlargement of community participation with increasing collaborative planning and governance.

2.1 Migration and Informality

Given a paucity of extensive and interdisciplinary research on migration to cities, urban policy making and planning have long assumed flawed premises. Rural to urban migration is widely [mis]understood as a one-way and permanent process that is largely responsible for sustained urban poverty and growing urban informality. This view prevails because narrow economic explanations of rural to urban migration, such as the Todaro (1969) and Harris and Todaro (1970) models, have dominated policy thinking in the developing world. These models narrowly considered low wages in the agriculture sector as the primary driver of urban migration, which exacerbated conditions in urban labor markets. Although the empirical validity of these models has been widely questioned, their persistent influence continues to encourage government policies that seek to restrict internal migration; and, in fact, such misguided policies have sharply increased since the 1990s (Fox 2014). Renewed interest in migration research in recent decades has illuminated the diversity and complexity of migration dynamics (Schmidt-Kallert 2012; Tacoli 2003). Therefore, an entrenched urban–rural policy dichotomy ignores the dynamic, cyclical, and interdependent nature of rural–urban linkages (Tacoli, McGranahan, and Satterthwaite 2015); yet, to manage internal migration better, how government policies should intervene or for what objectives is hardly any clearer today (Lall, Selod, and Shalizi 2006). National and local policies continue to discriminate against migrants when providing essential services and welfare support.

The upshot of rapid urbanization across the developing world, mostly due to rural to urban migration, was the proliferation of slums and squatter settlements. This was also at a time when states lacked effective planning capacity and policies to address informality. Extensive demolitions and evictions comprised the dominant state response to slums prior to the 1970s (Sumka 1987).

The preponderance of a dichotomous view of legality, which treats the informal as illegal, encouraged slum demolition and squatter eviction in developing economies. Such practices became legitimized and commonplace, but they have hardly prevented the emergence of slums because, for those affected, the benefits of proximity and access outweigh the risk of eviction. Although such practices are waning, they are still in effect. This is because many policymakers, public officials, and planners fail to appreciate that slums, usually, are the consequence of multiple push factors—economic, social, political, and environmental—as well as the inadequacy of urban services and affordable housing supply.

2.2 Shelter, Basic Services, and Informality

Beginning in the 1960s, influential writings by anthropologists like William Mangin and architects like John F.C. Turner, both of whom had for years closely observed informal settlements in Peru and elsewhere in Latin America, shed valuable light on slum origins, growth, and life (Mangin 1967; Turner and Fichter 1972). Turner's contributions were pivotal in advancing the idea of "self-help" as a housing policy alternative to improve the quality of life in indigent informal settlements, and in exhorting the global urbanization and shelter discourse to see informality's constructive side. Turner's philosophy of bottom-up, self-help housing was influenced by ideas expounded by urban thinkers such as Charles Abrams, Jacob Crane, Patrick Geddes, and Peter Kropotkin (Das 2020; Harris 1999; Harris 2003). Between 1960s and 1980s, Turner and others revealed how, with neither state support nor interference, squatters had incrementally improved their individual homes to sustain their livelihoods and cultures, thereby creating thriving communities with robust social networks (see, for instance, Perlman 1979). This fostered the notions of not displacing squatters to prevent their vital economic webs and social safety nets from fraying, and enabling the urban poor to build their own homes over time. Deep ethnographic research also started emerging from elsewhere—offering nuanced insights into the lives of people in informal urban settlements and their aspirations, trials and tribulations, social capital, and potential for collective action, as well as how urban development initiatives' quick "modernization" of the city often harm the poor (for example, see Guinness 1986 and

Jellinek 1991). Extensive research efforts in developing countries have underscored that *in situ* slum upgrading and even carefully designed "sites-and-services" projects should be prioritized within shelter policies because they embody the logics of self-help and incremental development (Gulyani 2016; King et al. 2017).

In the late 1960s, in preparing the city of Surabaya's first masterplan, Johan Silas, a young architect who shared Turner's views on self-help and community-driven development, proposed to preserve the city's *kampung* (traditional, slum-like neighborhoods that were poor and pervasive across much of the city) instead of demolishing and redeveloping them (Das and King 2019; Silas 1984). This radical departure from the common Indonesian urban development approach was meant to protect people's livelihoods and not upend their socioeconomic ties, and stoke a latent culture of collective self-help (Das 2020; Das and King 2019). Jakarta also initiated a similar project around the same time. These two projects saw the local governments deliver just physical infrastructure and services, such as roads, footpaths, water supply, drains, and community toilets. Nevertheless, these inputs by the state catalyzed gradual yet unprecedented investment by the people to upgrade their homes and habitats. This was feasible due to the flexibility derived from abandoning the rigid imposition of standardized land use regulations and building ordinances, and enabling community participation and autonomy at the neighborhood level. The long-sustained, citywide upgrading and preservation of *kampung* today makes Surabaya a rare city that offers its low-income residents affordable shelter and informal livelihood options even in central areas (Das and King 2019). The effectiveness of these pioneering *in situ* (at the original site) upgrading experiments encouraged the World Bank and other development agencies to fund several Kampung Improvement Programs (KIPs), whose countrywide implementation is estimated to have reduced Indonesia's urban poverty by about three-quarters. (Das and King 2019; Silas 1984).

Until the late 1980s, sites-and-services was another dominant policy that relocated entire squatter settlements to "serviced" sites on the urban fringe, with roads, water supply, sewerage, electricity, and even homes with property titles (Mayo and Gross 1987). Overall, these complex and heavily subsidized projects struggled to recover costs (Mayo and Gross 1987), harmed livelihoods and social networks (UN-Habitat 2003), and promoted downward raiding, whereby wealthier households supplanted the original beneficiaries (Gilbert 1997). However, some projects did succeed in Africa and Latin America (Buckley and Kalarickal 2006). In South Asia, as growth over 2 decades expanded the city outwards, the once fringed project sites transformed into thriving communities (Gulyani 2016). Besides broadening the urban poor's access to the housing market, successful sites-and-services projects created well-planned, well-serviced, livable, mixed income, and inclusive neighborhoods that developed incrementally. But sites-and-services projects were not predicated on community participation, something now deemed instrumental for more effective outcomes.

2.3 Property Rights, Tenure Security, and Informality

The rise of neoliberal policy thinking in the mid-1980s advocated rolling back the state from active development and service provision to allow for the growth of market actors. For example, the World Bank's "enabling markets to work" agenda for housing sector and institutional reform in developing countries (World Bank 1993) caused a shift from supply-side to demand-side approaches (Pugh 1997), and pushed complex shelter policy reforms toward integrating land development, finance, and social and economic development (Buckley and Kalarickal 2005). Expectedly, the 1990s and early 2000s saw strong calls for extending private property rights to the urban poor (De Soto 1989; 2000), almost as a panacea to resolve the urban informality and poverty conundrum, and a growing emphasis on developing housing finance and alternative financing options for the poor (Ferguson 1999; Ferguson and Smets 2010). However, by exposing the fallibility of the minimal state in shelter delivery, research has also challenged the notion that private property rights, titling, and home ownership improve credit access (Goldfinch 2015) and tenure security (Payne, Durand-Lasserve, and Rakodi 2009). Increased access to formal housing finance and property rights also exacerbated spatial and socioeconomic segregation (Monkkonen 2012). Indeed, as globalization and neoliberalism deepened, labor and shelter informality spread and worsened (Kundu and Kundu 2010). The retrenchment of public expenditures and services, liberal flows of global capital, and relaxed development controls to boost investment in urban development have caused a marked uptick in megaprojects, displacements, and peri-urbanization (Shatkin 2016), and hindered pro-poor efforts by making employment more precarious, services scarcer, and housing dearer (Rolnik 2014).

The institution of neoliberal policies, at the global and national levels, and their limited success reflected a largely dichotomous view of property rights, and a lack of understanding of the mechanics of slum formation as well as the dynamics of informal markets that govern slum real estate. For too long, it was not even recognized that there are myriad types of informal settlements distinguished by different formation pathways and structural characteristics (UN-Habitat 2003), or that not all dwellings are owner-built and that thriving rental markets exist in slums (Kumar 1996). Policies aimed at extending tenure security to informal settlements continue to be governed by a narrow ownership versus rental dichotomy emblematic of western property rights regimes, while ignoring alternative and traditional, non-western tenurial arrangements. However, ample research now exists to demonstrate how tenure security in informal settlements exists along and evolves through a continuum (Payne 2001; 2002). Recent planning scholarship shows in granular detail how the form and function of informal real estate markets are shaped by legal systems governing property rights, by national and local policy, and by historical and geographic particularities of specific neighborhoods (Birch, Wachter, and Chattaraj 2016).

Scholars have decried the formal–informal dichotomy as false and unproductive because it is state policies and market forces that create informal settlements (Birch, Chattaraj, and Wachter 2016), which often provide the only affordable rental option for poor migrants (Naik 2019). Current planning wisdom holds that the most effective pro-poor shelter intervention is slum upgrading (King et al. 2017), which should allow communities and other stakeholders to participate, offer rights to land or tenure security, recognize the needs of renters, help sustain livelihoods, build social capital, and be citywide in scale (Das 2015; Imparato and Ruster 2003; UN-Habitat 2003).

2.4 Livelihoods and Informality

While much research and policy action has focused on informal settlements as providers of affordable shelter and essential services, relatively less attention has been paid to another invaluable service they provide—the opportunity for the urban poor to pursue a range of livelihood options that would otherwise be unavailable to them. In general, though not all, most people who reside in informal settlements also work in the large informal urban economy. Recent research efforts suggest that informal employment accounts for 46% to 86% of total employment in several cities of Africa, Asia, and Latin America (Chen and Beard 2018). Though their estimates and shares vary considerably across cities, regions, and countries, a major chunk of informal employment is in the form of self-employment in home-based enterprises (HBEs) and micro and small enterprises

(Strassman 1987; Tipple 2005). HBEs are particularly important for women's empowerment and advancing the gender objective of inclusive planning because for many women, these are often the only livelihood opportunities available. Civil society organizations (CSOs) around the world have long concentrated on empowering the working poor, especially women, in the informal economy to secure their livelihoods through various kinds of support such as for labor rights, tenure rights, and microfinance (Baruah 2010; Horn 2010). Among them are Women in Informal Employment: Globalizing and Organizing (WIEGO), a global network of regional member networks, organizations, and individuals, and Self-Employed Women's Association (SEWA), a national trade union with several affiliate organizations. Their efforts have firmly placed the issue of informal livelihoods and women's interests on research, policy, and planning agendas for urban poverty reduction at all scales (Chen, Roever, and Skinner 2016; Ezeadichie 2012; Rakodi and Lloyd-Jones 2002). The focus on informal sector livelihoods is gaining increasing policy attention because of its critical role in enabling urban resilience, a concept that is now atop urban planning and development agendas.

2.5   Resilience and Informality

Concerns over global warming and the increasing frequency of disasters and extreme weather events have triggered a burgeoning research interest in and policy and planning action for urban resilience. Influenced by resilience-thinking, whose interdisciplinary roots lie in the ecological and social sciences (Davoudi et al. 2012), creating resilient communities is a major planning objective causing a rethink of contemporary urban management (Cutter et al. 2008: 599). Increasingly severe and frequent recurring disasters, such as floods, in Asian cities (Chan et al. 2012) have laid bare how rapid urbanization, weak infrastructure, and iniquitous development exacerbate disaster impacts and render the poor and the informal sector disproportionately more vulnerable (Miller and Douglass 2016). Resilience-thinking has also nudged planners and policy makers to think of issues that have traditionally not been concerns of urban planning, such as food security (Raja et al. 2021).

Scholars have also long cautioned against these vulnerabilities that expanding cities now face, and pointed out how haphazard urbanization raises flood risks, which disproportionately affects the urban poor (Havlick 1986; Hollis 1975). The accumulation of research evidence suggests a new conceptualization to understand and enable community resilience (Cutter et al. 2008)—one that (i) distinguishes between inherent and adaptive resilience of a place, and

(ii) emphasizes appreciating at once the interplay of multiple systems (human-environment, social, political) and dimensions (ecological, social, economic, institutional, infrastructure, community competence). To attain social resilience, which is now rightfully gaining attention, promoting cohesion, collective action, and state-civil society/community relationships for policy making and planning are indispensable. This, nevertheless, is challenging because, apart and together, the concepts of community and resilience underscore tensions between continuity and change, between resistance and adaptation, and between inclusion and exclusion (Mulligan et al. 2016).

2.6 Civil Society, Participatory Planning, and Capabilities

After the end of the Cold War, along with expanding market forces and information access, the spread of democracy and rise of civil society worldwide (Anheier, Glasius, and Kaldor 2001) stoked participation in planning, governance, and development in the Global South (Mansuri and Rao 2013). Emerging research that articulated the understanding of social capital and the benefits of leveraging it for development and poverty alleviation (for instance, see Mayer 2003; Rydin and Pennington 2000) also contributed to a significant growth in civil society participation in planning and governance in Asia (Cheema 2013; Cheema and Popovski 2010). The vast body of Nobel laureate Amartya Sen's seminal scholarship on capabilities, exclusion, justice, and social choice has intricately exposed how marginalized groups are beset by "unfreedoms" that hinder the development of individuals, groups, and indeed entire societies (Sen 1999a; 1999b)—a concept fundamental to understanding and engaging with urban informality and poverty. Complementary contributions by other scholars such as Mahbub ul Haq (1995) and Martha Nussbaum (2000) helped push both discourse and practice of development and poverty beyond narrow income-based metrics toward appreciating complexity. The welcome upshot of their efforts is the creation and adoption of the Human Development Index (HDI) and the Multidimensional Poverty Index, and the emergence of progressive notions of inclusive urban governance (see for instance, Alkire et al. 2015 and Moser 1998). Likewise, the logics of collective action and co-production expounded by Elinor Ostrom and others have afforded the understanding to improve urban service delivery (Mitlin 2008). It is important and urgent to recognize that these seminal ideas and proven logics must be embodied in our approaches to dealing with informality.

Progressive planning theory concepts that have emerged in recent years in the west—such as multiculturalism (Sandercock 1998), the "right to the city" (Harvey 2008), the "just city" (Fainstein 2010), and "spatial justice" (Soja 2010)—have implicated neoliberal urban restructuring for eroding publicness and stoking exclusion. The context-sensitive adaptation of these concepts can be instrumental in reforming planning's treatment of informality in developing economies. Yet, scholars have also called for decolonizing our ways of looking at the city by exploring distinct epistemologies that truly reflect urban transformations underway in the Global South—where urban institutions and complexities are distinct, and where planning, therefore, must include and not preclude informality (Robinson and Roy 2016; Roy 2005). Thus, in addition to progressive scholarship, the experiences and impacts of decentralization, globalization, democratization, and civil society expansion in developing economies have slowly but surely begun to change the state's attitude toward informality. Multilateral and bilateral development institutions are also being more proactive and supportive in this regard.

Global consensus about making urban planning and development inclusive of informality and the informal sector (especially, shelter and work) has emerged in the form of the United Nations Sustainable Development Goals (SDGs) and the New Urban Agenda (NUA) (Dahiya and Das 2020; Fraser 2018). The NUA and SDGs (especially, SDG 11) explicitly behoove urban policies to acknowledge and remedy the marginalization of oppressed and disadvantaged groups in our cities (United Nations 2017; Watson 2016). The NUA recognizes that along with development policies, spatial organization, accessibility, and design of urban space can either promote or hinder social cohesion, equality, and inclusion. Squatters and others in the informal sector are among the most oppressed, but Asian cities still render them invisible, ineligible for welfare support, or even subject them to violence (Das 2017). Improved awareness about informality, the emergence of new stakeholders in urban local governance, and enhanced state–civil–society interactions, therefore, now present the informal sector as a site for critical analysis (Banks, Lombard, and Mitlin 2019). Recent empirical investigations on the informal sector in emerging and developing economies reveal that a large informal sector impedes economic recovery after crises. Lowering informality requires policies to improve human development, social safety nets, financing and markets, and institutions; and informality's drivers and challenges are unique and require appropriately tailored approaches (Ohnsorge and Yu 2021).

While urban planning and management institutions largely ignore informality, some remarkable urban planning innovations for sustainable and inclusive development have emerged from the Global South, often motivated by the desire to ameliorate conditions for those in the informal sector and through their active involvement (Bhan, Srinivas, and Watson 2018; Corburn et al. 2020; Mahendra et al. 2021). Innovations that emerged in developing economies, such as microfinance from South Asia, participatory budgeting and bus rapid transit from Brazil, the Metrocable from Colombia, and instances of creative coproduction involving civil society actors in many countries have inspired similar attempts across the developing world and even spread to developed economies. Essentially, these innovations sought to overcome the marginalization of the informal sector and enable its integration into the urban mainstream. Likewise, scholars are recognizing that recent advances to engage with the informal sector in the Global South suggest that understanding the modes of informal urban development is also instructive for planning in advanced economies (Harris 2018).

For several decades, research on urban informality focused almost exclusively on developing economies, which likely encouraged the misplaced notion that it is not an issue of significance in the developed ones, which thereby does not deserve urban planning research and policy attention. However, the impressive scholarship on informality in developing economies—for its progressive planning ideas, eloquent frameworks, sophisticated arguments, and sheer volume—has inspired scholars in developed economies to draw policy attention to urban informality in rich-country cities (Mukhija and Loukaitou-Sideris 2014). Today, albeit at a modest scale, and often with the active involvement of civil society actors and community groups, creative modes of supporting urban informality are increasingly visible in the form of street vending, food trucks, pop-up or temporary urbanism, and tiny homes. Technological advancement is also proving to be a significant disruptor of the status quo, and urban informality is stimulating entrepreneurism and market-led innovation in unprecedented ways. Gojek, Indonesia's first unicorn and platform economy giant, is rapidly transforming urban mobility and livelihoods;[2] it was inspired by informal sector motorcycle taxis. Many other service apps in the platform economy, especially finance and social networking ones, are rapidly transforming the urban economy by altering how businesses of varying degrees of informality operate.

---

[2]   Gojek is a business startup valued at over $1 billion.

New research based on micro- and macro-level data, including individual and household indicators, from many countries suggests that policies must address vulnerabilities of the informal sector. Transition to formalization is gradual and incremental, and pathways in and out of informality and poverty are complex (OECD and ILO 2019). Indeed, there is still much scope to explore and illuminate the variability and dynamics of the urban informal sector in Asia—its relationship to various aspects of urban development; how formal urban planning, policy making, and governance have engaged with informality; and what shifts are likely to ensue from the experiences with the COVID-19 pandemic. We hope that this book advances this mission.

3. COVID-19, Development Institutions, and the Informal Sector in Asian Cities

The COVID-19 pandemic has had an unprecedentedly damaging effect on the economies of cities and countries around the world. It has impeded or even set back development efforts in developing economies. Yet, besides the pain caused by it, COVID-19 has also yielded a fortuitous upshot in developing regions and emerging markets by providing an important reality check. It has demonstrated the multiple, interconnected vulnerabilities of those who depend on the informal sector, stemming from a lack of access to shelter, services, and rights. The urban poor have not been rendered vulnerable by COVID-19; they were always vulnerable, and COVID-19 has just exposed their vulnerabilities much more. In particular, it has exposed the pervasiveness and precarity of informality across the Global South, including in Asian cities, where robust economic growth in recent decades might have had encouraged some complacency about the need to address informality directly and proactively. It has proven that merely relying on market forces to ameliorate informality, poverty, and inequality is insufficient, and underscored the need to strengthen public investment and engagement, create supportive policies, and enable coordinated and focused planning.

In discussing the impacts of the COVID-19 pandemic, recognizing a cruel irony is imperative. While the urban poor and those in the urban informal sector have suffered the worst, they were not responsible for the spread of COVID-19 (Bhan et al. 2020). Public health protocols to contain the spread of COVID-19 that were implemented briskly in the advanced economies (i.e., frequent handwashing, extensive use of sanitizers, and social distancing) are simply infeasible in most indigent informal settlements around the world. Slums are often characterized by unusually high densities and poor quality of water and sanitation services. Measures like strict lockdowns, paradoxically, do not just deal with the most severe economic blow on those in the informal sector but also deny them the opportunity to temporarily escape the epidemiologically risk-laden environs of their habitats (Khatua 2020). In the world's largest urban slums, scores of thousands of people living in tiny dwellings within a square kilometer of land is commonplace (Lall 2020).

Since early 2020, when COVID-19 was globally recognized and treated as a global pandemic, multilateral and bilateral development agencies, the United Nations organizations, private sector research institutions, and national and international CSOs have all tracked and documented the extensive impacts on the informal sector. These ongoing efforts are yielding a critical mass of empirical evidence that behooves us to transform the prevailing insouciance or ambivalence toward urban informality. The International Labour Organization (ILO), for instance, has produced extensive data, surveys, and analyses of how the global pandemic has affected employment across the world. Globally, in 2020, an estimated additional 30 million adults fell into extreme poverty (living on less than $1.90 per day in purchasing power parity) while being out of paid work. The number of extreme working poor—those who do not earn enough to stay above the poverty line— rose by 8 million (ILO 2022). The absence of comprehensive social protection systems also has compounded financial burdens for the already poor and vulnerable households, with cascading effects on their health and nutrition. The Organisation for Economic Co-operation and Development (OECD), an intergovernmental organization of mostly rich countries, has stressed the need to eliminate the "social vulnerability trap." Those who rotate frequently among precarious jobs are more vulnerable to all kinds of shocks, from individual- and household-level shocks to macroeconomic shocks due to global crises such as the COVID-19 pandemic (OECD 2020). Persistent high informality has hampered the consolidation of the middle class and a more inclusive labor market in Latin America. OECD (2020) is therefore calling for universal safety nets to protect the region's informal workers, two-thirds of whom have no access to any form of social safety nets.

A recent monitoring report finds that by the end of 2021, employment had returned to pre-pandemic levels in most high-income countries,[3] but labor markets in low- and middle-income countries,

---

[3]   Global employment and hours worked declined again in the first quarter of 2022 and is expected to stay that way through the year because of the Russia–Ukraine war that began in late-February 2022 (International Labour Office 2022). Any detailed discussion of the conflict and its impacts are beyond the scope of this book.

which were hit the hardest, have been recovering much slower (International Labour Office 2022). The report finds that informal sector workers have struggled the most. In the second quarter of 2020, informal jobs plunged by 20% or twice as much as formal jobs; informal wage employment still trails pre-crisis levels by 8%; women in the informal sector have fared disproportionately worse—women's employment fell by 24% as compared to men's 18%; and employment recovery for women has been slower than for men, thereby widening the global gender employment gap. By the end of 2021, more informal jobs had recovered than formal sector employment, increasing the former's share of employment (International Labour Office 2022). While growth in informal employment is welcome, given the circumstances, it is also a cause for concern because of the associated precarity. Labor experts seem to believe that the pandemic might be inducing structural changes in the labor market—more informal self-employment, more remote work, and changing trends in temporary work—which can be enduring and damaging in terms of the quality of working conditions (ILO 2022).

Based on its extensive experience of promoting development in slums worldwide as well as empirical evidence from responses to pact pandemics in recent times, the World Bank has advised governments to have appropriately differentiated responses to address COVID-19's impact on slums (World Bank 2020). It has stressed the need for a paradigm shift to incorporate strong health foci in traditional upgrading and resilience-building approaches in slums. Short-, medium-, and long-term responses would require phased, customized (to account for slum diversity), multisectoral, technology-aided, and evidence-based approaches, involving substantive community engagement. The World Bank Group (2020) has called on local governments to prioritize introducing robust measures to ameliorate the lives and livelihoods of the urban poor who live in slums and work in the informal economy, and to propose essential checklists to accelerate such moves. As strategies for post-COVID-19 recovery are being developed and implemented, UN-Habitat has renewed its efforts to scale up the implementation of the NUA, focusing primarily on its three flagship programs: (i) Sustainable Development Goals cities (SDG cities), (ii) RISE-UP: Resilient Settlements for the Urban Poor, and (iii) Inclusive Cities: Enhancing the Positive Impacts of Urban Migration. These are aligned with the objectives of UN-Habitat's strategic plan 2020–2030: (i) reduced spatial inequality and poverty in communities across the urban–rural continuum, (ii) enhanced shared prosperity of cities and regions, (iii) strengthened climate action and improved urban environment, and (iv) effective urban crisis prevention and response.

Efforts by multilateral institutions and CSOs to produce data and assess trends during the COVID-19 pandemic have helped illuminate hitherto unrealized and/or underestimated aspects of deprivation and unequal access. Disparities in access to and quality of education and food security disproportionately harm those in the informal sector, especially children, and hinder overall societal progress. Yet, in most developing Asian cities, these are not yet routine concerns or priorities of urban planning and development endeavors. Empirical evidence assembled during the pandemic (International Commission on the Futures of Education 2020) should now encourage action that actively incorporates such traditionally excluded foci in conventional urban planning and development practice. Extended lockdowns and school closures have been devastating for children's education, especially young children. Never had so many children been out-of-school simultaneously, which disrupted learning and upended lives, especially of the most vulnerable and marginalized in the informal sector. According to United Nations estimates, over 91% of school-going children across the world are estimated to have been affected by school closures (about 1.6 billion children and youth were out-of-school by April 2020), and nearly 369 million children lost access to school meals, often their primary source of daily nutrition (UNESCO n.d.). Research in education and psychology certainly have already begun to investigate the long-term cognitive development and behavioral impacts on children of prolonged, fully remote, online learning, with limited or no in-person interaction; but it is likely that gains made toward SDG 4 (to ensure inclusive and equitable quality education and promote lifelong learning opportunities for all) have suffered setbacks in most countries. Even before the pandemic, collaboration between the World Bank and the UNESCO Institute for Statistics had revealed that by 2030, less than 60% of SDG 4 would actually be met because of a myriad of preexisting challenges—for instance, over 260 million children worldwide had poor or no schooling; there was significant learning poverty outside the developed world;[4] and remote learning was infeasible for the vast majority (about 36% in low- and middle-income countries) (World Bank 2019b). Cities in South and Southeast Asia experienced some of the strictest and most protracted school closures in the world.

Recent years have seen a growing focus of planning and policy research on the nexus between urban resilience and food security. The COVID-19 pandemic has markedly boosted interest in understanding

---

[4]   For instance, 80% of children in the least developed countries and 53% in low-and middle-income ones were unable to read and understand simple text by age 10.

local food systems for urban food security (Béné 2020; Tacoli 2021). Since the onset of the pandemic, the Food and Agriculture Organization of the United Nations (FAO) has produced much data, research, and policy briefs that demonstrate the centrality of food security not just for the poor to cope during economic crises but for overall socioeconomic development and urban resilience. FAO's knowledge products have illustrated how the pandemic has compromised food security of informal workers due to job and income loss and inadequate safety nets; how supply chain disruptions harmed informal workers in the agriculture sector; and that women informal workers, youth, indigenous people, and migrant workers are likely the worse affected (FAO 2020a). FAO has also drawn attention to how governments and other stakeholders are attempting to build more resilient food systems in the Asia and Pacific region (FAO 2020b), which offer possibilities for urban planning and management in Asian cities to engage purposefully to reduce food security concerns.

The lockdowns and unprecedented mobility restrictions imposed during the COVID-19 pandemic also brought into sharp relief the vital contribution of other informally provided urban services, such as public transportation. Informal public transportation affords employment and livelihoods to many in developing economies and provides millions of city dwellers with affordable mobility options. Despite its pervasiveness, the institutions and practice of formal transportation planning rarely engage with informal transportation provision, treating it as peripheral and insignificant if not undesirable. Unfortunately, it took a global pandemic to realize that in the Global South, public transportation needs to be more equitable, inclusive, and sustainable, and underscore the indispensable role played by the informal providers of public transportation options (Surico 2021). Fortunately, opportunities now abound for the substantive inclusion of informal public transportation services, service providers, and workers in the formal plans and policies that could lead the recovery out of the COVID-19 crisis (GLI 2020) and beyond. It will not only enhance resilience by securing millions of livelihoods but also improve the efficiency and quality of transportation services for millions more (Calnek-Sugin and Heeckt n.d.; Surico 2021).

4. The Asian Development Bank and the Informal Sector

ADB's initial focus on the informal sector dates back about 2 decades. As part of an ADB technical assistance (TA), a 2002 study conducted in Papua New Guinea (PNG) was among the first ADB initiatives that recommended the need for it to support informal sector activities as part of its overall poverty strategy.[5] Public policy in PNG has long promoted the informal sector, including as a nursery of entrepreneurship that could help informal enterprises transition into the formal sector; yet, in practice, weak political support had yielded little implementation. Under this TA, ADB assessed the legal, regulatory, and procedural frameworks for governing urban informal activities in PNG and identified through field surveys actual and perceived obstacles to development of the informal sector. ADB also provided an international comparative review of informal sector development and supported the development of an action plan to implement the TA recommendations. The results supported core policy making for sustained implementation.

A few years later, a chapter in the book *Key Indicators of Developing Asian and Pacific Countries 2007* provided evidence that absolute inequality has risen in many countries in Asia, and incomes of the rich had grown faster than those of the poor (ADB 2007). Gainful employment is a key avenue out of poverty. Improving the labor market and opportunities for informal workers, which in turn can ameliorate inequality, is essential. In many Asian countries, the poor usually have informal employment such as subsistence jobs, secondary jobs, and occasional jobs as a coping mechanism. In tackling urban poverty and inequality, understanding and measuring the diversity of the informal sector is therefore vital to improving labor market opportunities for the urban poor. In recent years, this realization has guided ADB assistance to developing member countries (DMCs).

---

[5] Technical assistance (TA) is a mode of ADB support that facilitates the preparation, financing, and execution of development projects and programs. It helps ADB developing member countries (DMCs) improve their capacities and make better use of their development resources; See ADB Business Center. What Is ADB Technical Assistance. https://www.adb.org/business/how-to/technical-assistance; See also ADB. Review of Constraints to Informal Sector Development (TA 3507-PNG). https://www.adb.org/projects/documents/review-constraints-informal-sector-development.

A key challenge is that data on the informal sector and informal employment are either nonexistent or scant or unreliable. National accounts statistics cannot cover this sector, which results in distorted estimates of the structure of the economy. This lack of information also hinders the understanding of policy makers about several intertwined social and economic issues related to informal sector activities, such as the absence of social protections; limited access to credit, training, and markets; and big differentials in wages and working conditions. As such, policies and interventions aimed at reducing poverty by generating decent work might not yield the desired outcomes. To address this serious gap, ADB implemented a regional technical assistance to help develop and institutionalize the measurement of the informal sector and informal employment.[6] The regional TA involved developing a data collection strategy, data collection and analysis, and economic and methodological research using the informal sector survey data. The initiative produced a comprehensive handbook that can support National Statistics Offices interested in producing informal employment and informal sector statistics, and two country reports (Armenia and Indonesia) that heightened public awareness about informal employment and other informal sector issues. It also generated interest in new planning inputs within ADB. In 2016, using case studies from multiple Asian countries, ADB published a book that examined the need to boost working age productivity, reduce vulnerability, improve economic opportunity, and expand social protection coverage among informal sector workers (Handayani 2016).

ADB supports knowledge partnerships, and one such endeavor is with Monash University's Cooperative Research Center for Water Sensitive Cities. ADB provided assistance through the Revitalization of Informal Settlements and their Environments (RISE) project using a water-sensitive approach in Indonesia and in Fiji.[7] The project demonstrated the effectiveness of a water-sensitive approach to wastewater treatment, flood risk reduction, and urban environment improvement using decentralized green infrastructure to biologically treat polluted water. Monash University and ADB published three knowledge products from RISE, contributing relevant experiences and lessons from pilot studies and suggesting effective strategies, technical designs, implementation arrangements, and cost estimates

---

[6]   See ADB (n.d.).

[7]   See ADB (2021).

for upscaling future investment projects.[8] The project stoked interest in the governments of Australia and New Zealand to replicate and scale up such efforts in Indonesia and Fiji.

ADB's Strategy 2030 envisions Asian cities to be more livable, green, competitive, resilient, and inclusive. ADB is committed to enhancing inclusive and participatory urban planning and integrating climate resilience and disaster risk management considerations into urban planning processes. The conventional approach of providing large-scale centralized trunk infrastructure in cities has typically failed to service lower-income and informal areas, which often have insecure land tenure. Currently, ADB administers a $150 million multidonor trust fund (2013–2021) under the Urban Climate Change Resilience Trust Fund (UCCRTF) to enable cities to improve urban planning, better design climate-resilient infrastructure, and develop requisite institutional capacity. With funding from The Rockefeller Foundation and the governments of Switzerland and the United Kingdom, UCCRTF aims to reduce climate risks faced by the poor and other vulnerable groups in fast-growing Asian cities by helping them better plan and design infrastructure to thwart the potential impacts of climate change. The fund seeks to scale up investments in urban climate change resilience by focusing on the urban poor in 25 secondary cities across Asia. The technical assistance, financed by UCCRTF, has helped pilot multistakeholder, community-based, and community-led urban resilience planning processes, wherein the involvement of vulnerable groups has informed project design and implementation. The TA seeks to strengthen community voice and participation in the design of urban resilience projects; enable urban planning processes to address priorities and aspirations of the most vulnerable and marginalized groups; and emphasize gender justice and non-income dimensions of poverty.

---

[8]   See RISE. RISE - ADB Knowledge Product Series: Water-Sensitive Informal Settlement Upgrading. https://www.rise-program.org/archived/publications/rise-adb-knowledge-product-series.

5. The Book: Objectives, Emphases, and Organization

Advancing our understanding of urban informality—its contours, forms, consequences, constraints, and potentials—is the motivation for and objective of this book. By focusing mainly on select physical infrastructures and services, as well as approaches to provide financial and human development services, the book illuminates how informality operates within some key urban sectors, how digital technology can be transformative for the informal sector, and how COVID-19 offers cautionary lessons about ignoring the informal sector. In analyzing the status and contributions of informality in different sectors, the book's contributions clarify the need to vanquish the prevalent tendency to locate informality solely within sectors. The chapters contribute toward the emerging realization in planning research that for urban policies and planning to be effective, the prevalent, siloed treatment of informality must end. The book also emphasizes that informality transcends sectors, scales, and actors; equating informality with just urban poverty is problematic; and digital technologies can empower the informal sector and enable formal planning and management to engage constructively with it.

The following questions broadly guided the research, arguments, and findings presented by the chapters in this book:

- What is the landscape and status of informal sector services in Asian cities? How have these been affected by recent shifts— regulations and policies, civil society action, technological innovation, and changing local governance?

- In select sectors, how has the provision of informal services been evolving and how have urban planning and management been responding?

- How has the COVID-19 pandemic impacted the informal sector and those who depend on it? How has the pandemic altered the demand, supply, and organizational aspects of informal services? How has the informal sector responded? How can urban policies and planning better support the informal sector in the future?

- How has the pandemic affected informal sector actors' use of digital technologies? How does this augur for future urban planning and development?

This book comprises 11 chapters, which include this introductory chapter and a concluding chapter. These chapters' authors represent various disciplinary backgrounds, and their research reflects distinct research designs and methodologies—quantitative analyses, various qualitative approaches, mixed methods, and case-study-style inquiries. The authors include practitioners and academic scholars, which make for good balance and dialog among different perspectives within and across the chapters. Several chapters rely extensively on rich primary data collected through field research and different types of surveys in several countries, as well as highlight the experiences of recent innovative initiatives, all of which makes for rare and deep insights and nuanced analyses. Collectively, these chapters expand our knowledge and refine our perceptions of the different aspects of informality and informal services provision, and possibly disabuse some misconceptions. A valuable contribution of this book is that almost all the chapters provide quite detailed accounts of the impacts of the COVID-19 pandemic on the respective issues being discussed. Likewise, multiple chapters illustrate how local-level planning and development initiatives to address informality can benefit from innovative and more robust engagement of development partners[9]—a topic that in recent decades seems to have become largely peripheral to planning scholarship.

The chapters in this book can loosely be of three types. The next three chapters (Chapters 2, 3, and 4) emphasize the multidimensional nature of urban poverty and informality and demonstrate how reducing vulnerabilities and building resilience will require reforming extant planning practices. The foci of these chapters are issues related to deprivation, marginality, and vulnerability. Informed by diverse literatures, their qualitative analyses stress the need for citywide and regional level thought, action, and coordination; multidisciplinary understanding; and context-specific, localized, multistakeholder responses with active participation by those whose lives are tied to informality. Chapters 5 and 6 are also drawn upon qualitative research to highlight the interconnectedness of multiple capability deprivations and risks, but each of them focuses on a specific issue of urban poverty alleviation and informality, namely food security, water, and sanitation. Such nuanced discussion of urban food security is still rare in planning scholarship, and some of the innovative technologies and institutional arrangements discussed in regard to water and sanitation enrich

---

[9]   In this book, the term "development partner" is used to refer to multilateral, bilateral, and other international institutions that fund development initiatives in developing economies.

contemporary planning knowledge. Chapters 6 through 10 present research that is mostly quantitative in nature. They utilize survey data for econometric modeling to offer fine-grained and even some novel insights into the intersections of informality, digital technologies, COVID-19, and gender. Most chapters focus on a single country, whereas a few discuss cases from multiple contexts. Collectively, the chapters explore several Southeast and South Asian contexts to lend the reader a useful comparative perspective. Brief descriptions of the individual chapters are provided below.

By emphasizing the need to address urban poverty alleviation with a systems resilience approach, especially in light of compounding challenges due to climate change, Chapter 2 by Virinder Sharma and Joy Amor Bailey introduces a framework that sets the stage for discussions in subsequent chapters. The authors argue that the growing appreciation of the links between poverty and climate change has prompted efforts by state and non-state actors to address both issues in tandem. Yet, how community-level climate action can make urban poor communities more resilient is still unclear because literature on this is limited. This chapter examines community-led resilience projects financed by ADB's UCCRTF in the Philippines, which illustrate how the application of ADB's Resilience Framework attains both poverty alleviation and climate resilience goals. Its holistic approach seeks infrastructural, ecological, social and institutional, and financial resiliency. The evidence demonstrates that community-led processes can empower the urban poor to determine their vulnerabilities and enhance their own capabilities. Such community-driven, inclusive planning helps to identify, implement, and sustain actions that reduce risks and build urban systems resilience.

In Chapter 3, Joris van Etten and Tiffany M. Tran explore the overlap and distinction between urban informality and urban poverty through a focus on slum upgrading in Indonesian cities. They argue that given poverty's multidimensionality, slum upgrading—a popular tool for poverty alleviation—cannot focus anymore just on physical infrastructure. Instead, they recommend an integrated multidimensional approach to slum upgrading to address technical, institutional, and financial challenges of program implementation. Case studies from ADB's urban sector work in Indonesia illustrate key lessons learned from attempts to transform practice, and the authors reflect critically on the discrepancies between theory and practice.

In Chapter 4, Priyam Das, Lakpa Sherpa, and Ashok Das use qualitative evidence gathered through field research during the COVID-19 pandemic to argue that to enable urban resilience, planning and policy making must engage with informality to improve the urban poor's access to basic services and livelihoods. Faced with an uncertain climate future increasingly prone to extremes, it is important to critically evaluate how planning's status quo and departures from convention impact informality. The chapter examines primary data collected in Nepal amid the COVID-19 pandemic as well as findings from investigations of related issues elsewhere, and weaves together lessons learned from the authors' individual yet synergistic research agendas to draw critical inferences for practice. The analysis shows how the delivery of physical infrastructure (water, sanitation, and housing) and services (human and economic development) is enhanced when institutions of the state, community, and civil society are incentivized to work in concert. The chapter echoes emergent wisdom for rethinking prevailing assumptions of and conventional approaches to urban development, governance, and planning for building resilience.

John Taylor, Ashok Das, Janet Naco, and Saiful Momen in Chapter 5 seek to stimulate urgent policy and planning attention to focus on food security of the urban poor—an issue largely outside the realm of conventional planning priorities, but also one that has gained much attention with growing concerns about resilience and the impacts of the COVID-19 pandemic. Nuanced insights into the dynamics of food insecurity and nutritional behavior of poor communities in Dhaka, Bangladesh reveal a fragile status quo. Utilizing multiple qualitative research methods, it exposes food security's links to broader planning and governance issues. The findings clarify that (i) poor nutrition and not just inadequate food also causes food insecurity, (ii) women and other vulnerable groups suffer more during crises like COVID-19, (iii) spatial determinants and access to basic services influence food consumption, (iv) civil society can play an enabling role in ensuring food security, and (v) coping mechanisms observed during the COVID-19 pandemic suggest desirable policy and planning interventions.

Chapter 6 is by Penny Dutton, Isabel Blackett, Neeta Pokhrel, Lara Arjan, Christian Walder, and Ellen Pascua. It draws our attention to a pervasive and vital yet relatively less studied part of urban water and sanitation delivery—informal service providers. Active in slums and informal settlements throughout Asia, informal service providers often dominate the provision of water and sanitation services. Yet, we know little about how these intermediaries emerge and operate at the margins between suppliers of formal services (e.g., utilities) and communities that generate demand for informal services. Cases from Bangladesh, Cambodia, Nepal, and the Philippines illustrate how informal service providers can leverage their relationships with communities to deliver services sustainably and adapt quickly to innovate when confronted by external challenges such the COVID-19 pandemic.

Dil B. Rahut, Jeetendra Prakash Aryal, Panharoth Chhay, and Peter J. Morgan explain the characteristics of micro and small enterprises (MSEs) in Cambodia in Chapter 7. MSEs, including home-based enterprises, are often the mainstay of any informal urban economy, and provide livelihoods to millions of the urban poor globally. Individual and household-level financial, human, physical, natural, and social capital represent capabilities that determine participation in MSEs, but much more research into such dimensions is needed from different contexts in developing economies. This study contributes toward filling that gap by analyzing data from the Cambodia Socio-Economic Survey 2019–2020 to examine factors that influence participation and explore gender differences within MSEs in urban Cambodia. It finds that assets, education, and access to credit drive participation in MSEs. It also reveals that more women than men own MSEs in Cambodia, yet women face and overcome more challenges to be able to work in the informal sector. Cambodian women participate less than men in some subsectors of MSEs that are more demanding but lucrative, for having to perform dual roles within the household as breadwinners and caregivers. To strengthen MSEs in Cambodia, the authors recommend promoting skills training to enable women to participate equally in all sectors and improving access to credit.

In a similar vein, Chapter 8 by Shigehiro Shinozaki views formalizing informal micro, small, and medium-sized enterprises (MSMEs) as critical to boosting national productivity, creating quality jobs, and promoting inclusive growth. Using linear probability regression and descriptive analysis based on data obtained through year-long surveys (March 2020 through May 2021), the chapter examines the impact of the COVID-19 pandemic on informal MSMEs in Indonesia. The COVID-19 crisis and associated mobility restrictions led many informal MSMEs to accelerate digitalization. But digitally operated firms could not always operate successfully during the pandemic. The chapter assesses the digital transformation and challenges in MSMEs due to the pandemic and highlights policy implications.

Chapter 9 focuses on how the informal sector is being transformed due to technology and digitalization. In Chapter 9, Peter J. Morgan, Kim Kunhyui, and Long Q. Trinh examine how financial technology (fintech) services—a big part of digitalization and the fast-growing platform economy—and the provision of government aid have influenced firm performance, measured as continuation of business and changes in revenue during early stages of the COVID-19 pandemic. Data on informal sector firms are very scarce, and this study used new ADBI data from seven Southeast Asian countries. Overall, it finds that the use of fintech made informal firms more resilient during the pandemic, likely by making it easier to broaden the customer base, receive and make payments, and obtain financing. Although government aid for small firms was large and widely distributed, aid did not have a significant influence on either business continuity or sales. However, it finds that government aid for small informal firms is useful and calls for promoting fintech adoption.

In Chapter 10, Takashi Yamano, Yasuyuki Sawada, Shigehiro Shinozaki, Hyuncheol Bryant Kim, Syngjoo Choi, and Siho Park draw our attention to a significantly large and ubiquitous yet less noticed part of the informal economy in Asian cities—the providers of informal and quasi-formal transportation services. Strict measures that curbed mobility to contain the spread of COVID-19 suddenly and drastically reduced transport workers' earnings with little ridership. Using panel data, the authors assess the impacts of the pandemic and the lockdowns that ensued on tricycle drivers in the Philippines between 2019 and 2021. Work declined sharply for this group during quarantine periods, and despite work resuming in later months, incomes continued to languish well below pre-pandemic levels. The demand for informal public transport services might not return to pre-pandemic levels anytime soon, thereby signaling that tricycle drivers need more support to cope with the unforeseen burdens placed by the pandemic.

References

Alkire, S., J. M. Roche, S. Seth, and A. Sumner. 2015. Identifying the Poorest People and Groups: Strategies Using the Global Multidimensional Poverty Index. *Journal of International Development* 27 (3): 362–387. https://doi.org/10.1002/jid.3083.

Anheier, H., M. Glasius, and M. Kaldor, eds. 2001. Global Civil Society 2001. *Global Civil Society Yearbooks*. Oxford, UK: Oxford University Press.

Asian Development Bank (ADB). 2007. *Key Indicators 2007*. Vol. 38. Manila.

———. 2021. *Technical Assistance Completion Report: Revitalization of Informal Settlements and their Environments Using a Water-Sensitive Approach*. https://www.adb.org/projects/documents/reg-51290-001-tcr.

———. n.d. *Technical Assistance Completion Report: Measuring the Informal Sector, 2007– 2011*. https://www.adb.org/sites/default/files/project-document/60772/41144-012-reg-tcr.pdf.

Banks, N., M. Lombard, and D. Mitlin. 2019. Urban Informality as a Site of Critical Analysis. *The Journal of Development Studies* 56 (2): 223–238. https://doi.org/10.1080/00220388.2019.1577384.

Baruah, B. 2010. NGOs in Microfinance: Learning from the Past, Accepting Limitations, and Moving Forward. *Geography Compass* 4 (8): 979–992. https://doi.org/10.1111/j.1749-8198.2010.00362.x.

Béné, C. 2020. Resilience of Local Food Systems and Links to Food Security: A Review of Some Important Concepts in the Context of COVID-19 and Other Shocks. *Food Security* 12 (4): 805–822. https://doi.org/10.1007/s12571-020-01076-1.

Bhan, G., T. Caldeira, K. Gillespie, and A. Simone. 2020. *The Pandemic, Southern Urbanisms and Collective Life*. 3 August. https://www.societyandspace.org/articles/the-pandemic-southern-urbanisms-and-collective-life.

Bhan, G., S. Srinivas, and V. Watson, eds. 2018. The Routledge Companion to Planning in the Global South. *Routledge Companions*. London; New York, NY: Routledge.

Birch, E. L., S. M. Wachter, and S. Chattaraj, eds. 2016. *Slums: How Informal Real Estate Markets Work*. The City in the Twenty-First Century. Philadelphia: Penn, University of Pennsylvania Press.

Buckley, R. M., and J. Kalarickal. 2005. Housing Policy in Developing Countries: Conjectures and Refutations. *The World Bank Research Observer* 20 (2): 233–257. https://doi.org/10.1093/wbro/lki007.

_____. eds. 2006. Thirty Years of World Bank Shelter Lending: What Have We Learned? *Directions in Development*. Washington, DC: World Bank.

Calnek-Sugin, T., and C. Heeckt. n.d. Mobility for the Masses: The Essential Role of Informal Transport in the COVID-19 Recovery. *London School of Economics and Political Science* (blog). https://www.lse.ac.uk/Cities/publications/blogs/Mobility-for-the-Masses.aspx.

Cervero, R. 2000. *Informal Transport in the Developing World*. Nairobi: United Nations Centre for Human Settlements (Habitat).

Chambers, B. 2005. The Barriadas of Lima: Slums of Hope or Despair? Problems or Solutions? *Geography* 90 (3): 200–224.

Chan, F. K. S., G. Mitchell, O. Adekola, and A. McDonald. 2012. Flood Risk in Asia's Urban Mega-Deltas Drivers, Impacts and Response. *Environment and Urbanization Asia* 3 (1): 41–61. https://doi.org/10.1177/097542531200300103.

Cheema, G. S., ed. 2013. *Democratic Local Governance: Reforms and Innovations in Asia*. Shibuya-ku, Tokyo, Japan: United Nations University Press.

Cheema, G. S., and V. Popovski, eds. 2010. *Engaging Civil Society: Emerging Trends in Democratic Governance*. Trends and Innovations in Governance Series. Tokyo; New York: United Nations University.

Chen, M., and V. A. Beard. 2018. Including the Excluded: Supporting Informal Workers for More Equal and Productive Cities in the Global South. *Working Paper—Towards a More Equal City*. Washington, DC: World Resources Institute. http://www.wri.org/publication/towards-more-equal-city-including-the-excluded?utm_source=twitter.com&utm_medium=wricities&utm_campaign=socialmedia.

Chen, M., S. Roever, and C. Skinner. 2016. Editorial: Urban Livelihoods: Reframing Theory and Policy. *Environment and Urbanization* 28 (2): 331–342. https://doi.org/10.1177/0956247816662405.

Corburn, J., M. R. Asari, J. P. Jamarillo, and A. Gaviria. 2020. The Transformation of Medellin into a 'City for Life:' Insights for Healthy Cities. *Cities & Health* 4 (1): 13–24. https://doi.org/10.1080/23748834.2019.1592735.

Corburn, J. et al. 2020. Slum Health: Arresting COVID-19 and Improving Well-Being in Urban Informal Settlements. *Journal of Urban Health*. April. https://doi.org/10.1007/s11524-020-00438-6.

Cutter, S. L. et al. 2008. A Place-Based Model for Understanding Community Resilience to Natural Disasters. *Global Environmental Change* 18 (4): 598–606.

Dados, N., and R. Connell. 2012. The Global South. *Contexts* 11 (1): 12–13.

Dahiya, B., and A. Das, eds. 2020. *New Urban Agenda in Asia-Pacific: Governance for Sustainable and Inclusive Cities.* Advances in 21st Century Human Settlements. Singapore: Springer. https://www.springer.com/gp/book/9789811367083.

Das, A. 2015. Slum Upgrading with Community-Managed Microfinance: Towards Progressive Planning in Indonesia. *Habitat International* 47 (June): 256–266. https://doi.org/10.1016/j.habitatint.2015.01.004.

———. 2017. A City of Two Tales: Shelter and Migrants in Surabaya. *Environment and Urbanization ASIA* 8 (1): 1–21. https://doi.org/10.1177/0975425316686501.

———. 2020. *Affordable Housing for Hawai'i and Native Hawaiians: Exploring Ideas and Innovations.* Research Report. Honolulu, HI: Department of Urban and Regional Planning, University of Hawai'i at Mānoa. http://hdl.handle.net/10125/81703.

Das, A., and R. King. 2019. Surabaya: The Legacy of Participatory Upgrading of Informal Settlements. *Working Paper—Towards a More Equal City.* Washington, DC. https://www.wri.org/wri-citiesforall/publication/surabaya-legacy-participatory-upgrading-informal-settlements.

Davoudi, S. et al. 2012. Resilience: A Bridging Concept or a Dead End? 'Reframing' Resilience: Challenges for Planning Theory and Practice Interacting Traps: Resilience Assessment of a Pasture Management System in Northern Afghanistan Urban Resilience: What Does It Mean in Planning Practice? Resilience as a Useful Concept for Climate Change Adaptation? The Politics of Resilience for Planning: A Cautionary Note. *Planning Theory & Practice* 13 (2): 299–333. https://doi.org/10.1080/14649357.2012.677124.

De Soto, H. 1989. *The Other Path: The Economic Answer to Terrorism.* New York, NY: Basic Books.

———. 2000. *The Mystery of Capital: Why Capitalism Triumphs in the West and Fails Everywhere Else.* New York: Basic Books.

Ezeadichie, N. 2012. Home-Based Enterprises in Urban Spaces: An Obligation for Strategic Planning? *Berkeley Planning Journal* 25 (1). https://doi.org/10.5070/BP325112010.

Fainstein, S. S. 2010. *The Just City.* Ithaca: Cornell University Press.

Ferguson, B. 1999. Micro-Finance of Housing: A Key to Housing the Low or Moderate-Income Majority? *Environment and Urbanization* 11 (1): 185–200. https://doi.org/10.1177/095624789901100102.

Ferguson, B., and P. Smets. 2010. Finance for Incremental Housing: Current Status and Prospects for Expansion. *Habitat International* 34 (3): 288–298. https://doi.org/10.1016/j.habitatint.2009.11.008.

Food and Agriculture Organization of the United Nations (FAO). 2020a. Impact of COVID-19 on Informal Workers. *Policy Brief.* Rome, Italy. http://www.fao.org/documents/card/en/c/ca8560en.

————. 2020b. Impacts of Coronavirus on Food Security and Nutrition in Asia and the Pacific: Building More Resilient Food Systems. *Policy Brief.* Bangkok, Thailand. http://www.fao.org/documents/card/en/c/ca9473en.

Fox, S. 2014. The Political Economy of Slums: Theory and Evidence from Sub-Saharan Africa. *World Development* 54: 191–203.

Fraser, A. 2018. Informality in the New Urban Agenda: From the Aspirational Policies of Integration to a Politics of Constructive Engagement. *Planning Theory & Practice* 19 (1): 124–126. https://doi.org/10.1080/14649357.2018.1412678.

Gilbert, A. 1997. On Subsidies and Home-Ownership: Colombian Housing Policy during the 1990s. *Third World Planning Review* 19 (1): 51.

Global Labour Institute (GLI). 2020. *Informal Passenger Transport Beyond COVID-19: A Trade Union Guide to Worker-Led Formalisation.* London: International Transport Workers' Federation. https://www.itfglobal.org/sites/default/files/node/page/files/Formalisation%20Guide%20Covid_0.pdf.

Goldfinch, S. 2015. Property Rights and the Mystery of Capital: A Review of de Soto's Simplistic Solution to Development. *Progress in Development Studies* 15 (1): 87–96. https://doi.org/10.1177/1464993414546971.

Guinness, P. 1986. *Harmony and Hierarchy in a Javanese Kampung.* Singapore: Oxford University Press.

Gulyani, S. 2016. Success When We Deemed It Failure? Revisiting Sites and Services 20 Years Later. *Sustainable Cities* (blog). 23 June. http://blogs.worldbank.org/sustainablecities/success-when-we-deemed-it-failure-revisiting-sites-and-services-20-years-later.

Gulyani, S., and D. Talukdar. 2010. Inside Informality: The Links Between Poverty, Microenterprises, and Living Conditions in Nairobi's Slums. *World Development* 38 (12): 1710–26. https://doi.org/10.1016/j.worlddev.2010.06.013.

Handayani, S. W., ed. 2016. *Social Protection for Informal Workers in Asia.* Manila: ADB. https://www.adb.org/sites/default/files/publication/203891/sp-informalworkers-asia.pdf.

Haq, M. U. 1995. *Reflections on Human Development: How the Focus of Development Economics Shifted from National Income Accounting to People-Centred Policies, Told by One of the Chief Architects of the New Paradigm.* New York: Oxford University Press.

Harris, J. R., and M. P. Todaro. 1970. Migration, Unemployment and Development: A Two-Sector Analysis. *The American Economic Review* 60 (1): 126–142.

Harris, R. 1999. Slipping through the Cracks: The Origins of Aided Self-Help Housing, 1918-53. *Housing Studies* 14 (3): 281–309.

———. 2003. A Double Irony: The Originality and Influence of John FC Turner. *Habitat International* 27 (2): 245–269.

Harris, R. 2018. Modes of Informal Urban Development: A Global Phenomenon. *Journal of Planning Literature* 33 (3): 267–286. https://doi.org/10.1177/0885412217737340.

Harvey, D. 2008. The Right to the City. *New Left Review.* No. 53 (October): 23–40.

Havlick, S. W. 1986. Third World Cities at Risk: Building for Calamity. *Environment* 28 (9): 7–11, 41–45.

Hollis, G. E. 1975. The Effect of Urbanization on Floods of Different Recurrence Interval. *Water Resources Research* 11 (3): 431–435. https://doi.org/10.1029/WR011i003p00431.

Horn, Z. E. 2010. The Effects of the Global Economic Crisis on Women in the Informal Economy: Research Findings from WIEGO and the Inclusive Cities Partners. *Gender and Development* 18 (2): 263–276.

Imparato, I., and J. Ruster. 2003. *Slum Upgrading and Participation: Lessons from Latin America.* Washington, DC: World Bank.

International Commission on the Futures of Education. 2020. *Education in a Post-COVID World: Nine Ideas for Public Action.* Paris: United Nations Educational, Scientific and Cultural Organization (UNESCO). https://unesdoc.unesco.org/ark:/48223/pf0000373717/PDF/373717eng.pdf.multi.

International Labour Office. 2022. *World Employment and Social Outlook: Trends 2022.* Geneva: International Labour Organization. https://public.ebookcentral.proquest.com/choice/PublicFullRecord.aspx?p=6941163.

International Labour Organization (ILO). 2022. *ILO Monitor on the World of Work.* Newsletter 9th edition. Geneva. https://www.ilo.org/wcmsp5/groups/public/---dgreports/---dcomm/---publ/documents/publication/wcms_845642.pdf.

Jellinek, L. 1991. *The Wheel of Fortune: The History of a Poor Community in Jakarta.* Honolulu: University of Hawaii Press.

Khatua, S. 2020. Density, Distancing, Informal Settlements and the Pandemic. *Economic and Political Weekly* 55 (20). https://www.epw.in/journal/2020/20/commentary/density-distancing-informal-settlements-and.html.

King, R., M. Orloff, T. Virsilas, and T. Pande. 2017. Confronting the Urban Housing Crisis in the Global South: Adequate, Secure, and Affordable Housing. *Working Paper—Towards a More Equal City*. Washington, DC: World Resources Institute. https://www.wri.org/publication/towards-more-equal-city-confronting-urban-housing-crisis-global-south.

Kumar, S. 1996. Landlordism in Third World Urban Low-Income Settlements: A Case for Further Research. *Urban Studies* 33 (4–5): 753–782. https://doi.org/10.1080/00420989650011816.

Kundu, A., and D. Kundu. 2010. *Globalization and Exclusionary Urban Growth in Asian Countries*. Working Paper 2010/70. Tokyo, Japan: United Nations University; Helsinki, Finland: World Institute for Development Economics Research. http://core.ac.uk/download/pdf/6250325.pdf.

Lall, S. 2020. Yes, Cities Will Survive COVID-19. But They Must Manage Their Economic Geography. *Sustainable Cities, World Bank Blogs* (blog). 18 June. https://blogs.worldbank.org/sustainablecities/yes-cities-will-survive-covid-19-they-must-manage-their-economic-geography.

Lall, S. V., H. Selod, and Z. Shalizi. 2006. Rural-Urban Migration in Developing Countries: A Survey of Theoretical Predictions and Empirical Findings. World Bank Policy Research Working Paper WPS3915. http://papers.ssrn.com/sol3/papers.cfm?abstract_id=920498.

Lewis, O. 1963. The Culture of Poverty. *Trans-Action* 1 (1): 17–19.

Lloyd, P. 1979. *Slums of Hope? Shanty Towns of the Third World*. Manchester: Manchester University Press.

Mahendra, A., J. Du, A. Dasgupta, V. A. Beard, A. Kallergis, and K. Schalch. 2021. Seven Transformations for More Equitable and Sustainable Cities. *World Resources Report: Towards a More Equal City*. Washington, DC: World Resources Institute. https://doi.org/10.46830/wrirpt.19.00124.

Mahler, A. G. 2017. Global South. *Oxford Bibliographies—Literary and Critical Theory*. Oxford University Press. https://doi.org/10.1093/obo/9780190221911-0055.

Mangin, W. 1967. Latin American Squatter Settlements: A Problem and a Solution. *Latin American Research Review* 2 (3): 65–98.

Mansuri, G., and V. Rao. 2013. *Localizing Development: Does Participation Work?* Washington, DC: World Bank.

Mayer, M. 2003. The Onward Sweep of Social Capital: Causes and Consequences for Understanding Cities, Communities and Urban Movements. *International Journal of Urban and Regional Research* 27 (1): 110–132. https://doi.org/10.1111/1468-2427.00435.

Mayo, S. K., and D. J. Gross. 1987. Sites and Services—and Subsidies: The Economics of Low-Cost Housing in Developing Countries. *The World Bank Economic Review* 1 (2): 301–335. https://doi.org/10.1093/wber/1.2.301.

Miller, M. A., and M. Douglass, eds. 2016. *Disaster Governance in Urbanising Asia*. Singapore: Springer.

Mitlin, D. 2008. With and Beyond the State—Co-Production as a Route to Political Influence, Power and Transformation for Grassroots Organizations. *Environment and Urbanization* 20 (2): 339–360. https://doi.org/10.1177/0956247808096117.

Monkkonen, P. 2012. Housing Finance Reform and Increasing Socioeconomic Segregation in Mexico. *International Journal of Urban and Regional Research* 36 (4): 757–772. https://doi.org/10.1111/j.1468-2427.2011.01085.x.

Moser, C. O. N. 1998. The Asset Vulnerability Framework: Reassessing Urban Poverty Reduction Strategies. *World Development* 26 (1): 1–19. https://doi.org/10.1016/S0305-750X(97)10015-8.

Mukhija, V., and A. Loukaitou-Sideris, eds. 2014. *The Informal American City: Beyond Taco Trucks and Day Labor*. Urban and Industrial Environments. Cambridge, Massachusetts: The MIT Press.

Mulligan, M., W. Steele, L. Rickards, and H. Fünfgeld. 2016. Keywords in Planning: What Do We Mean by "Community Resilience"? *International Planning Studies* 21 (4): 348–361. https://doi.org/10.1080/13563475.2016.1155974.

Naik, M. 2019. Negotiation, Mediation and Subjectivities: How Migrant Renters Experience. *Radical Housing Journal* 1 (2): 45–62.

Nuissl, H., and D. Heinrichs. 2013. Slums: Perspectives on the Definition, the Appraisal and the Management of an Urban Phenomenon. *DIE ERDE–Journal of the Geographical Society of Berlin* 144 (2): 105–116.

Nussbaum, M. 2000. Women's Capabilities and Social Justice. *Journal of Human Development* 1 (2): 219–247.

Ohnsorge, F., and S. Yu, eds. 2021. *The Long Shadow of Informality: Challenges and Policies*. Washington, DC: World Bank. https://www.worldbank.org/en/research/publication/informal-economy.

Organisation for Economic Co-operation and Development (OECD). 2020. *Informality and Employment Protection During and Beyond COVID-19: Good Practices and the Imperative of Universal Safety Nets.* Background Note, OECD-LAC Virtual Social Inclusion Ministerial Summit. Paris. https://www.oecd.org/latin-america/events/lac-ministerial-on-social-inclusion/2020-OECD-LAC-Ministerial-Informality-and-employment-protection-during-and-beyond-COVID-19-background-note.pdf.

OECD and ILO. 2019. *Tackling Vulnerability in the Informal Economy.* Paris: Development Centre Studies, OECD. https://doi.org/10.1787/939b7bcd-en.

Payne, G. 2001. Lowering the Ladder: Regulatory Frameworks for Sustainable Development. *Development in Practice* 11 (2–3): 308–318.

Payne, G., A. Durand-Lasserve, and C. Rakodi. 2009. The Limits of Land Titling and Home Ownership. *Environment and Urbanization* 21 (2): 443–462. https://doi.org/10.1177/0956247809344364.

Payne, G. K. 2002. *Land, Rights and Innovation: Improving Tenure Security for the Urban Poor.* London: Intermediate Technology Development Group.

Perlman, J. E. 1979. *The Myth of Marginality: Urban Poverty and Politics in Rio de Janeiro.* Berkeley, California: University of California Press.

Pugh, C. 1997. The Changing Roles of Self-Help in Housing and Urban Policies, 1950–1996: Experience in Developing Countries. *Third World Planning Review* 19 (1): 91–106.

Raja, S., E. Sweeney, Y. Mui, and F. Boamah. 2021. *Local Government Planning for Community Food Systems: Opportunity, Innovation and Equity in Low- and Middle-Income Countries.* Rome, Italy: FAO. https://doi.org/10.4060/cb3136en.

Rakodi, C., and T. Lloyd-Jones, eds. 2002. *Urban Livelihoods: A People-Centred Approach to Reducing Poverty.* London; Sterling, Virginia: Earthscan Publications. http://site.ebrary.com/id/10128883.

Robinson, J., and A. Roy. 2016. Debate on Global Urbanisms and the Nature of Urban Theory. *International Journal of Urban and Regional Research* 40 (1): 181–186. https://doi.org/10.1111/1468-2427.12272.

Rolnik, R. 2014. Place, Inhabitance and Citizenship: The Right to Housing and the Right to the City in the Contemporary Urban World. *International Journal of Housing Policy* 14 (3): 293–300. https://doi.org/10.1080/14616718.2014.936178.

Roy, A., and N. AlSayyad, eds. 2004. *Urban Informality Transnational Perspectives from the Middle East, Latin America, and South Asia.* Lanham, MD: Lexington Books.

Rydin, Y., and M. Pennington. 2000. Public Participation and Local Environmental Planning: The Collective Action Problem and the Potential of Social Capital. *Local Environment* 5 (2): 153–169. https://doi.org/10.1080/13549830050009328.

Sandercock, L. 1998. *Towards Cosmopolis: Planning for Multicultural Cities*. Chichester, England; New York: John Wiley & Sons.

Schmidt-Kallert, E. 2012. Non-Permanent Migration and Multilocality in the Global South. *DIE ERDE–Journal of the Geographical Society of Berlin* 143 (3): 173–176.

Sen, A. 1999a. *Development as Freedom*. New York: Oxford University Press.

———. 1999b. The Possibility of Social Choice. *The American Economic Review* 89 (3): 349–378.

Shatkin, G. 2016. The Real Estate Turn in Policy and Planning: Land Monetization and the Political Economy of Peri-Urbanization in Asia. *Cities* 53 (April): 141–149. https://doi.org/10.1016/j.cities.2015.11.015.

Silas, J. 1984. The Kampung Improvement Programme of Indonesia: A Comparative Case Study of Jakarta and Surabaya. In *Low-Income Housing in the Developing World: The Role of Sites and Services and Settlement Upgrading*, edited by Geoffrey K. Payne, 69–87. New York: John Wiley & Sons.

Small, M. L., D. J. Harding, and M. Lamont. 2010. Reconsidering Culture and Poverty. *The ANNALS of the American Academy of Political and Social Science* 629 (1): 6–27. https://doi.org/10.1177/0002716210362077.

Soja, E. W. 2010. *Seeking Spatial Justice*. Minnesota: University of Minnesota Press.

Strassmann, W. P. 1987. Home-Based Enterprises in Cities of Developing Countries. *Economic Development and Cultural Change* 36 (1): 121–144. https://doi.org/10.1086/451639.

Sumka, H. J. 1987. Shelter Policy and Planning in Developing Countries: Introduction. *Journal of the American Planning Association* 53 (2): 171–175. https://doi.org/10.1080/01944368708976649.

Surico, J. 2021. Informal Transport Must Play a Bigger Role in Post-Pandemic Recovery. Here's How That Can Happen. *TheCityFix* (blog). 15 April. https://thecityfix.com/blog/informal-transport-must-play-a-bigger-role-in-post-pandemic-recovery-heres-how-that-can-happen/.

Tacoli, C. 2003. The Links between Urban and Rural Development. *Environment and Urbanization* 15 (1): 3–12.

———. 2021. Feeding All City Inhabitants. *International Institute for Environment and Development* (blog). 28 June. https://www.iied.org/feeding-all-city-inhabitants.

Tacoli, C., G. McGranahan, and D. Satterthwaite. 2015. Urbanisation, Rural–Urban Migration and Urban Poverty. Working Paper 10725IIED. *Human Settlements Working Paper*. London: International Institute for Environment and Development.

Tipple, G. 2005. The Place of Home-Based Enterprises in the Informal Sector: Evidence from Cochabamba, New Delhi, Surabaya and Pretoria. *Urban Studies* 42 (4): 611–632. https://doi.org/10.1080/00420980500060178.

Todaro, M. P. 1969. A Model of Labor Migration and Urban Unemployment in Less Developed Countries. *The American Economic Review* 59 (1): 138–148.

Turner, J. F. C. 1977. *Housing by People: Towards Autonomy in Building Environments*. New York: Pantheon Books.

Turner, J. F. C., and R. Fichter, eds. 1972. *Freedom to Build*. New York: Macmillan.

UNESCO. n.d. Sustainable Development Goals. 4 Quality Education. https://www.un.org/sustainabledevelopment/education/.

UN-Habitat. 2003. *The Challenge of Slums: Global Report on Human Settlements 2003*. London; Sterling, VA: Earthscan Publications.

United Nations. 2017. *New Urban Agenda*. New York.

Vijayan, P. 2020. Challenges in the Midst of the COVID-19 Pandemic. *Economic and Political Weekly* 55 (24). https://www.epw.in/journal/2020/24/commentary/challenges-midst-covid-19-pandemic.html.

Watson, V. 2013. Planning and the "Stubborn Realities" of Global South-East Cities: Some Emerging Ideas. *Planning Theory* 12 (1): 81–100.

Watson, V. 2016. Locating Planning in the New Urban Agenda of the Urban Sustainable Development Goal. *Planning Theory* 15 (4): 435–448. https://doi.org/10.1177/1473095216660786.

World Bank. 1993. *Housing: Enabling Markets to Work*. Washington, DC.

———. 2019a. *Global Economic Prospects, January 2019: Darkening Skies*. Washington, DC.

———. 2019b. Learning Poverty. https://www.worldbank.org/en/topic/education/brief/learning-poverty.

———. 2020. *COVID-19 and Slums WBG LAC: A Multisectoral Approach*. Washington, DC. https://thedocs.worldbank.org/en/doc/777881590683416399-0200022020/original/COVID19andSlumsWBGLAC.pdf.

World Bank Group. 2020. *COVID-19: Safeguarding Lives and Livelihoods—A Checklist Guide for Local Governments*. Washington, DC. https://thedocs.worldbank.org/en/doc/365441589388738131-0200022020/original/COVID19safeguardinglivesandlivelihoodsEnglish.pdf.

2

Applying Systems Resilience to Deliver Poverty Alleviation Outcomes in Vulnerable Communities

Virinder Sharma and Joy Amor Bailey

Abstract

There is a growing appreciation of the interlinkages between poverty and climate change. Consequently, state, and non-state actors are prompted to address both issues in parallel when developing policies and programs. However, there is limited literature on how climate resilience at the community level, particularly of the urban poor both in the formal and informal sector, can be achieved. This chapter examines the cases of community-led projects financed by the ADB Urban Climate Change Resilience Trust Fund (UCCRTF) in the municipalities of La Trinidad and Janiuay, Philippines. It illustrates how the application of ADB's Resilience Framework delivers both poverty and climate resilience outcomes. The framework is a holistic approach tackling four aspects of system resilience—infrastructural, ecological, social and institutional, and financial. The chapter further demonstrates the value of community-led processes that empower the urban poor to determine their vulnerabilities and enhance their capabilities in identifying, implementing, and sustaining climate change related actions toward reducing risks and building holistic resilience.

Keywords: poverty, climate change, system resilience, community led, UCCRTF, Philippines

1. Introduction

Levels of informality cut across sectors and differ in typology, but often there is a common attribute—poverty. This is manifested in the sustained expansion of informal settlements, as well as in precarious livelihoods that rely on the informal economy in rapidly urbanizing Asia. The lack of access to basic services in informal settlements and the absence of social protection in the informal economy are compounded by the urban poor's vulnerability to climate change and disaster related impacts. However, the policy formulation, program development, and investment prioritization by state and non-state actors rarely look at poverty alleviation and climate change as interconnected issues.

Commonly, dominant measures of poverty, which are mostly univariate and based on income, shape how policy makers and relevant stakeholders understand the complex phenomenon of poverty and formulate pertinent solutions. However, these measures are now recognized as imperfect (Greenberg 2009; Peter G. Paterson Foundation 2019). Various stakeholders have attempted to suggest poverty reduction measures that acknowledge the debilitating impact of climate change on marginalized sectors of the economy, and in exacerbating extreme poverty (Wilkinson et al. 2015).

Multiple frameworks have been developed to guide actions on climate change and development, such as the 21st Session of the Conference of Parties (COP21) in Paris, the Sendai Framework for Disaster Risk Reduction, and the Sustainable Development Goals (SDGs). The SDGs, for example, provide a comprehensive framework for implementing policies and programs that address the underlying causes of poverty, vulnerability, and climate change risks (UN DESA 2016). SDG 13 affirms the urgency of taking action to strengthen resilience and adaptive capacity. It also calls for the integration of climate change measures into national and subnational policies and recommends improving education and human resources and institutional capacities for climate change adaptation, among others (UN DESA 2016). The interlinkages between climate change and other aspects of development are also evident in the other SDGs. While the SDGs cut across multiple scales, they also emphasize the local level as the site where the effects of adverse climatic events are experienced and where interventions for mitigation should be implemented. Actions seeking to establish resilience and build adaptive capacities require focusing on the community level.

Despite the existence of literature on climate change and disasters as emergent factors underlying poverty, there is a gap between research knowledge and practice on how climate resilience ought to reshape existing poverty reduction measures. This chapter argues that poverty is a phenomenon experienced disproportionately by the marginalized and informal sectors, and exacerbated by climate change. To be relevant, the design of poverty alleviation measures needs to incorporate principles of resilience. The chapter does so by describing how the application of the Asian Development Bank (ADB) Resilience Framework has influenced the design and implementation of community-led projects (CLPs) financed through ADB's Urban Climate Change Resilience Trust Fund (UCCRTF). The ADB Resilience Framework is an approach that promotes system resilience across four key aspects of resilience—infrastructure, ecological, social and institutional, and financial. The chapter argues that climate resilience related factors need to be incorporated into the design, implementation, and monitoring of development programs to address the twin challenges of poverty and climate change.

2. Climate Resilience as a Missing Element in Poverty Alleviation

The Oxford Poverty and Human Development Initiative stresses that no single indicator could capture the multiple dimensions of poverty. Multidimensional poverty (MDP) goes beyond mere monetary deprivation; it also includes various other deprivations experienced by poor people in their daily lives. Townsend (1979) in his "Relative Deprivation Theory of Poverty" postulated MDP as follows:

> Individuals, families, and groups in the population can be said to be in poverty when they lack the resources to obtain the types of diet, participate in the activities, and have the living conditions and amenities which are customary, or at least widely encouraged or approved, in the societies to which they belong. Their resources are so seriously below those commanded by the average individual or family that they are, in effect, excluded from ordinary patterns, customs and activities (Townsend 1979: 31).

Chambers (1995) supplemented the concept of MDP by arguing that perceptions of poverty espoused by professionals were often universalist, reductionist, and standardized, whereas the poor themselves view poverty differently. Chambers (1995) noted that the realities of the poor are often local, diverse, complex, and dynamic, and recommended that participatory appraisal could confirm many criteria and dimensions of the disadvantage, ill-being, and well-being that people experience. Narayan et al. (2000) provided 10 interlocking dimensions capturing the poor's perspectives to show how ill-being exceeds material deprivation. They posited that these dimensions could cause or compound other dimensions of deprivations, thus creating and sustaining powerlessness and deprivations.

Similarly, the United Nations (UN DESA 1995) noted that poverty has various manifestations, such as the lack of income and sufficient resources to sustain livelihoods, hunger and malnutrition, ill health, limited or lack of access to education and basic services, increased morbidity and mortality from sickness, homelessness and inadequate housing, unsafe environments, and social discrimination and exclusion. It further emphasized that poverty is characterized by a lack of participation in decision-making, and in civil, social, and cultural life.

2.1 Understanding Threats and Vulnerabilities

The United Nations International Strategy for Disaster Reduction (2009: 24) defines resilience as "the ability of a system, community or society exposed to hazards to resist, absorb, accommodate to and recover from the effects of a hazard in a timely and efficient manner, including through the preservation and restoration of its essential basic structures and functions." Resilience could involve iterative and continually evolving processes; thus, it connotes the need for a better understanding of the interrelatedness of factors contributing to vulnerabilities, and the complexities of scale. The concept of resilience is about the relationship between risk and vulnerability, with the latter involving sensitivity, exposure, and adaptive capacity. Climate change and disaster impacts vary across geographies and scales, but they render the urban poor, especially those living in informal settlements and working in the informal economy, as among the most vulnerable.

Resilience is perceived as an essential component of any comprehensive climate action program given climate change's highly global and hyper-local scope (Center for Climate and Energy Solutions 2019). The Center for Climate and Energy Solutions (C2ES) noted that resilience is rooted in understanding threats and vulnerabilities of a particular phenomenon and its impact or consequences. It further noted that the prioritization of risks may vary based on the perspectives of individuals and institutions, depending on their vulnerabilities, and that the ability to recover from disruptive events varies according to the specific situations of different sectors at the local level. C2ES argued that wealth and social stability are significant predictors of resilience to shocks and stresses; the adaptation aspects of climate resilience will be rendered less impactful without mitigation and pre-planning for resilient and adaptive rebuilding; and the effects of inaction are more costly.

The Union of Concerned Scientists (UCS) developed a science-based framework showing that adaptation and mitigation are intrinsically linked, and that the narrowing of the climate resilience gap requires aggressive action on both climate mitigation and adaptation (UCS 2016). They recommended that decisions aimed at building resilience at all levels must be consistent with and responsive to the best-available science about climate change, and knowledge of how it affects human and natural systems (UCS 2016). UCS further urges decision makers to combine scientific rigor with systems thinking by consulting communities and beneficiaries, reflecting long-term visions, and establishing sound and responsive policies, among others.

While most of the abovementioned literatures are relevant, none truly emphasizes the need to incorporate climate resilience in poverty alleviation efforts. Despite the evident connections, not much scholarly research or practitioner wisdom yet embodies climate resilience as a key component of poverty alleviation.

2.2 Dismantling the Silos of Development and the Environment

The United Nations Department of Economic and Social Affairs affirmed that climate change is increasing the frequency and intensity of climate hazards which are likely to slow down economic growth, increase multiple forms of insecurities, and worsen health problems. Consequently, poverty and inequalities within and among nations will increase. The UN noted that climate change resilience can only be successful in attaining sustainable development if it addresses structural inequalities that perpetuate poverty, marginalization, and social exclusion, and increase vulnerability to natural hazards (UN DESA 2016).

Efforts to address poverty remain disconnected from efforts to meet environmental goals (UN DESA 2016). Most poverty alleviation efforts do not embody or are not informed by aspects of climate change resilience. Thus, often, socially and economically sound poverty alleviation projects or programs fail to consider the impacts of environmental or climatic conditions on development. As UN DESA (2016: 4) puts it: "Hence, there is much less experience and policy guidance on the integration of the various aspects of the environment into development policy. Building consistency across the economic, social and environmental dimensions of development policy will be a core challenge in building climate resilience and achieving sustainable development."

Attempts to systematically measure resilience have yielded resilience indices. For example, Arup, with support from The Rockefeller Foundation, has developed a City Resilience Index (CRI) to enable local governments to measure and monitor multiple factors that affect their resilience. The CRI identified the four most important dimensions—health and well-being, economy and society, infrastructure and environment, and leadership and strategy. Assessing these dimensions, according to Arup (2013), could help a city diagnose its strengths and weakness, set goals, and measure its relative performance over time. The metrics includes 52 indicators. Similarly, Subiyanto, Aldrian, and Boer (2020) have developed a climate resilience index which indicates that a system becomes more vulnerable when its level of exposure and sensitivity to disturbance—such as climate change or extreme weather—increases, while its capacity and opportunities for adaptation are low or reduced.

2.3   Investing in the Most Vulnerable

While concepts and policies strive to address climate resilience, actions should specifically target the urban poor, who are highly vulnerable to the impacts of climate-related disasters and have limited financial and social capital to recover from disruptive events. Many from this sector rely on the informal sector and have unstable incomes. It is estimated that about a billion people live in informal settlements and this figure is expected to double in the next decade (Vahapoglu 2019; Collier et al. n.d.). Regrettably, information on informal settlement communities remains largely inadequate, outdated, or nonexistent, making intervention targeting difficult (United Nations Children's Fund 2012).

Urban poverty is, likewise, often associated with working in the informal economy wherein people have little or no rights or social protection, making them vulnerable to external shocks. The International Conference of Labour Statisticians characterizes the informal economy as involving informal employment in unregistered or informal enterprises, informal employment in formal enterprises, and formal employment in informal enterprises. While there are low-income urban residents who do not live in informal settlements or work in the informal economy, and while residents of informal settlements and workers in the informal economy are not necessarily poor, there are many overlapping characteristics of poverty and informality that simultaneously contribute to higher levels of vulnerability.

According to the United Nations Economic Commission for Europe (2009), social exclusion and poverty are key drivers of the formation of informal settlements in most countries. Informal settlements are also considered "persistent features of urbanization" (UNECE 2009). Informal settlements are mostly established on illegally occupied lands that did not undergo regulatory and spatial planning procedures necessary in ensuring a well-planned, safe, and development-adherent community. These settlements have been built outside the formal system of laws and regulations covering land use, buildings, and infrastructure. Hence, informal settlements are deficient in amenities and are not included in urban development plans (UNECE 2016), and therefore do not comply with climate and disaster resilience standards. Informal settlements are deficient in infrastructures that ensure the well-being of residents, such as public recreational and commercial spaces, sewage systems, water supply, and safe and durable housing (Vahapoglu 2019; Collier et al. n.d.). Most informal settlements are situated in areas unsafe for human habitation, such as eco-sensitive environments, conflict zones, and locations vulnerable to extreme weather events and disasters (Vahapoglu 2019; Collier et al. n.d.).

Upgrading of informal settlements is considered essential for achieving resilient, inclusive, and low-carbon urban development. Sverdlik, Mitlin, and Dodman (2019) view such upgrading as a mitigative measure against climate risks, which can simultaneously provide socioeconomic development benefits. They further argue that upgrading in informal settlements comprises interventions that vary in scope—from single sector to multisectoral programs—and in the scale and levels of community participation. They also emphasize that climate friendly development has multiple benefits: (i) social benefits— which includes the promotion of gender equity, community pride, and social cohesion between local actors; (ii) health benefits—improved environmental quality, increased physical activity, and reduced vector-borne diseases; (iii) climate benefits and economic benefits—reduction of CO_2 emissions, adaptation to local climate risks, and improved air quality, among others; and (iv) economic benefits—protection of assets such as houses and livelihoods enhancement through potential cost savings.

Melore and Nel (2020) comparatively assessed the climate resilience of two informal settlements in Ethiopia and South Africa. Each community was assessed based on its environmental, social, economic, human, institutional, and physical capital in relation to climate change indicators. Both settlements encountered drought and poverty. The authors observed that the retention of indigenous knowledge in Konso (Ethiopia) greatly improved community resilience as compared to QwaQwa (South Africa), which relied on top-down approaches. Community members noted that deficits in all the identified forms of capital diminish their resilience to climate change. Konso's long-time reliance on indigenous knowledge systems in environmental conservation and traditional terracing, among others, improved its climate resilience. The authors concluded that top-down approaches, which dominate local planning processes, have failed to facilitate adaptive management—not recognizing indigenous knowledge that can augment local resilience.

Several studies show internationally funded interventions for climate change adaptation and vulnerability reduction have inadvertently reinforced, redistributed, and even created new sources of vulnerability (Eriksen et al. 2021). Commonly, four mechanisms that yield this maladaptive outcome, include (i) shallow understanding of the vulnerability context, (ii) inequitable stakeholder participation in both design and implementation, (iii) retrofitting of adaptation into existing development agendas, and (iv) a lack of critical engagement into how "adaptation success" is defined (Eriksen et al. 2021). Eriksen et al. (2021) suggest that these can be overcome by shifting the terms of engagement between adaptation practitioners and the participating local communities, and by expanding the understanding of local vulnerability to encompass global contexts and drivers of vulnerability. They recommend that instead of designing projects aimed at changing the practices of marginalized populations, learning processes within organizations and with marginalized populations must be at the core of adaptation objectives (Eriksen et al. 2021). Thus, consultative climate resilience programs and codesigns are vital.

3. Urban Climate Change Resilience and ADB

Institutions such as ADB have been actively supporting resilience-building activities. ADB is a multilateral development bank owned by 68 members, 49 of which are developing member countries (DMCs) from Asia and the Pacific. The DMCs have access to loans, technical assistance, grants, and equity investments to promote social and economic development. ADB's Strategy 2030, "Achieving a Prosperous, Inclusive, Resilient and Sustainable Asia and the Pacific," reflects the changing needs of the region while the preceding ADB Strategy 2020 focused on "Working for an Asia and Pacific Free of Poverty."

ADB (2018) contends that resilience can be achieved through several actions, and there is a need to build more measures on those actions over time. A key is to make resilience-building efforts reflective, redundant, robust, flexible, inclusive, resourceful, and integrated. According to ADB (2014), a city is climate-resilient when its (i) systems can survive shocks and stresses, (ii) people and organizations can accommodate such stresses into their day-to-day decisions, and (iii) institutional structures continue to support the capacity of people and organizations to fulfill their aims.

ADB (2014) noted that urban climate change resilience (UCCR) is evident in cities that have avoided system-wide collapse and those that have transformed how they function in the face of disruptions. To develop and sustain UCCR, action plans must encourage the generation and accumulation of knowledge from local experiences of actions and mechanisms. Engaging stakeholders, such as champions and entrepreneurs, government leaders, academe, and civil society is critical. Scaling up policies and plans, as well as investments and financing (from governments, external donors, and the private sector) can significantly contribute to UCCR.

3.1 Anchoring on a Resilience Framework

ADB (2019) promotes a resilience framework with four key aspects: systems-based holistic planning, multilevel governance strengthening, social networks, and financial management instruments (Figure 1).

(i) **Infrastructure resilience.** Identifying and understanding climate change and disaster risk information are crucial when planning, constructing, and operating infrastructure projects. Evidence-based decision-making must be done across the full project cycle. A holistic approach, rather than a narrow focus on physical or technical solutions, enables transformational resilience building.

(ii) **Ecological resilience.** Increasing attention to ecosystem services as part of a strategy to complement the built infrastructure, and to help people adapt to climate change and manage disaster risks.

(iii) **Social and institutional resilience.** Explicitly focusing on the social dimensions of resilience to reflect the mutually reinforcing nature of poverty and climate vulnerability, and their disproportionately high impact on vulnerable populations. Building partnerships and collective action across different scales and sectors through multistakeholder collaboration is key to a systems-based approach. A people-centered resilience approach needs to be grounded in political economy analysis to understand the local context and power relationships.

(iv) **Financial resilience.** Strengthening financial capacity and management of climate and disaster risks to support proactive adaptation measures, enable timely relief and recovery from disasters triggered by natural hazard, and incorporate measures to build back better.

Figure 1: Asian Development Bank Resilience Framework

ECOLOGICAL RESILIENCE

- Conservation, restoration, and rehabilitation of ecosystems
- Use of biodiversity and ecosystem services as part of an overall strategy of building resilience of communities and the economy

PHYSICAL RESILIENCE

Climate and disaster risk-informed infrastructure planning and development

FINANCE, KNOWLEDGE, AND PARTNERSHIPS

RESILIENCE

FINANCIAL RESILIENCE

Support for enhancing financial preparedness in a changing climate and disaster risk context

SOCIAL AND INSTITUTIONAL RESILIENCE

- Pro-poor and pro-vulnerable investments
- Multifaceted resilience solutions—livelihoods, social protection, skill development—at multiple scales (households, community, and local government)

Source: Asian Development Bank.

3.2 The Urban Climate Change Resilience Trust Fund

Cofinancing from other sources helps ADB perform its mandate. One of the multi-donor trust funds ADB administers is the $150 million Urban Climate Change Resilience Trust Fund (UCCRTF), which comprise contributions from the governments of the United Kingdom and Switzerland and The Rockefeller Foundation. UCCRTF aims to support fast-growing cities in reducing the risks that poor and vulnerable people face from floods, storms, or droughts, by helping cities to better plan, design, and invest in measures that address climate change. It also aims to scale up investments in UCCR in Bangladesh, Indonesia, Nepal, Pakistan, the Philippines, and Viet Nam. UCCRTF provides technical assistance and grant financing for climate change integration into city planning, implementation of both "hard" (infrastructure) and "soft" (policy or institutional) interventions and includes a strong knowledge component. Additionally, UCCRTF resources help enhance nature-based resilience approaches, stress the mobilization of communities as project partners, strengthen institutional capacity, and develop financial instruments for adaptation and disaster resilience.

The regional technical assistance (TA) on Promoting Urban Climate Change Resilience in Selected Asian Cities (2017–2022) is a flagship UCCRTF project.[1] It seeks to integrate community-led projects (CLPs) into ongoing or planned ADB projects in Bangladesh, Pakistan, and the Philippines. Selected collaboratively by ADB and the respective governments, the project sites are the municipalities of Bagerhat and Faridpur in Bangladesh; Abbottabad and Sialkot in Pakistan; and Del Carmen, Janiuay, La Trinidad, and Malay in the Philippines. To maximize the potential of community-driven development approaches and tools, the project collaborates with civil society organizations (CSOs); one such CSO is Oxfam GB, an international nongovernment organization dedicated to fighting inequality, advancing gender justice, and campaigning on climate.

---

[1]   See ADB. Promoting Urban Climate Change Resilience in Selected Asian Cities – Development of Pilot Activities and Project Development Support (Sub-project 3). https://www.adb.org/projects/48317-004/main (RETA 9329).

4. Research Design, Data, and Methods

Informed by the concept of multidimensional poverty (MDP), the ADB Resilience Framework serves as a scaffolding to generate holistic intervention strategies and project ideas to respond to multiple and unique forms of deprivations experienced by those in the informal sector. To apply the framework to analyzing resilience, this chapter utilizes empirical data gleaned from project documents, presentations, and reports. The analysis assembles multiple strands of evidence drawn from community stakeholders, CSO project implementers, UCCRTF as the source of funding, and ADB. Specifically, it examines two CLPs that are already at advanced stages of project implementation in Janiuay and La Trinidad in the Philippines. The aspects explored in each case include how vulnerability mapping is carried out, who are the agents of development, how social inclusion and climate resilience are integrated, and what actions are being implemented to enhance the communities' resilience from the impacts of climate change.

5. Building Resilient Urban Communities

This section clarifies how CLPs in the Philippines were designed and implemented. As of 2018, about 17.7 million Filipinos (or 16.7% of the country's population) did not earn enough to meet their basic food and nonfood needs. The National Economic and Development Authority (2014) estimates that there are over 1.5 million informal settler families; of these, 767,502 live in precarious locations deemed "danger area," such as along railroad tracks, *esteros* (estuaries), riverbanks, and high-tension wires; 378,517 occupy privately owned lands; and 265,361 are on government properties.

The municipalities of Janiuay and La Trinidad are typical of a country where a segment of the population lives in informal settlements and relies on the informal economy. Both local governments have limited resources and capacities to deliver optimal infrastructure services such as housing, livelihood, water supply, health care, and environmental services. Between 2014 and 2017, prompted by a myriad of challenges, these two municipalities, along with those of Del Carmen and Malay, actively collaborated with the Philippine Department of Environment and Natural Resources to access a proposed loan from the ADB-funded Solid Waste Management Sector Project. Recognizing that the municipalities have other needs too, ADB nominated them to be part of the regional TA.

The Municipality of Janiuay is in Iloilo Province, 33 kilometers northwest of Iloilo City, the provincial capital. It is estimated that Janiuay is 68.8 meters above mean sea level, and 55% of its land area is mostly plains with a maximum slope of 8%. The rest of its territory is mountainous and forested. With a population of 63,905 in 2015, Janiuay is politically subdivided into 60 barangays (villages). An inventory of informal settlers showed that 124 households reside in flood-prone areas and 456 households have settled in private lands, exposed to the threat of eviction (Flores and Taylor 2018).

The major sources of income for Janiuay are cultivation of rice, corn, sugar, copra, coffee, banana, abaca fiber; fishing; and raising game fowls, goats, cattle, and poultry. Rainfall influences the production of these crops and animals, as the region's two main rivers, Suage and Magape, run dry during the summer months. Only 37% of the population is served by the main water supply system; the rest relies on deep wells, undeveloped springs, and open dug wells (Flores and Taylor 2018). The municipality has one government hospital, one rural health unit, and 40 barangay health stations, wherein the physician to patient ratio both in the rural health unit and hospital is 1:12,781, which is far short of the World Health Organization standard of 1 doctor to every 435 patients (Flores and Taylor 2018).

The municipality of La Trinidad is the business district of Benguet Province. Located 256 kilometers north of Manila, the country's capital, La Trinidad covers an area of 81 square kilometers and comprises 16 barangays. In 2015, it had a population of 129,133, with an estimated annual growth rate of 4.09%. Due to its proximity to Baguio City, a highly urbanized and popular tourist destination, La Trinidad is considered a gateway to the southern lowlands of the Cordillera Region. This strategic location has made it one of the country's largest trading posts for agricultural produce, primarily vegetables and fruits. La Trinidad is characterized by its steep mountains and high terrain with a mean slope of 40% and elevation ranging from 500 to 1,700 meters. Spanning 250 hectares, its urban center is a valley crisscrossed by several bodies of water such as the Balili River, Wangal River, and Bolo Creek. Draining from the Busol Watershed are Ambiong Creek, Lubas Creek, and Tawang Creek. This urban part is vulnerable to flooding. Being the province's commercial, educational, and agro-tourism center also triggers land conversion (Manegdeg and Taylor 2018).

5.1 Building Resilience at the Community Level

In municipalities like Janiuay and La Trinidad, like elsewhere in the world, the approach to eradicate poverty focuses on providing access to basic services, and is centralized, funded by national coffers and designed at the national or local level. Sectoral in nature, many such initiatives do not reach the urban poor in informal settlements, diminishing the overall quality of life. An impetus to pursue resilience outcomes at the community level guided the design of the regional TA (footnote 1). It did not specify the projects to be delivered, rather it stressed a consultative process that encouraged the key stakeholders to self-determine their needs and priorities. This section now investigates how the four aspects of systems resilience—infrastructure, ecological, social and institutional, and financial—were pursued by the CLPs in Janiuay and La Trinidad.

Infrastructure Resilience

The degree of understanding of climate change and how it informs project identification, design, and funding varies across local governments in the Philippines. To balance this unevenness, ADB's UCCRTF brought together in 2017 the cities participating in the regional TA to the "Resilience Academy," an intensive 4-day workshop, to link interdisciplinary teams of local stakeholders, with place-based and technical expertise, to design solutions to address current and future risks in their respective areas (footnote 1). The exercise provided coaching on identifying shocks and stresses (including climate-related ones), mapping assets, determining vulnerable groups, applying resilience qualities in project design, engaging with stakeholders, and deciding on resilience outcomes and indicators. The workshop emphasized inclusion and urged the participants to think about how the poorest and most vulnerable were differently affected by various risks.

The teams from Janiuay and La Trinidad returned to their cities with lessons from the Resilience Academy to lead the "city profiling" process. City- and community-level information was consolidated to present each city's demographic, socioeconomic, physical, environmental, and institutional profiles, along with its development challenges and existing risks and vulnerabilities. The city's institutional and governance capacities, policy frameworks, and initiatives on disaster risk management and climate resilience were also documented.

With support from Oxfam and its local implementation partner, the Philippine Rural Reconstruction Movement (PRRM), a workshop in each city was conducted to rank vulnerable communities, choose a target community for the regional TA (footnote 1), identify an initial core group of stakeholders for the project, and set the criteria for selecting a CLP. A pilot community in each city was selected through focus group discussions, and objective vulnerability indicators such as poverty level and availability of an early warning system were identified. Likewise, the local stakeholders decided to rank communities based on qualitative indicators, such as their needs, willingness to commit and contribute to the project, and synergy with the city's vision on climate resilience.

The above processes correctly captured the primary threat and risk in Janiuay (periods of drought affecting the water supply) and identified the vulnerable population (43% or, approximately, 134 households in the village of San Julian are not connected to the water supply system). They rely on deep wells using an electric motor or manual/hand pump, open dug well, and undeveloped spring for their domestic water needs (Flores and Taylor 2020). Those who are connected to the main water supply have intermittent access, especially during summer months, and report water quality issues. Thus, the Janiuay CLP is focused on securing water supply. The project involves the construction of a community-managed water system with an overhead tank, storage tank, and piped distribution system, and rainwater harvesting facility with underground cistern, overhead storage tank, and treatment tank. The rainwater harvesting facility will augment the water supply for the target households during the rainy season and can serve as alternate water storage facility for the community.

On the other hand, in La Trinidad, flooding was identified as the leading threat. More than 500 small-scale and informal strawberry and vegetable growers in the village of Betag were identified as the most vulnerable group. The project feasibility study confirmed that flooding has a major impact on farmers' lives and livelihoods. Other underlying issues compounding their vulnerability concern land ownership and security of tenure as the land is rented on short-term arrangements from the Benguet State University. The farmers pay fees ranging from ₱6,250 ($125 at the end of October 2019) to ₱12,500 ($250) monthly for plots ranging from 250 to 500 square meters. During flooding episodes, these farms are inundated for almost 12 hours before the floodwater recedes, which destroys crops as they cannot withstand waterlogging for more than just a few hours (Manegdeg and Taylor 2020). The community, with expertise provided by the regional TA and the local government, pursued a flood risk reduction measure which involves the construction of three reinforced concrete box culverts. The technical design of the reinforced box culverts—which are wider, bigger, and thicker than the traditional culverts—aimed to improve the discharge of floodwaters out of the field's catchment area into Bolo Creek. The intervention is expected to last 50 to 75 years and handle projected increases in precipitation and flood volumes over the next 50 years due to climate change. During the periods of June to August and September to November, respectively, precipitation levels in La Trinidad are expected to increase by 18.5% and 26.3%.

Community-led project in Janiuay. A rainwater harvesting and storage tank, and cooperative office, constructed in 2021 complement the community-managed water supply system in the village of San Julian (photo by Philippine Rural Reconstruction Movement).

The municipalities successfully incorporated climate change and disasters data from various sources, including local indigenous knowledge, for determining key threats, identifying potential measures that could reduce risks, and using the information to design their community-led projects. However, in La Trinidad, a key challenge is that flooding in the village of Betag cannot be assessed based solely on flooding data within municipal boundaries; instead, the broader implications of climate change on the watershed, of which there is little information available for modeling purposes, need to be considered. Although small-scale infrastructure was delivered in both municipalities, infrastructure resilience within each of the communities was achieved only in part, and in some sectors. Limited financial resources, both at the municipal level and within the regional TA, prevented the financing of other resilience-building measures that the communities had identified.

Community-led project in La Trinidad. Climate-resilient concrete box culverts for flood risk reduction were constructed in three key sites in the village of Betag in 2021 (photo by Philippine Rural Reconstruction Movement).

Ecological Resilience

The CLPs were informed by increased attention to ecosystem services. In Janiuay, for example, the community-based water supply system design created an alternative, sustainable source of water for the community to respond to projected decreases in rainfall over the next 50 years. The longer periods of reduced rainfall in Janiuay may lead to drought events and inadequate water supply, adversely affecting agriculture and irrigation, water table replenishment, and water quality. These impacts could cause other problems such as heat-related illnesses, hunger, and malnourishment. The physical measures involved a combination of improved groundwater extraction and rainwater harvesting. For the groundwater source, a geo-resistivity test was conducted to find a stable aquifer. The rainwater harvesting facility will lessen groundwater depletion by reducing the amount of water extracted by the system from the ground and allow for some period for underground water recharge replenishment (Flores and Taylor 2020).

In Barangay Betag, in La Trinidad, the community discussions concluded that while flooding is localized in their valley, the capacity of natural bodies of water and constructed drainage systems to collect and drain floodwater is affected by the upstream neighboring city of Baguio. To complement the infrastructure, farmers were also provided training on clearing vegetation debris, to prevent the clogging of water bodies and drainage systems, and on elevated gardening. They also recognized that the ability of the watershed to store water and prevent runoff is dependent on a host of factors including forest cover. However, watershed management is complex as it transcends municipal boundaries and involves national government agencies. Hence, a key lesson from this experience is that attaining ecological resilience is challenging as it could require a transboundary approach.

Albeit small in scale due to the modest monetary investment, area affected, number of beneficiaries, and level of complexity, both CLPs adhered to the ADB Environmental and Social Safeguards Policy.

Social and Institutional Resilience

The regional TA identified people's lack of access to decision-making as a driver of urban poverty, inequality, and exclusion. Although the local government is the most proximate scale of government, the urban poor have few opportunities to influence policy-making processes in a meaningful way, particularly in determining spending priorities. The regional TA was designed to empower local communities by giving them a voice in decision-making through consultative means, such as focus group discussions (footnote 1).

Through the stakeholder analysis carried out in both project sites, various actors, sectors, and groups were identified and classified as either (i) decision makers, (ii) affected by decisions, (iii) traditionally excluded from local decision-making processes, or (iv) can play significant roles in implementing the project.

In each community, local stakeholders decided to form their respective ad-hoc committee, later named Community Stakeholder Group (CSG), to serve as an institutional and multisectoral mechanism for transparent and effective information sharing, decision-making, and implementation of community decisions and actions. It ingrained among CSG members a deep understanding of the issues that affect the community and, more importantly, its vulnerable members. In the village of San Julian, the CSG membership comprised representatives from women's groups, the elderly, single parents, persons with disability, farmers, families with overseas migrant workers, small and medium-sized enterprises, private sector employees, and local government. In the village of Betag, the CSG comprised representatives from farmer groups and associations, the youth, vendors, and stall owners, the elderly, women's organizations, recipients of the national government's social protection scheme called 4Ps, other civic groups, and the local government. Not only is the diversity of representation in these CSGs commendable, but also the fact that members contributed their time, skills, and knowledge without expecting any remuneration.

The CSGs led the community resilience planning process, oversaw project-related activities, led the implementation and sustainability of the project, and ensured meaningful community participation. The CSGs influenced the type and modalities of capacity development support that the regional TA had provided. A community development worker was mobilized as the project's community resilience officer at each site to guide the community on participatory approaches, particularly in (i) prioritizing what will be the community-led project (CLP), (ii) determining the scope of the feasibility study for the proposed CLP and which elements of the CLP design should be climate-resilient, (iii) explaining the procurement process, and (iv) determining the community's responsibilities during project construction and operation, and how the project can be sustained. These necessitated iterative processes, formal and informal dialogues, and workshops aimed at empowering the community.

Empowerment of people is a core tenet of sustainability. The regional TA demonstrated that the quality and consistency of capacity development inputs can empower communities to act on urban poverty and climate change challenges. What remains to be seen is whether the CSGs can (i) tackle other development issues in their communities beyond the ongoing project, (ii) influence planning and decision-making at the municipal level, and (iii) survive beyond the conclusion of the regional TA.

Financial Resilience

The regional TA helped CSGs in enhancing their financial management capacity for implementing adaptation measures related to climate and disaster risks. CSG members were trained on estimating investment costs for climate adaptation measures listed in the community's resilience plan and identifying potential sources of funding. They were also trained on preparing bid specifications and reviewing bids, and operating and maintaining community-owned assets, including financial sustainability. The regional TA also helped establish a Procurement Management Committee within the CSGs.

An ongoing exercise that CSGs undertake is the basic cost–benefit analysis. A limitation that has been observed is that CLPs provide a range of co-benefits not traditionally covered in standard cost–benefit analysis. Building resilience to the impacts of climate change at the community level does not only require monetary resources for small-scale infrastructure but also other forms of investments in equally vital components of the project, such as awareness raising, capacity building, and engaging with the private sector. The results of such investments are difficult to quantify in monetary terms.

In Janiuay, a preliminary cost–benefit analysis is being conducted to determine the value for money of the community-based water supply system and rainwater harvesting facility. The community-led project is expected to generate an average net annual revenue of ₱224,864.00 ($4,497.28 at the end of October 2019). The water tariffs proposed are expected to generate monthly revenues that can financially support the operation of the water system (Table 1). The profits will be used for system upkeep and upgrading, capital improvements, and maintenance and replacement of equipment and parts such as pumps and motors. This shows that the project has good revenue potential and cost recovery rate, and that it is likely sustainable.

Table 1: Estimated Revenue Based on Calculated Water Tariff

No. of Target Service Connections	Average Monthly Consumption per Household	Water Tariff (per m³/ month)	Average Monthly Revenue	Average Annual Revenue	Net ROI per Year
134 households (670 persons)	16.32 m³ (Equivalent to ₱408.00)	₱25.00 per m³. Required minimum consumption of 10 m³.	₱54,672.00	₱ 656,064.00	₱ 224,864.00 ($4,497.28)

m³ = cubic meter, ROI = return on investment.

Source: Feasibility Study Report of Brgy. San Julian Community-Managed Water Supply System, 2020.

The CLP is expected to generate revenues to cover the initial investment cost of $186,770 as well as the operating and maintenance costs. The positive benefit–cost ratio of 1.20—assuming that the Community-Managed Water Supply System will be in full operation over the next 50 years—indicates that the CLP is worth the money invested as it will help the community meet its immediate water supply needs and improve its climate resilience capacities. Aside from financial and economic benefits, social and environmental gains are also expected from the project, such as improved sanitation and better health outcomes; improved access to clean, potable, and stable water supply; and decreased time poverty, especially among women.

The project also registered positive return on investment of 20%, indicating potential cost-efficiency. Given its estimated annual revenue, the project is expected to recover the initial investment costs in its first 12 years of operation and then generate stable profits in subsequent years. The planning cost amounts to only $7.48 per beneficiary, which is highly economical as the amount covers the series of community consultations, community engagement, participatory planning, and design session with the community. The cost of capacity building and skills development is also low, at $6.41 per beneficiary. The cost of CLP investment is $137.63 per beneficiary, which is much lower than most investment projects. The modest costs and expected long-term gains indicate that CLPs are good value for money.

In La Trinidad, the construction of flood risk reduction box culverts was completed in July 2021, and the infrastructure's value was immediately realized when typhoon Fabian hit the area, which brought continuous rainfall for over 7 days, with 400 millimeters (mm) recorded on just the 23rd of July 2021. This 24-hour rate exceeded half the monthly average of 700 mm for July 2021. At that time, strawberry runners had been planted and lettuce and other vegetables were at various stages of growth. According to the CSG, the flooding subsided after 4 hours. Prior to the construction of the culverts, floodwaters could rise to 2 meters and inundate the whole valley floor for up to 12 hours before receding (Manegdeg and Taylor 2018). The CLP's performance demonstrated a marked improvement in the community's resilience and adaptive capacity to climate-related hazards that have destructive effects on their livelihoods and long-term economic well-being.

The CSG, with support from Oxfam and PRRM, is currently refining the cost–benefit ratio of the project by estimating the monetary value of economic losses avoided because of the project. For example, a farmer can have three production cycles of lettuce. Gross sales from each cycle are ₱80,000 ($1,600 at the end of October 2019) with an average production cost of ₱10,000 ($200). On the other hand, the production of strawberry—an annual crop usually planted in September in time for the December and summer harvests—costs around ₱100,000 ($2,000) with ₱350,000 gross sales ($7,000). Typhoon Ompong in 2018 cost local farmers almost ₱300,000 ($6,000) worth of income opportunity. The CLP has reduced the financial burden on farmers and residents in the area.

5.2 Delivering and Sustaining Results

The CLP projects in both Janiuay and La Trinidad were designed to be managed by the communities, thus their capacities for operation and maintenance were also enhanced through the regional TA. Despite the disruptions caused by the coronavirus disease (COVID-19) pandemic beginning in 2020, the CSGs continued to mobilize, complete construction, and jointly create sustainability plans. In Janiuay, a community-based water cooperative is being established to run the facility and will be supported by the barangay administration and municipal water supply provider. It will provide access to water for the urban poor, many of whom are informal settlers and were not connected to the main water supply system. Reliable and continuous water for drinking, domestic use, economic activities, and livelihoods addresses the twin challenges of poverty reduction and climate resilience and raises the quality of life. It also offers co-benefits such as preparing for drought, fire, and other disasters which are expected to increase in frequency and severity in the future due to climate change. Similarly, in Betag village, the CLP addresses the perennial problem of flooding, which affects the livelihood of low-income farmers, by improving flood drainage. Inspired and informed by strong community engagement and the tools used in the regional TA, the municipality has committed resources to improve the drainage system and tributaries in neighboring parts of the project site and in peripheral barangays.

6. Conclusion

Climate change has added to the vulnerabilities of urban poor communities, and the shocks and stresses thereof are becoming increasingly evident. Under the regional TA, ADB and CSOs, as development partners, have striven to offer holistic and transformative solutions to various economic, environmental, and social inequities in informal settlements to achieve the SDGs. This chapter demonstrates that the CLPs under the regional TA have upheld ADB's urban climate change resilience (UCCR) standards in achieving urban resilience outcomes. Linked with ADB's Resilience Framework, the community-led projects incorporated the vital UCCR elements which are used as nonnegotiable standards in the project design.

The authors conclude that pertinent issues such as social exclusion and climate change vulnerability, which remain peripheral, must be mainstreamed in poverty alleviation measures for the informal sector. These significant issues include tenure security, access to basic services, and sustainable livelihoods. Recognizing the multidimensional nature of poverty should be a prerequisite for urban planning and management. Community-level resilience interventions provide an opportunity to address deeper structural issues that contribute to vulnerability and informality of the urban poor. From a planning perspective, the application of more pro-poor and climate-resilient urban planning and investment programming could be an important first step toward more inclusive, climate-resilient urban economies.

This chapter has revealed the value of adopting a resilience framework that simultaneously investigates infrastructure, ecological, social, and institutional, and financial aspects of system resilience, to understand the complexity and multilayered needs of the urban poor. Development agents should therefore recognize that improving the quality of life for the urban poor should involve various forms of support to address those four aspects of resilience. The cases in Janiuay and La Trinidad demonstrate that the destructive impacts of climate- and disaster-related events can be minimized through CLPs, which can also prevent the reversal of developmental gains in the community.

Urban resilience cannot be achieved through a single action or in isolation. Actions need to be integrated across levels and must build on one another over time as lessons are learned about what works and does not toward enhancing urban resilience (ADB 2018). There is a need to improve climate resilience at different scales and with a range of different measures (Satterthwaite et al. 2020). When local communities are engaged in the design of urban resilience projects and planning processes, individuals and groups can agree on how climate and disaster risks specifically impact the local community, and how resilience initiatives can be developed to serve as local public goods. Such public goods have both tangible and intangible benefits. Tangible benefits include infrastructure resilience, for instance, the development of community-based water supply system in Janiuay and flood risk reduction measures in La Trinidad; and intangible benefits include greater inclusion of marginalized communities in decision-making, and increased empowerment and accountability of communities and local authorities alike for urban resilience planning.

The regional TA, through its community resilience planning processes and tools, used a combination of expert advice and local indigenous knowledge. The sociopolitical capital of local decision makers and policy makers was maximized so that the CLPs could embody multisectoral and cross-disciplinary perspectives. The resources spent on establishing and capacitating the Community Stakeholder Groups (CSGs) to enable social mobilization, community cohesion, and communication proved to be sound investments for social and institutional resilience. The sustainability of these small-scale projects, however, remains inconclusive as they could be affected by wider shifts in priorities, internal conflicts, transboundary issues, shifting political dynamics, and other challenges. The true test of sustainability will come once the external support from development partners such as ADB, UCCRTF, Oxfam, and PRRM ceases in December 2022.

A resilience approach that imbibes participation of non-state actors or agents at the community level could help identify and prioritize interventions and secure other sources of financing. Informal settlements and informal economies embody multidimensional poverty, and they often exist outside the ambit of formal policies and legal protection. As such, knowing specifically about how settlements are formed and how their unique living conditions impact settlers' lives, would help produce interventions particularly designed to address their needs (Simiyu, Cairncross, and Swilling 2018). However, the resources required to address the different aspects of underdevelopment affecting informal settlers exceed the financial capabilities of low- and middle-income countries, especially at the local government level (Shand et al. 2017). Commonly, not all resilience-building measures identified at the community level are financed. Hence, the CLPs discussed in this chapter attempted to achieve financial resilience.

An emphasis on building resilience at the community level is timely. A policy brief released by the UN Department of Economic and Social Affairs in October 2020 asserts that the COVID-19 pandemic and the ensuing global economic crisis will reverse years of gains in the reduction and alleviation of poverty, drastically undermining global efforts to meet the SDG goal of eradicating extreme poverty by 2030. The use of the ADB Resilience Framework could enable urban planners, engineers, and decision makers to identify individual dimensions of poverty without losing sight of its aggregate nature. Holistic and cross-disciplinary approaches, therefore, should not be arbitrary but systematic. This will be significant for addressing the deprivations of the urban poor exacerbated by the COVID-19 pandemic. Traditional urban planning tends to be top-down and overwhelmingly dominated by technical rationality, which alienates poor communities by excluding their knowledge and experiences. The resilience framework enables identifying complementary measures that can reduce the urban poor's deprivations and improve their coping mechanisms. Such measures are essential for effecting transformative recovery following climate- and disaster-related shocks and stresses.

References

Arup. 2013. City Resilience Index. https://www.arup.com/perspectives/publications/research/section/city-resilience-index.

Asian Development Bank (ADB). 2013. *Key Areas of Economic Analysis of Investment Projects*. Manila.

_____. 2014. *Urban Climate Change Resilience: A Synopsis*. https://www.adb.org/sites/default/files/publication/149164/urban-climate-change-resilience-synopsis.pdf.

_____. 2018. *ADB Strategy 2030: Achieving a Prosperous, Inclusive, Resilient, and Sustainable Asia and the Pacific*. Manila.

_____. 2019. *Building Resilient Infrastructure for the Future; Background Paper for the G20 Climate Sustainability Working Group*. Manila.

Center for Climate and Energy Solutions. 2019. *Climate Essentials: What is Climate Resilience and Why Does it Matter?* https://www.c2es.org/wp-content/uploads/2019/04/what-is-climate-resilience.pdf.

Chambers R. 1995. Poverty and Livelihood: Whose Reality Counts? *Environment and Urbanization* 7 (1). April.

Collier, P., E. Glaeser, T. Venables, M. Blake, and P. Manwaring. n.d. *Policy Options for Informal Settlements*. https://www.theigc.org/wp-content/uploads/2019/03/informal-settlements-policy-framing-paper-March-2019.pdf.

Eriksen, S. et al. 2021. Adaptation Interventions and Their Effect on Vulnerability in Developing Countries: Help, Hindrance, or Irrelevance? *World Development* 141 (2021): 105383. https://doi.org/10.1016/j.worlddev.2020.105383 0305-750X/! 2021.

Flores, R., and S. Taylor. 2018. Janiuay City Resilience Profile. Unpublished.

_____. 2020. Barangay Betag Community Resilience Plan. Unpublished.

Greenberg, M. 2009. It's Time for a Better Poverty Measure. *Center for American Progress*. 25 August. https://www.americanprogress.org/article/its-time-for-a-better-poverty-measure/.

Manegdeg, N., and S. Taylor. 2018. La Trinidad City Resilience Profile. Unpublished.

_____. 2020. Barangay San Julian Community Resilience Plan. Unpublished.

Melore, T. W., and V. Nel. 2020. Resilience of Informal Settlements to Climate Change in the Mountainous Areas of Konso, Ethiopia, and QwaQwa, South Africa. *Journal of Disaster Risk Studies* 12 (1): a778. https://doi.org/10.4102/jamba.v12i1.778.

Narayan, D., R. Chambers, M. Shah, and P. Petesch. 2000. *Voices of the Poor, Crying Out for Change*. Oxford: Oxford University Press.

National Economic and Development Authority. 2014. *Developing a National Informal Settlements Upgrading Strategy for the Philippines*. Manila.

Peter G. Paterson Foundation. 2019. How Do We Measure Poverty? Is There a Better Way to Do It? https://www.pgpf.org/budget-basics/how-do-we-measure-poverty-and-is-there-a-better-way-to-do-it.

Satterthwaite D. et al. 2020. Building Resilience to Climate Change in Informal Settlements. *One Earth* 2 (2): 143–156. 21 February. https://reader.elsevier.com/reader/sd/pii/S259033222030 0506?token=3E0A9E41CA57A9AEA9A62F824C903FDF21BB ACA717AA687E0CD16FDE1359D3EED271CA24C9AA5DA28 84E6C34527FA4A6&originRegion=eu-west-1&originCreation-=20220222105117 (accessed 24 October 2021).

Shand, W. et al. 2017. *Enabling Private Investments in Informal Settlements: Exploring the Potential of Community Finance*. London: UK Aid and Infrastructure and Cities for Economic Development. https://pubs.iied.org/sites/default/files/pdfs/ migrate/ G04180. pdf (accessed 20 October 2021).

Simiyu, S., S. Cairncross, and M. Swilling. 2018. Understanding Living Conditions and Deprivation in Informal Settlements of Kisumu, Kenya. *Urban Forum* (2019) 30: 223–241. https://doi.org/10.1007/s12132-018-9346-3.

Subiyanto, A., E. Aldrian, and R. Boer. 2020. Climate Resilience: Concepts, Theory, and Methods of Measuring. *Environment Asia* 13 (1): 1–13. DOI 110.14456/ea.2020.1. ISSN 1906-1714; ONLINE ISSN:2586-8861.

Sverdlik, A., D. Mitlin, and D. Dodman. 2019. *Realizing the Multiple Benefits of Climate Resilience and Inclusive Development in Informal Settlements*. New York: C40 Cities Climate Leadership Group. https://reliefweb.int/sites/reliefweb.int/files/resources/C40-Climate-Resilience-Inclusive-Housing.pdf.

Townsend, P. 1979. *Poverty in the United Kingdom*. London: Allen Lane and Penguin Books.

Union of Concerned Scientists (UCS). 2016. *Toward Climate Resilience, A Framework and Principles for Science-Based Adaptation*. https://www.ucsusa.org/sites/default/files/attach/2016/06/climate-resilience-framework-and-principles.pdf.

United Nations Children's Fund. 2012. *Children in an Urban World: The State of the World's Children 2012*. https://www.unicef.org/media/89226/file/The%20State%20of%20the%20World's%20 Children%202012.pdf.

United Nations Department of Economic and Social Affairs (UN DESA). 1995. Report of the World Summit for Social Development. https://www.un.org/development/desa/dspd/world-summit-for-social-development-1995/wssd-1995-agreements/pawssd-chapter-2.html.

_____. 2016. *World Economic and Social Survey 2016: Climate Change Resilience: An Opportunity for Reducing Inequalities.* https://www.un.org/development/desa/dpad/wp-content/uploads/sites/45/publication/WESS_2016_Report.pdf.

United Nations Economic Commission for Europe (UNECE). 2009. *Self-Made Cities: In Search of Sustainable Solutions for Informal Settlements in the United Nations Economic Commission for Europe Region.* https://unece.org/sites/default/files/2022-01/SelfMadeCities_E.pdf.

_____. 2016. *Informal Settlements in Countries with Economies in Transition in the UNECE Region.* https://unece.org/DAM/hlm/documents/Publications/Literature_Review_on_Informal_Settlements.pdf.

United Nations International Strategy for Disaster Reduction. 2009. *2009 UNISDR Terminology on Disaster Risk Reduction.* https://www.unisdr.org/files/7817_UNISDRTerminologyEnglish.pdf.

Vahapoglu, L. 2019. Strategies for Improving Informal Settlements. In *Global Health Equity Research in Translation,* edited by E. Boamah, K. Kordas, and S. Raja. New York: University of Buffalo.

Wilkinson, E., T. Tanner, C. Simmonet, and F. Pichon. 2015. The Geography of Poverty and Climate Extremes. In *Climate Extremes and Resilient Poverty Reduction: Development Designed with Uncertainty in Mind,* edited by E. Wilkinson and K. Peters. London: Overseas Development Institute.

3

Policies and Programs for the Urban Poor: Slum Upgrading in Indonesia

Joris van Etten and Tiffany M. Tran

Abstract

Approximately one-third of the world's urban residents live in informal settlements (King et al. 2017) characterized by lack of secure land or dwelling tenure, lack of access to adequate basic infrastructure services, and noncompliance with spatial plans or building regulations. Although national definitions may vary, slums are the most excluded form of informal settlements, with high levels of poverty and large expanses of unsafe housing located in hazardous areas (UN-Habitat 2015).

This chapter explores the overlap and distinction between urban informality and urban poverty through a focus on slum upgrading in Indonesian cities. Because poverty is multidimensional, slum upgrading programs cannot focus on physical infrastructure alone if they are targeted at the urban poor. For an integrated approach to slum upgrading, program development must prioritize the use of multidimensional approaches to address technical, institutional, and financial challenges of program implementation. Case studies from the Asian Development Bank's urban sector work in Indonesia illustrate the lessons learned from attempts to transform practice and reflect on the discrepancies between theory and practice.

Keywords: cities, informal settlements, slum upgrading, urban poor, policy

1. Introduction

Safe housing and urban infrastructure are fundamental to human well-being, environmental sustainability, and economic productivity—but the number of people without these basic services is growing. Since 1990, although the global share of slum population to urban population has declined, the global urban slum population has continued to increase in absolute numbers (King et al. 2017). Today, over a billion people worldwide live in urban informal settlements (UN-Habitat 2020) characterized by lack of secure land or dwelling tenure, lack of access to adequate basic infrastructure services, and nonconformance with spatial plans or building regulations (UN-Habitat 2015).

Beyond these defining characteristics, informal settlements are diverse. For instance, the original settlement of Jamestown in Accra, Ghana is legally recognized and historically significant. The favelas of Rio de Janeiro, Brazil have developed in the urban periphery due to displacement or migration. The humanitarian settlements in Cox's Bazar, Bangladesh have developed where refugees, asylum seekers, and internally displaced persons have sought safety from persecution.

The UN considers slums as the most excluded form of informal settlements, characterized by high levels of poverty and large expanses of unsafe housing in hazardous areas (UN-Habitat 2015). The persistence of slums in developing regions is mainly driven by the negative externalities of rapid urbanization, whereby land-use policies, spatial planning, housing provision, and basic service delivery have not kept pace with growth and demand (UN-Habitat 2020).

Asia has the world's largest share of the urban population living in slums and the highest projected growth rate for urban slums. In 2018, 36% of the world's urban population living in slums lived in East or Southeast Asia with another 22% in Central or South Asia (UN-Habitat 2020). Furthermore, for every 1% increase in urban population growth, the incidence of slums is projected to increase by 5.3%— five times faster (UN-Habitat 2020). Of the countries with reported data on the urban population living in slums, Indonesia has one of the largest slum populations at 44.9 million people (Table 1). However, Afghanistan[1] and Bangladesh had the largest shares of the urban population living in slums, with 73.5% and 47.6%, respectively. Investments in housing, living space, water, sanitation, and secure land tenure in Asian cities are therefore much needed.

---

[1]   ADB placed on hold its assistance in Afghanistan effective 15 August 2021; See ADB Statement on Afghanistan | Asian Development Bank (published on 10 November 2021). Manila; This report was prepared based on information available for Afghanistan as of 31 July 2021.

Table 1: Urban Population Living in Slums in Select ADB Developing Member Countries, 2018

Country	Percent of Urban Population (%)	Urban Slum Population (million)
Indonesia	30.4	44.9
Bangladesh	47.6	29.0
Philippines	44.3	22.1
Uzbekistan	58.5	9.6
Myanmar	57.1	9.4
Thailand	24.5	8.5
Afghanistan[a]	73.5	6.8
Viet Nam	13.5	4.7
Nepal	49.3	2.9
Cambodia	45.6	1.7

[a] ADB placed on hold its assistance in Afghanistan effective 15 August 2021; See ADB Statement on Afghanistan | Asian Development Bank (published on 10 November 2021). Manila; This report was prepared based on information available for Afghanistan as of 31 July 2021.

Source: UN-Habitat Urban Indicators Database. https://data.unhabitat.org/ (accessed 5 January 2022).

Addressing the challenge of providing access to adequate and affordable housing and infrastructure is critical to building livable cities and communities. Gaps in the provision of urban services can lead to informal, illegal, or unregulated self-provisioning by residents, posing high individual and societal costs and threatening human well-being, economic productivity, and environmental sustainability (Beard, Mahendra, and Westphal 2016). Unmanaged solid waste, for example, can clog drainage systems and increase risk of flooding and waterborne diseases from contaminated wastewater. Overcrowding and inadequate water supply during the coronavirus disease (COVID-19) pandemic has precluded implementation of safety measures including handwashing, physical distancing, and self-isolation, creating new risks to health and livelihood. The high rate of unregulated groundwater extraction in Jakarta is contributing to land subsidence and increasing flood risk for coastal communities, especially for the urban poor (World Bank 2011).

The international community—including nation states, multilateral organizations, and international nongovernment organizations (INGOs)—has established various global policies and targets to meet these urban development challenges. Since the 1970s, the United

Nations Human Settlements Programme (UN-Habitat) has spearheaded global policy for human settlements and urban development. Through international conferences such as the World Urban Forum and Habitat, UN-Habitat has facilitated a global agenda for the sustainable development of cities. Today, two global policy documents broadly represent international thinking on urban development: (i) the Sustainable Development Goals (SDGs) adopted by United Nations member states in 2015, specifically SDG 11 for sustainable cities and communities, which aims to make cities inclusive, safe, resilient, and sustainable; and (ii) the New Urban Agenda, which provides a road map to help countries implement, monitor, and report progress on SDG 11. To assist with policy implementation, donor countries and development finance institutions, including the Asian Development Bank (ADB), provide financing services such as grants and concessional lending to developing country governments or entities.

However, progress on slum improvement has been mixed. Voluntary National Reviews of SDG 11 in 2018 showed that while urban development features prominently in national agendas, over 90% of countries reported challenges related to adequate housing and proliferation of informal settlements (UN-Habitat 2020), with notable increases in Bhutan, Egypt, and Jamaica (UN DESA 2018). Moreover, few countries had presented policy interventions that leveraged the linkages between SDG 11 and New Urban Agenda (UN-Habitat 2020).

Given the complex policy and implementation experience for slum improvement, how can the international community support Asian cities in providing access to improved housing and urban infrastructure? Using select case studies from ADB's recent urban sector work in Indonesia, this chapter attempts to argue that multidimensional approaches to slum improvement may provide an answer to this challenging question. Because Indonesia's on-site slum upgrading policy served as an international model for over half a century (Das and King 2019), its recent policy shift toward urban renewal and slum redevelopment presents a unique opportunity to examine slum upgrading within the context of its rise and fall.

The chapter begins with a theoretical framework to motivate the discussion on informal settlements, followed by an introduction to the Indonesian context to provide background information for the case studies. The subsequent section presents three case studies highlighting lessons learned, followed by a policy discussion on those takeaways. The chapter concludes with reflections on the discrepancies between theory and practice, and implications for the future of informal settlements in Indonesia and beyond.

2. The Case for Multidimensional Approaches

This chapter's theoretical framework relies on literature at the intersection of urban informality and multidimensional poverty to analyze the complexities of informal settlements and slum improvement policies in Indonesia (Figure 1). Informal settlements and slums represent a unique spatial manifestation of urban informality and urban poverty. Urban informality in slums includes informal real estate transactions, self-construction of housing, and self-provisioning of urban services. Urban poverty in slums comprises multidimensional deprivation, from monetary to health, education, and infrastructure poverty (OPHI 2020). The tendency to focus on inadequate housing and infrastructure in slums lends itself to policies and programs that measure direct impacts of infrastructure interventions, such as rates of coverage and project maintenance.

However, to achieve long-term improvements to socioeconomic outcomes, slum improvement programs must take a multidimensional approach that targets multiple aspects of informality and poverty simultaneously. Successful slum improvement programs have taken this approach primarily by including multiple types of stakeholders in the upgrading process, particularly communities. These programs offer both physical and nonphysical interventions, including housing microfinance or livelihood development, and allow for flexibility in location of upgrading, whether on-site or elsewhere. Although coordinated by a national level agency, the Baan Mankong housing program in Bangkok, Thailand primarily relied on community-driven development and the combined action of central and local governments, community-based organizations, and households (Lucci et al. 2015). Moreover, the program allowed communities the flexibility to choose between types of upgrading options and thereby the location of interventions (Bhatkal and Lucci 2015). Integrated Urban Projects (PIUs) in Medellin, Colombia notably connected slums to the city by cable car and invested in comprehensive upgrading around the transit stations, including housing, increased public space, new libraries and schools, and economic development through training and employment in public works (Lucci et al. 2015).

In practice, however, multidimensional approaches are challenging to implement. Although participatory planning and community-driven development can build consensus among stakeholders, navigating the opinions and desires of diverse stakeholders can prolong and even paralyze project implementation. Moreover, while provision of physical and nonphysical interventions could address multiple deprivations at

Figure 1: Theoretical Framework

Urban Informality

- **Exclusion** from decision-making processes
- **Insecure** livelihoods and land tenure
- **Self-provisioning** of urban services

Slums

Spatial **concentrations** of urban informality and multidimensional poverty

Multidimensional Poverty

- **Monetary poverty**
- **Health** deprivations
- **Education** deprivations
- **Poor living standards**

WHO

Participatory planning with a diversity of actors and stakeholders

WHAT

Physical and nonphysical interventions at appropriate scale

HOW

In situ upgrading or relocation for environmental or safety concerns

Multidimensional Approaches

Source: Authors.

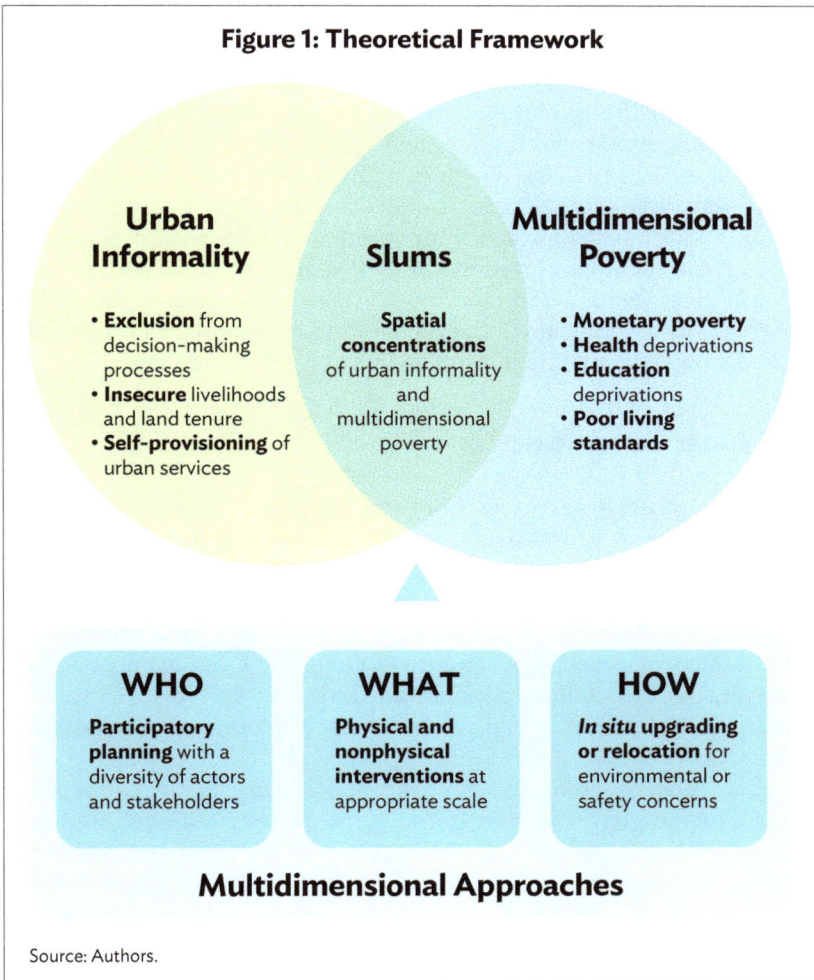

once, separate mandates for government agencies can disincentivize agencies from going beyond their jurisdictions. Conducting program monitoring and evaluation of multidimensional slum upgrading programs also requires monitoring a wide range of indicators to assess direct program impacts (e.g., coverage) and indirect program impacts (e.g., employment) (Duranton and Venables 2018; Field and Kremer 2008). The complexity of implementation, in turn, can lead to challenges for coordination, garnering political will, and allocating funds, causing project delays and community disillusionment. Last, while urban location has high socioeconomic value to slum dwellers, economic growth may create opportunities for governments to capture higher land values in slum areas through denser uses and land formalization to increase the tax base. The citywide benefits of land redevelopment must be weighed against the costs of resettlement (Harari and Wong 2020), which may differ even between slum areas within the same city. Housing policy therefore involves challenging tradeoffs. In this chapter, multidimensional approaches are framed as inputs at this unique intersection of informality and poverty structured around three considerations: "who," the actors and stakeholders involved; "what," the nature and types of improvements; and "how," the tradeoffs between on-site improvements and resettlement.

3. Slums in Indonesia

Similar to global trends over the past 25 years, the share of urban population living in slums has declined, while nearly doubling in absolute terms. Between 1993 and 2018, the proportion of urban population living in slums declined from 27% to 22%.[2] Moreover, the percentage of urban households with adequate housing declined from 98% to 65% between 2015 and 2021 (Figure 2). In absolute terms, however, the urban slum population has increased from 17.5 million persons to 32.1 million[3]—equivalent to nearly 1.5 times the population of Jakarta.

Slum improvement and housing policies are distinct, but slum criteria include housing indicators. In the current National Medium-Term Development Plan (RPJMN) 2020–2024, the Government of Indonesia is targeting improvements to water supply and sanitation, including access to clean water for all households; access to improved sanitation for 90% of households; and 10,000 hectares of slum alleviation (BAPPENAS 2020a). For housing, the Government of Indonesia also aims to provide public rental housing flats (RUSUNAWA) and public housing flats for sale (RUSUNAMI) that are integrated with the public transportation system. Aligned with the RPJMN, the Ministry of Public Works and Housing (MPWH) target for affordable housing provision is more than 51,000 public housing (RUSUN) units,

[2]   Statistics Indonesia (BPS). National Socio-Economic Survey (SUSENAS). https://www.bps.go.id/ (accessed 5 January 2022); Asian Development Bank. Key Indicators Database. https://kidb.adb.org/ (accessed 5 January 2022).

[3]   Calculated from Index Mundi. Indonesia – Urban Population. www.indexmundi.com/facts/indonesia/urban-population (accessed 5 January 2022).

with 70% of households occupying decent and affordable housing (MPWH 2020).[4] Moreover, the MPWH includes housing among the seven infrastructure criteria to define slum areas: water supply, sanitation, solid waste management, drainage, roads, fire protection, and housing (MPWH 2018). Local governments use these criteria, along with other factors including land ownership and the strategic value of the location, to designate slum areas. Slum improvement in Indonesia therefore hinges upon adequate housing provision.

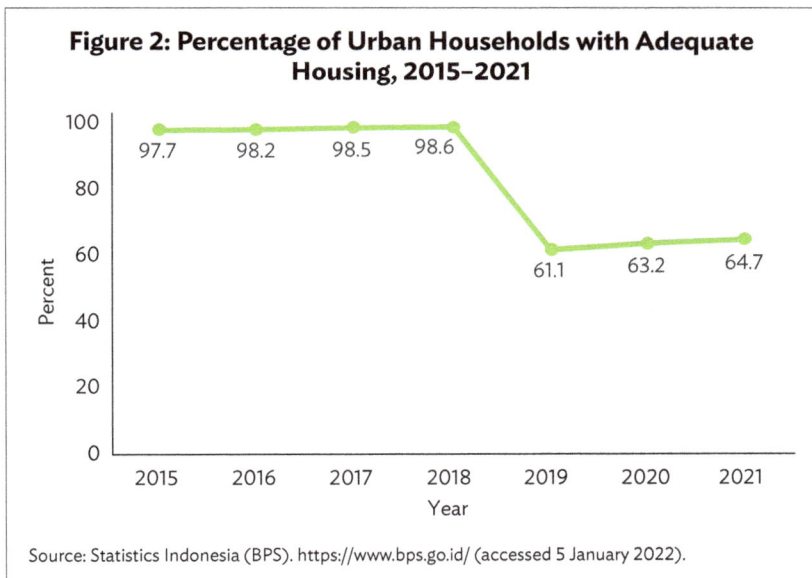

Figure 2: Percentage of Urban Households with Adequate Housing, 2015–2021

Source: Statistics Indonesia (BPS). https://www.bps.go.id/ (accessed 5 January 2022).

3.1 History of Slum Upgrading in Indonesia

Indonesia's history of slum upgrading can be simplified into two distinct phases: pre- and post-decentralization. Throughout, the central government has relied on national slum upgrading programs for slum improvement while local governments have been sources of upgrading innovation. Between the late 1960s and decentralization in 1999, Indonesia piloted and scaled up Surabaya City's Kampung

---

4   Outlined in Strategic Priorities (Sasaran Strategis) SS-3.

Improvement Program as a national and international model for on-site, participatory slum upgrading (Das and King 2019). Since decentralization, local or district governments such as cities (*kota*) and regencies (*kabupaten*) have taken on major responsibilities for spending and service delivery.

Local governments are responsible for slum upgrading and housing provision, but the central government continues to develop national programs. The Neighborhood Upgrading and Shelter Sector Project 2005–2011 (NUSSP), financed by ADB, aimed to improve access to shelter financing, deliver on-site improvements and new housing sites for the urban poor, and strengthen the institutional capacity of local government agencies for slum upgrading. In parallel, the National Program for Community Empowerment (PNPM, 2007–2014) aimed to improve the welfare and employment opportunities of the poor through capacity building for improved independence, welfare, and quality of life.[5]

The current national slum upgrading program, Cities without Slums (KOTAKU), includes three projects financed by various development finance institutions. The National Slum Upgrading Project (NSUP, 2016–2022), cofinanced by the World Bank and Asian Infrastructure Investment Bank (AIIB), supports infrastructure upgrades and community empowerment through revitalization of the Community Self-Help Organization (BKM), a government-recognized community empowerment body that coordinates various poverty reduction programs and funds from development partners including governments, NGOs, and the private sector.[6] A second National Slum Upgrading Project (NSUP, 2016–2021), financed by the Islamic Development Bank (IsDB), has supported slum improvement by way of community-driven development and local government participation. The Neighborhood Upgrading and Shelter Project Phase 2 (NUSP-2, 2014–2019), financed by ADB, has focused on helping local governments prepare citywide slum improvement action plans; providing both large- and neighborhood-scale basic infrastructure through community empowerment; and developing new housing sites to resettle slum households from disaster-prone areas.

In parallel, the Government of Indonesia initiated the One Million Houses (SJR, *Satu Juta Rumah*) policy to provide a million newly constructed homes through public and private financing. SJR primarily targets low-income households for government housing subsidies

---

[5]   See Government of Indonesia (2012).

[6]   See MPWH (2017).

financed through state or local government budgets. In addition, the National Affordable Housing Program (NAHP, 2017–2021), financed by the World Bank, aims to improve access to affordable housing through a mix of demand and supply-side interventions targeting both lower-middle income and lower-income households.

These national slum upgrading and housing programs have seen mixed success. National programs have had limited capacity to monitor activities implemented at the local levels. Although baseline survey methods have been standardized following guidelines from MPWH, discrepancies and sampling errors during baseline data collection have created challenges for monitoring and evaluation of program impacts. This in turn has disincentivized political support for slum upgrading at the national level.

Citing challenges of evaluating impacts of national slum upgrading programs such as KOTAKU, Indonesian central government ministries have begun to transition away from small-scale slum upgrading initiatives toward slum redevelopment, aiming for large-scale, integrated projects with expected citywide impact. This strategy, known locally as "urban renewal," relies on land consolidation to readjust land use and ownership in slum areas to allow for higher building density and transit-oriented development (BAPPENAS 2020b). Redeveloped sites would include market-rate and affordable housing, and slum households would be rehoused on-site.

Existing scholarship on slum improvement supports central government's preference for slum redevelopment over slum upgrading. Despite its relatively low-cost nature, slum upgrading can be unattractive to governments due to the challenges of cost-recovery, which tends to hinge upon the organizational structure of loan distributions and monthly service payments (Sanyal 2016). Moreover, without institutions for sustainable financing and operation and maintenance (O&M), upgrading projects have deteriorated over time (Sanyal 2016). In addition, new evidence from Indonesia suggests that on-site upgrading may have suppressed land values and prolonged the persistence of slums (Harari and Wong 2019). Slum upgrading thus has limitations.

Slum redevelopment, meanwhile, has the potential to generate revenue through land value capture including domestic resource mobilization, making it economically attractive to governments despite the complexities of assembling land and resettling slum communities. Subnational governments have already experimented with various levels of slum redevelopment, with much criticism. Between 2014 and 2016, the Basuki "Ahok" Tjahaja Purnama administration in Jakarta evicted and relocated over 25,000 people from slum areas to public housing rental units (RUSUNAWA) in high-rise residential towers. How slum redevelopment will be implemented given existing institutional, technical, and financial challenges at both national and local levels remains unclear.

3.2 Institutional Arrangements

In theory, governments have had different but complementary roles and responsibilities in slum alleviation and prevention since decentralization. The central government sets policy direction and priorities and allocates fiscal spending for poverty alleviation and housing provision through the Special Allocation Fund (DAK, Dana Alokasi Khusus).[7] Provincial governments act as regional representatives of the central government, responsible for communicating national policies, supervising development, and helping local governments to allocate their budgets. District governments are responsible for policy implementation, including construction, service delivery, and operation and maintenance.

Urban policies and plans in theory follow this decentralization of roles and responsibilities (Figure 3). With the exception of the Detailed Spatial Plan (RDTR), a planning document that regulates land use, density, and allowable development activities in special areas of a district (*kota* or *kabupaten*), key planning documents guiding local development are derivatives of their respective provincial and/or national plans. For instance, the Regional Medium-Term Development Plan (RPJMD) is the overarching development plan that references the RPJMN; the General Spatial Plan (RTRW) is a comprehensive plan that guides long-term development; and the Housing and Settlements Development Plan (RP3KP) guides housing provision activities. Each city is responsible for issuing local slum policies, including a Mayoral Decree on Slums (SK Kumuh) and a Slum Prevention and Quality Improvement Plan (RP2KPKP). The SK Kumuh enumerates the total hectares of slum area in the city and designates specific slum locations at the neighborhood and block levels (RW/RT). At the provincial level, a Gubernatorial Decree on Slums similarly enumerates the total hectares of slum area under provincial jurisdiction within each district.

---

[7]   The Special Allocation Fund (DAK) is an earmarked grant conditioned on specific sectoral spending priorities. The DAK Fisik supports capital investments while the DAK non-Fisik cofinances recurrent expenditures such as health and education assistance. To receive DAK, subnational governments must submit grant proposals to the central government.

Figure 3: Urban Policy and Planning Framework

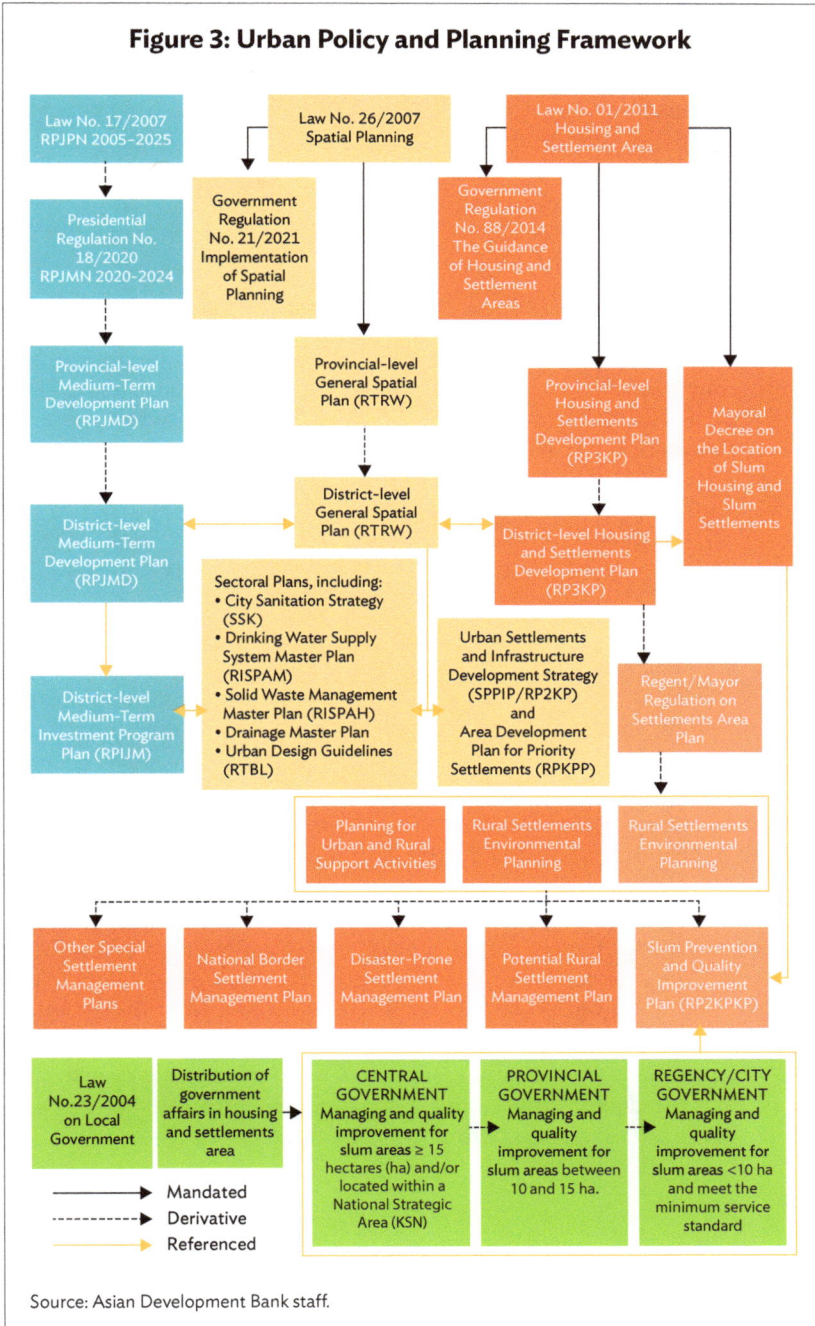

Law No. 17/2007 RPJPN 2005–2025	Law No. 26/2007 Spatial Planning	Law No. 01/2011 Housing and Settlement Area

Presidential Regulation No. 18/2020 RPJMN 2020-2024

Government Regulation No. 21/2021 Implementation of Spatial Planning

Government Regulation No. 88/2014 The Guidance of Housing and Settlement Areas

Provincial-level Medium-Term Development Plan (RPJMD)

Provincial-level General Spatial Plan (RTRW)

Provincial-level Housing and Settlements Development Plan (RP3KP)

Mayoral Decree on the Location of Slum Housing and Slum Settlements

District-level Medium-Term Development Plan (RPJMD)

District-level General Spatial Plan (RTRW)

District-level Housing and Settlements Development Plan (RP3KP)

Sectoral Plans, including:
• City Sanitation Strategy (SSK)
• Drinking Water Supply System Master Plan (RISPAM)
• Solid Waste Management Master Plan (RISPAH)
• Drainage Master Plan
• Urban Design Guidelines (RTBL)

District-level Medium-Term Investment Program Plan (RPIJM)

Urban Settlements and Infrastructure Development Strategy (SPPIP/RP2KP) and Area Development Plan for Priority Settlements (RPKPP)

Regent/Mayor Regulation on Settlements Area Plan

Planning for Urban and Rural Support Activities

Rural Settlements Environmental Planning

Rural Settlements Environmental Planning

Other Special Settlement Management Plans

National Border Settlement Management Plan

Disaster-Prone Settlement Management Plan

Potential Rural Settlement Management Plan

Slum Prevention and Quality Improvement Plan (RP2KPKP)

Law No.23/2004 on Local Government

Distribution of government affairs in housing and settlements area

CENTRAL GOVERNMENT Managing and quality improvement for slum areas ≥ 15 hectares (ha) and/or located within a National Strategic Area (KSN)

PROVINCIAL GOVERNMENT Managing and quality improvement for slum areas between 10 and 15 ha.

REGENCY/CITY GOVERNMENT Managing and quality improvement for slum areas <10 ha and meet the minimum service standard

→ Mandated
--→ Derivative
→ Referenced

Source: Asian Development Bank staff.

Despite decentralization of roles in slum policy, responsibility for policy implementation is shared among different levels of government depending on the total land area of each slum: for slum areas greater than or equal to 15 hectares (ha), the central government is the lead agency; for those between 10 and 15 ha, the provincial government is the lead agency; while for slum areas that are less than or equal to 10 ha, the local government is the lead agency. As a result, in cities with varying sizes of slum areas, multiple levels of government are responsible for issuing decrees to identify slum locations. In Makassar City, because the 20 slum areas (*kawasan kumuh*) range from 3 ha to 55 ha, all three levels of government are responsible for policy implementation in various slum areas. The city thus has multiple decrees on slum locations issued at different levels of government. Updated slum locations in the 2021 Mayoral Decree have now introduced discrepancies between the new decree and its provincial counterpart.

Moreover, cities are at different stages in creating derivatives of provincial-level plans or seeking approval for updating old plans. Many cities do not yet have a city-level RP3KP plan that references the RTRW and the Mayoral Decree on Slums. Cirebon City officials are currently referencing the outdated 2015 Mayoral Decree on Slums because the central government is still reviewing the proposed 2018 amendment with updated slum locations. These inherent delays in vertical coordination, compounded by the continuously changing boundaries of slum areas, create a vicious circle in which slum documents are constantly being updated and re-coordinated. As a result, governments are unable to keep pace with slum development.

Horizontal coordination across different government offices is similarly disjointed. Although the MPWH is responsible for both slum and housing policies, these policy areas are overseen by different directorates. The Directorate General of Human Settlements is responsible for settlement infrastructure (and thereby, slum upgrading), while the Directorate General of Housing Provision oversees housing policy.[8] These bureaucratic divisions create silos and disincentives for integrated policy implementation for slum upgrading. While the MWPH's strategic plan outlines a proposal for bureaucratic reform that would join the directorates under a singular program, this reform had not yet occurred as of this writing (MPWH 2020).

---

[8]   Other relevant directorates include the Directorate General of Water Resources and Directorate General of Housing Finance.

3.3 Technical Environment

Land availability is central to all slum improvement efforts, but land management and transfer systems in Indonesia remain tenuous. Approximately 40% of the nation's landmass, or approximately 77 million ha, is disputed (Aqil 2020). To receive financing for slum improvement projects, district governments in Indonesia must provide "clean and clear" land (i.e., assembled property with titles that are free from ownership disputes). In practice, identifying land for upgrading or assembling land for redevelopment is extremely complex, precisely due to overlapping claims. In Cirebon City, slums have developed on a combination of private lands, public lands, and informal land reclaimed using solid waste as backfill. Informally reclaimed plots have received formal land titles through the Cirebon City Land Administration Office (Kantah BPN), which issues land titles through the central government's land registration program, the Comprehensive Systematic Land Registration (PTSL). As a result, the informally reclaimed plots are recognized by the central government despite their nonconformance with local spatial planning, contributing to further confusion over land ownership. The complexity of tracking land ownership can create a tendency to prioritize slum upgrading in formal or legal settlements rather than in slum areas with greatest need (Taylor 2015).

The government has taken a digital approach to addressing land disputes by unifying spatial data. Indonesia's One Map policy aims to merge about 85 thematic maps related to land cover and land tenure across its 34 provinces. In Cirebon City, the Department of Information, Statistics, and Communications is developing a shared data hub for datasets across all local government agencies, including for spatial data. In Makassar City, the local government has recently launched an online GIS library for public access to its spatial data, though datasets are still very limited.

Participatory mapping efforts have helped to accelerate spatial data collection. In cities receiving the KOTAKU program (Cities without Slums), teams of consultants conduct household surveys of each block unit (RT, *rukun tetangga*), measuring each household against 16 indicators across the seven infrastructure criteria for determining slums. From this survey, a baseline percentage value is calculated for each indicator and then assigned a corresponding score of either 1, 3, or 5.[9] These scores are then totaled, and each *rukun tetangga* is assigned a corresponding level of high, moderate, or low

---

[9]   1 = 24%–50%; 3 = 51%–75%; 5 = ≥75%. Zero if not applicable or less than 24%.

to indicate the severity of slum conditions.[10] Officially, there are five slum types: over water, on the water, in the lowlands, in the highlands, and in disaster-prone areas (MPWH 2018).[11] Figures from the baseline survey are then formally endorsed by the mayor, who issues a Mayoral Decree on Slum Locations. The baseline data is intended to be updated regularly to monitor progress toward slum alleviation.

While participatory slum mapping allows for data transparency and consensus-building, it also introduces challenges. Although baseline survey methods have been standardized in regulations from MPWH, survey methods were inconsistent across Cirebon and Makassar cities. ADB consultants found discrepancies between baseline data prior to slum upgrading and their corresponding geospatial files. Some baseline data on slums prior to upgrading are biased due to sampling errors. Moreover, the collected data could not be combined with available poverty data due to incompatible administrative units. These data limitations create challenges for implementing slum improvements and evaluating their impacts.

To address these challenges, local governments should focus on improving spatial data collection methods and thereby the quality of spatial data, particularly for land tenure and slum areas. Nationwide systematic mapping and enumeration of slum areas conducted by an integrated task force or research group could potentially address the inconsistencies in slum data across cities—similar to the poverty mapping efforts conducted by the SMERU Research Institute. Mapping slum areas using administrative units that are compatible with existing socioeconomic datasets would enable wider engagement with slum data, including more rigorous slum improvement program design, monitoring, and evaluation.

3.4 Financial Arrangements

Decentralization has given local governments broad autonomy over spending, but constraints remain. Because district civil servants are part of the central civil service, local governments have limited influence over human resources decisions concerning their civil servants. For example, districts must seek central government approval to change the

---

[10]   Out of a possible score of 80: High = ≥60; Moderate = 38–59; Low = 16–37; Not Slum = ≤15.

[11]   Type 1 slums include those with stilt housing or similar structures; type 2 slums include those with structures in riparian or coastal areas, according to the Government of Indonesia.

number of civil service positions and have no control over setting base pay. Spending is thus largely consumed by civil servant wages, limiting district autonomy to manage service delivery.

Districts also have limited autonomy to raise own-source revenue to finance service delivery. In 2009, the central government significantly increased district discretion for setting local tax and user fee rates and conferred property taxation to districts. Property taxes have since become the most important source of district own-source revenue, representing 41% in 2017 (World Bank 2020). However, local tax compliance remains poor due to limited administrative enforcement capacity, and local tax-to-GDP ratios have not grown. Moreover, district dependency on intergovernmental transfers remains high. In 2018, intergovernmental transfers comprised 78% of district revenue (World Bank 2020).

The General Allocation Fund (DAU) is the main unconditional grant for fiscal equalization across subnational governments, but its allocation formulas have led to fiscal inefficiencies. DAU transfers make up the largest share of district revenues (over 60% in 2018) and are intended to support regional development, especially capital expenditure on infrastructure development and public services. However, allocation formulas assume an average fiscal need that is equal across districts, regardless of population size. As a result, smaller districts receive more funding per capita than larger districts. In 2017, local governments in the smallest population quintile received approximately five times more revenue per citizen than those in the largest population quintile (World Bank 2020). Densely populated urban areas therefore lack resources for housing and infrastructure provision. Moreover, because DAU transfer amounts are tied to the number of civil servants employed by a district, the allocation formulas create perverse incentives for districts to overspend on wages (World Bank 2020).

The Special Allocation Fund (DAK) is Indonesia's most important earmarked grant, conditioned on specific sectoral spending priorities, but it may not be reaching districts most in need. The DAK Fisik supports capital investments, while the DAK non-Fisik cofinances recurrent expenditures such as health and education assistance. To receive DAK, subnational governments must submit grant proposals to the central government. However, the DAK has reduced its targeting to low-capacity districts, perhaps suggesting that these districts are less capable of preparing eligible proposals (World Bank 2020).

While the Government of Indonesia spends an adequate amount of the state budget on the housing sector, it may not spend efficiently (World Bank 2020). The majority of public expenditure on housing comes from the central government, representing 71%, compared with 24% from districts and 5% from provinces. Approximately 70% to 85% of funding for low-income housing is dedicated to national ministries such as the MPWH and the Ministry of Agrarian and Spatial Planning/ National Land Agency (ATR/BPN). As a result, local governments have insufficient resources to develop and implement urban planning, housing programs, and data management systems.

Ensuring that local governments maximize opportunities for own-source revenue collection and improve their creditworthiness is key to increasing fiscal autonomy. Improving local land management systems, such as through enhanced property mapping, is critical to the implementation of slum improvement programs and the ability of local governments to mobilize domestic resources.

4. Multidimensional Approaches to Slum Upgrading: Attempts to Transform Practice

This section presents three case studies from ADB's recent urban sector work in Indonesia, selected to illustrate the challenges of multidimensional approaches to slum upgrading (Table 2): (i) Neighborhood Upgrading and Shelter Project Phase 2 (NUSP-2), (ii) Revitalising Informal Settlements and Their Environments (RISE), and (iii) Livable Settlements Investment Project (LSIP). NUSP-2 was an ADB investment loan completed in 2020, which had financed urban infrastructure and basic services in slum areas. RISE and LSIP were technical assistance provided by ADB to pilot innovative, multidimensional approaches to slum upgrading.

Table 2: Case Study Comparison

	Neighborhood Upgrading and Shelter Project Phase 2 (NUSP-2)	Revitalising Informal Settlements and Their Environments (RISE)	Livable Settlement Investment Project (LSIP)
Description	Infrastructure and access to basic services improved in slum areas in 20 Indonesian cities through: • Institutional capacity for managing pro-poor urban development strengthened • Infrastructure in slum neighborhoods upgraded • New settlements for poor families	• Neighborhood-scale, nature-based solutions for water and sanitation piloted in select slum communities in Makassar City	• Multidimensional urban resilience assessment (built, natural, human, social dimensions) to enable comprehensive understanding of Cirebon and Makassar cities
Support	• $74.4 million concessional sovereign loan	• $1.5 million in technical assistance (estimate)	• $150,000 in technical assistance (estimate)
Status	• Project completed • About 67,000 low-income households benefited • Four new settlements established	• Pilot location constructed • Detailed engineering design and due diligence prepared for six additional locations	• Urban resilience assessments • Multidimensional framework to assess city livability currently being piloted in Pontianak and Semarang

Source: Authors.

4.1 Neighborhood Upgrading and Shelter Project – Phase 2 (NUSP-2)

From 2014 through 2019, ADB financed the second phase of the Neighborhood Upgrading and Shelter Project with a $74.4 million concessional sovereign loan (Table 3). NUSP-2 aimed to improve infrastructure and access to basic services in slum areas in 20 Indonesian cities by helping local governments prepare citywide slum improvement action plans; providing both large- and neighborhood-scale basic infrastructure through community empowerment; and developing new housing sites to resettle slum households from disaster-prone areas. Approximately 67,000 low-income households benefited from the project.

Table 3: Neighborhood Upgrading and Shelter Project - Phase 2

Area	Description	Lessons
Who	Communities Local government Central government	• On-site upgrading strengthened community's sense of ownership and capacity • Community engagement is time-consuming
What	Urban infrastructure	• Need for strong monitoring and oversight to ensure consistency in construction quality
How	On-site and resettlement	• Important to create sufficient economic opportunities in resettlement areas • Important to have transparent selection of project beneficiaries • Important to create dedicated fiscal budget for O&M

Source: Authors.

Who: Communities and Government (for Participatory Planning and Mapping)

Central to NUSP-2's approach was a gradual planning process that mimicked the typical decentralized nature of Indonesian urban planning—starting at the city-level with a slum improvement action plan, followed by settlement-level neighborhood upgrading action plans and community action plans. With the MPWH as the executing agency, the central government and provincial implementation agencies were involved in all aspects of project implementation. Local governments also played an active role in identifying slum areas and facilitating complementary support programs.

Baseline data collection prior to slum upgrading was conducted in a community-led, participatory manner in slum neighborhoods through the Village Self Survey. The process was typically facilitated by the local BKM. Collectively, teams of residents surveyed the neighborhoods to document existing infrastructure conditions and identify potential infrastructure problems, using simple GPS coordinates and photo applications such as NoteCam. Community groups also facilitated the participatory planning process through community consultations to prepare neighborhood upgrading action plans and community action plans, which identified infrastructure investments to be financed by NUSP-2.

What: Urban Infrastructure

Once infrastructure investments were prioritized, the project utilized direct community contracting mechanisms between the city government and community implementation organizations (CIOs) to implement over 1,000 small-scale civil works packages. These ranged from upgrading of neighborhood streets and drains to the construction of small gardens. The CIOs then recruited community members as construction workers. Following construction completion, NUSP-2 established community groups for the operation and maintenance of small-scale infrastructure works.

For larger infrastructure works such as local roads and river embankments, NUSP-2 procured external contractors following ADB's procurement policy and regulation. CIOs organized community consultations, facilitated the dissemination of project information, and managed the grievance mechanism. Local governments would be responsible for the O&M of large-scale infrastructure while CIOs would be responsible for the O&M of small-scale infrastructure.

How: On-Site and Resettlement

NUSP-2 supported both on-site upgrading of slum neighborhoods as well as construction of new settlements to resettle poor families away from disaster-prone areas. On-site upgrading strengthened the community's sense of ownership, built community capacity to plan, and provided work opportunities that allowed additional income for the community. However, the approach required a strong monitoring mechanism from the central government, which was challenging to implement given their physical remoteness from the projects. Although community groups were enlisted to assist with monitoring, their capacity and commitment varied. As a result, construction quality varied across projects. Community consultation, training, and construction was also time-consuming. A professional construction safety inspector could potentially streamline future monitoring processes.

In four cities, NUSP-2 developed new sites to provide housing and facilities for resettled households. In total, 650 housing units were constructed with financial support from the Directorate General of Housing Provision. Beneficiaries interviewed in the new site development areas said their quality of life in these areas drastically improved due to (i) increased access to basic services, (ii) a safer environment because of less exposure to risks, and (iii) improved financial situation due to lower rent.

The overall success of NUSP-2's comprehensive resettlement strategy can be attributed to its multidimensional approach. NUSP-2 ensured sufficient economic opportunities in resettlement areas, using spatial data to analyze travel distances from new sites to potential new job centers. Moreover, the project's transparent selection of beneficiaries instilled trust in the resettlement process, while its involvement of beneficiaries in the design and management of the new sites created a sense of ownership among beneficiaries. These resettlement strategies were further supported by a dedicated budget for operations and maintenance of the new sites, making local governments responsible to the new communities.

4.2 Revitalising Informal Settlements and Their Environments Program

The Revitalising Informal Settlements and Their Environments (RISE) Program aims to pilot neighborhood-scale, nature-based solutions for water and sanitation in 24 slum communities in Suva, Fiji and Makassar, Indonesia (Table 4). Initiated by a Monash University-led consortium of partners including ADB, RISE focuses on neighborhood-scale, nature-based solutions (NBS) together with more traditional gray infrastructure to provide a water-sensitive approach to improving services in urban informal settlements. To monitor and evaluate program impact, the Monash research design used randomized controlled trials to measure the effects of environmental changes on health outcomes of children ages five and under. Indicators measured include pathogen burden, markers of intestinal inflammation and function, and drug-resistant markers in feces.

In 2018, a RISE demonstration site was constructed in Makassar City and detailed engineering designs were prepared to scale up the approach in additional neighborhoods. Thus far, RISE is the only slum-upgrading project in Indonesia to fully integrate climate adaptation strategies with physical infrastructure solutions.

Table 4: Revitalising Informal Settlements and Their Environments Program

Area	Description	Lessons
Who	Communities Local government Universities and knowledge institutions	• Community engagement key to develop infrastructure investments tailored to each slum • Partnerships with universities to inform design and understand health outcomes of improved infrastructure • Community engagement time-consuming and expensive
What	Water-sensitive infrastructure	• NBS enhanced resilience of infrastructure • NBS reduced operation and maintenance costs
How	On site upgrading	• Co-benefits of upgrading using nature-based solutions • Challenges of identifying land for nature-based solutions in densely populated slum areas • Need to build capacity among experts to facilitate codesign process and design nature-based solutions

Source: Authors.

Who: Local Residents, Local Government, and Local Universities and Knowledge Institutions (Community Codesign)

RISE emphasizes the codesign of infrastructure solutions together with each community to ensure that solutions are fit-for-purpose. Community facilitators, complemented by universities and knowledge partners, support the participatory planning process by recommending design solutions and undertaking research on the health outcomes of improved access to basic services. In Makassar, RISE also partners closely with the local government to ensure support, facilitate upscaling, and build capacity for understanding the research design. As a result of the intense community involvement in the design process, the project team observed improvements to the wider living environment of the informal settlement.

Partnering with universities and researchers greatly increased the innovative nature of the project and provided opportunities to systematically evaluate infrastructure impacts on health and well-being in target communities. RISE is a rare example of a slum upgrading project designed using randomized controlled trials, an experimental method that allows researchers to evaluate causal relationships—in this case, between the provision of sanitation infrastructure and children's health outcomes. However, given the project's novel approach and technologies, more capacity building on the codesign process itself and the design of nature-based solutions is needed.

While the codesign process allows for infrastructure investments to be tailored to the needs of each community, the intensity and frequency of the community consultations make the process very time-consuming and costly. In future upscaling, digital technologies could potentially decrease the transaction costs of participatory planning and streamline the codesign process.[12]

What: Nature-Based Solutions for Sanitation

RISE combines traditional gray infrastructure with green infrastructure solutions, using a water-sensitive design approach to reduce fecal contamination while managing stormwater, thereby improving health outcomes and urban resilience. Central to RISE's design is a sanitation "treatment train" whereby a combination of green infrastructure collects, cleans, and discharges stormwater, graywater, and blackwater within the slum itself (Figure 4). Smart-pressure sewer technology enables wastewater flows to be moderated based on climatic events, notably peak rainfall and flooding events. The nature-based design of the infrastructure increases its adaptive capacity to shocks and stressors, compared with traditionally engineered infrastructure. The project also harvests rainwater to improve water security for the urban poor.

Although yet to be evaluated, another expected outcome includes lower costs for O&M of nature-based infrastructure compared with traditional infrastructure. While traditional sanitation infrastructure typically relies on pumping technologies requiring electricity and regular replacement, RISE's nature-based solutions utilize natural processes to clean septage. As O&M of sanitation systems is typically the responsibility of local governments, reducing these O&M costs is crucial for long-term sustainability of a system.

---

[12]   For example, Makassar City, among others in Indonesia, has transitioned its annual participatory budgeting process (MUSRENBANG) from an in-person forum to an online portal.

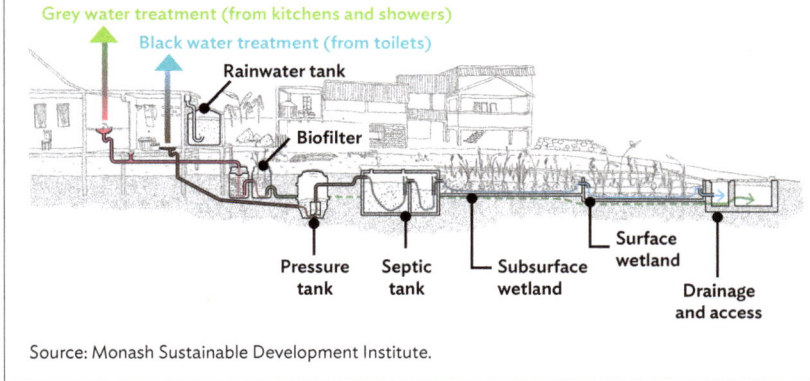

Figure 4: Sanitation "Treatment Train" Cross-Section Diagram

Grey water treatment (from kitchens and showers)

Black water treatment (from toilets)

Rainwater tank

Biofilter

Pressure tank

Septic tank

Subsurface wetland

Surface wetland

Drainage and access

Source: Monash Sustainable Development Institute.

How: On-Site Upgrading

As RISE emphasizes at-scale solutions, a determining factor for RISE's feasibility is the availability of land on-site—a daunting task in dense informal settlements. In Makassar City, the community identified available land through voluntary land contributions whereby landowners contributed small portions of their land for the construction of wetlands. While the voluntary nature of these land contributions was ideologically grounded, in practice, it triggered complex social safeguard requirements for ADB, which assume that land contribution from the urban poor reduces their value-generating assets. Because ADB is unable to finance projects that would negatively impact the urban poor, it proposed instead to sign 10-year land leases to secure land for construction of the nature-based infrastructure. However, signing these leases was very complex and expensive. Furthermore, the ADB investment grant for program scale-up had to be channeled through the central government, which was not keen to administer a grant that would only benefit a limited number of settlements. Ultimately, ADB could not provide the intended investment grant. Using the design work financed by ADB, the Australian Department of Foreign Affairs and Trade directly engaged Monash University in the construction of the RISE infrastructure. The trade-offs between at-scale solutions and land availability in dense informal settlements therefore need to be carefully considered. In some cases, off-site infrastructure may provide a more feasible solution.

4.3 Livable Settlements Investment Project

LSIP was a proposed $150 million slum upgrading program whereby ADB would finance slum upgrading and basic infrastructure in five Indonesian cities (Table 5). Originally called the Slum Improvement in Strategic Human Settlements Area (SISHA) Project and requested by the Directorate General of Human Settlements under MPWH, the potential loan would build on experiences from the completed NUSP-2 and related upgrading programs.

In early 2020, ADB mobilized a consultant team to develop the LSIP loan program, beginning with a situation assessment report on slum conditions in the proposed program cities. The team's task was to assess citywide livability to understand the relationship between slums and the wider city, starting with the cities of Cirebon and Makassar. Based on the literature for multidimensional poverty and urban resilience, the team developed the Livable Cities Framework, a multidimensional framework to assess city livability across four key dimensions: (i) built capital, including housing and infrastructure; (ii) natural capital, including land, air, and water resources; (iii) human capital, including well-being and education; and (iv) social capital, including governance and citizen engagement (Figure 5). The consultant team also experimented with two new partnerships to advance research on slums and urban vulnerability: a youth-led research team funded through ADB's Youth for Asia initiative, and a team of urban data specialists from Future Cities Laboratory based out of ETH-Zurich's Singapore campus.[13]

Key lessons for urban research emerged from the team's attempts to adapt to the uncertainties and limitations of the COVID-19 pandemic. First, the role of local partners became even more critical for effective community consultation and engagement. Second, through experimentation with digital tools and virtual methods for urban research, the team also learned new ways of collecting primary data remotely.

---

[13]   ETH-Zurich is a leading Swiss technical university.

Table 5: Livable Settlements Investment Project

Area	Description	Lessons
Who	Local experts	• Local experts played critical roles in engagement and local knowledge
	Local government	• Inability to engage formally with local government and communities due to reluctance on part of central government
	Youth	• Youth researchers and local youth ambassadors played innovative roles in collecting primary data and mobilizing support for youth-led research and youth vulnerability
What	Multidimensional urban resilience assessment (built, natural, human, social dimensions)	• Comprehensive urban resilience assessment allowed for contextual understanding of the city
	ur-scape database on slums	• Slum data in Indonesia is very coarse, containing sampling errors and discrepancies between tabular and spatial datasets
How	Local experts	• Informal engagement with local government agencies to collect secondary data
	ur-scape spatial planning software	• Digital tools to visualize and analyze cross-sectoral data supports integrated spatial planning
	Virtual research methods from youth team	• Innovation in data collection helps reach vulnerable groups

Source: Authors.

Figure 5: Multidimensional Livable Cities Framework

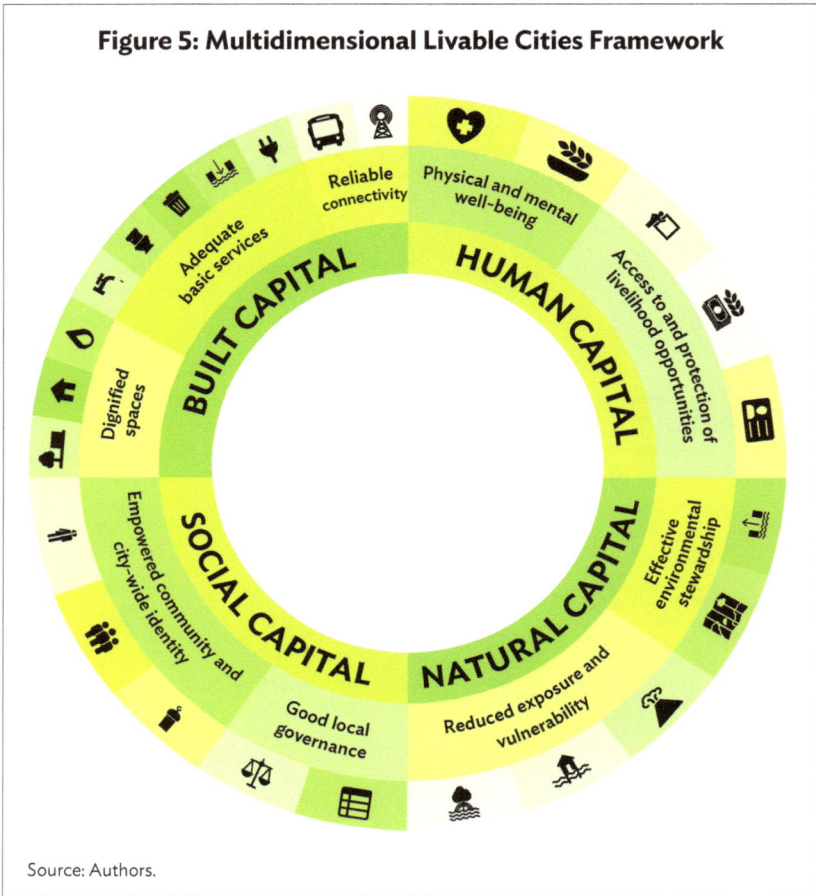

Source: Authors.

Who: Local Experts and Youth Researchers

Due to travel restrictions related to the COVID-19 pandemic, the team placed a premium on the ability to conduct in-person (albeit physically distanced) consultations. In efforts to build local champions for the project, the team recruited pairs of locally based consultants in Cirebon and Makassar cities. The project facilitator's role was to serve as the primary liaison to the local government, while the community mobilizer's role was to engage with NGOs and grassroots organizations.

A first lesson learned was that ADB's recruitment system is not set up for local recruitment. Most of the competent and skilled community activists did not meet ADB English-language requirements, nor did they know how to navigate ADB's Consultant Management System. Despite the administrative hurdles, the team persisted in recruiting teams with local knowledge and engagement skills. Recruitment and mobilization of the full consultant team took 6 months. Exploring ways to better align ADB's requirements for transparent recruitment with the skills of qualified community workers would greatly benefit future technical assistance.

The team also confirmed the value of a multistakeholder approach to understanding cities. Local experts played a critical role in stakeholder engagement and local knowledge, providing valuable insights and nuanced field observations to help foster a deeper understanding of the research context. Informal, in-person interactions with local government agencies led to Cirebon City's vice mayor's support for LSIP. Moreover, partnering with the youth researchers, who had separately mobilized more than 20 local youth ambassadors, allowed the consultant team to support youth-led research by exchanging knowledge and sharing networks.

What: Multidimensional Framework for Assessing Urban Livability

Guided by the Livable Cities Framework, the consultant team collected secondary data across 25 different indicators. From this assessment, the team intended to engage with local stakeholders to present findings and identify physical and nonphysical investment priorities related to improving slum communities to achieve four outcomes:

- Built capital: access to basic services and housing in priority slum areas increased

- Human capital: social and livelihood resilience for urban poor increased

- Natural capital: resilience of natural resources for urban poor improved

- Social capital: capacity of local government to plan, deliver, operate, and maintain basic services and livelihood support programs for urban poor increased

Stakeholder engagement at the local level stalled upon completion of the multidimensional livability assessment, due to MPWH's reluctance to move forward with LSIP loan processing. MPWH had since shifted its focus to improving the performance of ongoing development finance and using foreign lending only for investments with expected city-scale impact. As a result, slum upgrading, with its neighborhood-scale interventions, became less attractive to decision makers. Thus, despite support from local governments, the consultant team did not engage in formal consultations with them as planned. Given that financing for slum improvement still flows through the central government, a key lesson learned was that slum upgrading efforts deeply depend on garnering and maintaining political support of the central government. To date, central government counterparts have not decided to move forward with the LSIP loan program, so the outcomes of the multidimensional assessments are yet uncertain.

However, researching the cities through a multidimensional lens allowed the consultant team to develop and present a comprehensive assessment of urban livability in the project cities. More importantly, the multidimensional nature of the assessment helped to set a new standard for ADB loan processing documents, which until now had focused largely on individual infrastructure sectors. ADB is now piloting the Livable Cities Framework for situation assessment reports in the cities of Pontianak and Semarang, potentially transforming how ADB analyzes the urban context for its financing.

How: Digital Tools

Digital tools have expanded the research methods available to study cities. Restricted by travel limitations related to the COVID-19 pandemic, the consultant team experimented with digital tools to conduct remote field research. Youth researchers used KoBo Toolbox, Indeemo, and WhatsApp to identify, engage with, and collect primary data on vulnerable youth in Cirebon City. The innovative use of digital technologies enabled the youth researchers to identify and engage with vulnerable youths in Cirebon City during a period of very limited travel. The youth-led research team identified complex challenges facing Cirebonese youth related to their development and urban environment including unemployment, limited access to education, and poor waste management. Despite these challenges, the youth were excited to discuss ways to improve their lives and their community's well-being, especially entrepreneurial ways to repurpose materials and resources. These findings support the valuable role of young people in urban development. Building upon the pilots in Cirebon and Makassar cities, ADB is now further testing digital tools for field research in Pontianak and Semarang cities.

The team also experimented with digital tools for spatial data analysis. Urban data specialists from the Future Cities Laboratory provided technical support to analyze data through an open-source planning software called ur-scape. Unlike more popular GIS software, ur-scape has an attractive interface with built-in analytical tools, making it an accessible option for unsophisticated users. In both project cities, ur-scape allowed the team to overlay different spatial datasets to rapidly visualize and analyze spatial correlations between slum areas and their environs, then identify areas for further research. With great interest and support from the Cirebon City Government, the team is currently providing technical assistance to the Department of Information and Communications for training on ur-scape software as well as developing data management guidelines. In Makassar City, the government had already installed ur-scape in its control room, so the team focused on adding slum data layers to the existing database.

Alongside the spatial analysis, the team also piloted data visualization methods to create concise visual profiles of each slum area to distill information and support comparisons across slums. Infographics and a simple graphic format allowed for an efficient dissemination of findings to different types of audiences. In Cirebon City, these infographics will be incorporated into the city's One Map database for public access.

5. The Future of Slum Upgrading in Indonesia and Beyond

The nature of slums as a spatial concentration of urban informality and multidimensional poverty requires that upgrading efforts take a comprehensive approach that considers "who" is involved, "what" is improved, and "how" it will be delivered. Reflecting on the discrepancies between the theory and practice of multidimensional approaches to slum upgrading, this chapter presented three case studies from ADB's recent urban sector work in Indonesia.

Multidimensional approaches are indeed challenging multidimensional approaches are challenging to implement because of institutional, technical, and financial inefficiencies. The cumbersome regulatory bureaucracy for slum and housing policy has resulted in vertical and horizonal coordination failures. Poor data management for land ownership has led to complex land disputes that preclude financing for slum improvement programs. The limited capacity of local governments to raise own-source revenues has resulted in limited fiscal capacity for urban development.

The selected ADB case studies reveal important lessons for future slum upgrading policies and programs. In NUSP-2, although community construction can bring employment and skills training to communities, closely monitoring the quality of project implementation is key to ensuring public safety and sustainability of new construction. A key lesson from the RISE program is that on-site improvements, albeit innovative and nature-based, are intimately dependent on land availability. Moreover, the high transaction costs of community codesign can preclude investments by development finance institutions such as ADB. Streamlining partnerships for participatory planning is therefore of utmost importance in delivering at-scale solutions. Finally, with LSIP, a key lesson is that garnering and maintaining the political will and commitment of all levels of government is critical to slum upgrading efforts. Despite the commitment of local governments and the decentralization of responsibilities that would, in theory, give districts the fiscal autonomy to implement slum upgrading, dependence on the central government for civil service management and intergovernmental transfers has created barriers to financing urban infrastructure and services. Without political will from central government ministries, development finance for slum upgrading cannot transfer to local levels. Should priorities shift away from slum upgrading, as seen in LSIP, local governments have limited capacity to fill this financing gap.

Furthermore, where development partner lending could create fiscal space in local budgets, districts are still beholden to lender policies during implementation. In RISE, stringent social safeguards policies created unintended barriers to identifying and purchasing available land for neighborhood upgrading. Large development finance institutions may also not be institutionally equipped to recruit local experts and deliver community codesigned solutions. The institutional structure of the central government and development finance institutions is therefore limited in enabling the multidimensional approaches required for slum upgrading.

These lessons hold important implications for the future of slum upgrading and slum improvement more broadly: local governments and communities are best positioned to lead and monitor multidimensional approaches for slum improvement. From identifying slum locations, to monitoring civil works, to creating innovative sources of own-source revenue, local governments must be empowered with the institutional, technical, and financial tools required to effectively implement urban infrastructure and services. Making district governments the lead agency for all slum improvement efforts within their administrative boundaries would streamline policy implementation and give cities greater control over their own development. Building capacity for local governments and communities to collect, manage, and integrate spatial data would support property-mapping efforts and thereby improved urban planning and land management. Last, continuing to decentralize the intergovernmental transfer system would increase local government fiscal autonomy, allowing for more targeted urban development.

As its cities continue to urbanize, Indonesia will need to renegotiate the role of central government actors and of slum upgrading policy itself. With its small-scale interventions, on-site slum upgrading may have been an appropriate and effective policy for poverty alleviation in the early stages of urbanization (Harari and Wong 2020). However, economic growth will continue to create opportunities to capture higher land values in slum areas through denser uses. At what point in a city's development do the economic and environmental benefits of slum redevelopment—increased density, compact, and transit-oriented development—outweigh the social costs of resettlement? Moreover, the grand scale of typical slum redevelopment projects will require local governments to play an even more pivotal role in participatory planning, land consolidation, and resettlement. At what point does local government have sufficient institutional, technical, and financial capacity to lead such large-scale urban development? Ever a pioneer in slum improvement, Indonesia's complex tradeoffs between who, what, and how hold important implications for future slum improvement efforts across the globe.

References

Aqil, A. M. 2020. Concerns of Transparency, Inclusivity Raised as One Map Nears Completion. *Jakarta Post*. 4 September. https://www.thejakartapost.com/news/2020/09/04/concerns-of-transparency-inclusivity-raised-as-one-map-nears-completion.html.

BAPPENAS. 2020a. *Presidential Regulation (Perpres) No. 18/2020 on National Medium-Term Development Plan (RPJMN) 2020–2024*. Jakarta: Government of Indonesia.

_____. 2020b. *Urban Renewal: Integrated Revitalization*. Jakarta: Government of Indonesia.

Beard, V. A., A. Mahendra, and M. I. Westphal. 2016. *Towards a More Equal City: Framing the Challenges and Opportunities*. Washington, DC: World Resources Institute.

Bhatkal, T., and P. Lucci. 2015. *Community-Driven Development in the Slums: Thailand's Experience*. London: Overseas Development Institute.

BRAC Urban Development Programme. 2018. *Urban Development Programme Activity Update*. Khulna, Bangladesh: BRAC.

Buckley, R. M., A. Kallergis, and L. Wainer. 2016. The Emergence of Large-Scale Housing Programs: Beyond a Public Finance Perspective. *Habitat International* 54: 199–209. doi:10.1016/j.habitatint.2015.11.022.

Buckley, R. M., and J. Kalarickal, eds. 2006. Thirty Years of Shelter Lending: What Have We Learned? *Directions in Development: Infrastructure*. Washington, DC: World Bank.

Das, A., and R. King. 2019. *Surabaya: The Legacy of Participatory Upgrading of Informal Settlements—Towards a More Equal City*. Washington, DC: World Resources Institute.

Duranton, G., and A. J. Venables. 2018. *Place-Based Policies for Development*. World Bank Policy Research Working Paper 8410. Washington, DC: World Bank.

Field, E., and M. Kremer. 2008. *Impact Evaluation for Slum Upgrading Interventions*. Cambridge, Massachusetts: Harvard University.

Government of Indonesia. 2012. *PNPM Mandiri of 2012–2013*. Jakarta.

Harari, M., and M. Wong. 2019. *Slum Upgrading and Long-Run Urban Development: Evidence from Indonesia*. Working Paper. Philadelphia: The Wharton School, University of Pennsylvania.

_____. 2020. *Policy Memo for Slum Upgrading and Long-Run Urban Development*. Philadelphia: The Wharton School, University of Pennsylvania.

King, R., M. Orloff, T. Virsilas, and T. Pande. 2017. *Confronting the Urban Housing Crisis in the Global South: Adequate, Secure, and Affordable Housing—Towards a More Equal City*. Washington, DC: World Resources Institute.

Lucci, P., T. Bhatkal, A. Khan, and T. Berliner. 2015. What Works in Improving the Living Conditions of Slum Dwellers: A Review of the Evidence Across Fourth Programmes. *Development Progress*. London: Overseas Development Institute.

Michaels, G., D. Nigmatulina, F. Rauch, T. Regan, N. Baruah, and A. Dahlstrand. 2021. *Planning Ahead for Better Neighborhoods: Long Run Evidence from Tanzania*. Working Paper. doi:10.1086/714119.

Ministry of Public Works and Housing (MPWH). 2017. *Overview of Cities without Slums (KOTAKU) Program*. Jakarta.

———. 2018. *Ministerial Regulation (Permen) No. 14/2018 on Slum Prevention and Quality Improvement*. Jakarta: Government of Indonesia.

———. 2020. *Ministerial Regulation of Public Works and Housing (Permen) No. 23/2020 on Strategic Plan (Renstra) 2020–2024*. Jakarta: Government of Indonesia.

OPHI. 2020. *Global Multidimensional Poverty Index 2020 – Charting Pathways Out of Multidimensional Poverty: Achieving the SDGs*. England: University of Oxford.

Sanyal, B. 2016. Informal Land Markets: Perspectives for Policy. In *Slums: How Informal Real Estate Markets Work*, edited by E. L. Birch, S. M. Wachter, and S. Chattaraj. Philadelphia: University of Pennsylvania Press. pp. 177–194.

Taylor, J. 2015. A Tale of Two Cities: Comparing Alternative Approaches to Reducing the Vulnerability of Riverbank Communities in Two Indonesian Cities. *Environment and Urbanization* 27 (2): 621–636. doi:10.1177/0956247815594532.

United Nations Department of Economic and Social Affairs (UN DESA). 2018. *Voluntary National Reviews: Synthesis Report*. New York.

UN-Habitat. 2015. 22 – Informal Settlements. *Habitat III Issue Papers*. Nairobi.

———. 2020. *World Cities Report 2020: The Value of Sustainable Urbanization*. Nairobi.

World Bank. 2011. *Jakarta: Urban Challenges in a Changing Climate*. Washington, DC.

———. 2020. *Indonesia Public Expenditure Review*. Washington, DC.

4

Enabling Urban Resilience: Basic Services, Informality, and Livelihoods

*Priyam Das, Lakpa Sherpa, and Ashok Das**

Abstract

The last decade or so has witnessed a heightened focus on building urban resilience. It is buoyed by the compounding threats of climate change, accelerating urbanization in developing regions, deepening urban inequality, and a growing need for better urban planning. This chapter argues that to enable urban resilience, planning and policy making must engage with informality to improve the urban poor's access to basic services and livelihoods. To better prepare for a future that is increasingly prone to uncertainties and extremes, it is important to critically evaluate how planning's status quo and departures there from impact informality. By weaving together lessons learned from the authors' synergistic research agendas, the chapter examines primary data collected in Nepal amid the coronavirus disease (COVID-19) pandemic to draw critical inferences for practice, also informed by findings from investigations of related issues elsewhere. Specifically, the chapter explains how physical infrastructure (water, sanitation, and housing) and services (human and economic development) are enhanced when institutions of the state, community, and civil society are incentivized to work in concert. To enable resilience, the emergent wisdom suggests rethinking assumptions of and approaches to urban development, governance, and planning.

* The primary research presented here was supported by the 2020 Jagdish P. Sharma Memorial Scholarship, University of Hawai'i at Mānoa (for the second author). The authors are grateful to all the interviewees and facilitators for making this research feasible during the inordinately trying times of the COVID-19 pandemic.

Keywords: informality, urban resilience, basic services, livelihoods, land-use, urban governance, Kathmandu, Nepal

1. Introduction

Resilience is a term enmeshed in conceptual tensions. Nonetheless, it is now a popular "boundary object"—something that facilitates communication and understanding across disciplines, coordination among stakeholders, and consensus-building around policy issues (Brand and Jax 2007). It is even viewed as an emergent "bridging concept" that facilitates interdisciplinary and transdisciplinary inquiries (Baggio, Brown, and Hellebrandt 2015) and can strategically link different areas of work and practice (Davoudi et al. 2012). Consequently, in recent years, growing concerns over climate change, economic inequality, and social justice have helped push multiple prevailing and emerging debates in urban planning and policy under the umbrella of "urban resilience." A broad definition of urban resilience is the capacity of cities, their population, enterprises, and governments, and the systems on which they depend, to cope, adapt, and transform when faced with stresses and shocks (Satterthwaite et al. 2020).

Every third person is expected to live in cities by 2050 in what is being called an "urban century" (Avis 2016), and much of this urbanization is set to unfold in the Global South. Thus, in addition to protecting ecosystem health, ensuring access to basic services such as housing, water, sanitation, and wastewater management, among others, is central to building urban resilience. The local impacts of global climate change amid soaring inequality make addressing this issue urgent. As highlighted in the Fifth Assessment Report (AR5) of the Intergovernmental Panel on Climate Change (IPCC), sizeable proportions of the urban populations in low- and middle-income nations live in informal settlements that lack risk-reducing infrastructure and services (IPCC 2014: 14). Globally, as estimated by the United Nations Sustainable Development Goals (SDGs) report, 26% of the population or 2 billion people lacked access to a safely managed drinking water service in 2020; 46% or 3.6 billion lacked access to a safely managed sanitation service, with 494 million resorting to open defecation; and 44% of household water is not safely treated.[1] Another recent report by the World Resources Institute contends that closing the urban services divide in the Global South is vital—not just for accommodating over 2.5 billion additional

---

[1]   See UN DESA (2020).

urban residents by 2050, but also for recovering from the devastating socioeconomic impacts of the COVID-19 pandemic (Mahendra et al. 2021). The pandemic delivered a cruel shock to the world's poorest, who are already unfairly burdened by service deficits in the water and sanitation sectors. It is now widely accepted that investment in water and sanitation infrastructure and waste management practices could contribute to future pandemic-preparedness. For instance, UN-Habitat (2020: 1) points out that "without access to safe drinking water, people are at higher risk of water-borne diseases and therefore more susceptible to becoming seriously ill if infected by COVID-19." Not investing in these services foreshadows public health exigencies related to disasters triggered by natural hazard and economic shocks in developing regions.

To address the interconnected impacts of climate change and rapid urbanization, the World Bank recently announced its Climate Change Action Plan 2021–2025 to support green, resilient, and inclusive development by increasing climate finance to developing countries. In keeping with the goals of the Paris Agreement, it calls for an integration of climate and development goals and identification and prioritization of actions to mitigate and adapt by leveraging private capital (World Bank Group 2021).[2] While this could have far-reaching outcomes, it is imperative for governments to ensure that this new global agenda setting does not dilute the emphasis on the universal provision of basic urban infrastructure and services for the poor. In this chapter, we focus on fast-urbanizing cities of South Asia with relatively weak capacity for planning and governance to examine how access to services like water and sanitation affects urban resilience, with or without other overlapping shocks such as COVID-19. We mainly present primary qualitative evidence from a rapid study in Nepal conducted under restrictive conditions during the pandemic. The findings underscore planning's insouciant treatment of informality, consigning the urban poor to multiple and simultaneous vulnerabilities, and rendering them more fragile in the immediate aftermath of COVID-19. They also highlight the salience of basic services in efforts to safeguard cities from the deleterious impacts of extreme events. Physical infrastructure and services are enhanced when institutions of the state, community, and

---

[2]   The Paris Agreement is a legally binding international treaty on climate change. Its goal is to limit global warming to below 2 degrees Celsius, but preferably to 1.5 degrees Celsius, compared with pre-industrial levels. It was adopted by 196 Parties at COP 21 (the 21st Conference of the Parties) in Paris, on 12 December 2015 and entered into force on 4 November 2016. See UN Climate Change. The Paris Agreement. https://unfccc.int/process-and-meetings/the-paris-agreement/the-paris-agreement.

civil society are incentivized to work in concert. To enable resilience, it is critical to rethink assumptions of and approaches to urban development (to reduce sectoral separation—i.e., little coordination among agencies responsible for different services); governance (to overcome institutional insularity—i.e., local decision-making usually reflects little input from non-state stakeholders and communities, especially poor ones); and planning (to emphasize scalar specifics—i.e., land-use, environmental, and now climate adaptation plans are routinely conceptualized at the city or urban region level, mostly disconnected from settlement and neighborhood level ground realities). In recent decades, local civil society organizations (CSOs), including nongovernment organizations (NGOs) and community-based organizations (CBOs), have emerged as key stakeholders of urban poverty alleviation and development (Mitlin and Satterthwaite 2004), and feature prominently for driving equitable and empowering planning innovations in South Asia (Baruah 2010).

The remaining sections of the chapter are as follows: the second section reviews relevant literature in the areas of urban services, land-use plans and policy, and climate adaptation and resilience to provide a theoretical footing for our investigation. The third provides a summary note on research data and methods. The fourth analyzes how the interrelated issues of informality, basic services, and resilience played out during the COVID-19 pandemic using data collected from fieldwork in Kathmandu, Nepal, and presents the findings. A brief fifth section juxtaposes some key findings against past lessons from successes and failures, elsewhere in developing Asia, to reiterate wisdoms of planning practice for bolstering urban resilience. The conclusion remark on the pivotal role of urban planning in meeting the core objective of providing basic infrastructure and services so that cities can adapt to the increased incidence and intensity of adverse climate events and public health crises.

2. Literature Review

In much of the Global South, unequal access to urban services is among the problems that continue to beleaguer cities. While there are myriad factors for its persistence, the importance of scrutinizing modes and outcomes of urban development—mediated by formal plans, programs, and policies, and its impacts on settlements outside formal planning frameworks—cannot be overemphasized. A review of relevant literature on basic urban services in the Global South, with an emphasis on the intersection of informality and land-use plans, especially in light of the relatively recent scholarly inquiry on climate adaptation and resilience, is instructive as a framework for examining this issue.

2.1 Urban Services

Access to basic urban services transcends the formal-informal binary. Households in most cities encounter varying forms and degrees of privation in accessing services, ranging from aging infrastructure to absent or inadequate supply. Households receive municipal water two to three times a week for a few hours at a time. They have to augment supply by either installing a motor to pump water to a storage tank or purchasing water to meet their basic needs. In the slum settlements, safe sanitation facilities, whether they are individual or shared toilets, often do not connect to a sewerage system. Many small cities rely on septic tanks that are improperly maintained and present the risk of contaminating nearby water sources. Other services such as transport and electricity are also lacking or inadequate. Unequal access to essential infrastructure and services that are of high-quality, reliable, and affordable impairs productivity, human health, the natural environment, and perpetuates generational poverty (Mahendra et al. 2021).

When examining the intersection of urban resilience and urban planning, it is important to ask why physical infrastructure in cities is inadequate and how they could withstand the impacts of a changing climate; but to be able to address the inequality in access to such infrastructure and services, it is equally important to ask who is being impacted and how (Meerow and Newell 2019; Anguelovski et al. 2016; Vale 2014). Ample evidence indicates that the urban poor are being impacted disproportionately, particularly women. For instance, access to a piped network is considered the least costly option for poor households (Beard and Mitlin 2021). Beyond just the cost of the physical infrastructure and services, this calculation takes into consideration intangible costs such as time savings, health burdens, and the loss of employment. Yet, poor households that lack adequate access to water supply, sanitation, and wastewater management are also not connected to a piped network or sewers, and are often left to self-provide such services. Assuming that a household member needs 50 to 100 liters of water per day, affordability standards recommend that the cost of water and sanitation should not exceed 5% of a household's income (United Nations n.d.). In reality, households pay up to 52 times the cost of municipal supply when self-providing from alternate sources (Beard and Mitlin 2021), which, given their vulnerability to urban environmental hazards such as flash floods and heatwaves, and extreme events like the COVID-19 pandemic, could suddenly deplete their savings.

Households in low-income or informal settlements are unable to purchase sufficient quantities of water from public providers motivated by cost recovery (Mitlin and Walnycki 2019). Informal markets for water (and for other services) can be socially just or they can trap the poor in unjust arrangements (Wutich, Beresford, and Carvajal 2016). Rushed moves to privatize water supply in the 1990s led to riots in places like Cochabamba, Bolivia (Assies 2003) where the poor still struggle to access water. At the same time, several institutional arrangements involving stakeholders in the informal water sector, from organized neighborhood water committees to unionized water vendors, suggest that cooperation among multiple institutional actors across scales can influence the politics and practice of informal services delivery (Marston 2014; Wutich, Beresford, and Carvajal 2016). Similarly, in cities where homes are not connected to sewers, the responsibility of managing on-site fecal sludge falls on households and private providers, often promoting risky sanitation practices (Beard et al. 2022). Compared with wealthier households, coping costs are typically higher for low-income households (Majuru, Suhrcke, and Hunter 2016). For instance, before many were evicted and began moving into high-rise flats in 2014, residents of Jakarta's Kampung Melayu settlement had squatted for decades along the low-lying banks of the Ciliwung river. Every year they endured two to three episodes of flooding during which the waters would rise by one to two meters (Marschiavelli et al. 2008). Cleaning up a house after the waters receded could cost a household $60 to over $100 each time.[3]

Access to basic services needs to be viewed not simply as a symptom of failed urban planning warranting a solution but rather through a lens that is attentive to how historical, social, and economic processes mediate formal plans to provide resources. Occupation and co-construction of habitable space through infrastructural improvisation and self-organization is akin to claiming the right to the city (Amin 2014; Benjamin 2008; Caldeira 2012). Parnell and Pietrese (2010) call for establishing socioeconomic rights at the subnational level in addition to democratic rights—a right to affordable urban services, a safe environment, mobility, public space, and climate-secure cities. They point out that while the primacy of establishing a participatory democracy and protecting individual rights is well-meaning, it can ignore or subdue efforts to advance socioeconomic rights (Miraftab 2003)—those manifested in affordable urban services to poor households and neighborhoods. Realizing urban citizenship in cities of the Global South is challenging when subnational governments are feeble and well-articulated rights are absent (Das and Dahiya 2020). In Brazil, after a prolonged social movement in 2001, the right

---

[3] Revealed to the third author by residents during field visit to and transect walks in Kampung Melayu, 4 July 2014.

to the city was enshrined through national legislation—the Statute of the City. Nonetheless, translating it into material gains for the poor has been problematic (Fernandes 2007; Friendly 2017). Despite moves toward decentralization in developing countries, the discussion and articulation of rights (e.g., political, humanitarian, and developmental), as well as development agendas, continue to be led and realized at the national level. To achieve equity and inclusivity, as set forth in the New Urban Agenda (NUA) (UN-Habitat 2020), decentralization should catalyze subnational and local governments to undertake contextually appropriate urban planning and development endeavors that amount to *de facto* socioeconomic rights aligned with the NUA vision.

2.2 Land-Use Plans and Policy

Land-use plans direct urban growth, taking into account resources and their distribution over time and space. At the same time, planning modes and formal plans can render the poor invisible and even reinforce existing inequalities (Appadurai 2001; Das 2017; Miraftab 2009; Sandercock 1998). The making of formal plans constitutes a "techno-managerial" approach (Watson 2009); plans are authored by local planning staff in consultation with experts. They are insulated from the political context, leaving them misaligned with ground realities, and therefore, are challenging to implement. The common land-use plan details and instrumentalizes the attainment of a desired future of a city, as envisioned in the master plan, while regulatory tools like zoning ensure that all development conforms with the plans. Planning with master plans is at once deemed necessary and problematic, especially for its modernist approach that makes it inflexible, insensitive to the dynamics of informality, and even promoting informality (Todes et al. 2010). In the past, the transfer of models and processes of planning, such as master planning, from the imperial heartland to the colonial outposts, provided safe urban environments for expatriates, while tightening administrative control over indigenous populations. Today, master plans persist in much of the Global South despite gradually losing currency in countries of the North where they originated. Often, the widespread prevalence of informality in cities of the Global South is conveniently attributed to the absence of robust master plans. However, the persistence of urban informality and inequality is not for lacking detailed master plans but because power and perverse incentives disregarded and distorted them (Cowherd 2005). The "conflicting rationalities" between the state's governing and the poor's surviving create tensions in contested contexts where urban growth tends to overwhelm the capacity to provide services (Watson 2009). The prevalent perception that narrowly construes informality as illegitimate—especially when it involves the poor—continues to influence planning and policy for urban services. One view sees the answer in providing formal tenure and property rights to those without as the key to unlocking problems of informality and inequality (De Soto 2000); another finds regulations to be the culprit and celebrates informality as indicative of the potential of free markets (Bertaud 2018). Local governments' traditional unwillingness to provide essential services like water and sanitation to informal settlements for fear of encouraging more migration and informality is now deemed unproductive. Rather, the inclusion of various informal processes and actors is considered imperative for making cities in the Global South equitable (Mahendra et al. 2021).

Decades of empirical investigations have helped planning scholarship clarify that

(i)   informality and tenure rights are not binary entities but constitute a spectrum of various types and degrees (Payne 2002);

(ii)   the urban poor have long relied on informal markets and providers but pay disproportionately more compared with users of formal services (Birch, Wachter, and Chattaraj 2016; Crane 1994);

(iii)   the poor are willing to pay for occupancy rights without full property rights (Nakamura 2017); and

(iv)   applying zoning and planning regulations lightly and flexibly to informal settlements lets them flourish and become resilient with time, while also offering relatively more affordable residential options (Das and King 2019).

Informal settlements have experienced different interventions—*inter alia*, slum upgrading, resettlement, and land readjustment—with distinct benefits and challenges (Collier et al. 2019). Among them, in situ upgrading is highly recommended with alternatives that range from rudimentary to transformative, with varying degrees of government and community involvement and impacts (Satterthwaite et al. 2020). While the lowest rungs on the upgrading ladder, in some cases, entail displacement, the higher ones are more comprehensive and pay particular attention to anticipating risks from climate change and building resilience. Successful upgrading rests upon laying a solid foundation for building relationships of trust between the local government and informal settlement residents (Satterthwaite et al.

2020) and leveraging synergies among state-community-civil society actors (Das 2018; Mitlin and Satterthwaite 2004).

2.3 Climate Adaptation and Resilience

Climate adaptation plans and resilience strategies are gaining currency with local planning and policy institutions. To quite an extent, their efficacy is predicated upon the existing status of land-use planning, infrastructure, and basic services. In the Global South, where cities struggle to meet the current needs of their populations, the relationship between climate adaptation plans and routine planning is mutually reinforcing. Thus, they are often aligned with development co-benefits to make them politically expedient; however, like land-use plans, many are being criticized for privileging the elite and even creating new socio-spatial inequalities that can compromise the resilience of marginalized groups (Anguelovski et al. 2016). Such inequality implicates urban governance and institutions at multiple scales across multiple domains—social, ecological, and technological (Hamstead and Coseo 2020). Resilience thinking is well-intentioned; however, its overreliance on engineering and ecology metaphors amounts to advocating an instrumental approach that underplays sociopolitical complexities and, therefore, risks not addressing or reinforcing existing inequalities (Meerow and Newell 2019; Béné et al. 2018; Matin, Forrester, and Ensor 2018).[4] The social equity dimension of urban resilience is less well-understood (Meerow and Newell 2019) and, hence, relatively weakly emphasized. Few studies examine how bottom-up, grassroots approaches contribute to broader urban resilience. Among them, Jabeen, Johnson, and Allen (2010) document grassroots strategies for coping with extreme weather devised by the poor residents of Dhaka's Korail bosti. These range from household-level adaptation strategies to collective efforts toward neighborhood improvement, leveraging social capital, and temporary relocation, among others. They underscore the importance of local development plans and demonstrate the "built-in" resilience of the urban poor. Such strategies can be preventative and impact minimizing, or they can be post-event coping actions to reduce vulnerability (Wisner et al. 2004; Pelling and Wisner 2012). The complexity of extreme events makes it difficult to calibrate risk and translate it into spatial plans, thereby

---

4   Engineering and ecological metaphors of resilience assume a predetermined past or future steady state to bounce back or forward to resulting in technologically driven solutions (Vale 2014). See, for instance, Room for the River project by the Dutch.

prompting concepts like evolutionary resilience—the ability of complex social-ecological systems to change, adapt, and transform in response to stressors (Berkes, Colding, and Folke 2008; Meerow, Newell, and Stults 2016; Chelleri et al. 2015; Moglia et al. 2018). However, to reduce the vulnerability of the urban poor and enable communities to recover after extreme events, there is an urgent need to sharpen the policy and planning focus on social injustice—the inequitable access to resources and unfair allocation of risks and burdens (Vale 2014). Moreover, providing a normative dimension to resilience and acknowledging the associated trade-offs could correct the prevailing technical bias in resilience thinking and encourage better alignment with people, politics, and power for meaningful transformation (Bahadur and Tanner 2014).

Following a brief note on data and methods, we discuss the impacts of the COVID-19 pandemic on poor households in Nepal to illuminate how factors tied to the conditions of informality and access to basic infrastructure and services come to bear upon resilience.

3. Data and Methods

The methodological approach for the cases discussed in this chapter constitutes analyzing primary data and reviewing secondary sources. The guiding conceptual frame is informed by a range of secondary literature, including published scholarship based on the first and third authors' over 3 decades of mixed-methods research and extensive fieldwork in cities of South and Southeast Asia.[5] The case from Nepal constituted independent primary research; its analysis provides a richer understanding of the informality-resilience relationship, especially during the COVID-19 pandemic, by highlighting a broader set of factors and implications. Overall, the analysis presented in this chapter is informed by the purposive use of multiple qualitative methods, not only to capture the inherent complexities of the issue being investigated, but also to overcome limitations to research posed by the pandemic. The discussion of the case below includes further details of the respective data and methods used.

---

[5] The different mixed-methods approaches comprised, overall, archival research, document analysis, analysis of news media, semi-structured interviews, focus groups, transect walks and on-site observations, and various regression analyses using primary datasets generated from household surveys.

4. Informality, Resilience, and COVID-19: A Case from Nepal

Across the globe, the COVID-19 pandemic has impacted households with preexisting vulnerabilities. Despite a gradual relaxing of restrictions from around mid-2020, hardships persisted and later escalated as the COVID-19 Delta variant swept across the world in a devastating second wave of the pandemic (Chandran 2021). A rapid study conducted in Kathmandu, Nepal between June and August of 2021, amid restrictive protocols to control the pandemic, highlights some of the impacts due to COVID-19 endured by those in the informal sector and situates these within the broader context of access to basic infrastructure and services.[6]

4.1 Informality and the Poor in Kathmandu, Nepal

Informality, particularly informal work, in Nepal is not well-understood. Reliable data about informal dwellers and informal workers are yet unavailable. The World Bank now considers Nepal a lower-middle income country with a per capita income of $1,155 in 2020.[7] It has been steadily urbanizing over the last 2 decades with over 21% of its 30 million people living in cities and an urbanization rate of 2.1% (ADB 2021). Its current Human Development Index (HDI) of 0.602 makes it a medium HDI country, a result of sharp gains since 1990 (UNDP 2020).

In general, informal settlements in Nepal are characterized by poor quality housing, overcrowding, lack of land tenure, and insecure residential status. Many of them are located in environmentally hazardous areas such as along riverbanks and on public lands, steep slopes, and waste dumping sites, and the dwellings are often dilapidated or are temporary structures. Moreover, most of the informal settlements lack access to basic infrastructure such as municipal drinking water and sanitation. A poverty mapping exercise in 2010 estimated almost 20,000 informal dwellers residing along riverbanks, on public lands, and in public buildings in Kathmandu (UN-Habitat 2010). The number of informal dwellers in Kathmandu rose to 24,021 in 2013, and 46 informal

---

[6]   This study extended prior research conducted in 2020 by the second author for her capstone chapter toward her master's degree in urban and regional planning from the University of Hawai'i at Mānoa.

[7]   See World Bank. GDP per Capita – Nepal. https://data.worldbank.org/indicator/ NY.GDP.PCAP.CD?locations=NP.

settlements were recorded. By 2020, this number had grown to 52 informal settlements (Shrestha, Poudel, and Khatri 2021). The growth in informal settlements signals an increasing population of informal dwellers; however, their exact number is yet unknown. Without proper documentation of their residential status and without tenure security, these informal dwellers are vulnerable to state-led evictions. Forced demolitions and evictions over time have seen the emergence of CSOs that advocate for the rights of informal dwellers; among them are Lumanti Support Group for Shelter (Lumanti), Nepal Mahila Ekata Samaj (NMES), and Nepal Basobas Basti Samrakchan Samaj (NBBSS).

Environmentally hazardous areas. Many residents have no choice but to live in dilapidated temporary dwellings along a riverbank in Thapathali, Kathmandu (photo by Lakpa Sherpa).

The residents of informal settlements constitute the urban poor who mostly rely on the informal sector for living and working (Chen and Beard 2018). They engage in a range of low-paying and precarious income-generation activities, including self-employment, home-based enterprises, waste-picking, recycling, daily-wage unskilled labor, domestic worker, security guards, piece-rate work, and public transport related work (e.g., driving, fare collection, and transportation of building materials). Nepal has not yet introduced policies or developed mechanisms to include informal sector workers in the social protection system. The importance of expanding social protection to informal workers was realized during the COVID-19 crisis. A few CSOs, especially some member-based organizations (MBOs), are advocating for informal workers to have the right to access social protection;[8] however, until a legal framework enables a well-articulated social protection policy, informal workers remain vulnerable to daily work-related risk, income insecurity, harassment, and crackdowns. The COVID-19 pandemic only amplified these everyday stresses for those whose lives are marked by informality.

Lack of access to sanitation. Residents of Thapathali informal settlement in Kathmandu use a makeshift toilet (photo by Lakpa Sherpa).

To understand the impacts of COVID-19 and the lockdown in Kathmandu Valley's informal settlements, key informant interviews and a household survey were conducted. The study was approved by the University of Hawai'i at Mānoa Institutional Review Board. Five key informants representing different institutions were interviewed—one from Lumanti, one from UN-HABITAT, and three from NMES. Given the risk of contagion, the key informants were offered the choice of an in-person or phone interview. Eventually, only one interview was

---

8   A key distinction between MBOs and non-membership-based CSOs is in terms of ownership, with the latter being nonproprietary with no owners as such (Anheier 2005). In MBOs, membership is voluntary and non-compulsory, but MBOs allow greater decision-making by and demonstrate accountability toward their grassroots members who are also owners. Because of their greater democratizing potential, some deem MBOs to constitute the true third sector.

conducted in-person with COVID-19 safety measures. The second wave of COVID-19 in Nepal brought restrictions that discouraged in-person household surveys. Therefore, coordinating with NMES helped administer the household survey in informal settlements and gather data on households' sociodemographic characteristics and the impact of COVID-19 on people's lives. NMES introduced three focal persons from three informal settlements—Pathibhara, Manahara, and Bansi Ghat (Map 1). Between June and August 2021, these persons acted as the surveyors who collected data in their respective communities. The survey had 31 respondents, with at least 10 from each community. Since the surveyors were residents of their respective communities and members of NMES, they were trusted by the study participants. Initially, the survey was to be administered remotely via telephone or online platforms. However, since the surveyors had access to the community members, data collection was done in person.

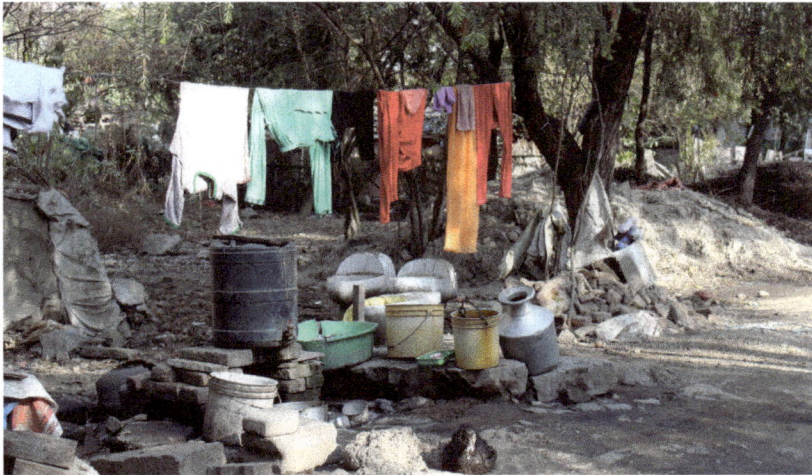

Lack of access to water. Residents share an open or common dishwashing area in Thapathali informal settlement, Kathmandu (photo by Lakpa Sherpa).

The survey was conducted not just to understand how the COVID-19 pandemic impacted the lives of informal settlement dwellers and informal workers but to also appreciate the status of shelter and services in informal settlements. Although a bigger sample and random sampling were initially intended, the persistence of restrictive conditions and access limitations eventually yielded a small sample with convenience sampling. These were adequate for the purpose of this research—to illuminate nuances of how dwelling in informality impacts the resilience of poor households and communities.

Map 1: Approximate Locations of Three Informal Settlements in Kathmandu
(chosen for the household survey, June–August 2021)

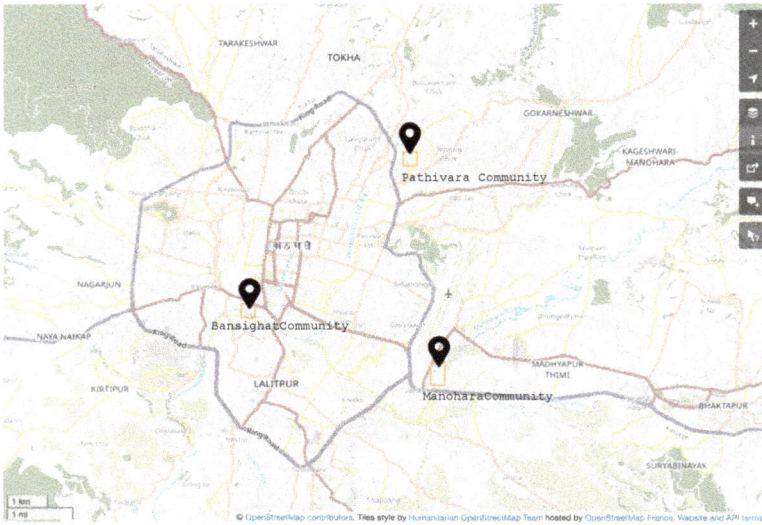

Source: Created by Lakpa Sherpa, using OpenStreetMap.

Table 1 presents various characteristics of the households surveyed in the three settlements. It is worth noting that households have resided in these settlements for a long time, on average 15 years or more. Yet they constantly live under the threat of eviction. A very high proportion, 90% or more, reported owning their homes (which does not imply any formal real estate transaction). The average household sizes range from 3.6 persons to 4.9, compared with Nepal's national average household size of 4.6 and 4.2 for urban households (Government of Nepal and UNDP 2016). Likewise, the average monthly household income in the three settlements is between $120 and $240—a range that is much lower than both Nepal's last available (2015) national average urban household income ($276) and overall national mean household income ($257) (CEIC n.d.). This indicates that these households are much more economically stressed.

Table 1: Characteristics of Households Surveyed
in Informal Settlements of Kathmandu

Household Characteristics	Settlements		
	Bansi Ghat	Manahara	Pathivara
Number of households	10	10	11
Average household size (persons)	4.9	4.1	3.6
Average length of residence in settlement (years)	17	16	15
Tenure status (% of households)			
Own	100	90	91
Rent	–	10	9
Employment status (average no. of working household members)	2.2	1	1.9
Average monthly household income ($; NRs in parentheses)[a]	240 (28,000)	120 (14,000)	205 (24,000)
Household access to soap, sanitizer, and personal protective equipment (%)			
Good	–	10	9
Limited	20	70	45
None	80	20	45
Economic impacts on households during COVID-19			
Had regular income (%)	–	10	27
Income status (%)[b]			
Stable	–	20	18
Declined	80	40	64
No income	20	30	9
Unemployed during COVID-19 (%)	70	80	64
Status of services			
Have access to water (%)	30	40	64
Sources of water (%)			
Hand pump/Tube well	–	100	64
Well	100	–	–
Jar (dispenser) water	100	100	100
Water tanker	70	–	–

– = zero.

[a] Currency equivalent applicable at the end of August 2021.

[b] Not all respondents answered this question, so the total % may not add up to 100.

Source: Field survey conducted by Lakpa Sherpa, June–August 2021.

Overall, almost 10% of the households surveyed lived in a one-room home that included a kitchen. Less than half of all households (45%) had two-room dwellings, and the remaining 45% had units with three or more rooms. The survey was unable to capture floor areas but did gather occupancy data. Interestingly, more rooms also resulted in higher occupancy per room—the average occupancy per room of single-roomed dwellings was 2.6 persons, two-room dwellings had an average occupancy of 4.14 persons per room, and the figure rose to 4.9 persons in homes with more than three rooms (29%). This is a valuable insight suggesting that larger dwellings likely suffer more overcrowding, which made the desired social distancing during the COVID-19 pandemic infeasible, if not impossible.

Almost every respondent had access to a private toilet, which was not anticipated (of course, the functional quality of toilets could not be ascertained). Access to running water varied considerably in the three settlements—from 30% to 64% (Table 1). The survey also revealed that respondents rely on different water sources for different uses such as drinking, cleaning, washing, and bathing. Moreover, access to or use of different water sources varies by settlement (Table 1), and households typically rely on some combination of water from hand pumps or tube wells, wells, and jars (plastic dispensers); only the residents of Bansi Ghat reported that they also rely on water tankers. All the households surveyed said they purchase jar water, which comes in 20-liter plastic dispensers that cost $0.35 each. Although expensive, it is an easily accessible and often the only reliable source of drinking water in Kathmandu. Likewise, buying potable water from water tankers is very expensive, and more so compared to jar water. Water tankers carry 7,000 to 12,000 liters. A community must have a facility to store such a large volume of water, and its operating costs are burdensome for informal dwellers.

Additional results from the household survey and the interviews are summarized in the following subsections to highlight how COVID-19 impacted the lives of Kathmandu's informal dwellers and informal workers.

Inability to Comply with Safety Protocols

When all of Nepal went into lockdown (late April to September 2021), many among the poor had little or no knowledge of the pandemic. Following the safety protocols—social distancing, isolation, regular handwashing, sanitizing, and mask-wearing—was burdensome. Overcrowded informal settlements and inadequate access to water and sanitation facilities made it difficult for the residents to comply. Protective face masks and sanitizers were expensive. One of the NMES members stated, "…..masks and sanitizers were very expensive and very unaffordable in the beginning of the COVID-19 lockdown. While households were hardly securing food for their families, masks and sanitizers were beyond their reach."[9] The containment measures made it challenging for informal dwellers and workers to obtain two meals a day, let alone afford soap, water, masks, sanitizer, or personal protective equipment (PPE). Table 1 presents the status of access to soap, sanitizer, and other essential protective supplies in the three informal settlements surveyed. The vast majority, 90% or more, stated they had limited or no access, and only 10% or less said they had good access. In general, informal settlements that have been upgraded are more centrally located or close to municipal water infrastructure, such as public standpipes, thus they were able to comply with safety protocols.

Job Loss and Food Insecurity

Members of many households are employed in the informal sector, which was completely disrupted by the lockdown. Of the households surveyed, 72% relied on informal work, and the rest were evenly split between holding formal sector jobs and being unemployed. During the lockdown, most informal workers lost their jobs and experienced declining earnings. Almost 68% of respondents reported being unemployed during the lockdown. In the three settlements, from almost three-quarters to all households reported having no regular income during the COVID-19 pandemic, less than 20% of households had incomes that stayed stable, and between 64% and 80% were unemployed in that period (Table 1). In Manahara and Pathivara, only 10% and 27% of households, respectively, had regular incomes during the lockdown, and none in Bansi Ghat.

Job loss and decline in earnings compromised the ability of those reliant on the informal sector to meet basic needs. For instance, a major hardship was felt in the ability to afford food. The nationwide lockdown compelled many to skip meals, medicines, and hospital visits. Most informal workers were unsuccessful in seeking alternative work. Many feared dying of hunger rather than from the virus. A resident in an informal settlement in Sinamangal, a residential district, said, "Rich people have managed to store food and can now spend some time at home with their families. It's like a vacation for them, but for working-class

---

[9]   Phone interview with NMES member, 5 June 2021.

people like us, if this situation prolongs, we will die of hunger" (Ojha 2020). Many informal workers—domestic workers, public transport drivers, home-based workers, and street vendors—lost their means of livelihood during the protracted national lockdown. According to an interviewee, "Job loss was one of the biggest challenges in the initial lockdown. The migrant workers remained jobless, and many had to return home. Because of the halt in tourism activities, many lost their incomes. Many living in squatter settlements lost their jobs. We also found families limiting their rations (eating just one meal a day). Food security was another issue. It is still the same [even] now."[10] With no regular income, it was extremely difficult for these families to survive in Kathmandu.

Poor Access to Education

Urban poor families faced extreme difficulties when the education system completely went online during the nationwide lockdown. Many children living in the informal settlements were unable to attend online classes given the deep digital divide that exists in these communities due to the lack of internet infrastructure or unaffordable smartphones or both. Without any steady income, many struggled to recharge their mobile phones, and children's online classes proved unaffordable. One interviewee mentioned, "While families were hardly securing food for [themselves] and masks and sanitizers were beyond their reach, another difficulty was providing online classes due to inaccessible smartphones, [computers], and WiFi services. Families even didn't have money to [send] their children to school and buy books/copies [notebooks]."[11]

Interventions and Responses during the Crisis

To address the impact of the COVID-19 pandemic, the Government of Nepal made efforts to raise awareness about the pandemic through educational programs and/or messaging using radio, posters, videos, and caller tunes. Similarly, to reduce the stress of food insecurity, they distributed both food and nonfood packages at the ward level. However, the unavailability of data on vulnerable populations impeded this response. Moreover, the food assistance provided by the government had not been adequate in the long run. An interviewee stated, "We received food assistance [5 kilograms of rice] from the Kathmandu municipality.

---

[10]   Phone interview with NMES member, 5 June 2021.

[11]   Phone interview with NMES member, 5 June 2021.

Although it was a relief at that period, it did not help in the long run. If one family has 10 people, then 5 kilograms of rice would finish in one or two days."[12] The government did acknowledge street vendors selling food, vegetables, and fruits as essential workers and allowed them to operate for limited durations during the lockdown. However, not all street vendors were allowed, and many experienced brutal police crackdowns.

Dealing with informal settlements and informal workers has almost always been challenging and unsatisfactory in developing countries, and Nepal is no exception. The COVID-19 crisis has underscored the importance of inclusive urban planning to address the issues of informality. Nepal's national and local governments have traditionally looked down upon and ignored the informal sector. There is much to do to build planning capacity and implement pro-poor policies. However, with the new 2015 Constitution, the restructuring of Nepal into a federal democratic republic with three tiers of government—federal, provincial, and local—has been conducive to promoting inclusive cities. The study's key informants all mentioned having sound working relationships with their ward representatives. This enabled them to collaborate with the local governments to implement projects that addressed the COVID-19 crisis in their communities. Research has demonstrated that most integration efforts by different stakeholders for building inclusive cities happens at the local level, and therefore the role of local government is crucial in addressing urban informality (Broadhead and Kierans 2019). In light of the COVID-19 crisis, this collaboration has been crucial; however, not all local governments responded similarly. An NMES member stated, "We also received support from a few ward offices that provided 25 kilograms [of] rice. It has varied from one ward to another. Some wards are reluctant to recognize slum dwellers and reluctant to provide relief packages. Since we worked together with ward offices, it has been easy to give the community members information about the time and location of relief distribution."[13]

Compared with other countries in South Asia, Nepalese CSOs are nascent and not as influential. Still, Nepalese MBOs have been supporting their members, who are informal dwellers and informal workers, since the beginning of the pandemic. Grassroots organizations and MBOs proved to be vital agents for providing their members with reliable and accessible information about health and safety protocols and in leading relief efforts, given the inadequacy of the government's relief

---

[12]   Phone interview with NMES member, 5 June 2021.

[13]   Phone interview with NMES member, 26 July 2021.

measures. Lumanti partnered with other organizations and distributed food, water, and other essential supplies in a few informal settlements in Kathmandu. To address households' financial insecurities, exacerbated by the pandemic, Lumanti, UN-HABITAT, the ILO, and UNDP led an effort to support grassroots-led savings and credit cooperatives. This enabled the vulnerable members of women's groups to seek loans that were used to invest in food and medicines, and support livelihoods to sustain their families during the lockdowns (Lumanti 2020). NMES and Lumanti initiated outreach efforts a week before the announcement of the lockdown to support their members to cope with the crisis. NMES trained young volunteers from different informal settlements about the safety measures like handwashing and wearing masks, so that they could, in turn, teach and inform their communities about the same. They also operated child learning centers in the squatter communities to help children attend online classes, complete their homework, and participate in other learning activities. Furthermore, they collaborated with a local NGO, Baideshik Rojgari Lok Kalyankari Kosh, to provide children books, notebooks, and stationery. MBOs have also helped their respective municipal wards to build isolation centers. The community members assisted each other during the crisis by collecting money to support the neediest families and sharing their supplies.

The COVID-19 pandemic has exposed the precarious state of informal settlements. Given the lack of basic infrastructure and services, even the simplest of preventive measures—washing hands regularly, self-isolation, and physical distancing—are infeasible in most slum communities. Planning that is inclusive of the informal sector and investments to upgrade informal settlements are urgently needed to enable the urban poor to become resilient. Grassroots organizations, slum federations, NGOs, and international NGOs are now working together in Kathmandu to mitigate the harsh impacts of the COVID-19 pandemic. The civil society representatives interviewed in this study mentioned collaboration with CBOs and local governments in responding to the crisis. This study has both tested the ability of coalitions of civil society stakeholders to be resilient and stressed their importance in coping with uncertainties of unseen magnitude. The lessons learned from this analysis are hardly unique to Kathmandu. Smaller and/or remote urban centers of larger countries with stronger economies also face similar challenges, and the burdens of inadequate infrastructure and services in low-income communities are significantly heightened during crises such as the COVID-19 pandemic.

5. Conclusion

Climate adaptation has been drawing much attention with cities adopting climate-proofing strategies and redoubling efforts to tap into climate financing offered by external agencies. Such responses have indeed become urgent in the wake of the increasing frequency of extreme events such as floods, droughts, and heat waves that have affected cities worldwide. Most of these strategies, at least in the Global North, tend to focus on the built environment—implementing nature-based solutions, encouraging resilient design through the adoption of new and improved building codes, and safeguarding critical infrastructure. This chapter has attempted to demonstrate and argue that in the Global South, which is home to most of the urban poor, climate proofing will entail strengthening the networks that promote the routine health, safety, and well-being of their populations during ordinary times, not just during or in the aftermath of extreme events. The COVID-19 pandemic has laid bare the unequal access to urban services spotlighting the need to strengthen and improve the role of urban planning in building urban resilience. Investing in access to water and sanitation, for instance, can catalyze compounded benefits in other sectors such as health, education, and employment.

Our research highlights three key takeaways. First, in the still developing cities, access to basic infrastructure and services remains the backbone of urban resilience, especially for the poor whose lives and livelihoods are primarily situated within the informal sector (Mahendra et al. 2021). Our study in Nepal provides a nuanced, grassroots-level picture of the impact of the COVID-19 pandemic on poor households that lack or have inadequate services. As extreme weather events collide with urbanization pressures, safeguarding cities and their inhabitants will require concerted planning to solidify not just physical infrastructure but also social infrastructure—services to support health, education, and livelihoods. Second, echoing lessons learned from successful local governments that attempted to provide infrastructure and services effectively and equitably proves that not only is the role of the local government critical but partnering with local non-state actors such as CSOs, community groups, and university departments and research centers is pivotal to enhancing the efficacy of state action (Das 2018; Das and King 2019). More attention needs to be given to intervening at smaller scales—urban, local, and even neighborhood— where unfavorable impacts of lacking resilience are experienced every day. At these scales, for instance, addressing local risks, realizing prudent land-use planning, and garnering funding to support local actors should be given priority. This emphasizes the need for sound urban planning that engages an expanded circle of capable local interlocutors and actors, especially in cities that are small and/or have limited resources (Lassa and Nugraha 2014).

Yet, in much of the Global South, urban planning institutions at the local level are largely inadequate and incapacitated to execute routine planning activities, and certainly unprepared to tackle the expanded mandate from threats of climate change and pandemics. Strengthening these institutions and investing in preparing the future generation of urban planners is critical. The capacity to produce professional planners is itself underwhelming. For instance, the entire country of Nepal has two university programs offering urban or regional planning degrees. However, it is not just the quantum of educational training that is insufficient. Planning education continues to be overwhelmingly technical and disproportionately focused on imparting hard skills. Little emphasis is given to acquiring the knowledge and skills indispensable for working for and with poor communities (Das 2019), such as understanding the dynamics of urbanization, migration, and informality; appreciating critical perspectives on social equity and spatial justice; learning from field experiences in informal settlements; and building participation, facilitation, and negotiation skills. This hinders the increasingly acknowledged need for formal planning to work with and not against informality (Bhan, Srinivas, and Watson 2018). Therefore, this chapter's third key takeaway concerns the creation of master plans. When drawing up citywide plans for guiding the development of infrastructure or climate adaptation, planners must identify and incorporate informal settlements to be able to address their needs and enable urban resilience.

As the case from Kathmandu illustrates, a common hurdle preventing local planning institutions from actively engaging with the urban poor in informal settlements is the nonexistent or poor data about them. The problem is acute in developing Asia's smaller urban centers with limited resources, often saddled by legacies of uneven development due to centralized planning or newer challenges of recent decentralization, or both. A necessary first step is, therefore, to generate citywide data that can be utilized to support development plans. To that end, successful examples from the Global South underscore the need for cities to facilitate collaboration between CSOs and poor communities, aided by local universities. High-quality data can be generated through community mapping, leveraging communities' human resources, and increasing accessible digital technologies (Ayson 2018; Padawangi et al. 2016). The Urban Resource Center in Karachi, Pakistan is one such endeavor that has successfully created and used grassroots data to influence urban policy and planning by advocating for the needs of the underprivileged and the informal sector (Hasan 2007). International civil society networks, such as the Asian Coalition for Housing Rights and Slum Dwellers International have also helped facilitate the spread of innovative community mapping and community-driven planning practices (Vergara-Perucich and Arias-Loyola 2021) honed in informal settlements by CSOs like Solo Kota Kita in Indonesia (Phelps et al. 2014), and programs like Baan Mankong in Thailand (Archer, Luansang, and Boonmahathanakorn 2012).

Providing physical infrastructures (water, sanitation, and housing) and services (human and economic development) is essential to building resilience in urban informal settlements. Incentivizing institutions of the state, community, and civil society to work in concert can help deliver the necessary infrastructures and services effectively and equitably. Enabling urban resilience will require rethinking prevalent assumptions and reforming urban development, governance, and planning.

References

Amin, A. 2014. Lively Infrastructure. *Theory, Culture & Society* 31 (7/8): 137–161.

Anguelovski, I. et al. 2016. Equity Impacts of Urban Land Use Planning for Climate Adaptation: Critical Perspectives from the Global North and South. *Journal of Planning Education and Research* 36 (3): 333–348. doi:10.1177/0739456X16645166.

_____. 2019. Opinion: Why Green "Climate Gentrification" Threatens Poor and Vulnerable Populations. *Proceedings of the National Academy of Sciences* 116 (52): 26139–26143. https://doi.org/10.1073/pnas.1920490117.

Anheier, H. K. 2005. *Nonprofit Organizations: Theory, Management, Policy*. London; New York, NY: Routledge.

Appadurai, A. 2001. Deep Democracy: Urban Governmentality and the Horizon of Politics. *Environment and Urbanization* 13 (2): 23–43. https://doi.org/10.1177/095624780101300203.

Archer, D., C. Luansang, and S. Boonmahathanakorn. 2012. Facilitating Community Mapping and Planning for Citywide Upgrading: The Role of Community Architects. *Environment and Urbanization* 24 (1): 115–129. https://doi.org/10.1177/0956247812437132.

Asian Development Bank (ADB). Data Library. Nepal, Key Indicators. https://data.adb.org/dataset/nepal-key-indicators (accessed 5 December 2021).

Assies, W. 2003. David versus Goliath in Cochabamba: Water Rights, Neoliberalism, and the Revival of Social Protest in Bolivia. *Latin American Perspectives* 30 (3): 14–36. https://doi.org/10.1177/0094582X03030003003.

Avis, W. R. 2016. Context: Urban Governance. *GSDRC Applied Knowledge Services*. November. https://gsdrc.org/topic-guides/urban-governance/concepts-and-debates/context/.

Ayson, D. 2018. Community Mapping and Data Gathering for City Planning in the Philippines. *Environment and Urbanization* 30 (2): 501–518. https://doi.org/10.1177/0956247818767338.

Baggio, J. A., K. Brown, and D. Hellebrandt. 2015. Boundary Object or Bridging Concept? A Citation Network Analysis of Resilience. *Ecology and Society* 20 (2). http://www.jstor.org/stable/26270178.

Bahadur, A., and T. Tanner. 2014. Transformational Resilience Thinking: Putting People, Power and Politics at the Heart of Urban Climate Resilience. *Environment and Urbanization* 26 (1): 200–214.

Baruah, B. 2010. NGOs in Microfinance: Learning from the Past, Accepting Limitations, and Moving Forward. *Geography Compass* 4 (8): 979–992. https://doi.org/10.1111/j.1749-8198.2010.00362.x.

Beard, V. A., and D. Mitlin. 2021. Water Access in Global South Cities: The Challenges of Intermittency and Affordability. *World Development* 147 (November): 105625. https://doi.org/10.1016/j. worlddev.2021.105625.

Beard, V. A., D. Satterthwaite, D. Mitlin, and J. Du. 2022. Out of Sight, Out of Mind: Understanding the Sanitation Crisis in Global South Cities. *Journal of Environmental Management* 306 (March): 114285. https://doi.org/10.1016/j.jenvman.2021.114285.

Béné, C., L. Mehta, G. McGranahan, T. Cannon, J. Gupte, and T. Tanner. 2018. Resilience as a Policy Narrative: Potentials and Limits in the Context of Urban Planning. *Climate and Development* 10 (2): 116–133.

Benjamin, S. 2008. Occupancy Urbanism: Radicalizing Politics and Economy Beyond Policy and Programs. *International Journal of Urban and Regional Research* 32 (3): 719–729.

Berkes, F., J. Colding, and C. Folke, eds. 2008. *Navigating Social-Ecological Systems: Building Resilience for Complexity and Change.* Cambridge: Cambridge University Press.

Bertaud, A. 2018. *Order without Design: How Markets Shape Cities.* Cambridge, Massachusetts: MIT Press.

Bhan, G., S. Srinivas, and V. Watson, eds. 2018. *The Routledge Companion to Planning in the Global South.* Routledge Companions. London; New York, NY: Routledge.

Birch, E. L., S. M. Wachter, and S. Chattaraj, eds. 2016. *Slums: How Informal Real Estate Markets Work.* The City in the Twenty-First Century. Philadelphia: Penn, University of Pennsylvania Press.

Brand, F. S., and K. Jax. 2007. Focusing the Meaning(s) of Resilience: Resilience as a Descriptive Concept and a Boundary Object. *Ecology and Society* 12 (1). http://www.jstor.org/stable/26267855.

Broadhead, J., and D. Kierans. 2019. INCLUSIVE CITIES: A Framework to Support Local Authorities and Communities to Build Inclusive Cities. University of Oxford. https://www.compas. ox.ac.uk/2019/inclusive-cities-framework/.

Caldeira, T. 2012. Imprinting and Moving Around: New Visibilities and Configurations of Public Space in Sao Paulo. *Public Culture* 24 (2): 385–419.

CEIC. n.d. Nepal Average Monthly Household Income: Whole Kingdom. https://www.ceicdata.com/en/nepal/household-budget-survey-average-monthly-household-income/average-monthly-household-income-whole-kingdom (accessed 19 March 2022).

Chandran. 2021. Delta Variant Clouds Developing Asia's Growth Outlook – ADB. *Reuters*. 22 September. https://www.reuters.com/world/asia-pacific/delta-variant-clouds-developing-asias-growth-outlook-adb-2021-09-22/.

Chelleri, L., J. Waters, M. Olazabal, and G. Minucci. 2015. Resilience Trade-Offs: Addressing Multiple Scales and Temporal Aspects of Urban Resilience. *Environment and Urbanization* 27 (1): 181–198.

Chen, M., and V. A. Beard. 2018. Including the Excluded: Supporting Informal Workers for More Equal and Productive Cities in the Global South. *Working Paper: Towards a More Equal City*. Washington, DC: World Resources Institute. http://www.wri.org/publication/towards-more-equal-city-including-the-excluded?utm_source=twitter.com&utm_medium=wricities&utm_campaign=socialmedia.

Collier, P., E. Glaeser, T. Venables, M. Blake, and P. Manwaring. 2019. *Informal Settlements and Housing Markets*. Policy Brief. London: International Growth Centre. https://www.theigc.org/wp-content/uploads/2019/01/informal-settlements-policy-brief.pdf.

Cowherd, R. 2005. Does Planing Culture Matter: Dutch and American Models in Indonesian Urban Transformation. In *Comparative Planning Cultures*, edited by B. Sanyal. New York: Routledge. pp. 165–192.

Crane, R. 1994. Water Markets, Market Reform and the Urban Poor: Results from Jakarta, Indonesia. *World Development* 22 (1): 71–83.

Das, A. 2017. A City of Two Tales: Shelter and Migrants in Surabaya. *Environment and Urbanization ASIA* 8 (1): 1–21. https://doi.org/10.1177/0975425316686501.

_____. 2018. Is Innovative Also Effective? A Critique of Pro-Poor Shelter in South-East Asia. *International Journal of Housing Policy* 18 (2): 233–265.

_____. 2019. For an Equitable Indonesian City: Reflections on Planning Practice and Education. *Ruang*. July.

Das, A., and B. Dahiya. 2020. Towards Inclusive Urban Governance and Planning: Emerging Trends and Future Trajectories. In *New Urban Agenda in Asia-Pacific: Advances in 21st Century Human Settlements*, edited by B. Dahiya and A. Das. Singapore: Springer. pp. 353–384.

Das, A., and R. King. 2019. Surabaya: The Legacy of Participatory Upgrading of Informal Settlements. *Working Paper: Towards a More Equal City*. Washington, DC. https://www.wri.org/wri-citiesforall/publication/surabaya-legacy-participatory-upgrading-informal-settlements.

Davoudi, S. et al. 2012. Resilience: A Bridging Concept or a Dead End? "Reframing" Resilience: Challenges for Planning Theory and Practice Interacting Traps: Resilience Assessment of a Pasture Management System in Northern Afghanistan Urban Resilience: What Does It Mean in Planning Practice? Resilience as a Useful Concept for Climate Change Adaptation? The Politics of Resilience for Planning: A Cautionary Note. *Planning Theory & Practice* 13 (2): 299–333. https://doi.org/10.1080/14649357.2012.677124.

De Soto, H. 2000. *The Mystery of Capital*. Basic Books.

Fernandes, E. 2007. Constructing the "Right To the City" in Brazil. *Social & Legal Studies* 16 (2): 201–219. https://doi.org/ 10.1177/ 0964663907076529.

Friendly, A. 2017. Urban Policy, Social Movements, and the Right to the City in Brazil. *Latin American Perspectives* 44 (2): 132–148.

Government of Nepal, Central Bureau of Statistics, National Planning Commission Secretariat and United Nations Development Programme (UNDP). 2016. Annual Household Survey 2015/16 (Major Findings). Kathmandu, Nepal. https://neksap.org.np/allpublications/annual-household-survey-2015-16.

Hamstead Z., and P. Coseo. 2020. How We Got Here: Producing Climate Inequity and Vulnerability to Urban Weather Extremes. In *Resilient Urban Futures*, edited by Z. A. Hamstead, D. M. Iwaniec, T. McPhearson, M. Berbés-Blázquez, E. M. Cook, and T. A. Muñoz- Erickson. Cham, Switzerland: Springer Link. pp. 11–28.

Hasan, A. 2007. The Urban Resource Centre, Karachi. *Environment and Urbanization* 19 (1): 275–292. https://doi.org/ 10.1177/ 0956247807076921.

IPCC. 2014: Climate Change 2014: Synthesis Report. *Contribution of Working Groups I, II, and III to the Fifth Assessment Report of the Intergovernmental Panel on Climate Change*, edited by Core Writing Team, R. K. Pachauri, and L. A. Meyer. Geneva, Switzerland. p. 151.

Jabeen, H., C. Johnson, and A. Allen. 2010. Built-in Resilience: Learning from Grassroots Coping Strategies for Climate Variability. *Environment and Urbanization* 22: 415.

Lassa, J. A., and E. Nugraha. 2014. From Shared Learning to Shared Action in Building Resilience in the City of Bandar Lampung, Indonesia. *Environment and Urbanization*. December. https://doi.org/10.1177/0956247814552233.

Lumanti. 2020. *COVID Crisis: Relief and Response to the Most Needy Urban Poor Women in Kathmandu Valley*. Lalitpur, Nepal. 12 September.

Mahadevia, D., A. Mishra, and Y. Joseph. 2017. Ecology vs Housing and the Land Rights Movement in Guwahati. *Economic and Political Weekly* 18-L11 (7): 58–65.

Mahendra, A., J. Du, A. Dasgupta, V. A. Beard, A. Kallergis, and K. Schalch. 2021. Seven Transformations for More Equitable and Sustainable Cities. *World Resources Report: Towards a More Equal City*. Washington, DC: World Resources Institute. https://doi.org/10.46830/wrirpt.19.00124.

Majuru, B., M. Suhrcke, and P. R. Hunter. 2016. How Do Households Respond to Unreliable Water Supplies? A Systematic Review. *International Journal of Environmental Research and Public Health* 13 (12): 1222. https://doi.org/10.3390/ijerph13121222.

Marschiavelli, C., M. P. Hadi, M. K. McCall, and N. C. Kingma. 2008. A Community-Based Vulnerability Assessment of Floods in Urban Areas of Kampung Melayu, Jakarta. *Indonesian Journal of Geography* 40 (2): 97–113.

Marston, A. J. 2014. The Scale of Informality: Community-Run Water Systems in Peri-Urban Cochabamba, Bolivia. *Water Alternatives* 7 (1).

Matin, N., J. Forrester, and J. Ensor. 2018. What Is Equitable Resilience? *World Development* 109: 197–205.

Meerow, S., and J. P. Newell. 2019. Urban Resilience for Whom, What, When, Where, and Why? *Urban Geography* 40 (3): 309–329. https://doi.org/10.1080/02723638.2016.1206395.

Meerow, S., J. P. Newell, and M. Stults. 2016. Defining Urban Resilience: A Review. *Landscape and Urban Planning* 147 (March): 38–49. https://doi.org/10.1016/j.landurbplan.2015.11.011.

Miraftab, F. 2003. The Perils of Participatory Discourse: Housing Policy in Postapartheid South Africa. *Journal of Planning Education and Research* 22 (3): 226–239. https://doi.org/10.1177/0739456X02250305.

———. 2009. Insurgent Planning: Situating Radical Planning in the Global South. *Planning Theory* 8 (1): 32–50. https://doi.org/10.1177/1473095208099297.

Mitlin, D., and D. Satterthwaite, eds. 2004. *Empowering Squatter Citizen: Local Government, Civil Society, and Urban Poverty Reduction*. London; Sterling, VA: Earthscan.

Mitlin, D., and S. Patel. 2020. Building Resilience to Climate Change in Informal Settlements. *One Earth* 2 (2): 143–156. https://doi.org/10.1016/j.oneear.2020.02.002.

Mitlin, D., and A. Walnycki. 2019. Informality as Experimentation: Water Utilities' Strategies for Cost Recovery and their Consequences for Universal Access. *Journal of Development Studies*. DOI: 10.1080/00220388.2019.1577383.

Moglia, M. et al. 2018. Urban Transformation Stories for the 21st Century: Insights from Strategic Conversations. *Global Environmental Change* 50: 222–237.

Nakamura, S. 2017. Tenure Security Premium in Informal Housing Markets: A Spatial Hedonic Analysis. *World Development* 89 (January): 184–198. https://doi.org/10.1016/j.worlddev.2016.08.009.

Ojha, A. 2020. Daily Wage Workers Are More Worried about Starving to Death than Covid-19. *The Kathmandu Post*. 26 March. https://kathmandupost.com/national/2020/03/26/daily-wage-workers-are-more-worried-about-starving-to-death-than-covid-19.

Padawangi, R., E. Turpin, Herlily, M. F. Prescott, I. Lee, and A. Shepherd. 2016. Mapping an Alternative Community River: The Case of the Ciliwung. *Sustainable Cities and Society* 20 (January): 147–157. https://doi.org/10.1016/j.scs.2015.09.001.

Parnell, S., and E. Pietrese. 2010. The "Right to the City": Institutional Imperatives of a Developmental State. *International Journal of Urban and Regional Research* 34 (1): 146–162.

Payne, G. K. 2002. *Land, Rights and Innovation: Improving Tenure Security for the Urban Poor*. London: Intermediate Technology Development Group (ITDG).

Pelling, M. and B. Wisner, eds. 2012. *Disaster Risk Reduction: Case Studies from Urban Africa*. London: Earthscan.

Phelps, N. A., T. Bunnell, M. A. Miller, and J. Taylor. 2014. Urban Inter-Referencing Within and Beyond a Decentralized Indonesia. *Cities* 39 (August): 37–49. https://doi.org/10.1016/j.cities.2014.02.004.

Roy, A. 2005. Urban Informality: Towards an Epistemology of Planning. *Journal of the American Planning Association* 71 (2): 147–158.

Sandercock, L., ed. 1998. *Making the Invisible Visible: A Multicultural Planning History*. California Studies in Critical Human Geography 2. Berkeley: University of California Press.

Satterthwaite, D., D. Archer, S. Colenbrander, D. Dodman, J. Hardoy, and S. Patel. 2018. *Responding to Climate Change in Cities and in their Informal Settlements and Economies.* Consultant report presented at the IPCC International Scientific Conference on Cities and Climate Change, Edmonton, Canada. London: International Institute for Environment and Development.

Satterthwaite, D. et al. 2020. Building Resilience to Climate Change in Informal Settlements. *One Earth* 2 (2): 143–156.

Shrestha, A., D. P. Poudel, and D. Khatri. 2021. Recognition and Reconciliation Remain Pivotal to Resolve Issues of Informal Settlers. *Southasia Institute of Advanced Studies* (blog). 4 June. https://sias-southasia.org/recognition-and-reconciliation-remain-pivotal-to-resolve-issues-of-informal-settlers_sias/.

Todes, A., A. Karam, N. Klug, and N. Malaza. 2010. Beyond Master Planning? New Approaches to Spatial Planning in Ekurhuleni, South Africa. *Habitat International* 34 (4): 414–420. https://doi.org/10.1016/j.habitatint.2009.11.012.

United Nations. n.d. The Human Right to Water and Sanitation. Media Brief. https://www.un.org/waterforlifedecade/pdf/human_right_to_water_and_sanitation_media_brief.pdf.

UN Department of Economic and Social Affairs (UN DESA). The Sustainable Development Goals Report 2020. https://unstats.un.org/sdgs/report/2020/#sdg-goals.

United Nations Development Programme (UNDP). 2020. *The Next Frontier: Human Development and the Anthropocene—Nepal.* Briefing Note for Countries on the 2020 Human Development Report. https://hdr.undp.org/sites/default/files/Country-Profiles/NPL.pdf.

United Nations Human Settlements Programme (UN-HABITAT). 2010. *Nepal Urban Housing Sector Profile.* Nairobi, Kenya. https://unhabitat.org/nepal-urban-housing-sector-profile.

———. 2020. The New Urban Agenda Illustrated. Nairobi, Kenya. https://unhabitat.org/sites/default/files/2020/12/nua_handbook_14dec2020_2.pdf.

Vale, L. 2014. The Politics of Resilient Cities: Whose Resilience and Whose City? *Building Research and Information* 42 (2): 191–201.

Vergara-Perucich, F., and M. Arias-Loyola. 2021. Community Mapping with a Public Participation Geographic Information System in Informal Settlements. *Geographical Research* 59 (2): 268–284. https://doi.org/10.1111/1745-5871.12458.

Watson, V. 2009. Seeing from the South: Refocusing Urban Planning on the Globe's Central Urban Issues. *Urban Studies* 46 (11): 2259–2275.

Wisner, B., P. Blaikie, T. Cannon, and I. Davis. 2004. *At Risk: Natural Hazards, People's Vulnerability and Disasters*. London: Routledge.

Wutich, A., M. Beresford, and C. Carvajal. 2016. Can Informal Water Vendors Deliver on the Promise of a Human Right to Water? Results From Cochabamba, Bolivia. *World Development* 79 (March): 14–24. https://doi.org/10.1016/j.worlddev.2015.10.043.

World Bank Group. 2021. *World Bank Group Climate Change Action Plan 2021–2025: Supporting Green, Resilient, and Inclusive Development*. Washington, DC. https://openknowledge. worldbank.org/handle/10986/35799 License: CC BY 3.0 IGO.

5

Nourishment at the Margins of a Megacity: How the Poor Eat in Dhaka, Bangladesh

John Taylor, Ashok Das, Janet Naco, and Saiful Momen*

Abstract

The routine struggle of the urban poor to access sufficient and nutritious food is yet poorly understood, and much less how nutrition deprivation perpetuates cycles of poverty and inequality. This chapter's nuanced discussion of the dynamics of food insecurity and nutritional behavior of poor communities in Dhaka, Bangladesh exposes a fragile status quo and seeks to stimulate urgent and focused policy and planning attention. It is based on qualitative research—focus group discussions, telephone surveys, and interviews—conducted in four municipalities. The following key findings clarify food security's links to other aspects of planning and governance: (i) even those among the poor who eat enough suffer food insecurity because of poor nutrition; (ii) more vulnerable groups such as women are worst affected during crises such as coronavirus disease (COVID-19); (iii) physical access influences food consumption, pointing to spatial determinants of food insecurity; (iv) lacking basic services impairs people's ability to consume hygienic and healthy food, further highlighting socio-spatial injustices; (v) pandemic-induced lockdowns made it evident that the role of the state, boosted by synergistic civil society support, is pivotal to food security; and (vi) coping mechanisms, such as urban agriculture, devised by the poor to withstand tribulations wrought by the pandemic point to potential policy and planning interventions.

---

*   The authors are extremely grateful to all who helped with field research—the surveyors, interviewers, and facilitators, and, especially, the people from Dhaka's informal settlements and the urban poor federations. Without them this research would not have been possible.

Keywords: food security, nutrition, urban informality, Bangladesh, COVID-19, gender, participatory planning

1. Introduction

As the introduction and other chapters of this book emphasize, the unfortunate consequences of the COVID-19 pandemic have, fortunately, made society realize how critical are the informal sector's contributions to the efficient functioning of our cities. Accumulating research evidence in urban planning and related social sciences disciplines, using various methods, has established how informality contributes both negatively and positively to dealing with urban poverty and inequity (Morgan 2013; Mui et al. 2018; Pothukuchi 2009; Raja, Morgan, and Hall 2017; FAO, WFP, and IFAD 2012). While the hardships experienced by the urban poor in the Global South—in terms of access to material infrastructure such as housing and basic services, as well as economic opportunities—are widely recognized, their routine struggle to access sufficient and nutritious food is yet poorly understood and hardly acknowledged (Raja et al. 2021). Much less appreciated is how nutrition deprivation perpetuates cycles of poverty and inequality. Globally, 820 million poor were chronically food insecure even before COVID-19, making food security intervention an imperative (FAO et al. 2019). The Food and Agriculture Organization of the United Nations (2006: 1) defines the condition of food security as "when all people, at all times, have physical and economic access to sufficient safe and nutritious food that meets their dietary needs and food preferences for an active and healthy life." Prior to the pandemic, living in extreme poverty, about a quarter of the Bangladeshi poor were unable to afford a basic food consumption basket (World Bank 2019: 23); and, during March 2020, the first month of pandemic-induced lockdowns, that figure rose to 60% (BRAC 2020). Since the start of the pandemic in early 2020, food prices have risen consistently in Asia and the Pacific due to supply chain disruptions, rising shipping costs, and bad weather (ADB 2021). Although, food inflation in Bangladesh has not been alarming, yet 3 months into the lockdown, prices of essential foods spiked in the capital, Dhaka (FAO 2020a), and with the pandemic continuing, food insecurity and malnutrition could worsen (FAO in Bangladesh 2020).

Bangladesh has made significant strides in reducing malnutrition and improving health indicators—for example, chronic malnutrition fell from 42% in 2013 to 28% in 2019 (BBS and UNICEF Bangladesh 2019). Despite Bangladesh's food security gains, a significant proportion of Dhaka's poor suffer from malnutrition and food insecurity, but systematic data do not exist to capture the extent of food insecurity. However, ascertaining urban food insecurity is difficult, in general; even global data on food security are not yet disaggregated into urban and rural (Ruel 2020). Perplexingly, despite spending significant household income on food, the poor are often unable to consume enough food to meet these needs.

The prolonged impacts of COVID-19 have only further hampered accessibility to food, and not just locally, but globally; everything from agricultural production to logistics, trade, and supply chains to household consumption has been impacted (World Bank 2020). The pandemic has exacerbated and exposed the tenuous food security situation, with women, children, and other vulnerable groups being most impacted by lost incomes, illnesses, and rising food prices (World Bank 2020). This chapter is a modest but an important endeavor to illuminate the challenges faced by the urban poor in Dhaka, exploring a combination of factors that constitutes food insecurity, including irregular and low earnings, inadequate access to housing and basic services, and the increasing pervasiveness of inexpensive, calorie-dense, yet unhealthy food. It asks the question: How well are the urban poor in Dhaka able to obtain and consume sufficient safe and nutritious food to meet their daily nutritional needs? The research looks at the factors that influence their ability to do so, how access may differ throughout the city, and which groups are most compromised. Our investigation into an ostensibly facile question reveals that the underpinnings, manifestations, and implications of food access are anything but simple. The chapter also explores the extent to which the urban poor's access to food has been impacted by the COVID-19 pandemic, and draws attention to the promising ways in which the urban poor's vulnerability to food and nutrition insecurity can be reduced.

This chapter is based on qualitative research—focus group discussions, telephone surveys, and interviews—conducted in four city corporations of the Dhaka metropolitan region, namely, Dhaka South, Dhaka North, Gazipur, and Narayanganj. It focuses on the lives of informal settlement dwellers and workers, and the activities of grassroots organizations, both before and during the pandemic. The research findings illuminate how low-income communities struggle to meet their nutritional needs as well as their remarkable but inequitable coping mechanisms. The following key findings clarify food security's links to other aspects of planning and governance: (i) even those among the poor who eat enough suffer food insecurity because they do not consume enough healthy food; (ii) more vulnerable groups such as women are worst affected during crises such as COVID-19; (iii) physical accessibility influences the consumption of nutritious food, pointing to spatial determinants of food insecurity; (iv) lacking basic services like water, sanitation, and electricity impairs people's ability to eat hygienic and healthy food, further highlighting how spatial injustices are manifested in food insecurity; (v) during the pandemic-induced lockdowns it became evident that the role of the state in enabling food security is pivotal, the efficacy of which is boosted by synergistic civil society support; and (vi) coping mechanisms devised by the poor, such as urban agriculture, to tide over the tribulations wrought by the pandemic point to areas for potential policy and planning interventions.

Including the introduction, the chapter is organized into six sections. The second section reviews the literature pertaining to the main issues and arguments to provide the chapter its theoretical framework; the third section is a note about the data and methods used. The fourth section is an essential backdrop to this chapter that introduces the reader to pertinent facets of Bangladeshi development, relevant aspects of governance and planning in metropolitan Dhaka, and key contextual features of the food landscape in question. The fifth section illustrates in detail and critically analyzes aspects of access, patterns of consumption, and impacts on nutrition that deepen food insecurity among those who exist in the marginalized confines of the informal sector. The sixth and final section provides a summary discussion of the key findings and concludes with policy and planning recommendations, and offers directions for future research. The recommendations call for more inclusive planning through institutional arrangements that foster participation among stakeholders and collaboration across levels of governance. Collectively, these suggestions can revamp and orient urban planning and policy making in Dhaka toward realizing healthier food environments, robust urban food systems, and equitable access to nutrition.

2. Theoretical Framework

The theoretical framework for this research draws from scholarship on urbanization and urban informality, food security and urban poverty, and progressive planning in the Global South that emphasizes synergistic collaboration between the state and non-state actors.

2.1 Urbanization and Urban Informality

The brisk urbanization of recent decades in developing Asia is predicted to not relent well into the second half of this century (Dahiya and Das 2020; Birch and Wachter 2011; UN-HABITAT 2010). Uneven development, disasters triggered by natural hazard, conflict, and now, climate change are factors that induce migration—a phenomenon that is still poorly understood. Rapid urbanization has significantly lowered poverty in Asia (Dahiya 2012), but poverty itself has become more urbanized—for instance, about 90% of poverty reduction in Bangladesh during 2010–2016 happened in rural communities (World Bank 2019). In most Asian countries urban inequality has been worsening lately, further constraining access to basic services (Mathur 2013). The urbanization of poverty and the widening inequality gulf are manifested in urban informality—by those who live and work in the informal sector.

Informal workers constitute the broad base of the global workforce and economy (Chen 2016). In many developing countries the informal sector employs most of the workforce, over 80% in Bangladesh.[1] That workforce contributes the majority of the urban gross domestic product (GDP). Nearly 80% of South Asia's urban residents work in the informal sector (Chen and Beard 2018), and over 30% resides in slums (King et al. 2017). Despite its ubiquity and significance to the economy, informality remains rather invisible due to unavailable or inadequate data on the sector's prevalence, contours, and the needs and challenges of informal sector workers and residents. The consequent weak understanding of informality helps sustain needlessly regressive policies that deny poor migrants basic urban services and welfare benefits (Chen and Beard 2018); even cities considered progressive persist with confoundingly imprudent policy approaches (Das 2017). Developing cities know little about their own informality; what precious little insights exist are usually estimates and locations of slum settlements, sometimes their populations, and maybe of coverage provided by services such as electricity, water, sanitation, immunization, and the provision of state-provided food supplies. But much of this information is informal and not officially recognized. Moreover, their capacity or initiative to understand about food security more nuancedly—how access, quality, and consumption patterns impact nutrition, health, and development outcomes—is yet nonexistent.

---

[1]   See ILOSTAT. Country Profiles. https://ilostat.ilo.org/data/country-profiles/ (accessed 12 January 2022).

2.2 Food Security, Urban Poverty, and COVID-19

Scholarship in urban studies and planning has long emphasized the need for cities to engage constructively with informality, and COVID-19's massive toll on lives and livelihood has clearly proved that great need. The heartrending media images of the massive exodus of poor migrants from cities caused by sudden and strict lockdowns have exposed their vulnerabilities, drawing attention to the need to make welfare benefits portable and upgrade slums and squatter settlements—steps toward making cities more inclusive. Although hard data and systematic research at larger scales are not yet available, still, much anecdotal evidence hinted at migrants leaving Bangladeshi cities, at least temporarily, owing to COVID-19. According to a survey by BRAC (2020), a large Bangladeshi nongovernment organization (NGO), sudden mass migration back to villages likely caused losses in rural incomes outstripping urban incomes. Estimates from multilateral agencies like the United Nations World Food Programme (WFP) and FAO suggest that during the first year of the COVID-19 pandemic, over 811 million people worldwide went undernourished, of which over half (418 million) were in Asia (FAO et al. 2020). Lockdowns, loss of employment, disruptions to national and intranational trade, and supply chain breakdowns due to COVID-19 not only impacted food security hugely (FAO et al. 2020) but exposed long-standing and deeply entrenched inequities in regard to food access in developed and developing countries alike (Ikhsan and Virananda 2021; FAO et al. 2019; O'Hara and Toussaint 2021; Zimmerer and de Haan 2020).

Higher food insecurity poses a compounding threat to fighting the pandemic and other future crises because of its detrimental effect on health and well-being and inducing migration (Smith and Wesselbaum 2020). Evidence from multiple low-income, food-deficient, food-importing, and drought-affected countries shows that food insecurity also impacts mental well-being, changes in the prevalence of undernourishment explain considerable variation in subjective well-being over time, and that food security can have developmental and political implications—thus, food security should be atop the policy agenda, which some countries have done by making the "right to food" a constitutional right (Kornher and Sakketa 2021). A flurry of research in different disciplines in the wake of the COVID-19 pandemic has produced an urgent and resonant call for building resilient food systems (Béné 2020; Paganini et al. 2020). In removing extant impediments to inclusive, innovative, and progressive policy making for addressing food security, it is important to understand, holistically, food systems (globally, regionally, and locally) and urban informality (Clapp and Moseley 2020; FAO 2020a; Rajan and Cherian 2021). The recent focus on food and nutrition is reiterating that malnutrition due to poverty and urban food insecurity causes both undernutrition and obesity among the urban poor; and, it is not just income but also the quality of housing and aspects of the surrounding built environment—connectivity, mobility, light and ventilation, open space, and exposure to hazards— that impair access to nutritious food (Tacoli 2021). COVID-19 made the challenge of adequate food and nutrition significantly more onerous for the urban poor, who are almost entirely reliant on the informal sector.

The impacts on food security due to COVID-19 have varied by country and city, depending on the control measures that were instituted and the resilience of food supply chains. In Addis Ababa, Ethiopia, despite job losses and falling incomes, overall food security had not declined although people reported consuming more staples than vegetables (Hirvonen, de Brauw, and Abate 2021). Around the same time, in some small Bangladeshi cities, which had a strict 9-week lockdown, the existing precariousness of food and nutrition security worsened considerably, and people reported resorting to more desperate coping strategies—such as curtailing consumption, relying on inexpensive starchy staples, allocating more of household income on food, having to take out emergency loans, and depending on relief aid (Ruszczyk et al. 2020). Even official social safety nets tend to be weaker in small urban centers, and formal and informal microenterprises are adversely impacted by the disruption of both supply and demand. Scholars investigating food insecurity during the COVID-19 pandemic have argued that climate change is yet an ignored factor that will exacerbate nutritional vulnerability and inequality everywhere, but much more so in poor countries (Raj et al. 2022).

2.3   Progressive Planning in the Global South and Multistakeholder Collaboration

Increasing democratization in the Global South in recent decades has burgeoned and strengthened civil society (Cheema and Popovski 2010), and decentralization has boosted localized planning by increasing direct participation by communities and non-state actors (Mansuri and Rao 2004, 2013; McCarney and Stren 2003). Cities where these moves have led to progressive, pro-poor transformative change—such as enhanced access to services and opportunities and improved institutional practices and performance across multiple sectors—are marked by effective governance that utilizes coalitions of various local actors in decision-making and execution of plans and policies (Mahendra et al. 2021). The communicative turn in planning theory stimulated collaborative planning (Healey 2003), which ought to be localized, democratic, and empowering (Fung and Wright 2003). Mixed experiences with collaborative and participatory planning at the local level indicate that reconfiguring institutional arrangements for greater downward accountability—by catalyzing synergies among state, community, and civil society stakeholders—is essential for improving outcomes (Mansuri and Rao 2013). Extensive, fine-grained evidence from field research on household-level participation and community-led planning for urban poverty alleviation—through shelter, social, and economic development interventions—have underscored the importance of empowering informal sector women by enabling their access to property rights, credit, organizing, decision-making, and leadership (Grantham and Baruah 2017). Women's education and health, and gender relations at the household and community levels impact their participation and, therefore, the quality of access to basic services in informal settlements (Beard and Cartmill 2007). Relatively less appreciated is the link between women's agency and household level food security. But evidence indicates that poor urban women often mitigate household food shortage through home-based enterprises that also directly provide food for consumption (Floro and Bali Swain 2013).

Vigorous engagement of Bangladesh's nonprofit sector, with its significant contribution to alleviating rural poverty (Roy 2010), can assist Bangladeshi cities and communities move toward becoming more inclusive and supportive of the informal sector. Since March 2020, the local government and its agencies, multilateral development organizations, civil society organizations (CSOs) such as nongovernment organizations (NGOs) and community-based organizations (CBOs), educational institutions, and other individuals and groups have initiated various efforts—at different degrees of coordination and/or collaboration—for assisting Dhaka's poorest. Recognizing the relevance and urgency of enabling civil society and NGOs to demonstrate alternative approaches to sustainable and equitable development, as in Bangladesh, is being emphasized even by influential market-oriented global institutions like the World Economic Forum (Saleh 2022). This is also urgent because whereas Bangladeshi NGOs and CBOs have been effective and critical in providing shelter and services, in megacities like Dhaka, entrenched structures of patronage, dependency, and intermediation involving state, civil society, and external actors also pose challenges for scaling up participation (Cawood 2021).

3. Data and Methods

This chapter draws from research undertaken for a larger study to attempt a comprehensive understanding of the relationship between urban poverty and food security in Greater Dhaka—the urban conurbation that is the metropolitan region surrounding the Bangladeshi capital. The study concentrated on four city corporations—Dhaka South, Dhaka North, Gazipur, and Narayanganj. The study utilized multiple methods and both qualitative and quantitative analyses, and this chapter is based upon the analysis of some of the qualitative data. Besides analyzing primary data from interviews, a market survey, and focus group discussions (FGDs), we also reviewed secondary literature and news media articles.

Most of the data collection through field research was accomplished by a team of the Dhaka Food System (DFS) Project, from the FAO Bangladesh office, led by the first and third authors of this chapter. This included the market survey, which was conducted almost weekly for about 14 weeks after the first day of the government-imposed lockdown on 24 March 2020. The survey collected information on food prices at fresh markets and local shops in 183 wet markets across the four city corporations. Between October 2020 and March 2021, at 14 mostly informal low-income settlements in these four city corporations, the team also conducted 19 FGDs involving 165 participants (142 women and 23 men) in collaboration with the local federation of grassroots organizations in each corporation (seven in Dhaka North, four in Dhaka South, four in Gazipur, and four in Narayanganj).[2] The FGDs aimed to understand household diets, access to and expenditure on food, strategies to feed families, and key factors behind food insecurity and inadequate nutrition. They probed food and non-food related and income and non-income dependent determinants, such as inadequate infrastructure and basic services, and lay specific emphasis on intra-household gender dynamics, especially for decision-making. Field visits to observe how people's housing conditions impact space and arrangements for cooking augment and help triangulate the aforementioned data. After data collection and analyses, a validation workshop in each city corporation with FGD participants and community leaders allowed the corroboration and finalization of the findings.

---

[2]   Local grassroots organizations and CBOs representing the urban poor and their settlements are often organized into "federations," which are registered as nongovernment entities, like many of their constituent organizations. For more information, see Cawood (2021) and Taylor (2020).

Between 29 March and 4 July 2020, mostly through women-led grassroots organizations of the urban poor federations, the DFS team also conducted over 250 phone interviews with residents of different slum areas to understand how COVID-19 was impacting their food security, jobs, and livelihoods; how they were responding to these challenges; and how they felt about the government's measures.[3] The findings generated a series of 16 weekly situation reports on food security in Dhaka's slums during this period. Additionally, in the last quarter of 2020, DFS launched a GIS mapping endeavor in the four city corporations, encompassing all 386 fresh markets therein, to provide data on indicators such as their basic services, market management, and planning.

4. Bangladesh and Dhaka: Some Background

Bangladesh is a country with approximately 147,000 square kilometers (km²) of area at the tip of the Bay of Bengal. Three large river systems— the Ganges, Brahmaputra, and Meghna—make most of the country deltaic. Low in elevation, almost a fifth of Bangladesh is less than 1 meter above the sea level (Huq 2001). Frequently beset by disasters, such as floods and cyclones, the compounding effects of climate change have increased migration to urban centers, proliferated informal settlements, and intensified the challenge of alleviating urban poverty (Banks, Roy, and Hulme 2011). Aside from 22 cyclones, at least eight major floods since the early 1970s inundated at least 30% of the country.[4] Lately, sea level rise and increased salinity have further stressed agriculture and other livelihoods along much of the country's over 700-kilometer-long coastline.[5]

With a population of 164.7 million in 2020 and 1,116 persons per square kilometer (km²), Bangladesh has the highest population density in the world and, consequently, only 480 square meters of arable land per capita.[6] Out of its 4 million landless households, 2.3 million are rural

---

[3]   The phone interviews resulted in 18 situation reports, one almost every week, and about 14 people were called for each.

[4]   See Bangladesh Meteorological Department. Historical Cyclones. http://live3.bmd. gov.bd/p/Historical-Cyclones/.

[5]   See Flood Hazard Research Centre. http://www.fhrc-bd.org/views/physical geography.php.

[6]   See World Bank. Bangladesh. https://data.worldbank.org/country/BD (accessed 12 January 2022); and FAO, cited in World Bank. Arable Land (hectares per person) – Bangladesh. https://data.worldbank.org/indicator/AG.LND.ARBL.HA.PC?locations =BD (accessed 12 January 2022).

(BBS 2019). Still, agriculture accounts for 40% of all employment (BBS 2018). The peasant mode of production has nearly disappeared, and migration out of rural areas is widespread (Thorner 1986).

Since 2000, Bangladesh's economy has grown at 6.15% annually, attaining a GDP of $306.5 billion in 2020.[7] A strengthening domestic economy buoyed by strong growth in the ready-made garments sector, prudent socioeconomic development policies, and expanding women's employment, complemented by remittances, have made Bangladesh being considered as the new Asian Tiger (The Financial Express 2021). Despite these impressive gains, two causes for concern that could hamper food security are the disproportionately high concentration of population and economic activity in the Dhaka metropolitan region, and rising inequality—the Gini coefficient rose from 0.458 to 0.483 between 2010 and 2016.[8]

One of the world's largest megacities, Dhaka draws people from across the country with its promise of economic opportunity and social mobility. The Dhaka of today originated about 4 centuries ago as an outpost of the Mughal empire on the north bank of the Buriganga river, and its population grew and declined at different times (Ahmed 2018). Its most defining phase came after Dhaka became the capital of newly independent Bangladesh in 1971. Today, metropolitan or greater Dhaka comprises Dhaka city, which is divided into two city corporations—Dhaka North and Dhaka South, and seven other municipalities or city corporations, including Gazipur and Narayanganj. Dhaka city covers an area just over 300 km² and has a population of over 8.5 million; the Dhaka metropolitan area covers an area of over 2,160 km² and houses over 18 million people.[9] In 1980, the population of the metropolitan area was only 3 million, which underscores the astounding pace and scale of growth (Bird et al. 2018). Such growth was accompanied by growing urban poverty and the number and population of slums. The 1997 Census of Slums estimated 1,579 slums and this number had ballooned to 3,394 in 2014. Currently, it is estimated that some 4 million people reside in about 5,000 slums in Dhaka (UNICEF Bangladesh n.d.).

---

[7]   See World Bank. GDP Growth (annual %) – Bangladesh. https://data.worldbank.org/indicator/NY.GDP.MKTP.KD.ZG?end=2019&locations=BD&start=2000 (accessed 12 January 2022).

[8]   As per the Household Income and Expenditure Surveys undertaken by the Bangladesh Bureau of Statistics (BBS). The World Bank (data.worldbank.org) however lists the Gini Index (Gini Coefficient times 100) for 2016 as 32.

[9]   Figures were taken from Bangladesh Bureau of Statistics. Population and Housing Census. http://www.bbs.gov.bd/site/page/47856ad0-7e1c-4aab-bd78-892733bc06eb/Population-and-Housing-Census

Map 1: Location of Slums and Fresh Markets in Dhaka North and Dhaka South

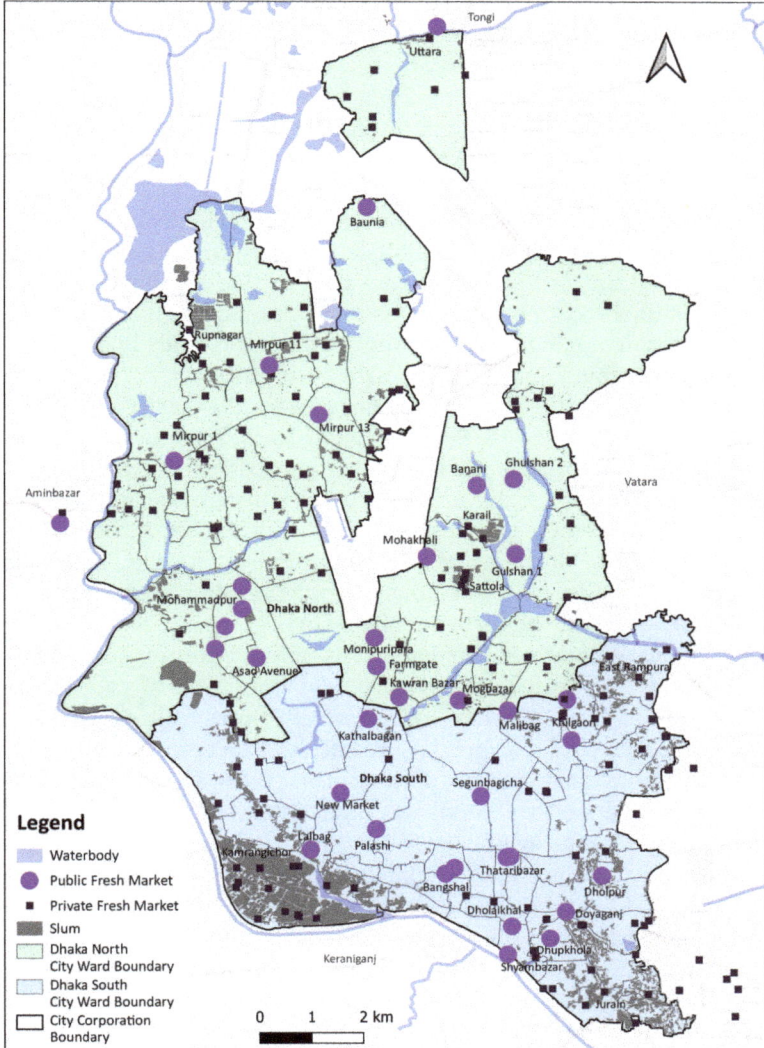

Note: Most large public fresh markets tend to be away from slums, which are served by smaller private markets.

Source: FAO Bangladesh (2020).

Map 1 shows the location of slums in Dhaka North and Dhaka South. Urban poverty in Bangladesh in 2016 was estimated at 18.9%, down from 21.3%, 5 years prior, but during this period rural poverty fell much more (BBS 2017). The population and conditions of the urban poor are likely underestimated because poverty calculations exclude some necessities of life, such as common property resources, which must be purchased in cities (Wratten 1995).

Food security has been a national policy priority since the country's independence in 1971, and much of the early efforts were focused on gaining self-sufficiency in rice production and stabilizing rice prices, which were aided by technological advancement and private sector investment in small-scale irrigation (Hossain, Naher, and Shahabuddin 2005). After the devastating floods in 1998 inundated two-thirds of the country and threatened the food security of tens of millions, active public policy interventions, such as trade liberalization, price stabilization, and food transfers to millions of households, tempered the impacts and further boosted food security (Del Ninno, Dorosh, and Smith 2003). Besides rice, fish is a staple of almost all Bangladeshis. Since the early 1980s, impressive strides made in aquaculture production have also expanded food security by raising employment, incomes, and consumption (Murshed-E-Jahan, Ahmed, and Belton 2010). However, as a country naturally prone to recurrent drought and floods, with very high population densities and limited arable land, climate change impacts—such as rising sea levels and temperatures, salt water intrusion, soil salinization, erratic rainfall, more intense and frequent typhoons, and migration of people—pose real threats to food security by negatively impacting water supply, fisheries, ecosystems, and the like (Faisal and Parveen 2004).

Multifarious institutions play various roles in urban planning and governance, service provision, and emergency response in the Dhaka metropolitan region. These institutions include the urban local governments (city corporations), the capital development authority (RAJUK), water supply and sewerage authority (DWASA), the water development board, and the home ministry (for fire and civil defense) among numerous others. There are also thousands of CSOs that support the urban poor, who themselves are well-organized into community groups and federations (Koli 2015). Despite the environmental stresses and disaster events, Bangladesh produces enough staples (rice, wheat, and corn) to meet domestic demand. The last 2 decades have witnessed a marked uptick in the poultry and aquaculture sectors; likewise, milk production has soared with thousands of new dairy farms in and around Dhaka (Asaduzzaman 2021). Although much improvement is possible, a decent transportation network helps the movement of agricultural produce across the country. Barring any severe countrywide shortage, Dhaka's grocery stores and wet markets are rarely undersupplied. However, wet markets serving informal settlements are fewer or farther, with limited and inferior offerings.

5. How Dhaka's Poor Eat: Access to Food and Nutrition

Urban poor households struggle to meet their nutritional needs due to a combination of factors characteristic of city life. These impact the availability and accessibility of healthy, nutritious, and safe food, and put the poor, especially women and children, at a distinct disadvantage in terms of their nutritional options.[10] Dhaka's food environment differs considerably from that of its surrounding rural and peri-urban areas and even that of smaller cities. Fast-food options are ubiquitous, mobile vendors ply their trade on busy streets, packaged and processed foods are pervasive and aggressively advertised, and, most importantly, food is more expensive. While food is generally more available and plentiful in cities than in rural communities, from where many of the urban poor migrate, the quality of their diets, ironically, tends to get worse.[11] Within the same urban poor household, it is not too uncommon to find one member to suffer from malnourishment and another from obesity—such is the confounding nature of food at the margins of a megacity. The following section explores a number of issues that influence how the urban poor are able to access food and nutrition, including household-level consumption patterns, where people access food, their livelihoods, access to basic services in poor communities, and the state's response to alleviate food insecurity during the COVID-19 lockdown. Recognizing gender inequities in terms of access to food is emphasized.

---

[10]   See Peters et al. 2019 and Pritchard, Mackay, and Turner 2017.

[11]   In the 2021 Global Hunger Index, Bangladesh ranks 76th of the 116 countries with a score of 19.1. WFP's Hunger Map 2021 estimates around 33.9 million people are living without enough food in Bangladesh, and an estimated 10 million people with insufficient food consumption in Dhaka division alone.

5.1 Household-Level Consumption Patterns

An FAO survey conducted in urban slums of Dhaka North in 2019, prior to the COVID-19 pandemic, demonstrated that food and nutrition security constitutes a spectrum.[12] While FAO's definition of food security stresses the need for three sufficient and regular meals to meet dietary needs, dietary diversity and balance, including animal protein, and vegetables and fruit for minerals and vitamins, are also important. Prior to the pandemic the average urban poor household in Dhaka would eat three meals a day, their staples included rice, potatoes, and lentils, which are cheap, accessible, and filling, but they also would eat more expensive leafy greens, vegetables, and dried fish. The survey of 69 women of different slum communities showed that while they ate enough food, protein-rich foods and leafy vegetables were limited; 85% of the respondents stated they filled themselves with rice and lentils, and did not feel they ate enough at meals and often experienced hunger, or ate neither sufficient nor diverse enough meals; and only 5% reported eating sufficient, healthy, and nutritious food regularly at each meal. Before the pandemic, at least, 65% indicated having experienced varying food insecurity levels at different times over the year (Figure 1). A respondent from Sattola bosti shared that, "Dal (lentil soup) is a must in every meal. Because we cannot eat more with just a small amount of vegetables but rather we can eat more with rice and dal. We have to fill our stomach." Meat, fresh fish, fruits, and dairy products are only consumed occasionally as these are expensive. The same person added, "We can only eat chicken or fish once in 2 weeks."[13]

During times of crisis, such as a family medical emergency, job loss, or prolonged uncertainties like the COVID-19 pandemic, the poor are forced to adopt multiple coping mechanisms that sharply reduce their nutritional intake. Interviews conducted both before and during the pandemic reveal that Dhaka's urban poor cope by reducing their number of daily meals to one or two, and they resort to inferior quality food to maximally stretch their meager incomes or savings to provide enough food for the family for as long as possible. During COVID-19, when we asked residents of different slum areas in our study area (across the four cities), 90% acknowledged having had experienced some form and degree of food insecurity (mild, moderate, or severe),

---

[12]   This chapter uses the terms slums, informal settlements, squatter settlements, and bosti (slums in Dhaka) interchangeably to refer to residential settlements of poor communities that, to different degrees and in different ways, exemplify urban informality. See Dhaka North Community Town Federation and FAO (2020).

[13]   FGD conducted at a respondent's residence on 21 October 2019.

which was much higher than that reported by about the two-thirds in Dhaka North before the pandemic (Figure 1). Many people reduced or eliminated chicken, fish, and meat, and even began consuming partially rotting vegetables. A respondent from Ershad Nagar, Gazipur shares, "We cannot eat good food, everything is pricey now. We cannot afford because we do not have income. It has been 8 to 9 months, [since] I have lost my income. We cannot even eat rice comfortably. The price of rice is Tk60 to Tk70 ($0.70–$0.83) per kilogram now." Another person says, "We could buy many things with Tk150 ($1.75) before, but it is not possible now. The current price of potato is Tk50 ($0.68) per kilogram and leafy vegetables is Tk60 ($0.70) per kilogram. Before the pandemic, the price of leafy vegetables was Tk15 ($0.18) and potatoes was Tk15 to Tk20 ($0.18–$0.23) per kilogram. We now buy 250 grams of what we bought 1 kilogram before."[14] Eating more starchy food, high in calories but low in other nutritional value, satiates and provides energy, but it especially mars the development of children, and the health of lactating women, the elderly, and persons with chronic health issues.

Figure 1: Self-Reported Food Insecurity by Residents of Dhaka Slums Before and during COVID-19 (%)

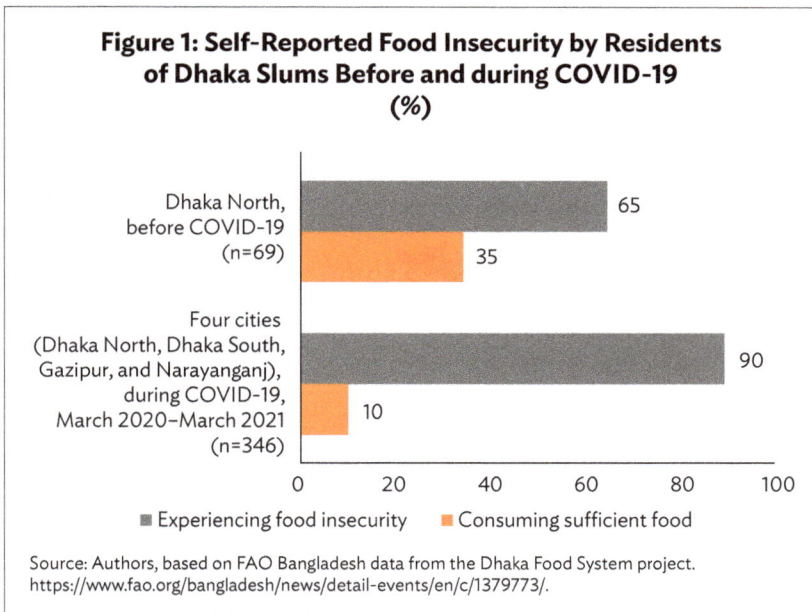

Source: Authors, based on FAO Bangladesh data from the Dhaka Food System project. https://www.fao.org/bangladesh/news/detail-events/en/c/1379773/.

---

[14] Telephone interviews conducted on 16 November 2020. Currency equivalents applicable at the end of February 2022.

Diets and Consumption Patterns of Women and Other Vulnerable Groups

How women make decisions about food for the household and how that, ultimately, affects their own nutrition is often overlooked. Our research substantiated that women mostly handle household decisions about spending on food, housing, education, and clothing, and are responsible for purchasing food from markets and cooking it. But when they are not the principal earners, they work within the limited budget they receive, often from their spouses or other male members, and have to make hard choices on how to distribute it. The women managing households often do not enjoy the same rights to property or in household matters as the men; also, often mothers-in-law make decisions on food purchases. Households that had experienced income loss reported food shortages, and women were the ones who reduced their food intake the most. Reflecting gendered traditional social protocols prevalent in much of South Asia, men and children eat first and are given proportionally more to eat, with women eating the least and last (Harris-Fry et al. 2017). A woman from Korail bosti, one of Dhaka's largest slums, said this about sacrificing her diet: "When there is a shortage of food, I do not let them know by saying that I do not feel like to eat. [My husband] is not seeing how much food is left. I cannot say to him that there is less food. I give him more food at that time because he works hard. I cannot give him less food. I have to keep him well. He is the family's pillar."[15] It is noteworthy that this account is from before the pandemic; conditions for women worsened during the lockdown. This inherent inequity in culturally steeped gendered expectations causes health problems, especially for pregnant or lactating women, such as anemia, bone fractures, and stunting in newborn children.[16] In addition, women spend 2 to 3 hours a day cooking meals, and women who also work outside the home have to cook for their families, either very early in the morning and/or late in the evening.

Other groups that have also suffered disproportionately during the pandemic include children, the elderly, and women-headed households. Like their parents, children too have been forced to eat the same starchy and filling foods such as rice, dal or mashed potatoes, sans the requisite nutrients and often only once a day. Such deficiency impacts children's physical, mental, and cognitive development (Aguayo and Menon

---

[15]   FGD conducted at a respondent's residence on 21 October 2019.

[16]   Bangladesh's first National Micronutrient Survey (2011–2012) revealed that, nationally, 26% of non-pregnant and non-lactating women were anemic—27.4% rural and 21.4% urban (IPHN 2014).

2016), and our respondents reported increasing health problems among children during the COVID-19 pandemic. The most common illnesses during and in addition to COVID-19 itself have been fever, cough, and dengue. Fearing these symptoms might be related to COVID-19, poor households have sought costly treatments and medicines more than they usually do.

A typical meal. A child street food vendor selling Alur Dom, a popular dish made from potatoes, at a slum in South Rellibagan, Narayanganj, February 2021 (photo by Fahad Abdullah Kaizer, FAO).

5.2 Access to Food

Residential location influences one's access to work, markets, security, basic services such as water and sanitation, as well as safe and nutritious food. Slums located away from fresh markets or work locations disproportionately disadvantage the poor compared with other groups in terms of their spending and options for accessing nutritious food (see Map 1). An FAO study found that 95% of Dhaka's poor households purchase food from fresh markets (FAO in Bangladesh 2021), which are located throughout the city and offer fresh fruits, vegetables, fish, and meat. Dry food items, such as grains and pulses, cooking oil, biscuits, and eggs are often purchased at more proximate, small neighborhood stores because they let regular customers buy food on credit, unlike vendors at larger markets. Informal mobile vendors who sell door-to-door are another important retail source for the urban poor, particularly for fruit and vegetables. Such vendors use hand carts or bicycle rickshaws to transport food items from fresh markets to slum communities, where they set up temporary stalls. Mobile vendors also allow food to be purchased in small quantities and sometimes even on credit.

An informal wet market. Early morning at Karwan Bazar, one of Dhaka's biggest fresh markets, December 2020. Dhaka residents usually shop at fresh markets in the early morning to buy fresh produce from vendors (photo by Fahad Abdullah Kaizer, FAO).

Poor households decide which food outlets to use based on several interrelated factors, such as the money available and convenience. Homes in slum communities are small, congested, and often lack electricity. Since storage space in these homes is scarce and refrigerators are a rarity, households generally buy small amounts of food every few days. For poor households, the monetary and time costs of accessing distant fresh markets by rickshaw can be prohibitive, so mobile vendors fill their unmet need, but often at a premium. Mobile vendors are more expensive, as a respondent from Bauniabadh, a slum in Dhaka North, reveals, "Mostly I buy vegetables from a mobile vendor. The price is at least Tk5 to Tk10 higher than the market."[17] A resident of Lokkhonkhola in Narayanganj also states, "I usually buy foods from mobile vendors

---

[17]   Telephone interview conducted on 24 December 2019.

because the distance to the market from my home is quite far...we can get foods on credit from mobile vendors in our area."[18]

Notwithstanding the convenience, the food items supplied by mobile vendors can lack quality (FAO 2021). They are transported and displayed in the open; exposed to the sun, dust, and pollution; and lack adequate and hygienic storage. Many mobile vendors buy from larger markets at the end of the day, when unsold goods are offloaded cheaply. For lack of alternatives to procure food, slum residents regularly forgo freshness and quality for convenience and affordability.

Food Insecurity during the Pandemic Has Prompted Interest in Alternative Food Sources

A possible alternative to healthy and fresh food is for slum communities to grow it themselves, either in communal plots, in individual micro-gardens, or vertically on walls or atop roofs. We observed that urban agriculture or gardening is not commonplace among poor households, although several households, mostly the women, do grow vegetables if they can. This is likely due to the lack of space and/or time. Leafy greens like spinach, and vegetables like taro (all parts of which are edible) can be planted, while climbers like various gourds (local delicacies) and beans can be cultivated on rooftops and walls. Urban agriculture, whether in dense urban settlements (where space is constricted) or in peripheral areas (with more land and water), cannot scale up to replace conventional food sources, but it can supplement consumption and nutrition of poor households, especially during economic and health crises like the pandemic. Selling surplus produce can also raise household incomes. During the pandemic urban agriculture has significantly expanded in Dhaka's poor communities. Our research conducted found that in Dhaka North, among those who do not yet grow food, 97% are interested in doing so; however, they cited limited space, lacking the know-how, and not having access to seeds as obstacles.

5.3   Livelihoods and Nutrition

The primary factor for urban poor households' food insecurity and inadequate nutrition is their low and irregular incomes, since they largely rely on labor-intensive and low-wage work in the informal sector. Research shows that in Dhaka, urban poor households can spend up to

---

[18]   FGD conducted on 7 December 2020 at a respondent's residence in North Lokkhonkhola, Narayanganj.

50% of their income on food, which trumps all other expenses (FAO in Bangladesh 2020). For the poor then, healthy diets are unaffordable. Not only are incomes low but living costs in the city are high. Poor households must pay for rising food prices, rent, utility bills, their children's education, and health-care costs, as well as put aside money for unexpected situations and shocks, including loss of employment and health emergencies. Our FGD participants shared that the average rent in slums is around Tk2,000 to Tk2,500 (about $23 to $29 at the end of November 2020) for one room (including electricity gas and water); most respondents live in one or two rooms. The monthly expenditure on food is around Tk5,000 (about $58), and the average cost of education is around Tk2,000 to Tk3,000 (about $23 to $35) per child. All women FGD respondents are members of either one or two community savings groups in which the minimum monthly deposit is around Tk50 to Tk100 each (about $0.60 to $1.20) depending on a household's income.

During economic hardships, as exemplified by the lockdown, food consumption is one of the first household expenses to be reduced, adversely and significantly impacting the urban poor's food security. A resident of Agargaon slum says, "First we think about the rent and our loan repayment and then food. Whatever we earn we can save only a little from that to pay the loan, and the rest goes to food."[19] Lacking nutritious food can compromise immunity and debilitate one's health and sense of well-being.

This precarious bind that characterizes the lives and livelihoods of low-income households worsened critically during the pandemic. FGD participants revealed that households reliant on irregular low incomes from the informal sector earn about Tk6,000 to Tk15,000 (around $72 to $180 at the end of November 2020) per month, or about Tk300 to Tk500 per day (around $3.50 to $5.80).[20] By comparison, garment factory workers who have steady wages earn between Tk10,000 and Tk12,000 per month (around $116 to $140).[21] Consuming two to three healthy meals a day, comprising chicken, fish, vegetables, pulses, and rice would cost poor households between Tk300 and Tk400 per day (around $3.50 to $4.70). Instead, their average daily expenditure on food is between

---

[19]   FGD held at a respondent's residence in Agargaon slum, Dhaka North on 12 December 2019.

[20]   About 4 million workers—both formal and informal—are employed in over 3,000 garment factories across Bangladesh's burgeoning ready-made garments sector, which is becoming more formalized and affording steadily improving working conditions. See Global Fund for Women (2019).

[21]   FGD held with urban poor respondents working in the garment industry at the community club office in Gazipur on 16 November 2020.

Tk100 and $150 (about $1.20 to $1.75). As mentioned earlier, this expenditure mostly gets lentils, potato, dried fish, some leafy vegetables, and, proportionately, much greater quantities of rice. Informal workers in physically demanding jobs—at construction sites or on the streets—seek out food high in carbohydrates that is filling, easy to consume, and relatively inexpensive such as buns and *singara*.[22] Such foods also tend to be packaged, of low nutritional value, and less hygienically sold.

Affording sufficient nutritious food became more difficult during the pandemic as garment factories closed down, and informal workers, such as daily laborers, rickshaw pullers, and vendors, were suddenly forced off the streets. Plus, food prices rose. Between 22 March 2020 (when the national government announced the lockdown to contain COVID-19) and May 2021, countrywide restrictions on transportation prevented farm supplies and workers from accessing food-producing regions, and farm produce from reaching markets. This disruption of food supply chains made the prices of even the most essential foods volatile. The average price of four eggs rose from Tk24 to Tk38 ($0.28 to $0.44), the price of rice rose 21%, lentils 30%, potatoes 49%, and chicken 24%.[23] A resident of Rajdighirpur in Gazipur states, "The way price of bare essentials such as rice, lentil, vegetables are rising, if it keeps going, we will die of hunger in the future with this minimum income."[24] Another respondent from the Ershadnagar slum shares, "We stopped eating fish and meat since Coronavirus hit the country and my husband lost his job. Now we have even cut down our vegetables consumption to around 50% because of high prices."[25] As the dire conditions became prolonged, many households were forced to sell their belongings and borrow money to afford enough food to eat. Although relatively invisible, this health emergency compounded the visibly fragile economic situation of many poor households, who not only reduced their food intake to below recommended levels, but also fell into debt.

The instability of employment and income, especially during the pandemic, helped us note gender biases, as discussed earlier, which first and foremost privilege meeting the dietary needs of men, traditionally regarded as bread winners, even when the women also work.

---

[22]   A traditional Bangladeshi snack that is a fried pyramid-shaped pastry, commonly stuffed with potato; it is the Bengali name for the South Asian delicacy popularly known as *samosa*).

[23]   See FAO (2020c).

[24]   Telephone interview conducted on 1 May 2020.

[25]   Telephone interview conducted on 21 June 2020.

The FGDs revealed that almost all urban poor households found it difficult to regain their jobs and raise their incomes to pre-pandemic levels. Women who worked as garment workers, domestic helpers, or home-based workers have been hit especially hard because these jobs continue to reel from the effects of COVID-19. For men, finding work pulling rickshaws or vending on the streets has been relatively easier. Overall, about 30 million urban slum dwellers in Bangladesh experienced social and economic shock because of the lockdown (UNDP in Bangladesh 2021).

5.4 Access to Basic Services in Poor Communities

Dhaka's poor are mostly cramped into high-density slum settlements lacking basic services, such as piped drinking water and sanitation—conditions that make preparing and consuming nutritious and safe food harder. The typical Dhaka settlement has small living quarters, narrow pathways, and negligible open space. Most households do not have individual kitchens, rather they share communal kitchens with up to 10 families. Unlike in metropolises elsewhere in South Asia, the communal kitchen is a facet peculiar to Dhaka's informal settlements. This is because unlike the common practice of squatting on public land, Dhaka's informal settlements are privately owned, and many owners or intermediaries provide communal kitchens and toilets (Rohekar 2016)—which makes for higher rents but also more living space in individual dwellings. Still, many of Dhaka's slums lack adequate connection to basic services. A survey carried out in Dhaka North and Dhaka South by UNDP in 2018–2020 found that 77% of slums lack adequate sanitation, 71% do not have proper drainage infrastructure, and 58% do not have adequate access to piped water supply.[26] Thus, water has to be pumped from the ground and transported by hand, and household waste ends up in septic tanks or is unsafely disposed. Without these environmental services, washing hands, cooking surfaces, and raw foods are a constant challenge that invites foodborne illnesses, whose transmission is a significant problem in Bangladesh that impacts about 30 million people each year (Al Banna et al. 2021; FAO, WFP, and IFAD 2012).

---

[26]   Participatory poverty mapping of urban slums (2018–2020) by the Livelihoods Improvement of Urban Poor Communities Project (LIUPCP), National Urban Poverty Reduction Programme of Local Government Division and UNDP. See LIUPCP. https://urbanpovertybd.org/.

Since cooking gas is expensive, slum dwellers commonly use firewood, which also adversely affects women's health due to smoke inhalation. The compact and crowded community kitchens present additional challenges. Because of fuel and time costs, households usually just cook once daily—a simple meal that is also stored to be eaten later but not in a refrigerator. It is almost always the women who wait in lines to take turns to cook for their entire families. The limited amount of time available to clean and cook adequately reduces food hygiene and the diversity of food consumed, therefore, households increasingly rely on ready-made foods that are quick to prepare and can be eaten on the go. A resident of Sattola bosti in Dhaka North states, "I share a common gas burner with other families. I often cannot get chance to cook in the morning, so I often buy something from local shop for my children. I mostly skip morning breakfast if there is no leftover from the previous day."[27] Although it is convenient to bring food to work, this strategy reduces people's intake of fresh food, and consuming more packaged and/or ready-to-eat foods makes them nutritionally deficient. Again, this is especially harmful to the health of children, pregnant and lactating women, and the elderly.

Community kitchens in Mohakhali Sat Tala slum, Dhaka North, March 2021. Several households use community kitchens at the same time, making access and cleanliness challenging (photo by Saikat Mojumder, FAO).

---

[27]   FGD conducted at the respondent's residence on 21 October 2019.

5.5 State Response to Alleviate Food Insecurity during the Lockdown

Bangladeshi cities are not mandated to provide emergency food supplies and address food security crises that impact the urban poor. The national government is responsible for these matters. However, during the pandemic, and especially during the lockdown, Dhaka's local governments coordinated with the national government on a number of actions that were instrumental in alleviating food security and addressing the needs of the most vulnerable. These actions included restricting mobility to contain the virus, launching public campaigns to raise awareness about COVID-19 transmission, moving fresh markets to outdoor public spaces to reduce transmission, setting up handwashing stations in poor communities, and coordinating with national government agencies to distribute food relief to the poor more effectively. Their impacts offer important lessons for ensuring food security for the poor, both during similar future shocks and normal times.

Coordination Between National and City Governments for Distributing Food to the Poor

The sharing of municipal-level information by Dhaka's local governments with national government agencies proved instrumental in coordinating humanitarian response actions effectively. The central government ministries, the Ministry of Food, and the Ministry of Disaster Management and Relief are charged with distributing food during humanitarian crises. Yet, these entities have little knowledge of urban poor populations, the sizes and locations of their communities, and inherent distribution challenges. Using mobile trucks, the central government operated the Open Market Sales (OMS) service, which offered poor households basic food staples, including rice, lentils, onion, soybean oil, sugar, and dates at very low prices—for example, at Tk10 per kilogram (approximately $0.12), rice was one-fourth the market price. To be eligible to buy from OMS trucks, the urban poor received ration cards from their respective municipal ward councilors, who first verified recipients' national identification cards to establish their status. Early on during the lockdown, the lack of knowledge on the location of areas with high demand had caused insufficient provision of food and poor crowd management. The Gazipur, Narayanganj, Dhaka North, and Dhaka South city corporations intervened to ensure better coordination with the national ministries for managing OMS, sharing information about the locations and spatial scales of slums in each ward, and their levels of demand. These moves let OMS acquire allocative efficiency to provide huge amounts of food the poor households desperately needed.

Emergency food distribution, April 2020. Community members of Agargaon slum wait in long lines for government subsidized food assistance through Open Market Sales (photo by Fahad Abdullah Kaizer, FAO).

State-Civil Society Coordination for Hunger Relief in Slums

In the city corporations we researched, and others too, good relationships preexisted at the ward-level between ward councilors and local NGOs and CBOs. Consequently, slum maps and censuses were easily available, and dialogue about the needs of the poor had already been established. In such wards, the government response to help the poor was swift and effective. Councilors enlisted the support of different local organizations—from large NGOs like BRAC to local pro-poor CSOs, such as the Urban Poor Federations of Dhaka North and Dhaka South— to create lists of the most vulnerable and needy community members. This helped distribute ration cards efficiently, and prioritized the most vulnerable (the elderly, children, and the very poor) for emergency food handouts.[28] A resident of Bihari Colony in Narayanganj conveys, "The ... councilor personally helped us. He gave us rice, pulse, and potato once. I have also received help from the government. I got to buy rice at the price of Tk10 to Tk30 (around $0.12 to $0.36) per kilogram." The relief distribution experience during the COVID-19 lockdown underscored how having an environment of good state–civil society understanding, coordination, and collaboration begets good governance and enables effective responses during crises. The existing relationships of trust enjoyed by local NGOs and CSOs with slum communities ensured that the food relief has reached those who needed it the most, and assured that future collaborations between the state and poor communities would help in addressing food insecurity.

6. Discussion and Conclusion

This chapter explored how the urban poor are able to nourish themselves with sufficient, nutritious, and healthy food in a megacity like Dhaka. An evident conclusion is that the urban poor struggle to consume enough nutritious food, particularly during critical periods. The chapter illuminates that the availability of food does not imply its adequacy and accessibility for all. This raises serious issues as malnutrition seriously impacts the health, productivity, and well-being of the poor, thereby trapping them in a vicious and debilitating cycle of poverty. Interviews and FGDs conducted before and during lockdown due to the COVID-19 pandemic enabled a deeper understanding of the poor's coping mechanisms and further underscored the implications of food insecurity during crises. This research revealed some key findings about poor Bangladeshis who depend on the informal sector for their livelihoods and shelter: (i) the urban poor suffer food insecurity in terms of both quantity and quality; (ii) even among the urban poor, certain groups such as women and children are more vulnerable, and they have suffered more due to the pandemic; (iii) spatial determinants such as the location and terrain of informal settlements impact access to nutritious

---

[28]   Ward councilors have played a role in supporting the urban poor to make use of vacant land for urban gardening purposes. For example, during 2021, in the Korail community, a large slum in Dhaka, urban poor residents approached the local ward councilor for permission to use the banks of Gulshan Lake for gardening purposes. While officially prohibited in the city's land use plans, the councilor granted a temporary easement to use the land to cultivate vegetables and fruits. The district agricultural extension officer then provided the community technical support on how to prepare the land properly. Such arrangements demonstrate a sympathetic relationship between the poor and city government, as well as a collaborative partnership between different government agencies.

food; (iv) nutrition and health quality also depend on the availability of basic services in informal settlements; (v) prompt state response during crises such as the COVID-19 pandemic is imperative, and is made more effective by synergistic collaboration with local civil society and community institutions; and (vi) coping mechanisms of the urban poor, especially during the COVID-19 pandemic, point to possible policy and planning interventions to ensure greater food security for the poor.

The ability of the urban poor to consume enough nutritious food, particularly during periods of crisis, is influenced by multiple factors. These include insufficient incomes, the fragility of the informal labor market, deficient access to basic public services such as water and sanitation, the generally inferior quality of food available to them, and the prohibitive costs of nutritious food. Price volatility and interruptions in food supply chains during the pandemic have repeatedly affected food affordability. While government interventions, such as giving food handouts to the most vulnerable and offering basic staples at subsidized prices to the poor, offered some relief, the protracted pandemic also exposed the limits of state intervention. Policies are needed to enable improved food and nutrition access routinely.

The pandemic inflicted disproportionately harsher impacts on certain vulnerable groups. Women who lost their employment and livelihood options, compared with men, for instance, became more economically and socially vulnerable. Usually the last to eat in the household, women reduced their food intake further, possibly compounding health problems for many—an issue that deserves deeper investigation. Furthermore, in addition to domestic work, the time women spend in dispensing caregiving responsibilities—toward children, the elderly, and sick family members—increased significantly, compounding the physical and mental pressures they endure. It is unclear which nutritional deficiencies incurred during and prior to the pandemic led to lasting debilitating impacts upon the health and productivity of the poor, and how exactly and by how much, especially upon children and young adults who may suffer the consequences for years to come.

The ability of the poor to access affordable and nutritious food also depends on their proximity to local fresh markets. Dhaka's rapid growth and the relative inattention paid to planning new food markets cause many slums to depend on informal vendors and delivery systems, which are often less hygienic and/or not fresh. The added costs involved in traveling to access nutritious food options make them prohibitive for the poor. Likewise, slum communities that occupy land with insecure tenure are likely to have inadequate access to basic services, such as water and sanitation, which, in turn, inhibits slum households' ability to prepare and store food hygienically. Thus, they rely on informal street vendors for their food, which tends to be unhygienic and unhealthy. The gravity of the inability to simply wash hands or food items, adequately and frequently, was widely realized during the pandemic.

Systematic and sustained policy focus by the state to strengthen urban food systems is largely absent. During the COVID-19 lockdown, the emergency measures undertaken by Dhaka's local governments helped sustain some degree of food security for the urban poor. Their responses demonstrated the value of coordination and communication among different government agencies, spanning the national and local levels, and synergistic partnerships with CSOs and slum communities. Particularly effective were efforts at the municipal ward levels to generate and share slum data with national agencies, and for public health messaging. However, despite quick action by the government and CSOs, which saved lives and ameliorated harsh conditions, the COVID-19 pandemic revealed that the urban poor's status quo of "existing" on the margins of the city exposes them to heightened social and economic vulnerabilities, especially during a prolonged crisis. Bangladesh's successful development outcomes in recent decades is widely attributed to the dynamism and stewardship of its civil society, enabled by principles of good governance premised on collaboration among sectors (Chowdhury et al. 2020; Roy 2010). This research suggests that improved governance and government responsiveness can also alleviate a hitherto ignored issue—the nutritional insecurity of the urban poor (Das and Dahiya 2020).

The COVID-19 pandemic forced people worldwide and indeed the urban poor in Bangladesh to devise varied coping measures, even unprecedented ones (Lemay et al. 2021; Ruszczyk et al. 2021). The most common coping mechanisms of reducing food intake and purchasing spoiled food are detrimental to health, but some hold promise. Urban agriculture, for one, expanded in Dhaka's informal settlements during the COVID-19 pandemic. Despite the recent spread of urban agriculture in some cities, agriculture in urban slums in South Asia has rarely been a policy focus, not even in slum upgrading programs, likely because land and water are scarce (Akaeze and Nandwani 2020). Moreover, government officials are usually reluctant to permit the use of vacant land for fear of inciting land ownership disputes or being perceived as encouraging squatting. Most public officials also share popular misconceptions that deem urban agriculture unsuitable for requiring large plots of land and abundant water, when, in fact, small lots, building walls and roofs, and modest water use make it a practical option for urban poor settlements. Urban agriculture allows the urban poor to bolster their food security, nutrition, and health, while also offering opportunities to recycle urban waste, augment their income, and improve the environmental quality of their communities (Lal 2020).

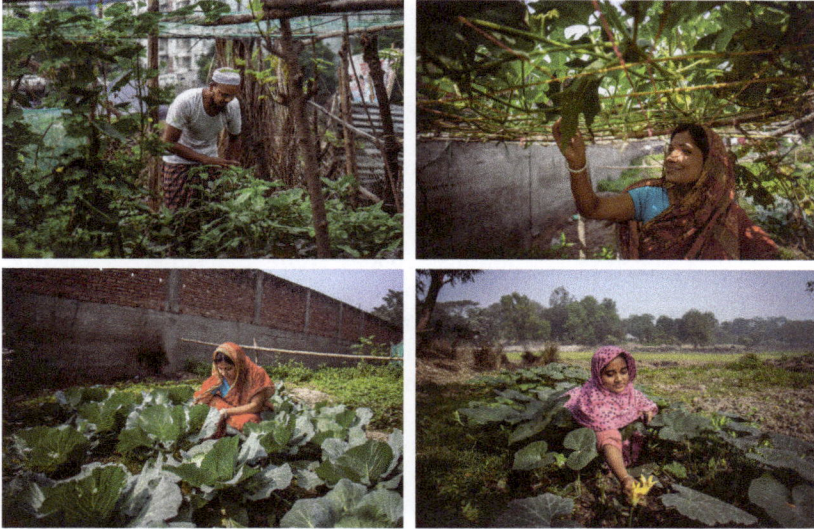

Urban gardening in Dhaka's slums, April 2020. Residents of various settlements grow their own vegetables—in Banani TNT Colony, Dhaka North (top left); West Kanaiya, Gazipur (top and bottom right); and Purba Nilerpara, Gazipur (bottom left) (photos by Fahad Abdullah Kaizer, FAO).

The observations and inferences from this research indicate three types of recommendations for potentially useful urban policy and planning interventions. First, nutrition related interventions are needed from different sectors to improve the poor's access to fresh, nutritious, and affordable food. These include infrastructural interventions, such as comprehensive slum upgrading, to upgrade physical conditions of slums and provide access to basic services, as well as social protection measures that ensure that the very poor are aware about nutrition and health, have financial safety nets, and access to health services (Das and King 2017; Taylor 2015). Urgently needed are campaigns directed at improving knowledge and practices of food hygiene and safety as well as reducing the intake of processed and overly starchy foods. Similarly, technical training for urban agriculture and promoting food sector livelihoods will be beneficial. Ultimately, nutrition-sensitive interventions should appreciate and address the causes of malnutrition. Hence, poverty reduction interventions should be multidimensional and multisectoral to improve the overall well-being and resilience of the poor. In Bangladesh, a number of government agencies, universities, local and international development institutions, and CSOs are already working toward addressing food insecurity and improving the food environment. Given the complex and multidisciplinary nature of food security, as discussed above, local governments should promote food-system planning by involving other institutions and actors such as landscape architects, urban designers, local environmental groups, urban poor CBOs, food and nutrition researchers, agricultural experts, and even consumer rights groups. Engaging a diverse range of actors will raise awareness in the public sphere, which will broaden participation and encourage innovation.

Second, besides promoting food-system planning, given the unfolding effects of urbanization and peri-urbanization, routine urban planning should be better informed and more concerned about food security issues. How cities are organized and managed—extant land use logics which influence the location of fresh markets, policies toward slums and informality, and zoning restrictions—influences food access. To reduce food and nutrition insecurity, urban planning must recognize and eliminate spatial disparities. Small steps like identifying locations for new markets closer to slum communities; promoting formal farmers' markets near informal settlements; policies promoting urban agriculture, including the temporary use of vacant plots for gardening by the poor; and upgrading water, sanitation, and electricity services can cumulatively have a big effect. Addressing the multiscale and multidimensional challenges requires both short-term and longer-term solutions. Multilateral agencies, such as FAO and ADB, international development organizations, and global and national NGOs, could work with local universities' planning and policy departments, local CSOs, and national and local government agencies to introduce the requisite emphases into planning education and research, regulations and guidelines, and practice. Heightened public awareness and concern urge institutions to act, something Dhaka's robust NGO sector and media outlets could also stimulate.

Third, administrative decentralization and good governance at the local level are essential to empowering the urban poor and enhancing their food security (Fung and Wright 2003; Das and Dahiya 2020). From the experiences of four local governments in Dhaka during the COVID-19 pandemic, this research found that good communication and coordination between government agencies and different levels of government, proximity between CBOs and local government officials, and dialog between organized urban poor communities and their municipal ward councilors all created favorable conditions to reduce food insecurity. Dhaka's experience stands in sharp contrast to what the urban poor experienced in places with weak local governance (Rajan and Cherian 2021). Good governance of food systems also demands better coordination among the private sector, public agencies enforcing food safety, NGOs and development organizations, consumer groups, local CSOs, and local universities. From advocacy and funding to research and technological innovations, each stakeholder can uniquely contribute to monitoring food security and poverty conditions. Further, bolstering the capacity of poor CBOs will enable them to voice their needs to local planning authorities and propose solutions to reduce their vulnerability and food and nutrition insecurity.

Robust food systems planning and governance should constitute platforms that will embody the enabling environment for the aforementioned recommendations. The institutional architecture for this already exists in Bangladesh, where civil-society-led efforts, encouraged by the state, have achieved impressive gains in poverty alleviation, empowerment of women, and education (Chowdhury et al. 2020; Roy 2010). In fact, in the field of food and nutrition, the same synergy and approach is already being directed toward the creation of urban food councils, city food charters, and a metropolitan-level food system governance platform.

Last, it is evident that much more research is needed to better understand how food security impacts urban poverty, and why it is vital to the urban economy at large. Most research on urban poverty in the Global South focuses on issues of housing and basic services, but it is becoming increasingly evident that although the dimension of food security is closely intertwined and consequential, it is yet poorly understood (Raja et al. 2021). More qualitative and mixed methods research can better examine and explain how the food system interacts with urban informality, including informal food delivery systems and supply chains, the lives and livelihoods of food vendors, access to financing and safety nets, as well as the impacts of demographic data and geospatial information on slums, or lack thereof, on food security of the poor. This chapter is a modest reminder that behooves us to move in that direction.

References

Aguayo, V. M., and P. Menon. 2016. Stop Stunting: Improving Child Feeding, Women's Nutrition and Household Sanitation in South Asia. *Maternal & Child Nutrition* 12 (1): 3–11. https://doi.org/10.1111/mcn.12283.

Ahmed, S. 2018. *Dacca: A Study in Urban History and Development.* London: Routledge. https://doi.org/10.4324/9781351186759.

Akaeze, O., and D. Nandwani. 2020. Urban Agriculture in Asia to Meet the Food Production Challenges of Urbanization: A Review. *Urban Agriculture & Regional Food Systems* 5 (1): e20002. https://doi.org/10.1002/uar2.20002.

Al Banna, M. H. et al. 2021. Factors Associated with Food Safety Knowledge and Practices among Meat Handlers in Bangladesh: A Cross-Sectional Study. *Environmental Health and Preventive Medicine* 26 (1): 84. https://doi.org/10.1186/s12199-021-01004-5.

Asaduzzaman, M. 2021. Agriculture in Bangladesh: The Last and the Next Fifty Years. *The Daily Star.* 26 March. https://www.thedailystar.net/supplements/celebrating-50-years-bangladesh/news/agriculture-bangladesh-the-last-and-the-next-fifty-years-2066689.

Asian Development Bank (ADB). 2021. *Food Inflation and Food and Nutrition Security Situation in Developing Asia During the COVID-19 Pandemic.* Manila. https://www.adb.org/news/features/food-inflation-food-nutrition-security-situation-developing-asia-covid-19-pandemic.

Bangladesh Bureau of Statistics (BBS), Ministry of Planning. 2017. *Preliminary Report on Household Income and Expenditure Survey 2016.* Dhaka, Bangladesh. http://bbs.portal.gov.bd/sites/default/files/files/bbs.portal.gov.bd/page/b343a8b4_956b_45ca_872f_4cf9b2f1a6e0/HIES%20Preliminary%20Report%202016.pdf.

————. 2018. *Report on Labour Force Survey (LFS) 2016-17.* Dhaka, Bangladesh. http://203.112.218.65:8008/WebTestApplication/userfiles/Image/LatestReports/LFS_2016-17.pdf.

————. 2019. *Preliminary Report on Agriculture Census 2019.* Dhaka, Bangladesh. https://bbs.portal.gov.bd/sites/default/files/files/bbs.portal.gov.bd/page/b343a8b4_956b_45ca_872f_4cf9b2f1a6e0/9beb0d821f582859681d77f76e89e321.pdf.

Bangladesh Rural Advancement Committee (BRAC). 2020. *Rapid Perception Survey on COVID19 Awareness and Economic Impact.* Dhaka, Bangladesh. https://reliefweb.int/sites/reliefweb.int/files/resources/Perception-Survey-Covid19.pdf.

Banks, N., M. Roy, and D. Hulme. 2011. Neglecting the Urban Poor in Bangladesh: Research, Policy, and Action in the Context of Climate Change." *Environment and Urbanization* 23 (2): 487–502. https://doi.org/10.1177/0956247811417794.

BBS and UNICEF Bangladesh. 2019. *Progotir Pathey: Bangladesh Multiple Indicator Cluster Survey 2019—Survey Findings Report.* Dhaka, Bangladesh. https://mics-surveys-prod.s3.amazonaws. com/MICS6/South%20Asia/Bangladesh/2019/Survey%20 findings/Bangladesh%202019%20MICS%20Survey%20 Findings_English.pdf.

Beard, V. A., and R. S. Cartmill. 2007. Gender, Collective Action and Participatory Development in Indonesia. *International Development Planning Review* 29 (2): 185–213.

Béné, C. 2020. Resilience of Local Food Systems and Links to Food Security – A Review of Some Important Concepts in the Context of COVID-19 and Other Shocks. *Food Security* 12 (4): 805–822. https://doi.org/10.1007/s12571-020-01076-1.

Birch, E. L., and S. M. Wachter, eds. 2011. *Global Urbanization: The City in the Twenty-First Century.* Philadelphia: University of Pennsylvania Press.

Bird, J, Y. Li, H. Z. Rahman, M. Rama, and A. J. Venables. 2018. *Toward Great Dhaka: A New Urban Development Paradigm Eastward.* Washington, DC: World Bank. https://doi.org/10.1596/978-1-4648-1238-5.

Cawood, S. 2021. Limits to and Opportunities for Scaling Participation: Lessons from Three City-Wide Urban Poor Networks in Dhaka, Bangladesh. *Environment and Urbanization* 33 (2): 396–412. https://doi.org/10.1177/09562478211026253.

Cheema, G. S., and V. Popovski, eds. 2010. *Engaging Civil Society: Emerging Trends in Democratic Governance.* Trends and Innovations in Governance Series. Tokyo; New York: United Nations University.

Chen, M. 2016. The Urban Informal Economy: Towards More Inclusive Cities. *Urbanet* (blog). 16 August. https://www.urbanet.info/ urban-informal-economy/.

Chen, M., and V. A. Beard. 2018. Including the Excluded: Supporting Informal Workers for More Equal and Productive Cities in the Global South. *Working Paper: Towards a More Equal City.* Washington, DC: World Resources Institute. http://www.wri.org/publication/towards-more-equal-city-including-the-excluded?utm_source=twitter.com&utm_medium=wricities&utm_campaign=socialmedia.

Chowdhury, T. A., A. B. Das, L. Chakraborty, and M. K. Barai. 2020. NGOs for Development: Experience of Bangladesh. In *Bangladesh's Economic and Social Progress: From a Basket Case to a Development Model*, edited by M. K. Barai. Singapore: Springer. pp. 351–380. https://doi.org/10.1007/978-981-15-1683-2_12.

Clapp, J., and W. G. Moseley. 2020. This Food Crisis Is Different: COVID-19 and the Fragility of the Neoliberal Food Security Order. *The Journal of Peasant Studies* 47 (7): 1393–1417. https://doi.org/10.1080/03066150.2020.1823838.

Dahiya, B. 2012. Cities in Asia, 2012: Demographics, Economics, Poverty, Environment and Governance. *Cities* 29, Supplement 2 (0): S44–61. https://doi.org/10.1016/j.cities.2012.06.013.

Dahiya, B., and A. Das, eds. 2020. *New Urban Agenda in Asia-Pacific: Governance for Sustainable and Inclusive Cities—Advances in 21st Century Human Settlements*. Singapore: Springer. https://www.springer.com/gp/book/9789811367083.

Das, A. 2017. A City of Two Tales: Shelter and Migrants in Surabaya. *Environment and Urbanization ASIA* 8 (1): 1–21. https://doi.org/10.1177/0975425316686501.

Das, A., and B. Dahiya. 2020. Towards Inclusive Urban Governance and Planning: Emerging Trends and Future Trajectories. In *New Urban Agenda in Asia-Pacific—Advances in 21st Century Human Settlements*, edited by B. Dahiya and A. Das. Singapore: Springer. pp. 353–384.

Das, A., and R. King. 2019. *Surabaya: The Legacy of Participatory Upgrading of Informal Settlements. Working Paper—Towards a More Equal City*. Washington, DC. https://www.wri.org/wri-citiesforall/publication/surabaya-legacy-participatory-upgrading-informal-settlements.

Del Ninno, C., P. A. Dorosh, and L. C. Smith. 2003. Public Policy, Markets and Household Coping Strategies in Bangladesh: Avoiding a Food Security Crisis Following the 1998 Floods. *World Development* 31 (7): 1221–1238. https://doi.org/10.1016/S0305-750X(03)00071-8.

Dhaka North Community Town Federation and FAO. 2020. *Defining and Measuring Food Security with the Urban Poor*. Dhaka. March.

Faisal, I. M., and S. Parveen. 2004. Food Security in the Face of Climate Change, Population Growth, and Resource Constraints: Implications for Bangladesh. *Environmental Management* 34 (4): 487–498. https://doi.org/10.1007/s00267-003-3066-7.

Food and Agriculture Organization of the United Nations (FAO). 2006. *Food Security*. Policy Brief Issue 2. Rome, Italy. https://www.fao. org/fileadmin/templates/faoitaly/documents/pdf/pdf_Food_ Security_Cocept_Note.pdf#page=1&zoom=auto,-134,848.

————. 2020a. *Impacts of Coronavirus on Food Security and Nutrition in Asia and the Pacific: Building More Resilient Food Systems*. Policy Brief. Bangkok, Thailand. http://www.fao.org/documents/card/ en/c/ca9473en.

————. 2020b. *Impact of COVID-19 on Food Security and Urban Poverty*. Situation Report 11. Dhaka, Bangladesh.

————. 2020c. Food Prices, Food Security and Urban Poverty. *Dhaka Food System Project Knowledge Series*. Special Edition 3. March– June.

————. 2021. *Food Systems Summit Independent Dialogue: The Role of Fresh Food Markets in Bangladesh's Food System*. 8 June. https://www.fao.org/bangladesh/news/detail-events/ zh/c/1410679/.

FAO Bangladesh. 2020. *Dhaka Fresh Markets Assessment Survey*. Dhaka Food Systems Project. Dhaka.

FAO, IFAD, UNICEF, WFP, and WHO. 2019. *The State of Food Security and Nutrition in the World 2021: Safeguarding Against Economic Slowdowns and Downturns*. Rome, Italy. https://www.fao.org/3/ ca5162en/ca5162en.pdf.

————. 2020. *The State of Food Security and Nutrition in the World 2020. Transforming Food Systems for Affordable Healthy Diets*. Rome, Italy. https://doi.org/10.4060/ca9692en.

FAO in Bangladesh. 2020. *The Urban Poor in Dhaka Spend up to Half Their Income on Food, According to New Research Presented Today*. 3 April. https://www.fao.org/bangladesh/news/detail- events/zh/c/1264912/.

————. 2021. *Food Systems Summit Independent Dialogue: The Role of Fresh Food Markets in Bangladesh's Food System*. 8 June. https://www.fao.org/bangladesh/news/detail-events/ zh/c/1410679/.

FAO, WFP, and IFAD. 2012. *The State of Food Insecurity in the World 2012: Economic Growth Is Necessary but Not Sufficient to Accelerate Reduction of Hunger and Malnutrition*. Rome, Italy. https://www.fao.org/3/i3027e/i3027e.pdf.

The Financial Express. 2021. An Asian Tiger in the Making. 16 December. https://www.financialexpress.com/opinion/an-asian-tiger-in- the-making/2380948/.

Floro, M. S., and R. Bali Swain. 2013. Food Security, Gender, and Occupational Choice among Urban Low-Income Households. *World Development* 42: 89–99. https://doi.org/10.1016/j.worlddev.2012.08.005.

Fung, A., and E. O. Wright, eds. 2003. *Deepening Democracy: Institutional Innovations in Empowered Participatory Governance.* London; New York: Verso.

Global Fund for Women. 2019. Empowering Garment Workers in Bangladesh. 15 April. https://www.globalfundforwomen.org/what-we-do/voice/campaigns/working-for-justice/building-a-coalition-of-advocates-in-bangladesh/.

Grantham, K., and B. Baruah. 2017. Women's NGOs as Intermediaries in Development Cooperation: Findings from Research in Tanzania. *Development in Practice* 27 (7): 927–939. https://doi.org/10.1080/09614524.2017.1349734.

Harris-Fry, H., N. Shrestha, A. Costello, and N. M. Saville. 2017. Determinants of Intra-Household Food Allocation between Adults in South Asia: A Systematic Review. *International Journal for Equity in Health* 16 (1): 107. https://doi.org/10.1186/s12939-017-0603-1.

Healey, P. 2003. Collaborative Planning in Perspective. *Planning Theory* 2 (2): 101–123. https://doi.org/10.1177/14730952030022002.

Hirvonen, K., A. de Brauw, and G. T. Abate. 2021. Food Consumption and Food Security during the COVID-19 Pandemic in Addis Ababa. *American Journal of Agricultural Economics* 103 (3): 772–789. https://doi.org/10.1111/ajae.12206.

Hossain, M., F. Naher, and Q. Shahabuddin. 2005. Food Security and Nutrition in Bangladesh: Progress and Determinants. *EJADE: Electronic Journal of Agricultural and Development Economics* 2 (853-2016–56126): 103–132.

Huq, S. 2001. Climate Change and Bangladesh. *Science* 294 (5547): 1617. https://doi.org/10.1126/science.294.5547.1617.

Ikhsan, M., and I. G. S. Virananda. 2021. *How COVID-19 Affects Food Security in Indonesia.* LPEM-FEBUI Working Paper 061. Jakarta: University of Indonesia, Salemba Campus. https://www.lpem.org/wp-content/uploads/2021/07/WP-LPEM-061_How_COVID-19_Affects_Food_Security_in_Indonesia.pdf.

Institute of Public Health Nutrition (IPHN). 2014. *National Micronutrient Survey 2011-12.* Final Report. Dhaka, Bangladesh. https://www.unicef.org/bangladesh/media/4631/file/National%20Micronutrient%20Survey%202011-12.pdf.

King, R., M. Orloff, T. Virsilas, and T. Pande. 2017. *Confronting the Urban Housing Crisis in the Global South: Adequate, Secure, and Affordable Housing: Working Paper—Towards a More Equal City.* Washington, DC: World Resources Institute. https://www.wri. org/publication/towards-more-equal-city-confronting-urban-housing-crisis-global-south.

Koli, A. 2015. Understanding Environmental Civil Society Activism in Bangladesh. In *Civil Society in Asia: In Search of Democracy and Development in Bangladesh*, edited by F. Quadir and Y. Tsujinaka. Farnham, Surrey, UK: Ashgate Publishing. pp. 99–124.

Kornher, L., and T. G. Sakketa. 2021. Does Food Security Matter to Subjective Well-Being? Evidence from a Cross-Country Panel. *Journal of International Development* 33 (8): 1270–1289. https://doi.org/10.1002/jid.3575.

Lal, R. 2020. Home Gardening and Urban Agriculture for Advancing Food and Nutritional Security in Response to the COVID-19 Pandemic. *Food Security* 12 (4): 871–876. https://doi.org/10.1007/s12571-020-01058-3.

Lemay, E. P. et al. 2021. The Role of Values in Coping with Health and Economic Threats of COVID-19. *The Journal of Social Psychology* 0 (0): 1–18. https://doi.org/10.1080/00224545.2021.1979454.

Mahendra, A., J. Du, A. Dasgupta, V. A. Beard, A. Kallergis, and K. Schalch. 2021. Seven Transformations for More Equitable and Sustainable Cities. *World Resources Report: Towards a More Equal City.* Washington, DC: World Resources Institute. https://doi.org/10.46830/wrirpt.19.00124.

Mansuri, G., and V. Rao. 2004. Community-Based and -Driven Development: A Critical Review. *The World Bank Research Observer* 19 (1): 1–39. https://doi.org/10.1093/wbro/lkh012.

———. 2013. Can Participation Be Induced? Some Evidence from Developing Countries. *Critical Review of International Social and Political Philosophy* 16 (2): 284–304. https://doi.org/10.1080/13698230.2012.757918.

Mathur, O. P. 2013. *Urban Poverty in Asia.* Manila: ADB.

McCarney, P. L., and R. E. Stren, eds. 2003. *Governance on the Ground: Innovations and Discontinuities in Cities of the Developing World.* Washington, DC; Baltimore: Woodrow Wilson Center Press; Johns Hopkins University Press.

Morgan, K. 2013. The Rise of Urban Food Planning. *International Planning Studies* 18 (1): 1–4. https://doi.org/10.1080/13563475.2012.752189.

Mui, Y., M. Khojasteh, K. Hodgson, and S. Raja. 2018. Rejoining the Planning and Public Health Fields. *Journal of Agriculture, Food Systems, and Community Development* 8 (B): 73–93. https://doi.org/10.5304/jafscd.2018.08B.004.

Murshed-E-Jahan, K., M. Ahmed, and B. Belton. 2010. The Impacts of Aquaculture Development on Food Security: Lessons from Bangladesh. *Aquaculture Research* 41 (4): 481–495. https://doi.org/10.1111/j.1365-2109.2009.02337.x.

O'Hara, S., and E. C. Toussaint. 2021. Food Access in Crisis: Food Security and COVID-19. *Ecological Economics* 180: 106859. February. https://doi.org/10.1016/j.ecolecon.2020.106859.

Paganini, N. et al. 2020. Growing and Eating Food during the COVID-19 Pandemic: Farmers' Perspectives on Local Food System Resilience to Shocks in Southern Africa and Indonesia. *Sustainability* 12 (20): 8556. https://doi.org/10.3390/su12208556.

Peters, R. et al. 2019. Nutrition Transition, Overweight and Obesity among Rural-to-Urban Migrant Women in Kenya. *Public Health Nutrition* 22 (17): 3200–3210. https://doi.org/10.1017/S1368980019001204.

Pothukuchi, K. 2009. Community and Regional Food Planning: Building Institutional Support in the United States. *International Planning Studies* 14 (4): 349–367. https://doi.org/10.1080/13563471003642902.

Pritchard, B., H. Mackay, and C. Turner. 2017. Special Issue Introduction: Geographical Perspectives on Food and Nutrition Insecurity in the Global South. *Geographical Research* 55 (2): 127–130. https://doi.org/10.1111/1745-5871.12227.

Raj, S., S. Roodbar, C. Brinkley, and D. W. Wolfe. 2022. Food Security and Climate Change: Differences in Impacts and Adaptation Strategies for Rural Communities in the Global South and North. *Frontiers in Sustainable Food Systems* 5. https://www.frontiersin.org/article/10.3389/fsufs.2021.691191.

Raja, S., K. Morgan, and E. Hall. 2017. Planning for Equitable Urban and Regional Food Systems. *Built Environment* 43 (3): 309–314.

Raja, S., E. Sweeney, Y. Mui, and F. Boamah. 2021. *Local Government Planning for Community Food Systems: Opportunity, Innovation and Equity in Low- and Middle-Income Countries*. Rome, Italy: FAO. https://doi.org/10.4060/cb3136en.

Rajan, S. I., and A. P. Cherian. 2021. COVID-19: Urban Vulnerability and the Need for Transformations. *Environment and Urbanization ASIA* 12 (2): 310–322. https://doi.org/10.1177/09754253211040195.

Rohekar, J. 2016. Slums on Rent. *Down to Earth*. 31 March. https://www.downtoearth.org.in/news/urbanisation/slums-on-rent-53291.

Roy, A. 2010. *Poverty Capital: Microfinance and the Making of Development*. New York: Routledge.

Ruel, M. 2020. *Growing Cities, Growing Food Insecurity: How to Protect the Poor during Rapid Urbanization*. 14 October. https://www.csis.org/analysis/growing-cities-growing-food-insecurity-how-protect-poor-during-rapid-urbanization.

Ruszczyk, H. A., M. F. Rahman, L. J. Bracken, and S. Sudha. 2021. Contextualizing the COVID-19 Pandemic's Impact on Food Security in Two Small Cities in Bangladesh. *Environment and Urbanization* 33 (1): 239–254. https://doi.org/10.1177/0956247820965156.

Saleh, A. 2022. *Development Needs to Change. Bangladesh Can Show Us How*. World Economic Forum. 18 January. https://www.weforum.org/agenda/2022/01/development-needs-change-bangladesh-can-show-us-how/.

Smith, M. D., and D. Wesselbaum. 2020. COVID-19, Food Insecurity, and Migration. *The Journal of Nutrition* 150 (11): 2855–2858. https://doi.org/10.1093/jn/nxaa270.

Tacoli, C. 2021. Feeding All City Inhabitants. *International Institute for Environment and Development (IIED)* (blog). 28 June. https://www.iied.org/feeding-all-city-inhabitants.

Taylor, J. 2015. A Tale of Two Cities: Comparing Alternative Approaches to Reducing the Vulnerability of Riverbank Communities in Two Indonesian Cities. *Environment and Urbanization* 27 (2): 621–636. https://doi.org/10.1177/0956247815594532.

Taylor, J. 2020. How Dhaka's Urban Poor Are Dealing with COVID-19. *International Institute for Environment and Development* (blog). 1 July. https://www.iied.org/how-dhakas-urban-poor-are-dealing-covid-19.

Thorner, D. 1986. Chayanov's Concept of Peasant Economy. In *A.V. Chayanov on the Theory of Peasant Economy*, edited by D. Thorner, B. Kerblay, and R. E. F. Smith, xi–xxiii. Madison, Wisconsin: The University of Wisconsin Press.

UNDP in Bangladesh. 2021. *Millions of Bangladesh's Urban Poor Took the Biggest Hit during the COVID Pandemic*. 25 January. https://www.bd.undp.org/content/bangladesh/en/home/presscenter/articles/2021/01/millions-of-bangladeshs-urban-poor-took-the-biggest-hit-during-t.html.

UNICEF Bangladesh. n.d. Children in Cities. https://www.unicef.org/bangladesh/en/children-cities%C2%A0 (accessed 12 February 2022).

UN-HABITAT. 2010. *The State of Asian Cities 2010/11*. Fukuoka, Japan.

World Bank. 2019. *Bangladesh Poverty Assessment: Facing Old and New Frontiers in Poverty Reduction*. Washington, DC. http://documents1.worldbank.org/curated/pt/793121572582830383/pdf/Bangladesh-Poverty-Assessment-Facing-Old-and-New-Frontiers-in-Poverty-Reduction.pdf.

World Bank. 2020. Food Security and COVID-19. 8 July. https://www.worldbank.org/en/topic/agriculture/brief/food-security-and-covid-19.

Wratten, E. 1995. Conceptualizing Urban Poverty *Environment and Urbanization* 7 (1): 11–38. https://doi.org/10.1177/095624789500700118.

Zimmerer, K. S., and S. de Haan. 2020. Informal Food Chains and Agrobiodiversity Need Strengthening—Not Weakening—to Address Food Security amidst the COVID-19 Crisis in South America. *Food Security* 12 (4): 891–894. https://doi.org/10.1007/s12571-020-01088-x.

6

Meeting the Demand for Water and Sanitation Services in Asia's Informal Urban Areas

Penny Dutton, Isabel Blackett, Neeta Pokhrel, Lara Arjan, Christian Walder, and Ellen Pascua*

Abstract

Informal service providers play a key role in water supply and sanitation services in informal settlements and slums throughout Asia. Yet, little research exists on how these intermediaries develop and operate at the margins between suppliers of formal services, such as utilities, and the community that has the demand for those services. This chapter examines water supply and sanitation cases in Bangladesh, Cambodia, Nepal, and the Philippines. It illustrates how service providers can leverage their relationships with communities to deliver sustainable services and adapt quickly to innovate when confronted by external challenges such as the coronavirus disease (COVID-19) pandemic. It offers some general policy recommendations for involving intermediaries in water and sanitation projects.

Keywords: informal, urban, water, sanitation, service providers

*   The authors are especially grateful to Elsa Rousset, Suzanne Assane-Aly, and Wilma Duguran (Eau et Vie); Anjanette Bansao and Alexandra Knezovich (Toilet Board Coalition); and Eva Leneveu (1001fontaines) who collected the primary data, shared valuable insights, and prepared a report from their studies. The key contributions of the following are also highly appreciated: Joanna Brewster (consultant) who copyedited and finalized the manuscript; and Aimee Hampel-Milagrosa and Jasmin S. Sibal of Asian Development Bank, and Ashok Das and Priyam Das of University of Hawaii who served as reviewers.

1. Introduction

Asia is home to more than half of the urban slum and informal settlement population of the world—about 590 million people (UN Habitat 2021). While the population living in informal settlements is a diminishing proportion of Asia's 2.3 billion urban inhabitants, the number of people in informal settlements is growing. As these settlements grow, so does the need for safe and sustainable water and sanitation. About 300 million people in Asia lack access to safe water supply, and 1.5 billion lack access to adequate levels of sanitation (ADB 2017). Accessing clean water and sanitation is a constant challenge for city dwellers living in informal settlements and marginal areas (United Nations General Assembly 2010).[1] In Dhaka, Bangladesh, for example, more than 50% of slum residents reported poor water quality and taste, and 12% of residents experienced periods when the water was unusable. Likewise, an average of 16.2 households shared a sanitation facility, and only 8.6% of households were able to access improved sanitation (Arias-Granada et al. 2018).

The health and social development impacts of such lack of services are well-documented (CRC for Water Sensitive Cities 2018)—as are the many economic, spatial, social, institutional, and political barriers to delivering services to informal settlements (Sinharoy, Pittluck, and Clasen 2019; Roaf et al. n.d.). Different technology options such as water kiosks or prepaid meters have been proposed as solutions, but often these make the utility as the main service provider (Souter and Orams 2019).

For most residents of informal settlements and marginal areas, informal local water and sanitation service providers meet these basic needs. These local entrepreneurs or enterprises provide services paid for directly by the clients. They are not planned, authorized, supervised, or acknowledged by the formal authorities as part of the official system (IGI Global 2021). Their services may include water provided by tankers for collection, bottled water delivery, provision and management of shared or community latrines, container-based sanitation, or piped water to a private household or shared tap. These providers have emerged in response to a significant essential service gap (Garrick et al. 2019).

There is also little understanding of how these informal service providers, or intermediaries, operate in the space between formal

---

[1]   Informal settlements are unplanned areas that lack secure tenure, basic services, and urban infrastructure. Marginal areas include settlements on steep slopes, floodplains, riverbanks, and mangroves.

providers, such as utilities and consumers.[2] Intermediaries in this context are service providers who overcome the water and sanitation service delivery barriers faced by formal providers, and by doing so deliver services in informal settlements through innovative, flexible, and community-responsive models. Most of the available literature on informal service providers focuses on Africa (Mwanza 2001; O'Keefe et al. 2015; WSUP 2018) or the Pacific (Schrecongost and Wong 2015), with relatively little on Asia. A study of small-scale private water providers in Asian cities highlights the key role of informal providers in meeting the water gap, but the study is outdated, has a narrow focus on entrepreneurs, and excludes sanitation service providers, nongovernment organization (NGO) supported ventures, and social enterprises (Conan 2004).

This chapter explores the role of informal water and sanitation services in some Asian cities, as well as their demand, supply, development, and evolution. Using case studies from Bangladesh, Cambodia, Nepal, and the Philippines, it explores the effectiveness of intermediaries—and the extent to which they have demonstrated nimbleness and flexibility by adapting their delivery models to the challenges of the COVID-19 pandemic.

This chapter's findings suggest that governments, water supply and sanitation utilities, and development financing institutions, including the Asian Development Bank (ADB), should incorporate intermediate service providers as partners in large-scale investments in water and sanitation service delivery in Asia.

Much research shows that informal water and sanitation services do not exist in isolation. They have developed from interacting with formal services, and the evolution of service models. This chapter starts by outlining the broad demand and supply for informal water and sanitation services in Asia and the Pacific (Figure 1, level 1). The supply-side and provision of services by small-scale providers in South and Southeast Asia (Figure 1, level 2) then provide the context into which specific country case studies from Bangladesh, Cambodia, Nepal, and the Philippines are situated (Figure 1, level 3). The impact of the COVID-19 pandemic on informal water and sanitation service

---

[2]   The term "intermediary" is used in different ways (for example, see Lardoux de Pazzis and Muret 2021). In this chapter, it means small or medium-sized private sector enterprises, social enterprises, NGOs, and community-based organizations (CBOs). The term is used to describe the function an intermediary plays between a formal utility or government provider and communities. It is not biased toward a particular legal structure or arrangement. In this chapter, the terms small and medium-sized enterprises (SMEs), social enterprise, NGO, and CBO are used deliberately and alternately to illustrate the range of activities that organizations may undertake in such an intermediary role.

models in these case studies supplies lessons for the wider provision and sustainability of informal services in South and Southeast Asia (Figure 1, level 4).

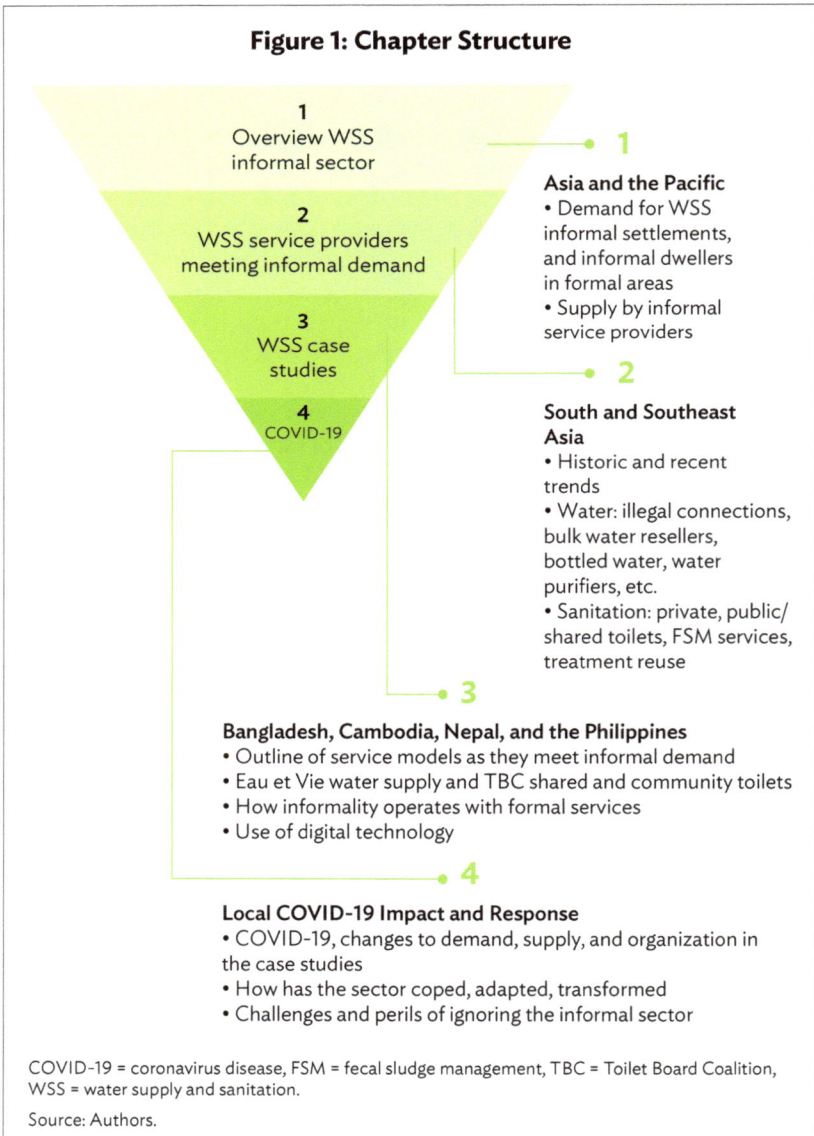

Figure 1: Chapter Structure

1
Overview WSS informal sector

2
WSS service providers meeting informal demand

3
WSS case studies

4
COVID-19

1

Asia and the Pacific
• Demand for WSS informal settlements, and informal dwellers in formal areas
• Supply by informal service providers

2

South and Southeast Asia
• Historic and recent trends
• Water: illegal connections, bulk water resellers, bottled water, water purifiers, etc.
• Sanitation: private, public/shared toilets, FSM services, treatment reuse

3

Bangladesh, Cambodia, Nepal, and the Philippines
• Outline of service models as they meet informal demand
• Eau et Vie water supply and TBC shared and community toilets
• How informality operates with formal services
• Use of digital technology

4

Local COVID-19 Impact and Response
• COVID-19, changes to demand, supply, and organization in the case studies
• How has the sector coped, adapted, transformed
• Challenges and perils of ignoring the informal sector

COVID-19 = coronavirus disease, FSM = fecal sludge management, TBC = Toilet Board Coalition, WSS = water supply and sanitation.

Source: Authors.

1.2 Understanding Formal and Informal Settlements, Water Supply, and Sanitation

At the outset, it will be useful to clarify and operationalize the oft-mentioned terms and phrases used in this chapter:

Informal settlements. Informal settlements are residential areas where inhabitants lack security of tenure, basic services, and urban infrastructure. Their dwellings may not comply with planning and building regulations and are often situated in geographically and environmentally hazardous areas. Slums are the most deprived and excluded informal settlements, characterized by poverty and large agglomerations of dilapidated housing often located in the most hazardous urban land, with slum dwellers exposed to eviction, disease, and violence (UN Habitat 2015).

Formal settlements and housing. Formal settlements are zones or areas designated for residential housing, usually in an urban plan. The land is legally registered and formally owned and typically has ready access to basic urban infrastructure and services, such as roads, water and sewerage, electricity, refuse collection, and street lighting. Housing is usually built to meet planning regulations and building codes.

Informal water and sanitation service providers. Informal water and sanitation service providers are individual entrepreneurs or enterprises that provide a service—in this case, water and sanitation—paid by the clients but is not planned, authorized, supervised, paid, or acknowledged by the formal authorities to be part of the official system (IGI Global 2021). The service providers include water vendors (by bottles, containers, carts, or tankers), unregistered latrine builders and plumbers, retailers of non-standardized products, illegal connections to water or sewerage mains, and manual or mechanical emptiers of pit latrines and septic tanks.

Formal service providers. Formal service providers are duly registered, legal companies that usually pay taxes. The term primarily refers to government-owned utilities and businesses, which operate under regulation and provide mostly piped services. However, it can also include private sector businesses that are formally contracted, delegated, regulated, and/or licensed to provide the services.

Typical characteristics of informal and formal settlements and services are described in Table 1. It should be noted, however, that informal settlements vary depending on the local and geographic context, and not all their characteristics are universal. Evidence indicates it is inaccurate to stereotype informal services as illegal, inefficient, traditional, expensive, or unsustainable. They often have a co-production relationship with formal services, and many may be stable, dynamic, expanding, and profitable businesses (Ahlers et al. 2014). While there are typical characteristics of informal settlements and services, as the case studies show, the reality is often more complex, and the boundaries of informal and formal are unclear.

Table 1: Typical Characteristics of Informal and Formal Settlements and Water Supply and Sanitation

	Informal	Formal
Settlements and housing	• Unplanned, unzoned • No or limited government services • Basic housing • High population density, overcrowding, or lower density in peri-urban areas • Often on marginal land, e.g., flood-prone, steep slopes • Mixed, low, or very low income levels	• Cadastral surveyed land • Planned settlements with laid-out, defined housing plots • Registered owners • Formal services such as roads, water, sewerage, power, transport, and telecommunications • Low-medium population density • Diverse income levels, but usually not very low
Water and sanitation services	• Self-provision or services obtained from an informal service provider • Shared or communal facilities (e.g., toilets and water points) • Overused services, some with queuing • Treated or untreated water • Low-quality pit or tanks • Unregistered or unknown water sources and poor quality • Unreliable services of variable quality *In some places, there are also* • Illegal connections • Extortionate control	• Formal provision by government entities and utilities or the registered designated private service providers • Household-level services to house or plot • Piped, treated water • Licensed service providers • Maintained and reliable services • Controlled prices through regulation • Accountability (of utilities to regulators)

Source: Authors.

2. Background
2.1 Evolution of Informal Urban Water and Sanitation Services

The growth in informal services has been driven by urbanization and migration, a shift to commercial services, global commitments to water and sanitation, and the COVID-19 pandemic.[3]

Asia's urban population increased at an average of 3.4% per year from 1970 to 2017 (ADB 2019). Urban growth has resulted from people seeking refuge from conflict, disasters triggered by natural hazard, climate change, and improved employment and education opportunities, as well as natural growth. It is projected that by 2050, Asia's urban population will increase by more than 1.1 billion, reaching about 3.0 billion (ADB 2019). Because of the lack of available and affordable formal housing, many migrants are forced to live in informal settlements (Baeumler et al. 2021). Birkmann et al. (2016) reported that each week, about 1.5 million people migrated to cities and peri-urban fringes, with the fastest growth in small to medium-sized cities where infrastructure and governance capacity lagged. Thus, informal water markets too have grown and thrived in response to increased demand where formal piped water systems have struggled to keep pace (Garrick et al. 2019).

Another driver has been the shift to commercial services. Since the 1990s, for water supply in particular, a shift in policy from state provision to commercial services has opened a door for informal services (Ahlers et al. 2014). Water sector commercialization aims for cost recovery and increased access to water; however, in practice, commercialization "has been an instrument for governments to relinquish their responsibility for funding investments in network expansion" (Dagdeviren 2008, 103). The pressure on utilities for cost recovery, economic investments, and higher tariffs has created tension with the delivery of affordable, quality services to low-income communities (Mitlin and Walnycki 2020). Utility hesitancy to service these informal areas has created a gap that informal services have stepped in to fill.

---

[3] Commercialization refers to the adoption of private sector principles and practices by public water providers, wherein management institutions (rules, norms, customs) are reworked to create conditions for operation at arms-length from government influence, cost-recovery, competitive bidding, cost-benefit analysis, performance-based salaries, and demand-driven investment (Tutusaus, Surya, and Schwartz 2019; McDonald and Ruiters 2007). Commercialization is the first step in a continuum to ultimate privatization, where the state sells its asset, along with operation and maintenance obligations, to a private company. Public–private partnerships are hybrid arrangements where some utility functions and responsibilities are transferred to the private sector.

Since 2000, an increase in the efficiency of water utilities has involved reducing nonrevenue water, which includes water "stolen" through illegal connections in slums and informal settlements. However, ADB has identified that the volumes "stolen" are relatively low compared, for example, with losses and leakages from poor quality joints and connections (Frauendorfer and Liemberger 2010). The same study found the prohibition on formally providing these communities with water caused illegal connections and subsequent losses.

A third driver of the rise of informal services has been the global water and sanitation targets. The Millennium Development Goals had aimed to halve the number of people without sustainable access to safe drinking water and basic sanitation by 2015 (Ahlers et al. 2014). That momentum continues through the 2030 Sustainable Development Goals (SDGs), which aim to achieve universal and equitable access to safe and affordable water, sanitation, and hygiene. Although global political commitment to the SDGs is strong and reflected in many national development plans, access does not always equate to service delivery (Singh 2019).

Where formal services have been extended, this has often been triggered locally by increased utility efficiency, as in the case of Phnom Penh Water Supply Authority in Cambodia (Sitha 2021). In some cities, such as those in Cambodia and Indonesia, informal settlements are now tolerated. However, they can be removed to make way for formal, high-impact or high-value developments, such as shopping centers, hotels, and housing, as seen in Jakarta in recent decades.

Due to the universal service ambitions of the SDGs and the International Decade for Action on Water for Sustainable Development (2018–2028), development banks have increased their focus on connecting "last mile" customers.

A recent driver of informal water and sanitation services has been the COVID-19 pandemic, which has highlighted, according to the United Nations, a "vital need to guarantee access to water and sanitation, particularly to those in the most vulnerable situations" (Office of the High Commissioner for Human Rights 2020, 1). During and after COVID-19 lockdowns and curfews, public health and behavior change messages have increased both awareness and practice of good hygiene, increased demand for water for handwashing, and triggered rapid sanitation solutions such as container-based toilets, which are emerging as alternatives to formal sewers. ADB makes the case that protecting the vulnerable is necessary to protect everyone during a pandemic, and increasing water, sanitation, and hygiene investments to the poorest communities requires the removal of barriers and application of established and innovative solutions, including greater use of digital technology (Bauer 2020).

2.2 Informal Demand

Informal demand for services comes from people who cannot access formal water supply and sanitation services provided by water and sewerage or sanitation utilities or by the registered, legal private sector. The reasons for lack of access to formal services include the legal, physical, and perceived barriers for the water and sanitation utility, as well as the housing and living circumstances of informal community residents. The main barriers to providing and accessing services are summarized in Table 2.

Table 2: Common Utility and User Barriers to Services

Utility barriers to providing water supply and sanitation services in informal communities	
• Water and sanitation service areas and networks are limited and do not include the whole city or town • Lack of tenure (ownership) or landlords' agreement • Not in utility mandate to serve informal areas; not the full water or sanitation service chain • High density is difficult for infrastructure (e.g., pipelines, wide roads for fecal sludge management trucks) • Fecal sludge management treatment facilities are unavailable near the service area • Limited capital resources to expand services into new areas • High service levels that are expensive and do not meet demand	• Underdeveloped billing and revenue collection systems limit operating revenue • A billing address is required • Political lack of will to charge adequate water and sanitation tariffs • A perception that poor customers will not pay • Concern about increasing unrecoverable operation and maintenance costs • Lack of experience working in low-income communities • Fear of legitimizing settlements by providing services • Violence, personal safety, community conflict, risk for utility staff
User barriers to accessing water supply and sanitation services in informal communities	
Water services • No piped water service in the area • Housing tenant (renter), lack of house or land tenure, or the landlord does not permit • Resident in a multistory dwelling with no piped water service • Unaffordable water connection charge • Unaffordable water tariff • No address for regular bills	**Sanitation services** • No sewers in the area • No space to build a latrine • Housing tenant (renter), lack of house or land tenure, or the landlord does not permit • Multistory dwelling with no sewers • Unaffordable sewer connection charge • Unaffordable sewerage tariff and desludging charge • Dense housing without adequate access to empty pits or tanks • High groundwater

Sources: Authors; and Conan (2004).

The most visible informal demand comes from the estimated 597 million residents of informal settlements and slums across Asia (UN-Habitat 2021). These settlements lack adequate, reliable, safe, affordable water and sanitation services, and most residents rely on shared facilities such as common toilets or standpipes (Sinharoy, Pittluck, and Clasen 2019).

Residents of informal settlements work in informal and formal jobs. Like everyone, they need water and sanitation services while at home, at work, at school, and at the terminuses of long commutes to work. Informal service providers mostly provide these services (Chen and Beard 2018).

There is also a demand for informal water and sanitation services from within formal areas of cities (McIntosh 2003). One part of this demand is from homeless people, pavement dwellers, and squatters who often live in the city centers and small settlements scattered among formal middle-class areas.

Informal demand is also generated by migrant day workers and informal vendors who provide goods such as food, drinks, and other fast-moving consumer products, as well as services, such as water and emptying latrines and septic tanks, to the formal sector workers and residents (Figure 2).

A final part of this demand is from residents of formal settlements with unreliable or inadequate formal water and sanitation services. Wherever sewers and licensed fecal sludge management (FSM) services are unavailable to formal housing and businesses, a vast demand for informal services is created. Similarly, if the utility piped water supply is intermittent or unreliable in formal areas, significant demand is generated for water services, such as by cart or tanker delivery and storage infrastructure to meet the needs of residents and businesses.

In some Central, West, and East Asian countries with high levels of quality, affordable, and reliable urban water and sanitation access, informal demand is lower. However, in most countries—including Organisation for Economic Co-operation and Development (OECD) countries—street-dwellers, migrants, and unregistered occupants of illegal or semi-legal properties daily require water supply and toilets. Official statistics often exclude street dwellers and migrants.

Figure 2: What Informal Workers Need from Inclusive Cities

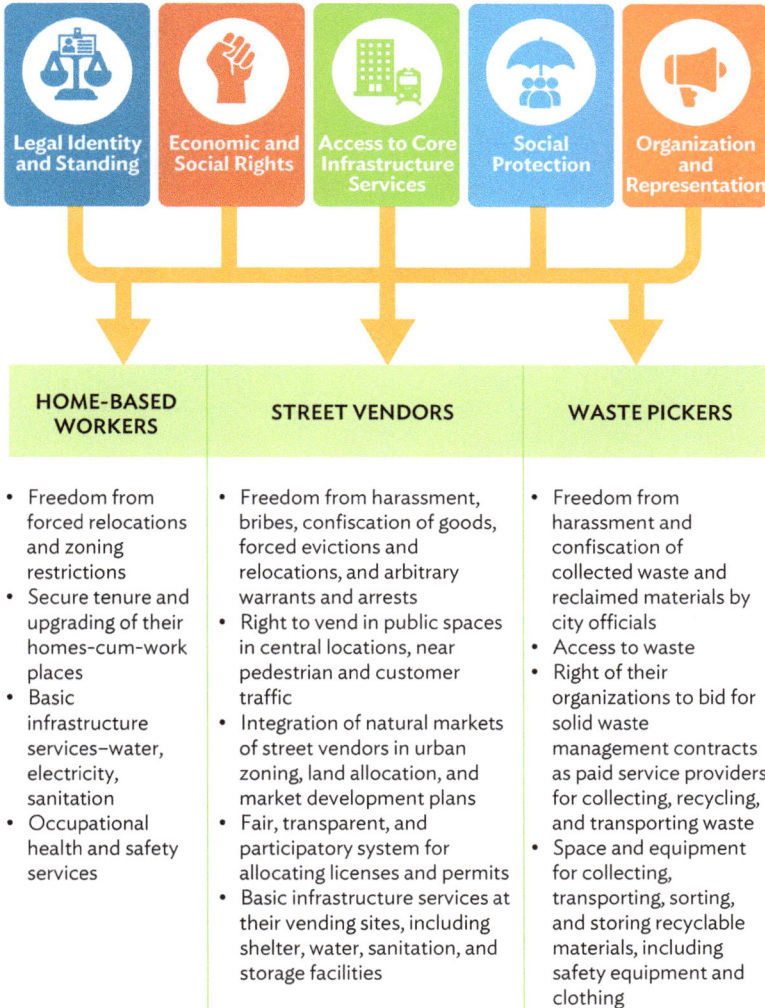

Legal Identity and Standing	Economic and Social Rights	Access to Core Infrastructure Services	Social Protection	Organization and Representation

HOME-BASED WORKERS	STREET VENDORS	WASTE PICKERS
• Freedom from forced relocations and zoning restrictions • Secure tenure and upgrading of their homes-cum-work places • Basic infrastructure services–water, electricity, sanitation • Occupational health and safety services	• Freedom from harassment, bribes, confiscation of goods, forced evictions and relocations, and arbitrary warrants and arrests • Right to vend in public spaces in central locations, near pedestrian and customer traffic • Integration of natural markets of street vendors in urban zoning, land allocation, and market development plans • Fair, transparent, and participatory system for allocating licenses and permits • Basic infrastructure services at their vending sites, including shelter, water, sanitation, and storage facilities	• Freedom from harassment and confiscation of collected waste and reclaimed materials by city officials • Access to waste • Right of their organizations to bid for solid waste management contracts as paid service providers for collecting, recycling, and transporting waste • Space and equipment for collecting, transporting, sorting, and storing recyclable materials, including safety equipment and clothing

Source: Chen and Beard (2018).

2.3 Informal Supply

Informal service providers supplying water and sanitation services across Asia usually fill formal sector gaps. The need, extent, and nature of the supply of informal services vary across countries. The level of informal demand primarily depends on factors such as local access, quality, reliability, and affordability of formal piped (or non-piped) water and sanitation services. The informal water and sanitation market encompasses simple as well as complex services involving diverse informal providers using different operational and service delivery models. Informal services are supplied throughout the water and sanitation service chains.

Informal sanitation services are present at containment, collection, transport, treatment, and reuse or disposal stages along the sanitation chain (Figure 3). In the absence of formal sewerage systems or official, regulated FSM services, residents and businesses have no choice but to self-supply, to avoid open defecation. The self-supply of sanitation may include wastewater disposal through illegal sewer connections or direct overflow (from toilets, septic tanks, or pits) to stormwater drains, as seen in megacities like Dhaka, Jakarta, and Manila. Residents and businesses construct substandard latrines and septic tanks and pay for septage removal by informal manual or mechanical FSM service providers. Such informal sanitation services are ubiquitous in informal settlements. They are also used in many established city centers and formal residential areas that lack sewerage.

Informal water supply services may be present at the source, treatment, storage, distribution, and/or consumption point of water along the supply chain (Figure 4). Their role is often connected to the water services provided by water utilities. Informal small-scale providers fill gaps left by inadequate piped water supplies and may constitute significant market share. Moreover, informal services may be the only option in fragile and conflict-affected areas (McIntosh 2003). In a middle-upper-class neighborhood, water may be informally sold from a formal connection or water from a utility supply stored in the household (McIntosh 2003). In some cities such as Shanghai, where the utility provides reliable and affordable water service, informal services may be limited to bottled water sales (McIntosh 2003).

Figure 3: Typical Informal Services along the Sanitation Service Chain

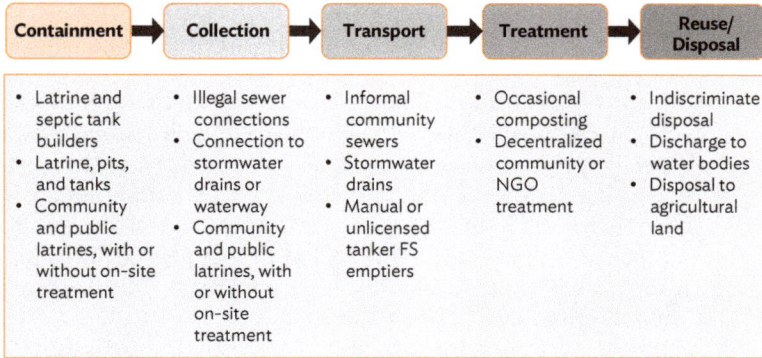

Containment	Collection	Transport	Treatment	Reuse/Disposal
• Latrine and septic tank builders • Latrine, pits, and tanks • Community and public latrines, with or without on-site treatment	• Illegal sewer connections • Connection to stormwater drains or waterway • Community and public latrines, with or without on-site treatment	• Informal community sewers • Stormwater drains • Manual or unlicensed tanker FS emptiers	• Occasional composting • Decentralized community or NGO treatment	• Indiscriminate disposal • Discharge to water bodies • Disposal to agricultural land

FS = fecal sludge, NGO = nongovernment organization.

Source: Authors.

Figure 4: Typical Informal Services along the Water Supply Service Chain

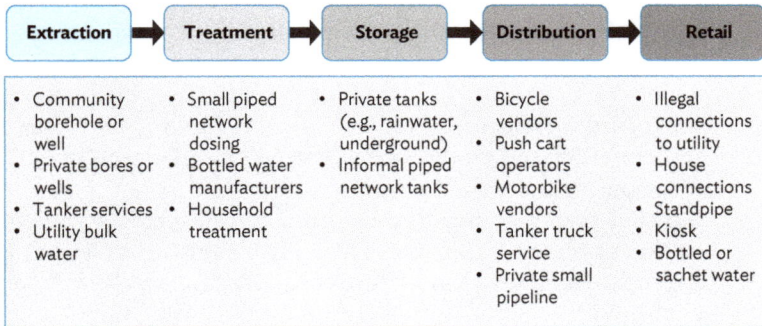

Extraction	Treatment	Storage	Distribution	Retail
• Community borehole or well • Private bores or wells • Tanker services • Utility bulk water	• Small piped network dosing • Bottled water manufacturers • Household treatment	• Private tanks (e.g., rainwater, underground) • Informal piped network tanks	• Bicycle vendors • Push cart operators • Motorbike vendors • Tanker truck service • Private small pipeline	• Illegal connections to utility • House connections • Standpipe • Kiosk • Bottled or sachet water

Source: Authors.

2.4 Formal–Informal Services Interaction

Informal sanitation services can be present throughout the sanitation chain (as shown in Figure 3) or be connected to formal services. Figure 5 illustrates typical sanitation linkages between informal and formal sanitation chains in South and Southeast Asia (orange lines, Figure 5). Common practices include

- **Illegal connections to sewerage systems.** Households and businesses informally or illegally connect their wastewater outlet to the storm drain and sewer system, for example, in Siem Reap, Cambodia (Cambodia News English 2021).
- **Emptying of substandard unregistered septic tanks or pits by registered FSM service providers.** Septic tanks or pits are not built to standards or are constructed by informal builders or households themselves; the concerned authorities do not inspect construction; and/or no formal system exists for registering on-site sanitation systems. This is common in many Asian cities, including Banjarmasin, Jakarta, and Bandung in Indonesia, Thu Dau Mot and Da Lat in Viet Nam (World Bank Group and Water Sanitation Program 2015), Siem Reap in Cambodia, and Dhaka in Bangladesh.
- **Disposal of waste by informal FSM service providers in formal treatment facilities.** Informal FSM service providers discharge their vacuum trucks of fecal waste into utility sewage or fecal sludge treatment works.

Conversely, formal sanitation services may be connected to informal services in the following ways (dashed lines, Figure 5):
- **Well-built toilets and septic tanks discharge informally into stormwater drains and water bodies.** This can be due to a lack of space for on-site disposal, the absence of sewers, or an expensive or obscure process for connecting legally to a sewer. Such connections are seen in Surakarta (Solo), Indonesia; in Phnom Penh, Cambodia; and in Dhaka, Bangladesh (DOHWA Engineering Co. Ltd. 2021).
- **Septic tanks are emptied by informal manual or vacuum tanker service.** This includes, for example, informal pit emptiers from low castes in cities in Bangladesh (World Bank et al. 2019).
- **Licensed FSM service providers discharge fecal sludge indiscriminately to land, water bodies, or agricultural land.** This may be because no fecal sludge treatment is available, the treatment is located too far away (more than a 30-minute haulage distance), hours of operation are incompatible with the services provided (for example, evening or early morning), or disposal is too expensive.

Figure 5: Examples of Formal and Informal Services Linkages along the Sanitation Service Chain

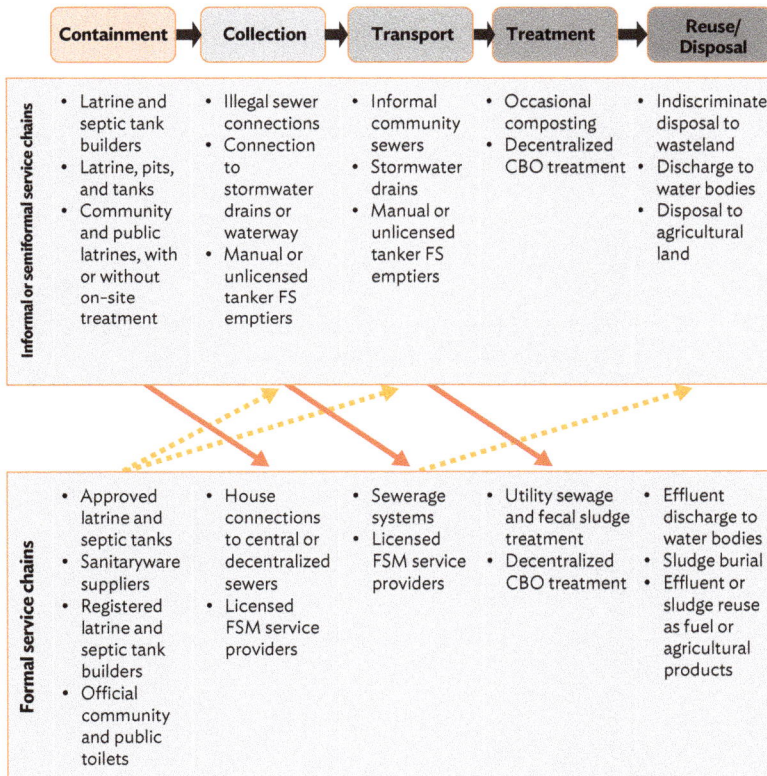

| Containment | Collection | Transport | Treatment | Reuse/Disposal |

Informal or semiformal service chains

- Latrine and septic tank builders
- Latrine, pits, and tanks
- Community and public latrines, with or without on-site treatment

- Illegal sewer connections
- Connection to stormwater drains or waterway
- Manual or unlicensed tanker FS emptiers

- Informal community sewers
- Stormwater drains
- Manual or unlicensed tanker FS emptiers

- Occasional composting
- Decentralized CBO treatment

- Indiscriminate disposal to wasteland
- Discharge to water bodies
- Disposal to agricultural land

Formal service chains

- Approved latrine and septic tanks
- Sanitaryware suppliers
- Registered latrine and septic tank builders
- Official community and public toilets

- House connections to central or decentralized sewers
- Licensed FSM service providers

- Sewerage systems
- Licensed FSM service providers

- Utility sewage and fecal sludge treatment
- Decentralized CBO treatment

- Effluent discharge to water bodies
- Sludge burial
- Effluent or sludge reuse as fuel or agricultural products

CBO = community-based organization, FS = fecal sludge, FSM = fecal sludge management, NGO = nongovernment organization.

Source: Authors.

For water supply, the linkages between the formal and informal sectors are predominantly in one direction, through water supplied from a formal utility to informal service providers. This may be by connecting to a bulk water supply from a utility to extend an informal piped network within a community. Or it may be illegal offtakes from a utility pipeline by water vendors. Where the water source is locally developed, such as a community borehole, interaction with formal services might be limited to regulation of the water source, if at all. Informal water services can operate completely disconnected from formal services. The linkages from informal services back to formal services are rare, except for informal vendors selling formally produced bottled water— such as those selling Pepsico Aquafina on the street corners of Ha Noi, Viet Nam.

Unlike informal services, formal water services are capital intensive, involve large-scale infrastructure, and use modern technologies. For example, desalination and wastewater recycling are officially recognized formalized entities, often with state backing, and can potentially deliver high-quality water services (Figure 6).

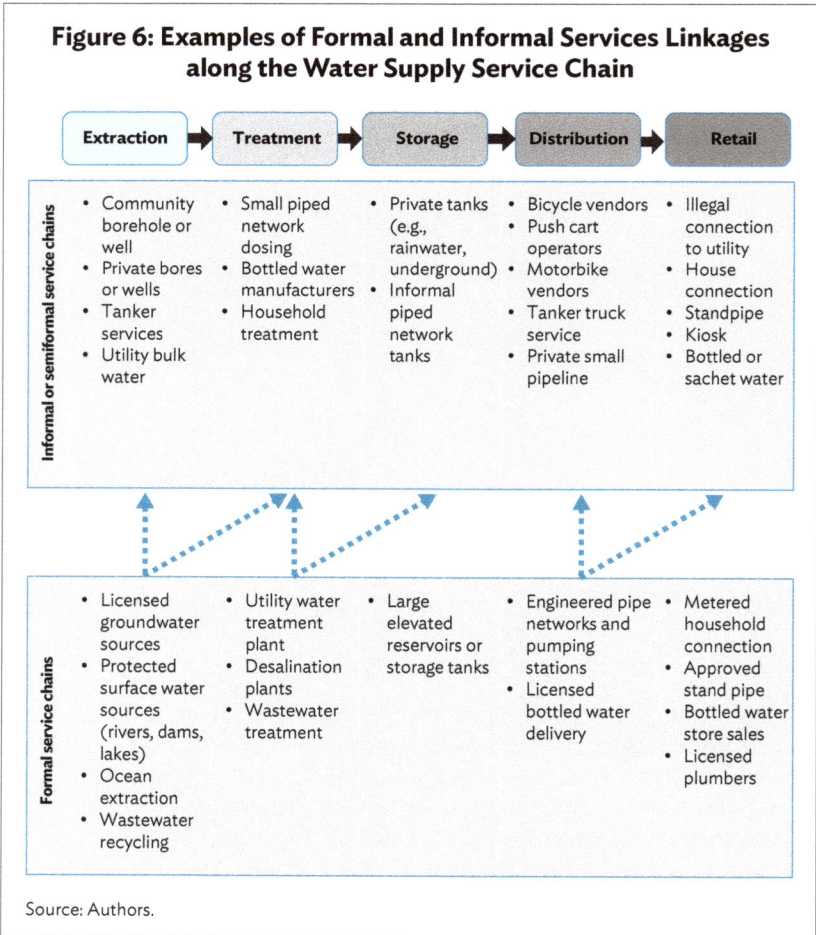

Figure 6: Examples of Formal and Informal Services Linkages along the Water Supply Service Chain

Extraction	Treatment	Storage	Distribution	Retail

Informal or semiformal service chains

• Community borehole or well • Private bores or wells • Tanker services • Utility bulk water	• Small piped network dosing • Bottled water manufacturers • Household treatment	• Private tanks (e.g., rainwater, underground) • Informal piped network tanks	• Bicycle vendors • Push cart operators • Motorbike vendors • Tanker truck service • Private small pipeline	• Illegal connection to utility • House connection • Standpipe • Kiosk • Bottled or sachet water

Formal service chains

• Licensed groundwater sources • Protected surface water sources (rivers, dams, lakes) • Ocean extraction • Wastewater recycling	• Utility water treatment plant • Desalination plants • Wastewater treatment	• Large elevated reservoirs or storage tanks	• Engineered pipe networks and pumping stations • Licensed bottled water delivery	• Metered household connection • Approved stand pipe • Bottled water store sales • Licensed plumbers

Source: Authors.

3. Methodology

The overview of water and sanitation services in Asia and service providers meeting demand in South and Southeast Asia draws from published literature and other secondary data sources, supplemented by ADB staff interviews and the authors' pooled experience from research and practice.

Field research was necessary to obtain insights on different service providers. Case studies in Bangladesh, Cambodia, Nepal, and the Philippines illuminate how informal demand is being met. Data for most of the water supply and sanitation case studies are drawn from fieldwork commissioned by ADB to the Toilet Board Coalition (TBC) and Eau et Vie. TBC is a business-led, membership-based global nonprofit organization that works with private businesses, entrepreneurs, investors, and governments to scale up market-based solutions to progress toward universal access to sanitation. Eau et Vie is a French NGO that helps establish social enterprises and local associations to improve water, sanitation, and waste conditions in deprived neighborhoods of Bangladesh and the Philippines.

Supplementary information for Southeast Asia is provided by a case study on a rural water kiosk model in Cambodia, with data drawn from reports by 1001fontaines—a French NGO working to improve the health of vulnerable populations by supporting small enterprises to produce and deliver affordable, safe drinking water.

The case studies and data collection methods, along with a description of the services, users, and the relationship with formal services, are summarized in Table 3.

The case studies were selected to explore viable and sustainable water and sanitation service provision in poor urban informal housing areas in South and Southeast Asia. The primary data were collected through surveys, semi-structured key informant interviews, and focus group discussions (FGDs). Gender inclusion was an important element in the survey and FGD methodology, with data disaggregated by gender where possible.

TBC's case studies were selected if they met four criteria: the service provider was operational before the COVID-19 pandemic (prior to March 2020); facilities or services are provided in informal settlements or low-income communities; a unique business model or sanitation solution is offered; and service providers are willing to participate in the study. From the five selected service providers, business leaders (owners, managers, or representatives), frontliners (workers who clean and maintain toilet facilities and/or deal directly with sanitation facility users), and customers (people who use the sanitation facilities or service) participated in the study. The five business leaders (one per enterprise) completed a brief survey, participated in a semi-structured interview with TBC, and joined an FGD. Frontliners—5 female and 10 male employees—completed a short survey. Customers—160 female and 148 male—were selected using simple random sampling, and completed a short survey on sanitation use and priorities.

Eau et Vie selected their case studies based on shared characteristics: (i) same number of beneficiaries, (ii) both connected to the water network in 2018, and (iii) same period of intervention by Eau et Vie. Data collection methods included women-only and community-level FGDs (31 women and 9 men participated in Bangladesh, and 21 women and 11 men in the Philippines), as well as key informant interviews with four government stakeholders and two water delivery providers.

Fieldwork for both TBC and Eau et Vie was conducted from October to November 2021. Secondary data sources, such as operational reports, previous publications, and previous surveys, were also used.

Primary data collection at the seven case study locations included information on COVID-19 impacts and responses. It is supplemented by ADB's 2021 *COVID-19 and Water in Asia and the Pacific Guidance Note*. The primary research itself was impacted by COVID-19, requiring fieldwork to be conducted using social distancing and hygiene best practices, following local regulations effective at the time.

Table 3: Summary of Water and Sanitation Case Studies and Data Collection Methods

Service Provider (SP)	Location	Service(s) Provided	Service Area and Population Served	Relationship to Formal Services	Data Collection		
					Surveys	KIIs	FGDs
TPA Social business	Guizo, Mandaue City, Cebu, Philippines	Household piped water connection	1,400 people/308 households served by 282 connections	TPA buys bulk water from MCWD under a 10-year memorandum of agreement		x	x
SJP Social enterprise	9 Number Bridge, Chattogram, Bangladesh	Household piped water connections, household latrines or shared toilets blocks	1,900 people/447 households served by 450 contracts	SJP buys bulk water from CWSA		x	x
Bhumijo Social enterprise	Dhaka, Rangpur, Khulna, Narayanganj, Bangladesh	Community and public toilet operations	250–260 users/day Over 15 facilities at 6,000 people/day	Connected to sewerage if available; land provided by local governments	x	x	x
Aerosan Social enterprise	Swoyambhu, Nepal	Female-focused and inclusive community sanitation facility with treatment	Six locations with approx. 400 users/day pre-COVID-19	Working with local government on the provision of land during the pandemic	x	x	x
Laguna Water, A joint venture of PGL and Manila Water	Barangay San Antonio, Santa Rosa City, Laguna, Philippines	Sanitation and water service utility, including desludging of septic tanks	Desludging services provided to Laguna Water customers; 5,500 households	Laguna Water is a formal utility	x	x	x
1001fontaines Social enterprise working with local entrepreneurs	Cambodia	Water kiosks provide a 20-liter container drinking water delivery service	270 water services supplying 25% of the rural population	Extracts and treats water in cooperation with local governments	Report only		

CWSA = Chattogram Water and Sewerage Authority, FGD = focus group discussion, KII = key informant interview, MCWD = Metropolitan Cebu Water District, PGL = Provincial Government of Laguna, SJP = Shobar Jonno Pani, TPA = Tubig Pag Asa Inc.

Source: Authors.

4. Discussion and Analysis

4.1 Informal Service Providers in South and Southeast Asia

Across South and Southeast Asia, informal service providers perform a critical supply function where formal services cannot affordably serve the entire urban population.

Sanitation

Informal household sanitation includes builders and owners of unhygienic hanging latrines in Manila, Philippines; Pekalongan and Tegal, Central Java, Indonesia; and Dhaka, Bangladesh, as well as builders and users of unimproved, unhygienic, dry pit latrines in Ambon, Indonesia.[4] There is also a rural market for fecal sludge from urban areas as a valuable soil supplement. Likewise, there are formal initiatives to safely reuse treated fecal sludge in Bangladesh, Cambodia, and Indonesia (Blackett and Hawkins 2017).

Informal sanitation. Overhung or hanging latrines such as this one in Pekalongan, Indonesia are suspended above water bodies. They are unhygienic and pollute rivers, canals, and the sea (photo by Isabel Blackett).

Water

Informal water providers in Asia's urban areas are highly heterogeneous. Services include private companies or cooperatives serving thousands of households through small piped networks or tanker truck delivery (for instance, in Ho Chi Minh City), community-initiated neighborhood providers of basic water services (paid or free), resellers (in Manila, Cebu, and Jakarta), street vendors of untreated water in South Asia, and bottled water sellers in tourist hot spots such as Siem Reap, Cambodia and Bali, Indonesia. Most providers

---

[4]   A hanging toilet or latrine is a toilet built over a sea, river, or other bodies of water into which excreta drops directly (UNICEF and WHO 2018).

are independent and entrepreneurial, without formal recognition from local authorities, yet effective at serving hard-to-reach places in urban areas (McIntosh 2003).

A smaller and possibly overlooked group of informal water providers is domestic households and businesses. These self-suppliers harness hand-dug wells, tube wells, boreholes, and rainwater to meet water needs. They may differentiate between water sources and qualities for different purposes, such as using well water for washing clothes and piped water for drinking and cooking. Examples of this are found in major Asian cities and medium-sized towns in the Lao People's Democratic Republic and Viet Nam.

4.2 Delivering Services to Informal Areas

Two Modes of Delivery

The case studies illustrate two predominant modes of service delivery for water and sanitation in informal areas: private household facilities (piped water, private latrines) and shared facilities at the community level (shared taps and community sanitation hubs).

Private Services

Almost all families aspire to have private water and sanitation services for convenience, control of use, and privacy. For private services, the household accepts responsibility for paying regular bills and operating and maintaining their facilities. The Eau et Vie case studies in Bangladesh and the Philippines show that an intermediary can make this aspiration possible at an affordable price and at scale through a delegated management arrangement with a local service operator, such as Shobar Jonno Pani (SJP) or Tubig Pag Asa Inc. (TPA) (WSUP 2013).

Community Services

Where household-level services are not possible due to cost, space, or other constraints, shared community or public facilities can overcome many barriers to services outlined in Table 2. Such community sanitation and water facilities can also provide additional value and benefits such as laundry facilities; sale of soap and menstrual hygiene management products; and opportunities for employment, social interaction, and information dissemination. They can also be well-constructed and overcome challenging environments, for example, regular flooding or high groundwater. However, communal facilities require an intermediary or other entity to pay water, electricity, and sewerage bills and to manage, operate, clean, and maintain the facilities.

The Case for Intermediaries

For informal urban residents in Bangladesh, Cambodia, Nepal, and the Philippines, water and sanitation service delivery often involves small and medium-sized enterprises (SMEs) as intermediaries between residents and the formal sector. These SMEs range in legal status from informal to formal businesses.

Unlike large utilities at scale, social enterprises, SMEs, and NGOs can be flexible, creative, and innovative in response to the needs of particular informal settlements and can deliver decentralized services in support of the SDGs. These service providers see daily needs as a business or social enterprise opportunity. They have developed many ways to overcome service delivery barriers. The case studies reveal the following common aspects among these suppliers:

- **Formalized relationships.** The suppliers have strong formal ties with local government or utility services, which may be based on a memorandum of agreement or understanding and include formal business registration and operating permits. Good working relationships with local government and utilities are essential for approving land for communal, shared, or public facilities and for preventing obstruction of operations.
- **Capacity for scale.** The suppliers have the capacity to deliver, at scale, quality, clean, reliable, sustainable, and affordable water and sanitation services to the whole community.
- **Responsive services.** The suppliers can provide adaptable, flexible, and responsive services to meet the circumstances and needs of poor households, such as decentralized communal facilities, payment methods that match the ability to pay, and agility in responding to changed circumstances.
- **Community relations.** The suppliers have the potential for long-term, deep community relations and meaningful community engagement. The physical presence of social enterprises in the community, regular meetings, and community interaction build social capital and trust.
- **"Parent organization" relationships.** The suppliers have an established connection to an international, parent organization that provides support and adds value to the services offered.

These organizations can provide critical setup support and capital costs, ongoing capacity building, networking among similar organizations, and specialist technical advice.

An example of a social enterprise as an intermediary is SJP in Bangladesh, which operates between the city utility and the community and households (Figure 7). A local NGO—Water and Life Bangladesh, which is part of the international Eau et Vie organization—assisted with setting-up and capital costs, provided capacity building, and delivers complementary activities, including hygiene promotion, firefighting, and community empowerment.

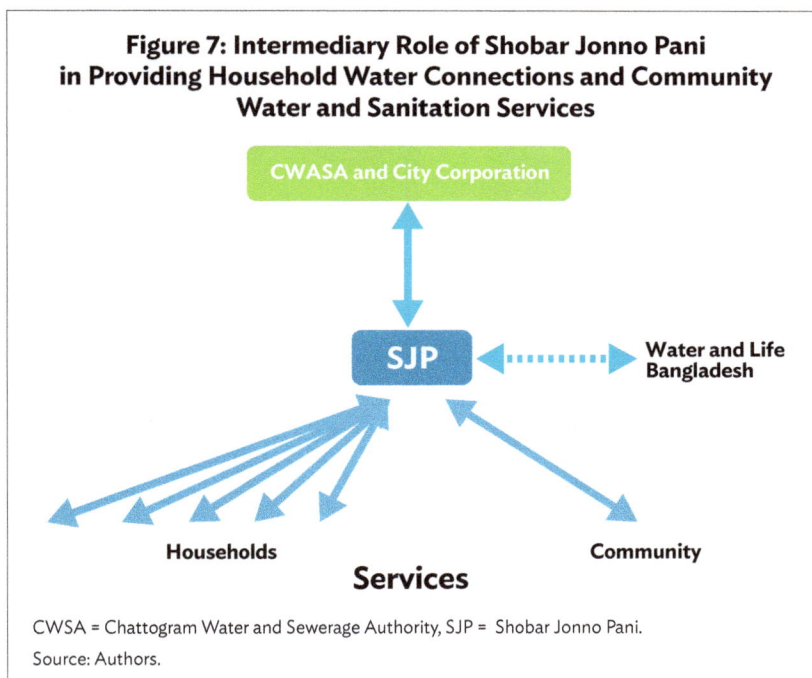

Figure 7: Intermediary Role of Shobar Jonno Pani in Providing Household Water Connections and Community Water and Sanitation Services

CWSA = Chattogram Water and Sewerage Authority, SJP = Shobar Jonno Pani.
Source: Authors.

The aforementioned five common aspects of the case studies may raise questions about the scalability, capacity, and financial sustainability of services provided by intermediaries. However, the evidence mostly quells these concerns.

The case studies vary by the number of customers served per day (Table 3) but show actual or potential to scale when the enterprises' number of sites is considered. For sanitation, Aerosan in Nepal has six locations averaging 800 customers per day and Bhumijo in Bangladesh has 15 locations serving 6,000 people per day. For water supply, Laguna Water in the Philippines has 116,000 customers across three cities, which provides an opportunity to scale its sewerage service. Under the Eau et Vie banner, TPA in the Philippines has, since 2008, scaled up to 18 communities serving 6,058 households; and SJP in Bangladesh has two locations serving 2,200 low-income households. 1001fontaines in Cambodia has 272 water kiosk services throughout the country, and in 2019, it expanded to Viet Nam and Myanmar. However, 1001fontaines (2020) estimates 20% of local operators or entrepreneurs fail despite a largely successful model, even with the parent organization's oversight and support.

Ongoing capacity building is a feature of the case studies, particularly where the parent organization has a strong and continuing presence, such as an international NGO (Eau et Vie, 1001fontaines, TBC) or links to research organizations. For example, 1001fontaines trains entrepreneurs and provides ongoing support through technical platforms in three areas of Cambodia. Eau et Vie brings to Bangladesh valuable international technical expertise on water, sanitation, and hygiene

Public sanitation facilities. An Aerosan toilet center in Kathmandu, Nepal serves nearby market customers and is clean and well lit (photo by AeroSan).

and water quality treatment. Ongoing support focused on learning, sharing, and capacity development for some sanitation case studies.

Typically, in most Asian and OECD countries, the capital investment costs of water and sanitation systems are fully or heavily subsidized. However, businesses and enterprises can only survive by paying the full management, operating, and maintenance costs from revenue earned from customers. Table 4 outlines the common funding sources for different categories of water and sanitation service providers. The table demonstrates that the private sector and NGOs have fewer and less-secure options for operation and maintenance costs, and this is a driver for efficiency, good billing and collection, and high-quality services for which customers are willing to pay. The case studies show that customers are willing to pay for better, safer, cleaner, and more reliable services—at affordable prices—instead of free but poor quality, inconvenient, or more expensive alternatives (WaterAid 2016).

**Table 4: Funding Sources for Public, Nongovernment,
and Private Water Supply and Sanitation Services**

Financing Requirement	Funding Sources for Water and Sanitation Services		
	Government Departments and Utilities	NGOs and CBOs	Private Sector (including social, small, and medium-sized enterprises)
Capital infrastructure investments	International loans to central governments, national budgets from taxes, customer receipts, private capital	Local and international grants, often linked to an international or local NGO	Private loans, savings, profits, innovation grants
Management, operation and maintenance of services	Customer tariffs and revenue, inter-government transfers and subsidies	Customer fees, tariffs, and income from complementary services	Customer revenue, profits, and diverse product offerings
Institutional and staff capacity building	National budgets, grants as part of international loans, international technical assistance project	International or local NGO support, grants from foundations and institutes	Revenue and profits, technical assistance project implementation, research grants

CBO = community-based organization, NGO = nongovernment organization.
Source: Authors.

4.3   Innovations and Transformative Interventions in Serving Informal Settlements

As outlined in Section 2 and Table 2, poor, informal urban communities face many barriers to accessing formal services. Overcoming these barriers requires service providers to innovate and take risks. The case studies highlight how intermediaries address the service provision gap and achieve scale.

Sanitation Hub Facilities

Sanitation hubs are public or community facilities that include toilets, bathing, laundry, and water supply. Typically, these are women-centered and disability-friendly (Aerosan in Nepal and Bhumijo in Bangladesh). They usually include good lighting, access ramps, female caretakers, dispensers for sanitary products, and diaper changing tables.

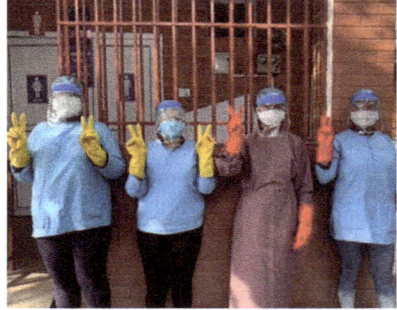

Worker protection. Informal services can still be safe and clean as demonstrated by the personal protective equipment worn by female staff of Aerosan toilets in Nepal (photo by Aerosan).

Water is sourced from public piped supplies where possible. Otherwise, water is delivered by tanker to storage (Bhumijo), or rainwater and recycled water are used (Aerosan).

Where possible, the sanitation hubs and toilets are connected to sewers (Bhumijo); elsewhere, waste is treated on-site in septic tanks (Bhumijo) or biodigesters (Aerosan).

The Aerosan sanitation hubs are environment friendly and include water-saving, graywater recycling, rainwater harvesting, energy-saving, and solar lighting. They are also kept very clean. Aerosan refers to their team as "hygiene hosts," akin to flight attendants.

Sanitation services. Laguna Water Staff emptying a septic tank in Laguna, Philippines (photo by Laguna Water).

Other operating innovations include monthly family subscriptions (not pay per use) and digital payments.

The Laguna Water Utility provides FSM septic tank emptying services to all customers where a sewerage connection is impossible. Laguna Water takes full responsibility for the wastewater generated from the water they supply. All customers pay for water and sanitation services, which they receive irrespective of whether sewers are in their neighborhood.

Quality Water Supply Services

The water supply case studies from Bangladesh and the Philippines demonstrate innovation in providing quality service by setting performance criteria: access to legal and reliable water sources (such as city utilities like the Dhaka Water Supply and Sewerage Authority), a sufficient quantity with at least 50 liters of water per person per day with 24/7 availability, meeting national standards for water quality, and an affordable price for low-income inhabitants. A connection policy for extremely poor households (Bangladesh) further reduces remaining barriers to inclusive access.

Since taking over poorly run urban water supplies in 2009, Laguna Water has improved its service levels to help ensure that safe and affordable water is accessible and available to all—through good pressure, 24-hour supply of high-quality water meeting national quality standards to an increased service area.

The social enterprises operate as "mini utilities," providing water treatment, water testing (1001fontaines), network operations and maintenance (SJP and TPA), billing, and customer support (1001fontaines, SJP, and TPA). Adding chlorine treatment guarantees quality water (to a better standard than the utility supplying the water). This production and delivery of consistently high-quality drinking water is also a feature of 1001fontaines in Cambodia. Water is treated and tested monthly in the NGO's laboratory and biannually by the Cambodian Ministry of Mines and Energy.

Household connections are the mode of service delivery in Bangladesh and the Philippines. They are regulated by individual, high-quality, precision meters placed in clustered meter cages to prevent vandalism. Such focus on quality compliance and quality service delivery produces loyal customers who trust the social enterprise.

Another innovative feature is the long-term memorandum of agreement with the utility. These have been in place for 10 years in Bangladesh between SJP and Chattogram Water and Sewerage Authority, and

Asset protection. Shobar Jonno Pani (SJP) protects clusters of water meters in locked cages in Bangladesh (photo by SJP).

between TPA and Metro Cebu Water District in the Philippines; some arrangements in the Philippines are for up to 15 years. Such long-term commitment allows social enterprises to recover operational expenditure costs and cover ongoing technical assistance.

A reliable water source in low-income communities can also improve emergency and firefighting responses, which are especially critical in densely populated informal settlements where fires prove devastating.

Firefighting and women's empowerment. With access to a reliable water supply, women in Bangladesh learn how to operate firefighting equipment and hoses—critical to emergency response in dense poor settlements (photo by Shobar Jonno Pani).

With water supply provided by the social enterprises SJP and TPA, Water and Life, an NGO, delivers firefighting equipment and training to volunteers, with support from local fire authorities. Volunteer brigades are then able to respond in case of fire.

Digital Technology

The service providers being discussed were early adopters of digital technology, including e-toilets with automation, remote monitoring, and digital water supply billing systems.

The COVID-19 pandemic accelerated and increased the use of digital technology in the informal and formal water and sanitation sectors. It also boosted automation and remote-control processes in formal utilities and increased socially distanced customer-utility interactions conducted via phone, apps, or the internet (Butler et al. 2020). Change is evident in the following areas:

Staff and company management. All the service providers reported using multiple platforms to communicate between management and staff, including WhatsApp, MS Teams, Viber, Telegram, Messenger, and Zoom, as well as mobile calls and texts. Staff meetings were held on MS Teams or Zoom.

User engagement and communication. Enterprises communicated with their customers in even more ways. Digital communications included Facebook, messaging via Barangay Information channels (Laguna), WhatsApp, Zoom, phone calls, Messenger, and office mobile

(Bhumijo). They also used physical signs and messages boards at the toilet facilities (Aerosan). During the lockdown, community water awareness sessions were conducted via phone, instead of community meetings (TPA).

Billing and revenue records. While bill collectors still go door-to-door in most cases (except Laguna), the billing list is downloaded onto a phone or tablet. Using specific software, household payments are entered digitally at the point of payment.

ভূমিজ পাবলিক টয়লেট সেবার
চার্জ পরিশোধ করা এখন আরো সহজ

Payments made easy. Bhumijo's introduction of payment by Bcash improved user experience and boosted the brand (photo by Bhumijo).

Digital payments. All the sanitation service providers have introduced online and digital payment methods, including radio-frequency identification cards, QR codes, and mobile app-based payments. Bhumijo said the payment innovations boosted the brand and users' experience, with some likening it to a "five-star hotel" experience. Prior to the pandemic, Bhumijo and Laguna Water had developed plans to introduce digital payments. They accelerated those plans, and most have launched the service. Aerosan is in the initial stages of establishing online payments, as most of its customers are comfortable paying cash.

The shift to online payments and the reduction in cash is evident in Laguna Water's accounts, with a decline in cash since April 2019 offset by a commensurate increase in online payments through a local app called GCash (Figure 8).

New technologies and payment options can help bridge the gap between suppliers and users. However, social enterprises reported the apps were not useful for improving bill payments when households suffered financial difficulties, which many did from the economic fallout of the COVID-19 pandemic.

Figure 8: Reduction in Laguna Water Cash Payments

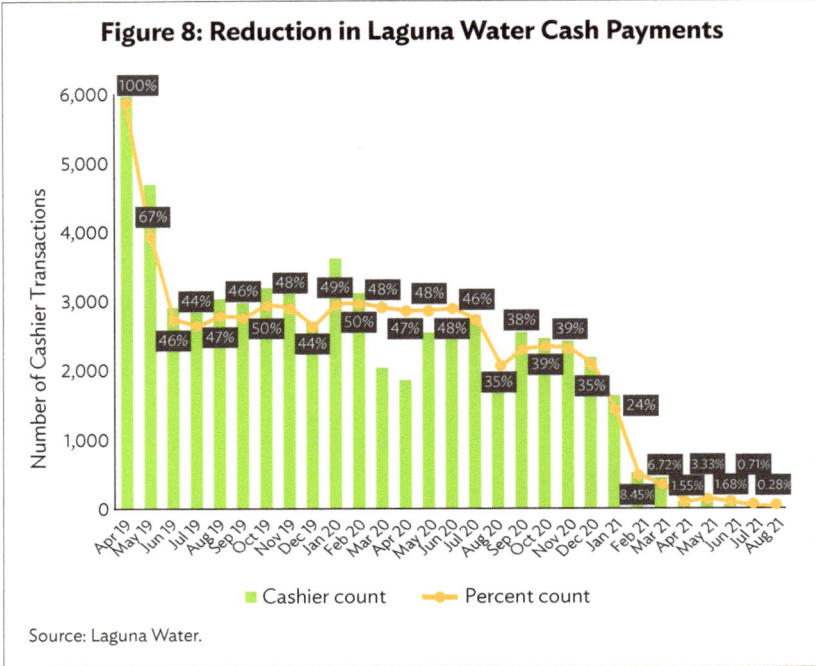

Source: Laguna Water.

4.4 Impacts and Benefits

This research also revealed that services in informal settlements provided by intermediaries can yield several significant benefits, such as the following:

Reliable service provision. Provide reliable, clean, and safe services for residents excluded from formal services due to lack of land and house tenure, space to build, or low income.

Public health benefits. Improve public health by reducing open defecation; addressing the lack of potable water; increasing water availability for bathing, laundry, and handwashing; and providing hygienic water storage.

Improved safety for women. Promote dignity and security for women and girls by circumventing the need for open defecation or using undignified, dirty facilities. In-house or proximate water supply makes for hygienic household water management by relieving women from the time-consuming and costly chore of collecting water from distant, unreliable, or crowded sources. Clean, private, and convenient toilets enable dignified, hygienic menstrual hygiene management.

Positive social outcomes. Through organized, equitable, and fairly priced water services, promote positive social outcomes, such as reduced community conflict over water (TPA), suppression of criminal networks exploiting the water market (SJP), and reduced vandalism of water infrastructure (TPA).

Environmental benefits. Promote a cleaner environment and help address climate impacts. 1001fontaines estimates an averted 17,000 tons of carbon dioxide emissions annually through climate-positive water production (including solar power) compared with household treatment of water by boiling (1001fontaines).

Community engagement and trust. Improve community engagement and trust through decentralized, resilient services that are customer-focused, and communicate effectively.

Employment creation. Create local jobs and employment for marginalized community members, which in turn boosts the local economy. In Cambodia, 1001fontaines (Teuk Saat 1001) employs more than 900 people (about 3 per service); in Bangladesh, SJP employs 98% of staff from the local areas (50% from within the area of intervention), 35% of whom are women; and intermediaries in the Philippines and Bangladesh create local opportunities for plumbers, bill collectors, community organizers, caretakers, engineers, branch managers, and field coordinators.

Add-on services. Offer many more add-on services than typical utility-style water and sanitation services. With support from their partners, intermediaries offer a platform for complementary actions— hygiene promotion, firefighting and emergency management, and solid waste management.

4.5 Learning from the Impact of COVID-19

Local lockdown policies for the COVID-19 pandemic varied but had the largest effect on sanitation hub services provided in markets and city centers due to the lack of customers as people stayed at home (Aerosan). Community water and sanitation services, however, were mostly sustained (SJP, TPA, Bhumijo, and Laguna Water), and even expanded in some places because people stayed home more (Bhumijo) or had returned home, such as returning migrants to Cambodia (1001fontaines) from Thailand. Figure 9 illustrates the changes in the use of sanitation facilities, which were not all uniform and depended on the services' location.

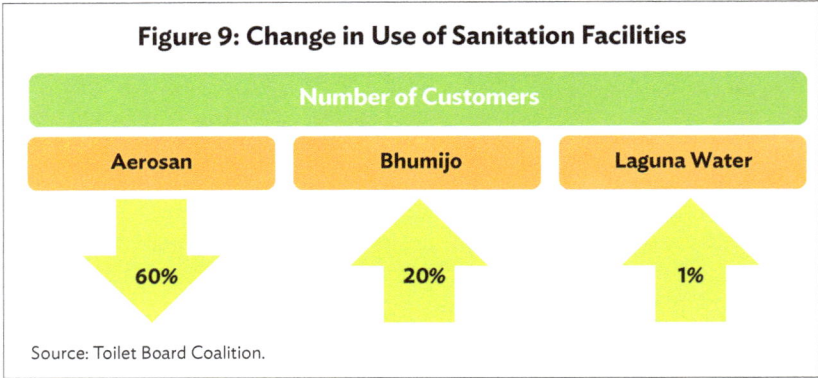

Figure 9: Change in Use of Sanitation Facilities

Number of Customers

Aerosan	Bhumijo	Laguna Water
60%	20%	1%

Source: Toilet Board Coalition.

Most water supply and sanitation services were sustained as basic needs. Most bulk water supply utilities continued to supply water to the intermediaries (Eau et Vie and Laguna Water).

In communities, the use of both water and sanitation services was maintained or increased (TBC, Eau et Vie, 1001fontaines). However, in Nepal, Aerosan users adapted to only occasionally using public toilets due to limited mobility (Figure 10). They reported using "open areas," "jungle areas," or "bushes" as open defecation and urination alternatives (TBC 2021).

Desludging septic tanks was not considered an essential service in the Philippines. Such

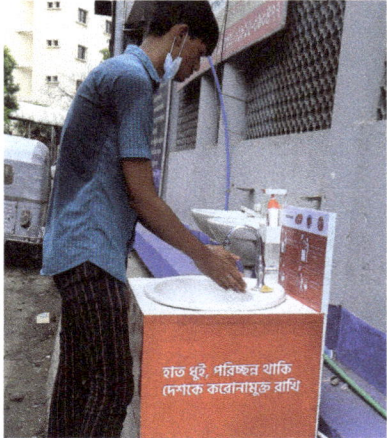

Contactless hygiene products. Pedal-operated handwashing basins are part of the new smart hygienic technology developed (photo by Bhujimo).

services were paused during the strictest COVID-19 lockdown in 2020 until an exception could be secured from the government.

The pandemic stoked innovations in the sanitation business sector. In Bangladesh, Bhumijo installed user feedback devices and footfall counting to facilitate remote monitoring and inform cleaning schedules. Bhumijo and Laguna Water reassigned staff to their innovative research and development teams.

Figure 10: Frequency of Sanitation Facility Use

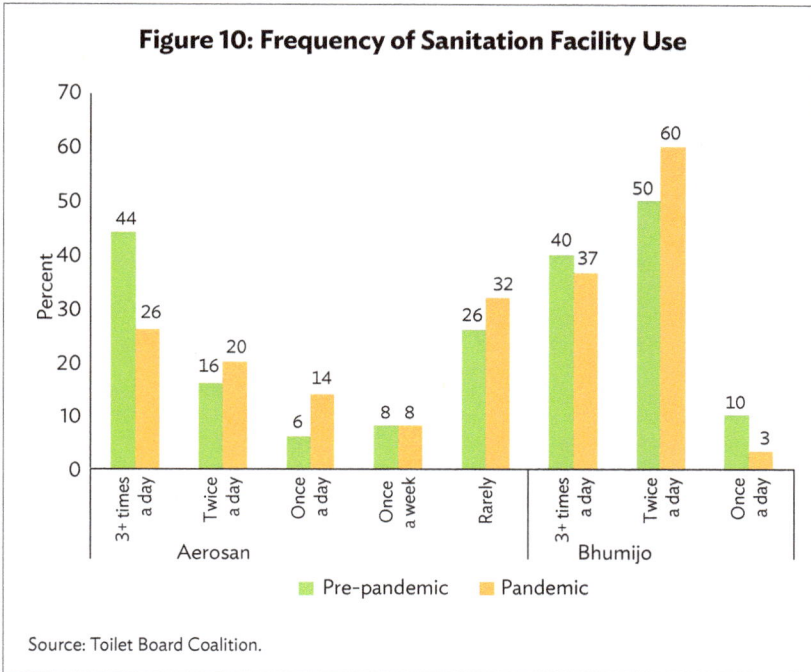

Source: Toilet Board Coalition.

The pandemic also accelerated investment in smart hygienic technology, such as air hand-dryers, sensors, and pedal-operated taps. Aerosan installed footfall counting devices, diaper changing stations, and sensor-based urinals. Bhumijo created a new pedal-operated flushing system and pedal-operated handwashing stations. They sold these devices to government bodies, local businesses, and development organizations. The sales helped stabilize their cash flow.

Innovations in water supply delivery were driven by the need to continue this essential service within the constraints of social distancing and lockdowns. Meter readings ceased, a phone hotline was installed to report emergency repairs, and payment arrears policies were adapted to extend repayment time (SJP and TPA).

A water fund (supported by development partners) enabled households to access 7.5 cubic meters of free water for 2 months during COVID-19 lockdowns (Bangladesh and the Philippines). This was to ensure people could access convenient quality water rather than having to use inferior quality or hazardous water sources or make illegal connections to the system. In Cambodia, 1001fontaines worked with

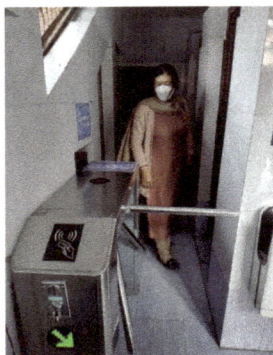

Monitoring technology. Footfall counting devices were installed to monitor user numbers and cleaning needs (photo by AeroSan).

Women-centered. Sensor-operated hand-washing basins, menstrual hygiene management facilities and nappy changing stations benefit women (photo by Aerosan).

commune[5] authorities to identify households that are most in need and provided them with free 20-liter bottles, hygienic products, and safe water refills for 3 months through kiosk entrepreneurs.

Water and sanitation intermediaries were important in distributing hygiene infrastructure and materials—handwashing stations, water, soap, sanitary pads, and masks—and awareness messages on the status of the services and the importance of handwashing and social distancing. These intermediaries provided critical communication links between local authorities and the community. In the case of TPA in the Philippines, these essential service providers were the only connection informal settlers had to the outside world during the mandatory COVID-19 lockdowns.

4.6 Existing and Future Challenges

Aside from the benefits and potentials of intermediaries, the case studies also highlight real-world threats and challenges experienced by service providers, both from within their organizations (internal) and beyond their spheres of direct influence (external), as well as in scaling up their operations.

---

[5]   The commune is the lowest (third) level of local administration in Cambodia (United Cities and Local Government and OECD 2016).

Internal

The financial viability of social enterprises is threatened by weak or uncertain financial sustainability and recovery of operational costs. For water supply, this starts with having a fair or discounted bulk water rate, to which the social enterprise must add their overheads.

Informal service providers rely on external support for financing capital investments, capacity building, and ongoing technical support. This support is susceptible to fluctuating funding trends and, hence, is less secure and less visible than what larger state-run utilities enjoy. In the case of water supply, ongoing support may be provided by highly subsidized NGOs (Eau et Vie, 1001fontaines).

External

Climate change and disasters, such as flooding in the Philippines and landslides in Bangladesh, threaten water and sanitation infrastructure and housing. Climate-related water resources depletion threatens the quantity of water supplied by utilities, and shortages will have knock-on effects on the services of social enterprises.

Informal settlements remain vulnerable to changing political stances, with the threat of evictions being constant in most places. Political conflicts and the souring of relationships with local government are other challenges. Stringent government regulations (Laguna Water) were also seen to adversely impact financial sustainability. Within communities, vandalism and theft of infrastructure, intimidation, and standover tactics (Bhumijo, TPA) tend to harm emerging social enterprises.

Scaling Up

Besides the internal and external threats to intermediaries mentioned above, other challenges to scaling up service delivery are posed by a lack of the following:

- **Land**. The availability of suitable land for construction of facilities with access to utilities, and sanitation locations that are convenient for and highly visible to customers.
- **Will to collaborate**. The willingness of water and sanitation or sewerage utilities and local governments to partner or engage with informal SMEs and social enterprises to serve informal demand. Including these nonconventional agents may require additional support and simplified procurement processes.

- **Capital**. Capital investment for water and sanitation infrastructure that includes nonconventional components (such as contracts with local enterprises) to enable services to informal settlements.
- **Capacity building**. During construction and setup, with continued support as needed during the early stages of operation.
- **Long-term commitment.** Support for social enterprises by highly subsidized NGOs involved in water supply—such as Eau et Vie and 1001fontaines—demands a long-term commitment.

5. Conclusion

The challenges of providing water and sanitation services for informal settlement residents remain formidable, and, in many Asian cities, will likely increase with continued urban growth. However, intermediaries provide an alternative to formal utilities to serve these underserved or excluded residents. While the appropriate types of intermediaries will vary in different contexts, their roles will broadly be similar.

The case studies that inform this chapter suggest that, by collaborating with formal water and sanitation utility services and local governments, intermediaries such as social enterprises and SMEs have proven to be effective and complementary service providers. They can sustainably serve the needs of informal settlement residents by accessing bulk water or sewerage services from utilities and larger private providers, and by leveraging external grant funding. However, development financing institutions, such as banks and multilateral and bilateral agencies, do not yet widely recognize the fact that the option of leveraging intermediaries offers significant benefits.

This chapter has provided evidence of the innovation, agility, and resilience that diverse and decentralized social enterprises and SMEs bring to the water and sanitation sector, and their roles in bridging formal services and customers in Asia's informal settlements. It also highlighted how using intermediaries offers multifarious benefits that frequently extend beyond technical gains to include social and gender equity gains. Amid pressures of the COVID-19 pandemic, and the associated burden on service providers, these social enterprises remained dedicated to providing and sustaining quality services, with sensitivity, to the vulnerable communities they serve. Rather than collapsing during the pandemic, these social enterprises found innovative ways to adapt, which underscores their resiliency.

Recommendations for Improving Development Partner Effectiveness

ADB, other development financing institutions, and bilateral development partners can support the transformation of service delivery to informal communities in several ways, including the following:

- **Supporting utility partnerships with small and medium-scale local service providers.** Financing institutions and development partners should actively encourage client utilities to seek opportunities to supply bulk water and connect sewerage systems to small and medium-scale businesses, social enterprises, CBOs, and NGOs to fulfill SDG objectives and serve informal settlements and slums. This can benefit the utilities' revenue, enabling the extension of services, increasing sales, and reducing nonrevenue water, with minimal additional billing and revenue collection and without the operations and maintenance workload.

- **Applying effective "intermediary" models and examples from proximate or comparable countries.** Development banks and partners can use their knowledge platforms to share regionally about these models. They can also support the tailoring of these models to different situations or countries, and in demonstrating their scalability.

- **Adopting less bureaucratic procurement and related processes to enable nonconventional service providers to apply and compete for contracts and funding.** Development banks and partners can facilitate these to be less demanding for small local subcontracts, and therefore include a wider range of service providers, while maintaining transparency and accountability.

- **Investing in capacity development of informal service providers to build skills and help sustain services.** This could involve reserving places for SMEs, social enterprises, NGOs, and CBOs in capacity-building activities of internationally financed projects (even if the intermediary is not a direct project beneficiary), as well as including them in development-partner-initiated study tours, webinars, and workshops on water and sanitation topics. The participation of women should be emphasized.

- **Encouraging CBOs and NGOs.** CBOs and NGOs should be encouraged to pursue scaling up, reduce dependency, and seek full cost recovery of local management, operation, and maintenance costs from the start. These prudent actions are possible even when serving the poorest customers.

The lessons learned from the case studies should encourage governments, water supply and sanitation utilities, and development financing institutions, including ADB, to incorporate intermediate service providers as valuable partners in large-scale investments in water and sanitation service delivery. These case studies provide important, previously undocumented evidence of the flexibility and resilience of intermediaries and highlight their vital role toward achieving the SDG goals in Asia's towns and cities.

References

1001fontaines. 2020. *Cambodia Economic Sustainability Report*. Paris.

———. n.d. *Water Kiosk Delivery Service: Bridging the Safe Drinking Water Gap in Underserved Areas*. Paris.

Ahlers, R. et al. 2014. Informal Space in the Urban Waterscape: Disaggregation and Co-Production of Water Services. *Water Alternatives* 7 (1): 1–14.

Arias-Granada, Y. et al. 2018. *Water and Sanitation in Dhaka Slums: Access, Quality, and Informality in Service Provision*. Policy Research Paper 8552. Washington, DC: World Bank.

Asian Development Bank (ADB). 2017. *Meeting Asia's Infrastructure Needs*. Manila.

———. 2019. *Asian Development Outlook 2019 Update: Fostering Growth and Inclusion in Asia's Cities*. Manila.

Baeumler, A. et al. 2021. *Demographic Trends and Urbanization*. Washington, DC: World Bank.

Bauer, G. K. 2020. An Effective Response to COVID-19 Requires Innovative Water and Sanitation Services. *Mobile for Development*. 22 April. https://www.gsma.com/mobilefordevelopment/programme/digital-utilities/an-effective-response-to-covid-19-requires-innovative-water-and-sanitation-services/.

Birkmann, J. et al. 2016. Boost Resilience of Small and Mid-Sized Cities. *Nature* 537: 605–608.

Blackett, I. and P. Hawkins. 2017. *FSM Innovation*. Seattle: Bill & Melinda Gates Foundation.

Butler G. et al. 2020. *The Impact of COVID-19 on the Water and Sanitation Sector*. Washington, DC: International Finance Corporation, The World Bank.

Cambodia News English. 2021. Siem Reap Residents Illegally Connecting Sewers to New Network. *Cambodia News English*. 17 March. https://cne.wtf/2021/03/17/siem-reap-residents-illegally-connecting-sewers-to-new-network/.

Chen, M. A., and V. A. Beard. 2018. *Including the Excluded: Supporting Informal Workers for More Equal and Productive Cities in the Global South*. Working Paper. Washington, DC: World Resources Institute.

Conan, H. 2004. *Small Piped Water Networks: Helping Local Entrepreneurs to Invest*. Manila: ADB.

CRC for Water Sensitive Cities. 2018. *Strengthening the Delivery of WASH in Urban Informal Settlements: Addressing Multiple Exposure Pathways in Urban Environments*. Melbourne, Australia: Cooperative Research Centre for Water Sensitive Cities.

Dagdeviren, H. 2008. Waiting for Miracles: The Commercialization of Urban Water Services in Zambia. *Development and Change* 39 (1): 101–121.

DOHWA Engineering Co. Ltd. 2021. *Dhaka Water Supply Network Improvement Project (DWSNIP) Consultancy for Project Development Facility (PDF).* Contract No. DWSNIP / PDF / 03.5. Feasibility Report.

Frauendorfer, R., and R. Liemberger. 2010. *The Issues and Challenges of Reducing Non-Revenue Water.* Manila: ADB.

Garrick, D. et al. 2019. *Informal Water Markets in an Urbanising World: Some Unanswered Questions.* Washington, DC: World Bank.

IGI Global. 2021. *What Is an Informal Service Provider?* https://www.igi-global.com/dictionary/existing-realities-and-sustainable-pathways-for-solid-waste-management-in-ghana/78894.

Jones, P. 2017. Formalizing the Informal: Understanding the Position of Informal Settlements and Slums in Sustainable Urbanization Policies and Strategies in Bandung, Indonesia. *Sustainability* 9 (8): 1436.

Lardoux de Pazzis, A., and A. Muret. 2021. *The Role of Intermediaries to Facilitate Water-Related Investment.* OECD Environment Working Papers. No. 180. Paris: OECD Publishing.

McDonald D. A., and G. Ruiters. 2007. Rethinking Privatisation: Towards a Critical Theoretical Perspective. *Beyond the Market: The Future of Public Services.* Amsterdam: Transnational Institute.

McIntosh, A. C. 2003. *Asian Water Supplies: Reaching the Urban Poor.* ADB and International Water Association.

Mitlin, D., and A. Walnycki. 2020. Informality as Experimentation: Water Utilities' Strategies for Cost Recovery and their Consequences for Universal Access. *The Journal of Development Studies* 56 (2): 259–277.

Mwanza, D. 2001. *Water and Sanitation Services to the Urban Poor.* 27th WEDC Conference: People and Systems for Water, Sanitation and Health. Lusaka, Zambia.

Office of the High Commissioner for Human Rights. 2020. COVID-19 Pandemic and the Human Rights to Water and Sanitation. *UN Water.* 17 November. https://www.unwater.org/covid-19-pandemic-and-the-human-rights-to-water-and-sanitation/.

O'Keefe, M., C. Lüthi, I. Tumwebaze, and R. Tobias. 2015. Opportunities and Limits to Market-Driven Sanitation Services: Evidence from Urban Informal Settlements in East Africa. *Environment & Urbanization* 27 (2): 421–440.

Roaf V., A. Potter, I. Ngunjiri, and B. Schreiner. n.d. *Human Rights and Water Integrity Implications for Informal Settlement Water and Sanitation.* Water Integrity Network and Socio-Economic Rights Institute.

Schrecongost A., and K. Wong. 2015. *Unsettled: Water and Sanitation in Urban Communities of the Pacific.* Washington, DC: World Bank.

Singh, S. 2019. *Achieving Sustainable Sanitation in Asia.* Policy Brief. No. 2019-4. Tokyo: ADB Institute.

Sinharoy, S., R. Pittluck, and T. Clasen. 2019. Review of Drivers and Barriers of Water and Sanitation Policies for Urban Informal Settlements in Low-Income and Middle-Income Countries. *Utilities Policy* 60.

Sitha, S. 2021. Phnom Penh Water Supply Authority's Path to Progress. *The Source Magazine.* 26 November. International Water Association (IWA). https://www.thesourcemagazine.org/phnom-penh-water-supply-authoritys-path-to-progress/.

Souter, S., and P. Orams. 2019. *Water and Sanitation Services for Informal Settlements in Honiara, Solomon Islands.* Washington, DC: International Bank for Reconstruction and Development, The World Bank.

Toilet Board Coalition (TBC). 2021. *Impact of the COVID-19 Pandemic on the Sanitation Service Provision and Delivery in Informal Settlements in Asia.* Geneva.

Tutusaus, M., R. A. Surya, and K. Schwartz. 2019. Degrees and Forms of Commercialization: Community-Managed Water Operators in Lamongan Regency, Indonesia. *Water.* 11 (10): 1985.

UN-Habitat. 2015. Informal Settlements. *Habitat III Issue Papers* 22.

_____. 2021. Urban Indicators Database. https://data.unhabitat.org/pages/housing-slums-and-informal-settlements (accessed 9 November 2021).

United Cities and Local Governments and OECD. 2016. Cambodia profile. https://www.oecd.org/regional/regional-policy/profile-Cambodia.pdf

United Nations Children's Fund (UNICEF) and World Health Organization (WHO). 2018. *Core Questions on Drinking Water, Sanitation and Hygiene for Household Surveys: 2018 Update.* New York.

United Nations General Assembly. 2010. *Human Right to Water and Sanitation.* Resolution 64/292.

Water and Sanitation for the Urban Poor (WSUP). 2013. *Getting to Scale in Urban Water Supply.* Topic Brief. London.

_____. 2018. *Improving the Performance of Water Entrepreneurs in Urban Kisemu, Kenya.* Practice Note. London.

WaterAid. 2016. *Water: At What Cost? The State of the World's Water 2016.*

World Bank, International Labour Organization, WaterAid, and World Health Organization. 2019. *Health, Safety and Dignity of Sanitation Workers: An Initial Assessment.* Washington, DC: World Bank.

World Bank Group and Water and Sanitation Program. 2015. *Improving On-Site Sanitation and Connections to Sewers in Southeast Asia: Insights from Indonesia and Vietnam.* Washington, DC: World Bank.

7

Examining Micro and Small Enterprises from a Gender Perspective in Urban Cambodia

Dil B. Rahut, Jeetendra Prakash Aryal, Panharoth Chhay, and Peter J. Morgan

Abstract

Micro and small enterprises (MSEs) provide livelihood opportunities for a large population, especially for the poor. Participation in MSEs depends on the individuals' and households' financial, human, physical, natural, and social capitals. As the literature on developing countries has found that men and women have differential access to and ownership of productive resources, this study uses the Cambodia Socio-Economic Survey 2019–2020 to examine factors influencing participation in MSEs and the associated gender differences in urban Cambodia. The current study's findings suggest that assets, education, and access to credit are crucial drivers of participation in MSEs. Applying Blinder–Oaxaca decomposition showed a gender gap in MSE participation, with women owning more MSEs than men. However, the differences in participation vary across sectors. While women have higher participation rates in retail and wholesale, restaurants, and smaller enterprises, men are more likely to participate in manufacturing, construction, and repairs. Another crucial finding of this study is that a large proportion of men-owned enterprises fall under the petty trading categories (i.e., the lowest stratum of the MSEs), indicating that gender policies also need to consider poorer and less skilled sections of society. Government policies to promote the development of MSEs should focus on two aspects: (i) skills training to enable women to also be equally able to participate in manufacturing, construction, and repairs sectors; and (ii) improved access to credit, so both men and women can participate in enterprises requiring bigger investments.

Keywords: gender, micro and small enterprise, women's participation, urban Cambodia, Blinder–Oaxaca decomposition

1. Introduction

Micro and small enterprises (MSEs) have a crucial role in sustaining the livelihoods of millions of people worldwide, providing them ways to diversify their sources of income (Erdin and Ozkaya 2020; Karlstrom 2018). More importantly, they are one of the major sources of employment in the informal sector of developing countries. In the emerging economies, micro, small, and medium-sized enterprises (MSMEs) comprise approximately 90% of total employment (Lessidrenska 2019; International Labour Office 2018).[1] In developing economies, most MSEs are informal, offering alternative sources of livelihood for the poor. An estimated 70% of the total workforce of developing countries is involved in the informal economy, either through self-employment or working in businesses that are not legally registered and considered as informal enterprises. Due to flexibility in their operations, informal sector businesses provide opportunities for the poor to work, and MSEs contribute significantly to poverty reduction (Hammond et al. 2007). Therefore, the promotion of small and micro business enterprises contributes to the achievement of multiple UN Sustainable Development Goals (SDGs), including ending poverty (SDG 1) and attaining gender equality (SDG 5).

Many MSMEs are owned by women. For instance, the International Finance Corporation (IFC 2014) estimates that there are about 9.34 million formal women-owned MSMEs (or 33% of all) in some 140 countries. Among the regions in Asia and the Pacific, East Asia and the Pacific have the highest number of women-owned MSMEs, while South Asia has the fewest (IFC 2014). Women-owned MSMEs are more likely to be in sectors such as retail and wholesale, health care, beauty and cosmetics, hotels and restaurants, and services and trade, but they are less likely to be in manufacturing and construction sectors. Despite the high level of women-owned and/or women-led MSMEs, only a small

---

[1]   While this chapter aims to empirically examine the gender gap among MSEs, some statistics from the literature are only available for MSMEs. Thus, both of these terms are shown in this chapter.

portion of them are prepared to scale up (ADB 2020). Women-owned and/or women-led MSMEs often face multiple challenges, including limited access to formal financial institutions, lower business skills, limited access to social and economic networks, competing demands on women's time beyond formal work, lack of ability to travel, limited access to technology, and unequal rights within legal frameworks (Leahy et al. 2017; IFC and EU 2010). Therefore, a deeper understanding of prospects and barriers in small business enterprises through a gender lens is crucial to strengthening the capacity of women-owned or women-led enterprises and achieving multiple SDGs, particularly SDG 1 (no poverty), SDG 2 (zero hunger), SDG 5 (gender inequality), and SDG 10 (reduced inequality).

Gender differences in economic participation and entrepreneurship remain a critical issue in development debates, mainly due to the existing social norms and their residual effects. Until recently, women-owned businesses used to face gendered challenges strongly influenced by prevailing gender inequalities, such as in educational attainment, levels of literacy, insufficient funds availed for women's MSMEs, lack of property ownership, and the resultant inability to meet collateral requirements, as well as discriminatory practices that prevent them from accessing vital information and business networks (ADB 2014). Such challenges were further aggravated by social and cultural norms prevailing in some developing countries. However, recent research shows rapid changes in gender relations and the status of women entrepreneurs, especially in the urban areas of Cambodia (Huot and Jensen 2022). Women entrepreneurs in Phnom Penh and other urban centers tend to be more educated, liberal, and confident than those living in rural areas of the country (IFC 2019).

Given this background, Cambodia serves as a special case to examine how gender issues affect MSEs, as women own almost 61% of all businesses in the country (IFC 2019). Moreover, 90% of the MSEs managed by women were profitable in 2018 (IFC 2019). Nevertheless, as in many other developing countries, this economic participation does not necessarily reflect equal opportunities for women.

Gender inequalities, owing to Cambodia's *Chbab Srey* custom[2] (traditional "Code of Women"), limit women's economic independence and opportunities to a large extent (Leahy et al. 2017). However, the traditional values related to gender have changed drastically in Cambodia, and since 2015 the country has made significant progress toward improving gender equality (IFC 2019), evidenced by various international indexes. For instance, in Asia and the Pacific, in terms of progress toward gender equality, Cambodia is one of the leading countries with an improvement of +4.7 points on the Gender Equality Index, which is a little behind Nepal (+6.7 points) and Tajikistan (+5.0 points) (Equal Measures 2022). Although Cambodian society has become more open and women are actively participating in the income-generating activities of the family, the existing negative gender stereotypes still prevent women from reaching their full potential and from succeeding in businesses (IFC 2019).

While the MSEs, particularly micro enterprises, are an important source of livelihood and can play an important role in achieving SDGs concerning poverty, gender equality, and zero hunger, they are inadequately understood. There are limited empirical studies using large datasets that examine gender differences in MSEs. Therefore, this chapter analyzes data from the Cambodian Socio-Economic Survey 2019–2020 to investigate gender gaps in MSE ownership by size and types (manufacturing, construction, repairs, wholesale and retail, food and accommodation, and professional). This study uses (i) a large individual-level dataset to understand the gender difference in ownership of micro enterprises in urban Cambodia, and (ii) the Blinder–Oaxaca model to better understand the gender gap in running MSEs in urban Cambodia.

The next section gives a brief background of MSEs in Cambodia and their significance to Cambodia's economic growth; Section 3 provides a conceptual framework; Section 4 outlines the data and methodologies; Section 5 discusses the empirical results; and Section 6 offers key takeaways and policy recommendations.

---

[2]   According to Anderson and Grace (2018) *Chbab Srey* (Code of Conduct for Women) is an important piece of Khmer (traditional Cambodian language and culture) literature outlining the expected behavior from girls and women in Cambodia. *Chbab Srey* is a poem about a mother advising her newly married daughter. It was orally passed down from 14th through 19th century, and then codified in written form. The mother advises her daughter to maintain peace within the home, walk and talk softly, and obey and respect her husband. The persistence of *Chbab Srey*, despite the Khmer Rouge's violent attempts to wipe out Khmer culture, and its inclusion in the new education system and curriculum, are indications of the poem's importance in Cambodian society.

2. Background

After Cambodia gained its independence in 1953, the following four decades saw periods of fragility and conflict. The advent of democracy, which began in 1993, stimulated the rise of civil society organizations (CSOs). Since the late 1990s, Cambodia had undergone brisk economic growth and development transition, and attained the lower middle-income status in 2015 (World Bank 2022). Between 1998 and 2019, Cambodia's economic growth was among the strongest in the world, growing annually at a rate of 7.7% (World Bank 2022). However, this economic growth has been narrowly based (mainly driven by garment exports and tourism), and unevenly distributed (EIC 2006). While the majority of the population lives in rural areas, economic growth and development have concentrated in urban areas.

According to the General Population Census in 2019, the total population in Cambodia is approximately 15.5 million, of which around 39% is urban (NIS 2020). The General Population Census in 2019 shows that nearly half of the Cambodian population (48.9%) lives in the Central Plains region, and the second most populated (31.4%) is the Tonle Sap (Southeast Asia's largest freshwater lake) region in the lower Mekong basin; the rest is distributed across its mountainous and coastal regions (NIS 2020). As per the NIS (2020), the majority of the employment in Cambodia is in the informal sector, which constitutes approximately 67.7% of the total employed population.[3] The proportion of women in the informal sector (70.1%) is higher than that of men (65.4%). The International Labour Office however estimates the informal sector's share of overall employment in Cambodia is much higher, at over 93% (International Labour Office 2018). The share of the informal sector in the Cambodian economy had decreased—which was 82.6% in 2008 and 67.7% in 2019. This is mainly due to a decline in the share of unpaid family workers, especially among rural women.

---

[3]   Informal sector consists of those working as own-account workers or unpaid family workers.

2.1   Micro and Small Enterprises and Their Significance to Cambodia's Economic Growth

MSEs are defined in several ways. The World Bank defines MSEs based on the number of employees: micro (1–9 employees), small (10–49), and medium-sized (50–249) (Kushnir, Mirmulstein, and Ramalho 2010). In Cambodia, business enterprises are defined not only by number of employees but also by asset value. For instance, the Cambodia Inter-Censal Economic Survey 2014 used assets to categorize firms: (i) micro enterprise (under \$50,000); (ii) small enterprise (\$50,000 to \$250,000); (iii) medium-sized enterprise (\$250,000 to \$500,000); and (iv) large enterprise (over \$500,000).

This study's dataset does not have information on the number of employees and assets. Therefore, the annual operating cost was used to categorize enterprise by cost quintile, as it allows granular examination of the enterprise (Table 1). Of the 2,072 enterprises in the sample, 46% were owned by men and 54% were owned by women.[4] Men were mostly engaged in the smallest (quintile 1) and women in quintiles 2–4, and there is not much difference in quintile 5. Overall, contrary to widespread belief, the percentage of women running Cambodian MSEs is higher than that of men.

Table 1: Classification of Enterprise Size by Operating Cost

Quintile	Amount ($)	Classification	Overall (%)	Men (%)	Women (%)
1	Less than 3,915	Petty	20	27.1	14.6
2	3,915 to 10,837	Micro	20	16.9	22.4
3	10,838 to 22,346	Micro	20	17.8	21.8
4	22,347 to 51,247	Micro	20	17.8	21.7
5	More than 51,247	Small and medium-sized	20	20.4	19.6
		All	100	44	56

Source: Authors' calculation based on the Cambodia Socio-Economic Survey 2019–2020.

---

[4]   This study used the gender of the person primarily running the business to determine whether it is owned by women or men.

In 2014, there were 513,759 enterprises in Cambodia (NIS 2014), with MSEs constituting almost 98% of all enterprises in the country. The share of medium-sized and large enterprises is less than 2%. This dominance of MSEs in Cambodia suggests that they have a major role in providing livelihood security to a majority of the population. Micro enterprises employ nearly 58% of the total labor force, while small and medium-sized enterprises employ only 13% (NIS 2014).

Recent estimates show that women own almost 62% of the micro enterprises, while their share in small and medium-sized enterprises is about 26% (NIS 2014). The same study showed that 74% of the small and medium-sized enterprises are men-owned. It is estimated that 84.2% of women-owned businesses and about 70% of men-owned businesses are operated with one or two individuals (ADB 2015). Women-owned businesses in Cambodia are largely micro and informal, and 76% of micro businesses and 31% of SMEs are home-based enterprises—small businesses operated at home.

2.2 Informal Sector and COVID-19

The coronavirus disease (COVID-19) has severely impacted the lives and livelihood of millions of people, particularly those dependent on the informal sector in developing countries, including Cambodia (Huot and Jensen 2022). Many small and micro enterprises in developing Asia are informal with limited resources, and are generally not registered with the government. The informal sector enterprises include both salaried and self-employed employees, and the share of the informal economy is highest in developing Asia and Africa. Informal entrepreneurship in developing countries is often driven out of necessity to survive. Informal enterprises in developing Asia include street vendors, small groceries, small restaurants, food stalls, rickshaws, and local transport, which rely on daily economic activity, indicating their vulnerability to lockdown and other shocks. A recent study by the International Labour Organization (ILO) found that the majority of the 2 billion people in the informal sector are own-account workers, and an estimated 76% (1.6 billion) have been hit hard due to COVID-19 and related lockdowns (ILO 2020). The same study highlights that women in the high-risk sectors are higher than men.

In Cambodia, one in five informal workers have lost their jobs due to the COVID-19 pandemic. Unemployment among women (22%) was much higher than among men (13%), and nearly two-thirds of all informal sector workers reported that they were unable to meet their basic needs (Vinh 2021). In 2020, the Cambodian economy shrunk by 3.1%, its worst performance since 1994 (World Bank 2022). Amarthalingam (2022: para. 19) pointed out that according to Vorn Pao, president of Independent Democracy of Informal Economy Association (IDEA), "70%–80% of female street vendors faced bankruptcy between early 2020 and March 2021, and 90% of IDEA members were doing two to three jobs to make ends meet." Furthermore, compared to pre-COVID-19 incomes, whereas informal sector men in Cambodia found their incomes reduced by 15%, the corresponding decline for women (29%) was almost twice as much (Amarthalingam 2022). Due to limited data availability, this chapter does not examine the effect of COVID-19 on the informal sectors. UN ESCAP (2020) confirmed that COVID-19 adversely impacted the informal sector in Cambodia, particularly those run by women. Unemployment, poverty, and inequality, all of which rose in Cambodia because of COVID-19, continue to be higher than pre-pandemic levels (World Bank 2022).

2.3 Transition from Informal to Formal

Under the normal assumption of a perfectly competitive market (free entry and exit), some enterprises exit while others continue to grow and transition into formal enterprises over time. Formalization is a process that helps bring the informal enterprise under regulation, which involves certain rewards and responsibilities (ILO 2021). However, in developing countries, the majority of the enterprises are informal and established by individuals due to various constraints as a coping response. Therefore, many informal enterprises neither earn enough profit to reinvest and grow nor have access to credit from formal financial institutions to invest. Further, most informal entrepreneurs do not have the social, financial, and technical capital to transform their enterprise into formal ones. Sometimes, enterprises in developing countries are reluctant to register themselves due to red tape. To support people in informal sectors, some Asian countries have initiated programs to provide them with pensions and insurance and integrate them into the banking sector.

3. Conceptual Framework

Contrary to common belief, women now play a key role as decision makers and leaders of several economic activities, including MSEs and agricultural cooperatives in Cambodia (UNIDO and UNWOMEN 2021). Cambodian women own more than 62% of the micro enterprises (NIS 2014); and they make up almost 60% of members of agricultural cooperatives in the country, whose boards of directors constitute 34% women (UNIDO and UNWOMEN 2021).

However, despite increasing gender equality and changing social norms, women in Cambodia spend more than twice as much time as men on unpaid household work. A recent study by Pike and English (2022) shows that women's increasing participation in paid work in Cambodia has not been accompanied by a corresponding change in the gender division of unpaid labor in the household and community. Such an unequal division of household responsibilities influences several aspects of women's participation in the economy, from disproportionate representation in the informal economy to their relatively weak use of technology to build on and expand their businesses (OECD 2017). Overall, while assessing the role of gender on entrepreneurial women, the collective interplay of history, culture, policy, and marketing, and their dynamic effects on entrepreneurial women in transitioning Cambodia needs to be examined (Ardrey, Pecotich, and Shultz 2006).

Unequal power relations between men and women often place women at a disadvantage in owning medium-sized and large enterprises— a basic reason why they are more involved in MSEs. This sort of inequality is also observed in natural resource management in Cambodia, such as in women's participation in fisheries management (Kwok et al. 2020). Therefore, culture accounts for multifarious differences in women's entrepreneurship across societies and the success of their business activities. Indeed, many barriers and constraints that women entrepreneurs experience are gender-specific, stemming from cultural values, norms, and customs (Bullough et al. 2022).

Figure 1 shows the framework for participation in MSEs in the context of developing countries. The livelihood assets possessed by households, set against the backdrop of the sociocultural context, influence participation by men and women in MSEs. However, households and individuals differ in livelihood assets owned, which significantly influences their livelihood strategies.

The livelihood assets can generally be grouped into five categories: social, natural, human, physical, and financial. These assets reflect the "capability" of an individual or a group manifested in terms of financial, human, physical, natural, and social capital (Sen 1992; Sugden 1993). They play an important role in choosing between low return and high return enterprises (Berdegué et al. 2001). These five categories are particularly important in accessing MSEs with a high entry barrier. Desperation and poverty push individuals to participate in low-return enterprises, as opposed to participating in high-return ones that maximize revenues (Rahut and Micevska Scharf 2012).

Figure 1: Conceptual Framework

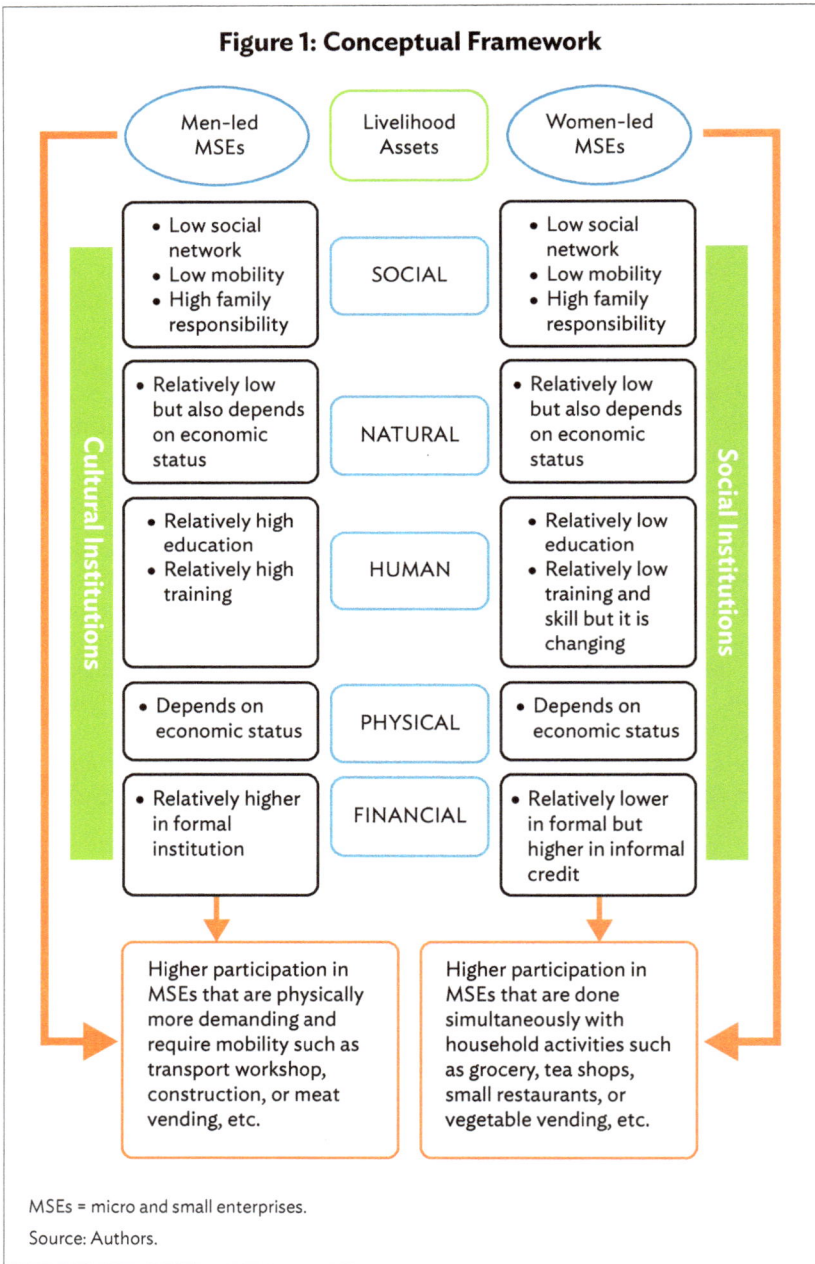

Men-led MSEs	Livelihood Assets	Women-led MSEs

Cultural Institutions

Social Institutions

Men-led MSEs		Women-led MSEs
• Low social network • Low mobility • High family responsibility	SOCIAL	• Low social network • Low mobility • High family responsibility
• Relatively low but also depends on economic status	NATURAL	• Relatively low but also depends on economic status
• Relatively high education • Relatively high training	HUMAN	• Relatively low education • Relatively low training and skill but it is changing
• Depends on economic status	PHYSICAL	• Depends on economic status
• Relatively higher in formal institution	FINANCIAL	• Relatively lower in formal but higher in informal credit

Higher participation in MSEs that are physically more demanding and require mobility such as transport workshop, construction, or meat vending, etc.	Higher participation in MSEs that are done simultaneously with household activities such as grocery, tea shops, small restaurants, or vegetable vending, etc.

MSEs = micro and small enterprises.

Source: Authors.

Besides livelihood assets, social and cultural institutions also influence women's ability to participate in MSEs. Social and cultural norms restrict women from accessing livelihood assets in some communities and from participating in livelihood activities, including MSEs. However, sociocultural norms in several communities have also evolved, significantly increasing women-owned MSEs. Working toward the SDGs, public policies also support women entrepreneurs through training and access to credit, helping increase women-owned MSEs.

The conceptual framework in Figure 1 guides a larger set of ongoing studies, from which the analysis presented in this chapter is excerpted. It uses recent household datasets from Cambodia to examine the factors influencing men's and women's participation in MSEs, and the gender gap in MSE participation by enterprise size and sector.

4. Data and Methodology

4.1 Data and Sampling

The Cambodia Socio-Economic Survey (CSES) 2019–2020 is nationally representative, and the data collection involves a multistage random sampling strategy. The sampling frame is stratified by province (24 provinces and one capital, Phnom Penh); and within each province, it is further classified as urban or rural, which yields 49 strata. First, the sample was allocated to each province and Phnom Penh by a power allocation of the number of households within each province. Second, the sample size within each province was allocated proportionally over urban and rural areas. Finally, the urban and rural allocation was adjusted so that the urban part of the sample was 30% of the total sample. Based on the sampling frame, around 24% of Cambodian households live in villages classified as urban.

From each selected village frame, the primary sampling unit, one enumeration area was selected by simple random sampling. In total, 1,008 villages were selected (706 rural and 302 urban).[5] In each of the selected enumeration areas from step 2, all households are mapped. Finally, 10 households are selected from each enumeration area by

---

[5]   Urban villages refer to those villages located in urban areas. The Cambodia Socio-Economic Survey 2019–2020 defines urban areas using commune-level data with the following criteria: "(a) population density exceeding 200 per km2; (b) percentage of male employment in agriculture below 50 percent; and (c) total population of the commune should exceed 2000" (NIS 2020: 13).

circular systematic sampling, resulting in a sample of 10,080 households (7,060 rural and 3,020 urban).

Since the focus of this study is urban businesses, the sample was limited to individuals living in an urban area and working-age individuals, age 16 and above. The total sample for the analyses is 11,604 individuals (2,074 with ownership of MSEs and 9,530 without).

Although their formality status is unknown, it can be inferred that most businesses in the sample are informal, due to their low annual operating costs. Moreover, as stated in Section 2, the informal sector, which is narrowly defined as consisting of own-account workers or unpaid family workers, constituted approximately 67.7% of the total employed population in 2019. If this study defined the informal sector as those businesses without formal registration, then the share of the informal sector would be even larger. Therefore, it is reasonable to assume that the findings of this study largely reflect the current state of informal businesses in urban Cambodia.

4.2 Methodology

Logit and Multinomial Logit

To examine the gender-based probability of running a business, this study employs the following logistic regression model:

$$\Pr(Y_i = 1 \mid G_i, X_i) = F(\alpha G_i + X'_i \beta)$$

$$\Pr(Y_i = 1 \mid G_i, X_i) = \frac{1}{1 + \exp[-(\alpha G_i + X'_i \beta)]} \quad (1),$$

where Y_i is the binary outcome variable that equals 1 if the individual i is running a business; G_i is a binary variable indicating gender, which equals 1 if the individual i is female; X_i is a vector of other observed individual and household characteristics (including but not limited to age, education, access to credit, asset index, and geographic zone fixed effects); and F is the cumulative standard logistic distribution function.

To further understand the prevalence of female entrepreneurship by business size and sector, the study limits the sample to those individuals owning a business and uses the multinomial logistic model to analyze whether the prevalence of female entrepreneurship is more concentrated within any specific enterprise size or sector. The multinomial logistic model used for this analysis is

$$\Pr(S_i = j \mid G_i, X_i) = \frac{\exp(\alpha_j G_i + X'_i \beta_j)}{\sum_{h=1}^{j} \exp(\alpha_h G_i + X'_i \beta_h)} \quad j = 1, 2, ..., J \quad (2),$$

where S_i is the categorical variable for business size or sector. As stated earlier, the study generated a size indicator by dividing the sample into quintiles based on the expenditure of the business, with the 1st quintile showing the lowest expenditure and the 5th quintile showing the highest expenditure.[6] Overall, the businesses are divided into seven sectors: manufacturing, construction and repair, wholesale and retail, transport and storage, accommodation and food, professional, and others.

Blinder–Oaxaca Model

To better understand the prevalent gender gap in running a business, this study employs the Blinder–Oaxaca decomposition technique, which considers a separate regression model process for male and female samples and examines the relative contributions of all the measurable characteristics in the model. For linear regression, the standard Blinder–Oaxaca decomposition of the gender gap in the average value of the outcome variable Y is

$$\overline{Y}^M - \overline{Y}^F = [(\overline{X}^M - \overline{X}^F)\,\hat{\beta}^M] + [\overline{X}^F\,(\hat{\beta}^M - \hat{\beta}^F)] \quad (3),$$

where $\overline{X}^j$ is a row vector of average values of the independent variables and $\hat{\beta}^j$ is a vector of the coefficient of estimate for gender j. However, since the outcome variable of interest is a binary variable, this standard technique cannot be used directly. Following Fairlie (1999), the Blinder–Oaxaca decomposition of the gender gap for a logit model can be written as

$$\overline{Y}^M - \overline{Y}^F = \left[\sum_{i=1}^{N^M} \frac{F(X_i^M\,\hat{\beta}^M)}{N^M} - \sum_{i=1}^{N^F} \frac{F(X_i^F\,\hat{\beta}^M)}{N^F}\right] + \left[\sum_{i=1}^{N^F} \frac{F(X_i^F\,\hat{\beta}^M)}{N^F} - \sum_{i=1}^{N^F} \frac{F(X_i^F\,\hat{\beta}^F)}{N^F}\right] \quad (4),$$

where N^J is the sample size for gender j, and F is the cumulative standard logistic distribution function. The first term on the right-hand side of equations 3 and 4 captures the difference in the outcome due to observable characteristics X, whereas the second term indicates the different effects in the estimated coefficients.

---

[6] Due to the lack of information on the number of employees and capital, the sample could not be divided based on the formal definition of enterprise size. Since the majority (97.6%) of businesses in Cambodia are micro enterprises (IFC 2019), it can be inferred that most of the businesses in the sample are also micro enterprises. The presence of small, medium-sized, and large enterprises, if any, is in the 5th quintile.

5. Results and Discussion

5.1 Descriptive Statistics

Table 2 presents the descriptive statistics of the variables used in the analyses. Column 1 shows the means and standard deviations of the variables for the whole sample, which includes working-age individuals living in urban Cambodia, while Columns 2 and 3 show the characteristics of the business and no-business subsamples, respectively. Column 4 presents the results of a simple statistical test of the difference in means of each variable between the business and no-business subsamples. Columns 5 and 6 show the characteristics of women and men who run a business, respectively, while Column 7 presents the results of a simple statistical test of the difference in means of each variable between the two subsamples.

Approximately 18% of individuals in urban Cambodia run some business. Women comprise about 53% of the sample. Table 2 also shows that the average age of the sample is roughly 39, and the average formal education is approximately 7.4 years. About 64% of individuals in the sample are married. The average education of household heads is approximately 6.5 years, while the average age of household heads is about 51. Female-headed households are about 20%. On average, about 33% of all households have debts from financial institutions.

Table 2: Summary Statistics

Variable	Whole Sample (Standard deviation) (1)	Own a Business (2)	No Business (3)	Difference (Δ) (4)	Women-Owned Business (5)	Men-Owned Business (6)	Difference (Δ) (7)
Own a business	0.18 (0.38)						
Female	0.53 (0.50)	0.56 (0.50)	0.52 (0.50)	-0.04***			
Age (years)	39.14 (16.25)	42.70 (12.22)	38.36 (16.90)	-4.33***	42.50 (0.36)	42.94 (0.38)	0.44
Age-squared	1795.80 (1469.53)	1972.26 (1125.31)	1757.40 (1531.60)	-214.85***	1966.03 (33.98)	1980.29 (35.79)	14.26
Years of schooling	7.40 (4.61)	6.95 (3.88)	7.50 (4.75)	0.544***	6.46 (0.11)	7.59 (0.12)	1.13***
Years of schooling-squared	76.04 (78.47)	63.40 (62.03)	78.79 (81.35)	15.39***	56.32 (1.68)	72.54 (2.19)	16.21***
Married	0.64 (0.48)	0.84 (0.37)	0.60 (0.49)	-0.23***	0.76 (0.01)	0.92 (0.01)	0.16***
Head's years of schooling	6.54 (4.43)	7.13 (4.12)	6.41 (4.49)	-0.72***	7.16 (0.12)	7.08 (0.12)	-0.08
Head's age (years)	50.64 (13.17)	47.76 (12.82)	51.26 (13.16)	3.51***	49.16 (0.38)	45.94 (0.41)	-3.22***
Female-headed household	0.20 (0.40)	0.18 (0.39)	0.21 (0.40)	0.02***	0.27 (0.01)	0.06 (0.01)	-0.21***

continued on next page

Table 2 continued

Variable	Mean (Standard deviation)		No Business (3)	Difference (Δ) (4)	Mean		Difference (Δ) (7)
	Whole Sample (1)	Own a Business (2)			Women-Owned Business (5)	Men-Owned Business (6)	
Working-age adults (no.)	3.40	3.03	3.48	0.45***	3.06	2.99	-0.06
	(1.63)	(1.40)	(1.67)		(0.04)	(0.04)	
Elderly aged > 64	0.31	0.23	0.32	0.09***	0.26	0.19	-0.06***
	(0.59)	(0.53)	(0.60)		(0.01)	(0.01)	
Children aged < 5	0.40	0.41	0.40	-0.01	0.39	0.42	0.02
	(0.63)	(0.62)	(0.64)		(0.01)	(0.02)	
Access to credit	0.33	0.36	0.32	-0.04***	0.33	0.40	0.06***
	(0.47)	(0.48)	(0.47)		(0.01)	(0.01)	
Asset index	1.41	1.88	1.30	-0.57***	2.05	1.65	-0.40***
	(2.73)	(2.60)	(2.75)		(0.07)	(0.08)	
Zone: Phnom Penh	0.25	0.26	0.24	-0.01*	0.26	0.25	-0.01
	(0.43)	(0.44)	(0.43)		(0.01)	(0.01)	
Zone: Plain	0.23	0.19	0.24	0.05***	0.19	0.17	-0.02
	(0.42)	(0.39)	(0.43)		(0.01)	(0.01)	
Zone: Tonle Sap	0.21	0.23	0.20	-0.02***	0.21	0.24	0.03**
	(0.41)	(0.42)	(0.40)		(0.01)	(0.01)	
Zone: Coastal	0.12	0.13	0.11	-0.02***	0.13	0.12	-0.01
	(0.32)	(0.34)	(0.32)		(0.01)	(0.01)	
Zone: Plateau/Mountain	0.20	0.19	0.20	0.00	0.19	0.19	0.00
	(0.40)	(0.39)	(0.40)		(0.01)	(0.01)	

continued on next page

Table 2 continued

Variable	Mean (Standard deviation)		No Business	Difference (Δ)	Mean		Difference (Δ)
	Whole Sample	Own a Business			Women-Owned Business	Men-Owned Business	
	(1)	(2)	(3)	(4)	(5)	(6)	(7)
Business sector:							
Manufacturing		0.10			0.07	0.13	0.06***
		(0.30)			(0.01)	(0.01)	
Construction and repair		0.05			0.00	0.10	0.10***
		(0.22)			(0.00)	(0.01)	
Wholesale and retail		0.51			0.67	0.29	−0.37***
		(0.50)			(0.01)	(0.01)	
Transport and storage		0.14			0.00	0.32	0.32***
		(0.35)			(0.00)	(0.01)	
Accommodation and food		0.10			0.14	0.03	−0.11***
		(0.30)			(0.01)	(0.01)	
Professional		0.03			0.01	0.04	0.03***
		(0.17)			(0.00)	(0.01)	
Others		0.07			0.08	0.05	−0.03***
		(0.26)			(0.01)	(0.01)	
Total observations	11,604	2,074	9,530		1,169	905	

Note: *** p<0.01, ** p<0.05, * p<0.1.

Source: Authors.

The results in Column 4 show that there are significant differences in most variables between those running a business and those who do not.[7] For instance, women constitute 56% of those who are running a business and 52% of those who are not running a business. The average individual's age in the business sample is 43, versus 38 in the no-business sample. Those who own a business have completed an average of 7 years of formal education, as opposed to 7.5 years for those who do not, a rather small difference in magnitude. This may be due to the inverted U-shaped relationship between education and running a business, as discussed in the next section. On average, about 84% of those who run a business are married, while approximately 60% of those who do not run a business are married.

On the lower panel of Column 2 of Table 2, the summary statistics of each business sector are presented. The manufacturing sector constitutes approximately 10%; construction and repair sector about 5%; wholesale and retail sector roughly 51%; transport and storage sector about 14%; accommodation and food sector about 10%; the professional sector just about 3%; and the remaining 7% are classified as "others," comprising mainly "other personal service activities."

The results in Column 7 show that there are significant differences between men and women who run a business, in terms of their education level, marital status, access to credit, assets, and sector of business. For instance, women who run a business have about 1.1 fewer average years of schooling than men who run businesses. Approximately 92% of men who have a business are married, compared with only about 76% of women who have a business. Similarly, approximately 27% of women and only 6% of men who run a business belong to female-headed households. Moreover, the level of access to credit among women entrepreneurs is about 6 percentage points lower than that of their male counterparts. Interestingly, women running a business have a higher asset index than men who run a business. Since the asset index is constructed using the principal component analysis on a set of household-level socioeconomic variables such as ownership of a car or a refrigerator, number of rooms, or the use of electricity or piped water, this result may reflect higher earnings in families where both the husband and wife are employed. The difference between the asset indexes for men and women, in general, is not statistically significant.

---

[7]   The differences are statistically significant at the 1% level for most variables, except the variable Tonle Sap zone which is statistically significant at the 5% level.

Figure 2 shows the distribution of enterprise ownership by gender. Women are primarily engaged in wholesale and retail. Around 67% of women micro and small entrepreneurs are involved in wholesale and retail, followed by accommodation and food (14.7%) and manufacturing (7%). Men are primarily involved in transport and communication (32.2%), followed by wholesale and retail (29.3%), manufacturing (13.7%), and construction and repair (10.9%). This study finds that women dominate wholesale and retail and accommodation and food, while men dominate transport and storage, manufacturing and construction, and repairs, likely due to the nature of those jobs.

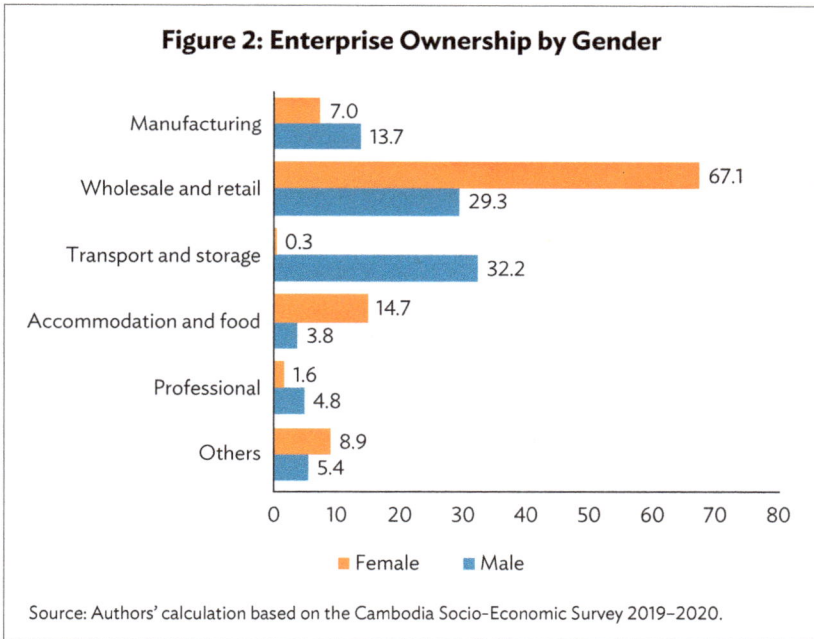

Figure 2: Enterprise Ownership by Gender

Source: Authors' calculation based on the Cambodia Socio-Economic Survey 2019–2020.

5.2 Empirical Results

Gender and Business Ownership

The decision to run a business is modeled using logistic regression analysis (Table 3). Coefficients are reported as average marginal effects, showing estimates of the effect of a change in a particular variable on the probability that a working individual is running a business. Standard errors are presented in parentheses. The results indicate that in urban Cambodia, women are more likely to run an MSE than men. Specifically, the probability of women running a business is approximately 5.82 percentage points higher than their male counterparts. According to IFC (2019), most businesses in Cambodia (61%) are owned by women, and micro and small businesses are run mostly by women. Compared with other countries in the Association of Southeast Asian Nations (ASEAN), Cambodia is the only country where working women are more likely to be self-employed than working men (OECD 2017). Poverty and family income security are the main plausible factors pushing Cambodian women to engage in income-generating activities. However, due to the lack of education and skills, women have fewer opportunities to find jobs (Emerging Markets Consulting 2017). These factors push women to enter a low entry-barrier business, as suggested by the fact that most women-owned businesses in Cambodia are micro enterprises. Furthermore, although Cambodian women are highly active in income-generating activities in their families, the burden of housework and childcare still falls disproportionately on them (Van der Vaeren 2017). This also poses a major barrier to women's participation in the paid economy. As a result, running a micro or small business, especially a home-based one, is favorable for most women, since they can seek to manage household chores and childcare simultaneously, while opportunities in the paid economy are limited for them.

Table 3: Average Marginal Effects: Own a Business

Variable	Own a Business
Female	0.0582***
	(0.0085)
Age (years)	0.0255***
	(0.0021)
Age-squared	−0.0002***
	(0.0000)
Years of schooling	0.0271***
	(0.0032)
Years of schooling-squared	−0.0023***
	(0.0002)
Married	0.0531***
	(0.0125)
Head's years of schooling	0.0038***
	(0.0015)
Head's age (years)	−0.0026***
	(0.0005)
Female-headed household	0.0383***
	(0.0123)
Working-age adults (no.)	−0.0259***
	(0.0032)
Elderly aged > 64	0.0013
	(0.0092)
Children aged < 5	0.0156**
	(0.0068)
Access to credit	0.0278***
	(0.0087)
Asset index	0.0253***
	(0.0019)
Zone: Plain	−0.0386***
	(0.0127)
Zone: Tonle Sap	0.0175
	(0.0125)
Zone: Coastal	0.0155
	(0.0144)
Zone: Plateau/Mountain	-0.0211
	(0.0131)
Log Likelihood	−4304.78
LR chi2	1263.72
Pseudo R2	0.1280
Total observations	9,365

Notes: Standard errors are presented in parentheses.
*** $p < 0.01$, ** $p < 0.05$, * $p < 0.1$.
Source: Authors.

The associations between running a business and some important covariates are discussed below. Individuals' age and years of schooling have an inverted U-shaped relationship with the status of owning a business. People are more likely to run a business if they have accumulated experience and capital through time; however, they are less likely to start one after reaching a certain age. Similarly, individuals with a higher level of education are more likely to run a business. However, those possessing the highest level of education are less likely to be self-employed. With a high level of education, people can work as professionals in the formal sector, making stable wages and, hence, are less likely to run a business.

Being married is positively associated with owning a business, suggesting that help and support from a spouse are likely key to running a business, especially home-based micro enterprises. Besides individual characteristics, this study also controlled for household-level characteristics and geographic zones. The results show that households with more assets and access to credit are, expectedly, more likely to own a business. Except for the plains zone, the effect of the geographic zone itself is not statistically significant. However, the plains zone shows significant negative effects, indicating that individuals living there are less likely to run a business than those living in Phnom Penh. Most people living in the plains zone are engaged in agricultural activities, since it is favorable for agricultural production.

Table 4: Gender Gap in Business Ownership

	Own a Business
Male	0.1891***
	(0.0058)
Female	0.2525***
	(0.0065)
Overall difference	−0.0633***
	(0.0087)
Difference in endowments	−0.0127**
	(0.0052)
Difference in coefficients	−0.0806***
	(0.0090)
Difference in interaction	0.0300***
	(0.0062)
Total observations	9,365
Males	4,591
Females	4,774

continued on next page

Table 4 continued

			Own a Business
Decomposition	**Endowments**	**Coefficients**	**Interaction**
Age (years)	0.0065	0.0424	0.0004
	(0.0063)	(0.1506)	(0.0015)
Age-squared	−0.0031	−0.0154	−0.0002
	(0.0050)	(0.0721)	(0.0009)
Years of schooling	0.0330***	0.0360	0.0086
	(0.0057)	(0.0436)	(0.0106)
Years of schooling-squared	−0.0465***	0.0122	0.0047
	(0.0078)	(0.0231)	(0.0088)
Married	0.0039***	0.0166	0.0020
	(0.0010)	(0.0174)	(0.0022)
Head's years of schooling	0.0018**	−0.0651***	−0.0037**
	(0.0008)	(0.0216)	(0.0016)
Head's age (years)	0.0003	−0.1451***	0.0011
	(0.0003)	(0.0483)	(0.0010)
Female-headed household	−0.0088***	−0.0393***	0.0202***
	(0.0020)	(0.0067)	(0.0031)
Working-age adults (no.)	−0.0033***	−0.0227	−0.0014
	(0.0010)	(0.0193)	(0.0013)
Elderly aged > 64	0.0002	0.0044	−0.0005
	(0.0003)	(0.0047)	(0.0006)
Children aged < 5	0.0002	−0.0033	−0.0001
	(0.0002)	(0.0051)	(0.0002)
Access to credit	0.0001	0.0115**	0.0003
	(0.0001)	(0.0054)	(0.0004)
Asset index	0.0026*	−0.0124***	−0.0012
	(0.0016)	(0.0045)	(0.0008)
Zone: Plain	0.0000	−0.0058	0.0001
	(0.0002)	(0.0057)	(0.0003)
Zone: Tonle Sap	0.0000	0.0026	−0.0001
	(0.0001)	(0.0048)	(0.0002)
Zone: Coastal	0.0003	−0.0057*	−0.0005
	(0.0003)	(0.0031)	(0.0005)
Zone: Plateau/Mountain	0.0001	−0.0036	0.0002
	(0.0002)	(0.0051)	(0.0003)
Constant		0.1123	
		(0.0967)	

Notes: Standard errors are presented in parentheses.

*** $p < 0.01$, ** $p < 0.05$, * $p < 0.1$.

Source: Authors.

Table 4 shows the results of the Blinder–Oaxaca decomposition analysis, which is used to further understand the differences between men and women in regard to the strengths of the various factors in the regression model. It shows that the mean probability of owning a business for the male and female samples are, respectively, 18.91% and 25.25%. The overall difference in these means is also shown, followed by the difference in endowments, the difference in coefficients, and the difference in their interaction. The model finds the gender gap in running a business to be –6.33%, meaning that women are more likely to run a business than men. This overall difference is explained largely by the differences in the gender effects (coefficients), as the difference in coefficients is –8.06 percentage points, whereas the difference due to the endowment gap is only –1.27 percentage points. The difference in endowments suggests that if women had characteristics identical to men, then the mean probability of women owning a business would reduce by about 1.27 percentage points. The difference in the coefficient (the gender effects) reflects the unobservable inherent distinctions between both genders that cannot be explained by their endowments.

Gender and Business Size

To further understand the prevalence of female entrepreneurship by business size, the study limits the sample to those individuals owning a business and then generates a size indicator by dividing the sample into quintiles based on the expenditure of the business, with the 1st quintile showing the lowest expenditure and the 5th quintile showing the highest. Due to the lack of information on the number of employees and capital, it should be noted that, in this analysis, the variable for enterprise size does not conform to its formal definition. Since the majority (97.6%) of businesses in Cambodia are micro enterprises (IFC 2019), it can be inferred that most of the businesses in the sample are also micro enterprises. Small, medium-sized, and large enterprises, if any, belong to the 5th quintile.

The multinomial logistic model is used to analyze whether the prevalence of female entrepreneurship is more concentrated within any specific enterprise size. The coefficients in Table 5 are the average marginal effects, showing estimates of the effect of a change in a particular variable on the probability that an entrepreneur is running a business of a different size; standard errors are presented in parentheses. Table 3 shows that women are less likely to run the 1st quintile businesses but more likely to run those in the 2nd and 3rd quintiles. For the 4th and 5th quintile businesses, there are no significant differences in ownership by gender. The prevalence of female entrepreneurship is higher among micro enterprises, except for the lowest-cost quintile. In the lowest-cost quintile, the largest share is transport and storage businesses, such as motorcycle taxis and tuk-tuk services, which tend to be run almost exclusively by men and require the lowest daily costs.

Although the sample consists mostly of micro enterprises, Table 5 shows that the prevalence of women-owned businesses declines as business expenditure increases. This is an existing challenge that hinders the growth of women-owned MSEs, and reflects prevailing gender inequalities that disadvantage women, including lower educational attainment, inadequate business skills, lack of property ownership, inability to meet collateral requirements, limited access to social and economic networks, competing demands on women's time beyond formal work, limited ability to travel, limited access to technology, and unequal rights within legal frameworks (Leahy et al. 2017; IFC and EU 2010). The lack of education, for instance, can hinder the growth of MSEs in several ways. According to the United Nations ESCAP (2017), lower education attainment can affect the type and size of a business, the level of innovation of products and services, access to finance (due to lack of information), the ability to internationalize (due to lack of information and language barriers), and the capacity to apply research and development findings to the business.

Table 5: Average Marginal Effects: The Choice of Business by Size

Variable	Cost1 (1)	Cost2 (2)	Cost3 (3)	Cost4 (4)	Cost5 (5)
Female	−0.1190***	0.0487**	0.0572***	0.0137	−0.0007
	(0.0207)	(0.0206)	(0.0210)	(0.0212)	(0.0195)
Age (years)	−0.0078*	−0.0082*	0.0025	0.0089	0.0046
	(0.0047)	(0.0050)	(0.0055)	(0.0058)	(0.0054)
Age (squared)	0.0001*	0.0001	0.0000	−0.0001**	0.0000
	(0.0001)	(0.0001)	(0.0001)	(0.0001)	(0.0001)
Years of schooling	0.0014	−0.0132*	−0.0073	−0.0029	0.0220***
	(0.0075)	(0.0076)	(0.0077)	(0.0080)	(0.0078)
Years of schooling (squared)	−0.0003	0.0005	0.0007*	−0.0001	−0.0008*
	(0.0005)	(0.0005)	(0.0004)	(0.0005)	(0.0004)
Married	0.0434*	−0.0650*	0.0175	0.0027	0.0014
	(0.0258)	(0.0348)	(0.0316)	(0.0312)	(0.0307)

continued on next page

Table 5 continued

Variable	Cost1 (1)	Cost2 (2)	Cost3 (3)	Cost4 (4)	Cost5 (5)
Head's years of schooling	0.0045	0.0091***	−0.0004	−0.0025	−0.0107***
	(0.0035)	(0.0034)	(0.0035)	(0.0035)	(0.0034)
Head's age (years)	0.0025**	0.0015	0.0004	−0.0009	−0.0036***
	(0.0012)	(0.0012)	(0.0013)	(0.0012)	(0.0012)
Female-headed household	0.0321	−0.0477*	−0.0414	0.0629*	−0.0060
	(0.0320)	(0.0287)	(0.0305)	(0.0347)	(0.0297)
Working-age adults (no.)	−0.0036	−0.0021	0.0024	0.0011	0.0022
	(0.0074)	(0.0078)	(0.0078)	(0.0077)	(0.0070)
Elderly aged > 64	−0.0082	0.0101	0.0355	−0.0200	−0.0174
	(0.0205)	(0.0216)	(0.0217)	(0.0235)	(0.0217)
Children aged < 5	0.0031	0.0121	−0.0102	0.0031	−0.0081
	(0.0146)	(0.0157)	(0.0168)	(0.0160)	(0.0151)
Access to credit	−0.0210	−0.0045	0.0096	−0.0439**	0.0598***
	(0.0184)	(0.0202)	(0.0211)	(0.0200)	(0.0201)
Asset index	−0.0420***	−0.0274***	−0.0097**	0.0271***	0.0520***
	(0.0045)	(0.0048)	(0.0047)	(0.0044)	(0.0039)
Zone: Plain	−0.0760***	−0.0325	−0.0665**	0.0672**	0.1077***
	(0.0215)	(0.0274)	(0.0265)	(0.0323)	(0.0339)
Zone: Tonle Sap	0.0091	0.0275	−0.0385	−0.0166	0.0186
	(0.0251)	(0.0289)	(0.0270)	(0.0283)	(0.0283)
Zone: Coastal	−0.0541**	−0.0308	−0.0036	0.0569	0.0317
	(0.0258)	(0.0310)	(0.0322)	(0.0352)	(0.0322)
Zone: Plateau/ Mountain	−0.0604***	−0.0344	0.0039	0.0249	0.0660**
	(0.0234)	(0.0281)	(0.0300)	(0.0315)	(0.0318)
Log Likelihood	−3080.72				
LR chi2	508.05				
Pseudo R2	0.0762				
Total observations	2,072				

Notes: Standard errors are presented in parentheses. The base outcome is the 1st quintile based on the business expenditure.

*** p<0.01, ** p<0.05, * p<0.1.

Source: Authors.

Table 6 shows the gender gap in the choice of business by size. Similar to Table 4, the analysis limits the sample to individuals who own a business, then generates a size indicator by dividing the sample into quintiles based on business expenditure, with the 1st quintile being for the lowest and the 5th for the highest expenditure. Column 1 compares the highest-cost businesses (5th quintile) with the rest of the sample. Column 2 compares businesses in the 4th quintile with businesses in the 3rd, 2nd , and 1st quintiles. Column 3 compares businesses in the 3rd quintile with businesses in the 2nd and 1st quintiles. Column 4 compares businesses in the 2nd quintile with businesses in the 1st quintile.

Table 6: Gender Gap in the Choice of Business by Size

	Cost Quintile 5 with 4, 3, 2, and 1 (1)	Cost Quintile 4 with 3, 2, and 1 (2)	Cost Quintile 3 with 2 and 1 (3)	Cost Quintile 2 with 1 (4)
Male	0.204***	0.224***	0.288***	0.384***
	(0.013)	(0.016)	(0.019)	(0.024)
Female	0.196***	0.270***	0.371***	0.606***
	(0.011)	(0.014)	(0.018)	(0.024)
Overall difference	0.008	-0.046**	-0.083***	-0.221***
	(0.017)	(0.021)	(0.027)	(0.034)
Difference in endowments	0.001	-0.031**	0.009	0.004
	(0.011)	(0.013)	(0.018)	(0.023)
Difference in coefficients	-0.029	-0.020	-0.106***	-0.183***
	(0.022)	(0.033)	(0.037)	(0.053)
Difference in interaction	0.036*	0.005	0.015	-0.043
	(0.020)	(0.028)	(0.033)	(0.047)
Total observations	2,072	1,658	1,244	829
Males	905	720	559	398
Females	1,167	938	685	431

Notes: Standard errors are presented in parentheses.

*** $p<0.01$, ** $p<0.05$, * $p<0.1$.

Source: Authors.

Column 1 of Table 6 shows that in the highest-cost quintile there is no significant difference in the mean probability of owning a business between male and female samples, suggesting that no gender gap exists in running a business in the highest-cost quintile. However, significant differences are found in Columns 2, 3, and 4. In Column 2, the gender gap in running a 4th quintile business is −4.6%, meaning that businesses in the 4th quintile are more likely to be run by women than men. This overall difference is explained largely by the difference in endowments of −3.1 percentage points, whereas the total difference due to gender effects is only −2.0 percentage points and it is not statistically significant at conventional levels. The difference in endowments suggests that if women had characteristics identical to men, then the mean probability of women owning a business in the 4th quintile would reduce by about 3.1 percentage points. Larger gender gaps are found in Columns 3 and 4, which limit the sample to lower-cost quintiles. In Column 3, the gender gap in running a 3rd quintile business goes up to −8.3%. This overall difference is explained largely by the difference in the gender effects, as the difference in coefficients is −10.6 percentage points, but the difference due to the endowments gap is only 0.9 percentage points. Similarly, in Column 4, the gender gap in running a 2nd quintile business rises to −22.1%. Again, this overall difference is largely owing to differences in gender effects, as the total difference in coefficients is −18.3 percentage points, and the difference due to the endowments gap is only 0.4 percentage points.

Gender and Business Sector

To confirm whether female entrepreneurship is concentrated within any specific sector, the study undertook an analysis similar to those presented in Tables 5 and 7, where the dependent variable is changed from the expenditure-based size to the business sector. Table 7 shows that women are more likely to own a business in the wholesale and retail, accommodation and food, and "others" sectors. On the other hand, men are more likely to run a business in the manufacturing, construction and repair, transport and storage, or professional sectors.

Table 7: Marginal Effects after Multinomial Logit: Business Sectors

Variable	Manufacturing (1)	Construction and Repair (2)	Wholesale and Retail (3)	Transport and Storage (4)	Accommodation and Food (5)	Professional (6)	Others (7)
Female	-0.0665***	-0.1035***	0.3908***	-0.3202***	0.0972***	-0.0227***	0.0249**
	(0.0163)	(0.0144)	(0.0247)	(0.0229)	(0.0136)	(0.0070)	(0.0126)
Age (years)	0.0020	-0.0031**	0.0071	0.0008	0.0079*	-0.0019	-0.0128***
	(0.0050)	(0.0013)	(0.0067)	(0.0012)	(0.0042)	(0.0016)	(0.0034)
Age (squared)	-0.0000	0.0000*	-0.0001	0.0000	-0.0001	0.0000	0.0001***
	(0.0001)	(0.0000)	(0.0001)	(0.0000)	(0.0000)	(0.0000)	(0.0000)
Years of schooling	-0.0028	0.0012	-0.0035	0.0046*	0.0008	-0.0024	0.0022
	(0.0068)	(0.0021)	(0.0098)	(0.0024)	(0.0058)	(0.0023)	(0.0061)
Years of schooling (squared)	-0.0001	-0.0001	0.0006	-0.0003**	-0.0003	0.0003***	-0.0001
	(0.0004)	(0.0001)	(0.0006)	(0.0001)	(0.0004)	(0.0001)	(0.0003)
Married	0.0331	0.0084	-0.0452	-0.0019	0.0042	-0.0019	0.0032
	(0.0261)	(0.0066)	(0.0383)	(0.0081)	(0.0223)	(0.0099)	(0.0221)
Head's years of schooling	0.0010	0.0011	-0.0068	0.0002	0.0040*	0.0003	0.0002
	(0.0033)	(0.0011)	(0.0044)	(0.0011)	(0.0024)	(0.0011)	(0.0025)
Head's age (years)	0.0012	0.0004	-0.0027*	0.0002	0.0001	0.0003	0.0006
	(0.0011)	(0.0003)	(0.0016)	(0.0003)	(0.0009)	(0.0004)	(0.0009)
Female-headed household	-0.0143	-0.0026	-0.0398	0.0201	0.0303	0.0068	-0.0004
	(0.0289)	(0.0092)	(0.0412)	(0.0133)	(0.0268)	(0.0122)	(0.0228)
Working-age adults (no.)	-0.0035	-0.0026	-0.0065	0.0026	0.0055	0.0052	-0.0008
	(0.0069)	(0.0020)	(0.0097)	(0.0017)	(0.0055)	(0.0022)	(0.0059)

continued on next page

Table 7 continued

Variable	Manufacturing (1)	Construction and Repair (2)	Wholesale and Retail (3)	Transport and Storage (4)	Accommodation and Food (5)	Professional (6)	Others (7)
Elderly aged > 64	-0.0116	-0.0009	0.0346	0.0002	-0.0034	-0.0006	-0.0181
	(0.0198)	(0.0049)	(0.0278)	(0.0044)	(0.0162)	(0.0068)	(0.0176)
Children aged < 5	-0.0101	0.0018	0.0355*	0.0002	-0.0110	-0.0149**	-0.0015
	(0.0141)	(0.0034)	(0.0204)	(0.0030)	(0.0128)	(0.0060)	(0.0120)
Access to credit	0.0445**	-0.0049	-0.0247	0.0060	0.0015	0.0005	-0.0228
	(0.0186)	(0.0043)	(0.0258)	(0.0045)	(0.0153)	(0.0063)	(0.0150)
Asset index	-0.0029	0.0016	0.0083	-0.0047***	-0.0030	-0.0024*	0.0031
	(0.0038)	(0.0010)	(0.0054)	(0.0017)	(0.0032)	(0.0014)	(0.0032)
Zone: Plain	0.0138	0.0110	-0.0339	-0.0182***	-0.0126	0.0431*	-0.0032
	(0.0272)	(0.0096)	(0.0398)	(0.0066)	(0.0208)	(0.0261)	(0.0225)
Zone: Tonle Sap	0.0427	0.0157	-0.1196***	-0.0109**	-0.0091	0.0732**	0.0080
	(0.0277)	(0.0099)	(0.0393)	(0.0052)	(0.0206)	(0.0307)	(0.0223)
Zone: Coastal	-0.0294	0.0086	-0.0996**	0.0015	0.0508*	0.0447	0.0234
	(0.0263)	(0.0107)	(0.0444)	(0.0062)	(0.0292)	(0.0329)	(0.0277)
Zone: Plateau/Mountain	-0.0219	0.0147	-0.0394	-0.0191***	0.0020	0.0468*	0.0170
	(0.0243)	(0.0104)	(0.0402)	(0.0068)	(0.0226)	(0.0270)	(0.0246)
Log Likelihood	-2614.27						
LR chi2	1108.64						
Pseudo R2	0.1749						
Total observations	2,074						

Notes: Standard errors are presented in parentheses. The base outcome is manufacturing sector.

*** p<0.01, ** p<0.05, * p<0.1.

Source: Authors.

Table 8 shows the gender gap in the choice of business by sector. The sample is limited to those individuals owning a business, and each business sector is used as the dependent variable. The mean probability of owning a business for women is found to be higher than that of men in the wholesale and retail, accommodation and food, and "others" sectors, where gender gaps in owning a business are, respectively, −37.78%, −10.96%, and −3.48%. On the other hand, the mean probability of owning a business for women is lower than that of men in the manufacturing, construction and repair, transport and storage, and professional sectors, where the gender gaps in owning a business are 6.69%, 10.51%, 31.90%, and 3.13%, respectively. It should be noted that all overall differences are explained largely by differences in the gender effects (coefficients), as the differences due to the endowment gaps are very small compared with the differences in coefficients. It is quite likely that the lack of women's engagement in these sectors is mainly due to social norms, societal perceptions, higher risk, and physical strain pertaining to women, and their time poverty (given women's reproductive and unpaid care roles within the household). While these findings may not be unique to Cambodia, it is evident that, even in a country where the level of women's entrepreneurship is relatively high, a large gender gap exists in the manufacturing, construction and repair, transport and storage, and professional sectors, which happen to generate relatively more revenue than others.

Table 8: Gender Gap in the Choice of Business by Sector

	Manufacturing (1)	Construction and Repair (2)	Wholesale and Retail (3)	Transport and Storage (4)	Accommodation and Food (5)	Professional (6)	Others (7)
Male	0.1370***	0.1094***	0.2928***	0.3215***	0.0376***	0.0475***	0.0541***
	(0.0115)	(0.0104)	(0.0151)	(0.0156)	(0.0064)	(0.0070)	(0.0075)
Female	0.0701***	0.0043**	0.6707***	0.0026*	0.1471***	0.0163***	0.0890***
	(0.0075)	(0.0019)	(0.0137)	(0.0014)	(0.0104)	(0.0037)	(0.0083)
Overall difference	0.0669***	0.1051***	-0.3778***	0.3190***	-0.1096***	0.0313***	-0.0348***
	(0.0137)	(0.0105)	(0.0204)	(0.0156)	(0.0122)	(0.0079)	(0.0112)
Difference in endowments	0.0077	-0.0026	0.0137	0.0002	-0.0137	0.0049	-0.0105
	(0.0078)	(0.0017)	(0.0126)	(0.0015)	(0.0103)	(0.0038)	(0.0067)
Difference in coefficients	0.0487**	0.1163***	-0.3940***	0.3458***	-0.1192***	0.0410***	-0.0357**
	(0.0194)	(0.0163)	(0.0324)	(0.0312)	(0.0138)	(0.0141)	(0.0162)
Difference in interaction	0.0104	-0.0087	0.0024	-0.0270	0.0233*	-0.0146	0.0114
	(0.0172)	(0.0119)	(0.0287)	(0.0276)	(0.0135)	(0.0117)	(0.0136)
Total observations	2,074	2,074	2,074	2,074	2,074	2,074	2,074
Males	905	905	905	905	905	905	905
Females	1,169	1,169	1,169	1,169	1,169	1,169	1,169

Notes: Standard errors are presented in parentheses.

*** p<0.01, ** p<0.05, * p<0.1.

Source: Authors.

6. Conclusion and Policy Recommendation

Micro and small enterprises (MSEs) are pervasive in developing countries as a source of livelihood and as a vehicle to improve people's well-being and help them escape from poverty. For some individuals and families, MSEs offer lucrative opportunities to maximize their revenue (pull factor), while for others, they are a means to secure food and shelter (push factor). Despite the relatively low entry barriers for informal MSEs, a poor household with little resources or capital—be it human, financial, social, or physical—is able to participate only in petty enterprises whose entry barrier is very low, while those with more capital can engage in enterprises that require higher financial and human capital. Further, as is also seen in Cambodia, women have limited access to resources in some communities, and sociocultural norms restrain their participation in MSEs.

This chapter analyzed data from the Cambodia Socio-Economic Survey 2019–2020 and used the nonlinear Blinder–Oaxaca model to examine gender differences in participation in microenterprises in urban Cambodia. This study finds that, unlike what is seen in many other developing countries, women in Cambodia generally tend to participate in microenterprises as owners, and more so than men. Further analyses also show that a large proportion of men-owned enterprises fall under the petty trading categories (i.e., the lowest stratum of the MSEs). The Blinder–Oaxaca decomposition finds the gender gap to be negative and significant in MSEs in expenditure-based quintiles 2, 3, and 4, indicating that women are more likely to own MSEs than men. However, the difference is insignificant in quintile 5, highlighting the nonexistence of the gender gap in larger enterprises. Differences in quintiles 2 and 3 are due to unobserved factors, while quintile 4 is due to the endowment factor (livelihood assets). Further sectoral analysis shows that due to the nature of the jobs, women tend to participate mostly in retail, wholesale, food and accommodation businesses, while men participate more in manufacturing and construction and repairs. Since most microenterprises are operated by the owners themselves without hired employees, women are less likely to participate in businesses that need greater physical strength and mobility. They are also generally responsible for caregiving of children and sick and elderly family members. This restrains women's mobility, so they participate more in MSEs that are operated from home or in close proximity—enterprises such as grocery shops, retail stores, and eateries. Results also suggest that the country's sociocultural institutions and public policies tend to be supportive of women's participation in MSEs.

To further aid women entrepreneurs in expanding and transitioning into formal enterprises, Cambodian public policy should focus on providing training to bolster the entrepreneurial capacity of women, so that they can be empowered to participate in sectors that require higher skills and generate higher revenues. Moreover, since the findings show that households with access to credit are more likely to own a business, the policy should promote measures that will provide more access to financial resources for women, helping them overcome barriers to participating in enterprises that require higher capital. Although the impact of the COVID-19 pandemic was not specifically included in the analysis presented here, the pandemic's impacts on informal sector livelihoods and MSEs in other developing Asian countries have been discussed extensively in other chapters of this book. Given Cambodia's relatively large share of employment in the informal sector and the economy's strong dependence on tourism, the burdens and challenges experienced by women in the informal sector have been more pronounced. Evolving tools and measures to pursue the aforementioned policy goals would benefit from the inputs of various stakeholders who have been engaged in understanding and/ or responding to the challenges on the ground—civil society actors, multilateral institutions such as ADB, and researchers at universities and other institutions.

References

Amarthalingam, S. 2022. Cambodia's Informal Economy Slips through the Cracks. *The Phnom Penh Post*. 3 February. https://www.phnompenhpost.com/special-reports/cambodias-informal-economy-slips-through-cracks.

Anderson, E., and K. Grace. 2018. From Schoolgirls to 'Virtuous' Khmer Women: Interrogating Chbab Srey and Gender in Cambodian Education Policy. *Studies in Social Justice* 12 (2): 215–34. https://doi.org/10.26522/ssj.v12i2.1626.

Ardrey, W. J., A. Pecotich, and C. J. Shultz. 2006. Entrepreneurial Women as Catalysts for Socioeconomic Development in Transitioning Cambodia, Laos, and Vietnam. *Consumption Markets and Culture* 9: 277–300. https://doi.org/10.1080/10253860600921811.

Asian Development Bank (ADB). 2011. *Cambodia: ADB Civil Society Briefs*. Phnom Penh, Cambodia. https://www.adb.org/sites/default/files/publication/28965/csb-cam.pdf.

_____. 2014. *Gender Tool Kit: Micro, Small, and Medium-Sized Enterprise Finance and Development*. Manila. https://www.adb.org/sites/default/files/institutional-document/34125/gender-tool-kit-mse-finance-development.pdf.

_____. 2015. *Promoting Women's Economic Empowerment in Cambodia*. Manila.

_____. 2020. *Asia Small and Medium-Sized Enterprise Monitor 2020 Volume I—Country and Regional Reviews*. https://www.adb.org/publications/asia-sme-monitor-2020-country-regional-reviews.

Berdegué, J. A. et al. 2001. Rural Nonfarm Employment and Incomes in Chile. *World Development* 29: 411–425.

Bullough, A., U. Guelich, T. S. Manolova, and L. Schjoedt. 2022. Women's Entrepreneurship and Culture: Gender Role Expectations and Identities, Societal Culture, and the Entrepreneurial Environment. *Small Business Economics*. 58: 985–996. https://doi.org/10.1007/s11187-020-00429-6.

Economic Institute of Cambodia (EIC). 2006. *Decent Work in the Informal Economy in Cambodia: A Literature Review*. International Labour Office.

Emerging Markets Consulting. 2017. *Unlocking the Potential of the Cambodian Private Sector*. http://www.mekongbiz.org/wp-content/uploads/2017/07/Cambodia-private-sector-assessment-report.pdf.

Equal Measures. 2022. Back to Normal Is Not Enough: The 2022 SDG Gender Index. *Equal Measures 2030*. https://www.equalmeasures2030.org/2022-sdg-gender-index/.

Erdin, C., and G. Ozkaya. 2020. Contribution of Small and Medium Enterprises to Economic Development and Quality of Life in Turkey. *Heliyon* 6: e03215.

Fairlie, R. W. 1999. The Absence of the African-American Owned Business: An Analysis of the Dynamics of Self-Employment. *Journal of Labor Economics* 17 (1): 80–108. https://doi.org/10.1086/209914.

Hammond A. L. et al. 2007. The Next 4 Billion-Market Size and Business Strategy at the Base of the Pyramid. *Innovations: Technology, Governance, Globalization*. Washington, DC: World Resources Institute and International Finance Corporation.

Huot, S., and L. Jensen. 2022. Gender Implications of COVID-19 in Cambodia. In *Gender, Food and COVID-19 Global Stories of Harm and Hope*, edited by P. Castellanos, C. E. Sachs, and A. R. Tickamyer. Oxfordshire, England: Routledge.

International Finance Corporation (IFC). 2014. *Women-Owned SMEs: A Business Opportunity for Financial Institutions—A Market and Credit Gap Assessment and IFC's Portfolio Gender Baseline.* Washington, DC.

_____. 2019. *Exploring the Opportunities for Women-Owned SMEs in Cambodia.* Washington, DC.

International Finance Corporation (IFC) and European Union (EU). 2010. Understanding Cambodian Small and Medium Enterprise Needs for Financial Services and Products. *Cambodia Agribusiness Series* No. 2. Phnom Penh, Cambodia.

International Labour Office. 2018. *Women and Men in the Informal Economy: A Statistical Picture*. Third Edition. Geneva.

International Labour Organization (ILO). 2018. *Women and Men in the Informal Economy: A Statistical Picture*. Third Edition. Geneva.

_____. 2020. Impact of Lockdown Measures on the Informal Economy. *ILO Brief.* Geneva.

_____. 2021. Transition from the Informal to the Formal Economy — Theory of Change. *ILO Brief.* Geneva.

Karlstrom, C. 2018. *The Sustainable Development Goals — A Framework for Everyone, Even SMEs*. London: Royal Society for the Encouragement of Arts, Manufactures and Commerce (RSA). https://www.thersa.org/blog/2018/06/the-sustainable-development-goals--a-framework-for-everyone-even-smes.

Kushnir, K., M. L. Mirmulstein, and R. Ramalho. 2010. *Micro, Small, and Medium Enterprises around the World: How Many Are There, and What Affects the Count?* Washington, DC: IFC (World Bank Group).

Kwok, Y. K. E., K. Bahadur KC, J. J. Silver, and E. Fraser. 2020. Perceptions of Gender Dynamics in Small-Scale Fisheries and Conservation Areas in the Pursat Province of Tonle Sap Lake, Cambodia. *Asia Pacific Viewpoint.* 61: 54–70. https://doi.org/https://doi.org/10.1111/apv.12225.

Leahy, C., J. Lunel, M. Grant, and J. Willetts. 2017. Women in WASH Enterprises: Learning from Female Entrepreneurship in Cambodia, Indonesia, and Lao PDR. *Enterprise in WASH.* Working Paper 6. Sydney: Institute for Sustainable Futures, University of Technology.

Lessidrenska, L. 2019. SMEs and SDGs: Challenges and Opportunities. *Development Matters.* Paris: Organisation for Economic Co-operation and Development (OECD). https://oecd-development-matters.org/2019/04/23/smes-and-sdgs-challenges-and-opportunities/.

National Institute of Statistics of Cambodia (NIS). 2014. *Cambodia Inter-censal Economic Survey 2014.* https://www.stat.go.jp/info/meetings/cambodia/pdf/c14ana01.pdf.

_____. 2020. *General Population Census of the Kingdom of Cambodia 2019: National Report on Final Census Results.* https://www.nis.gov.kh/nis/Census2019/Final%20General%20Population%20Census%202019-English.pdf.

Organisation for Economic Co-operation and Development (OECD). 2017. *Strengthening Women's Entrepreneurship in ASEAN: Towards Increasing Women's Participation in Economic Activity.* https://www.oecd.org/southeast-asia/regional-programme/Strengthening_Womens_Entrepreneurship_ASEAN.pdf.

Pike, K., and B. English. 2022. And Roses Too: How "Better Work" Facilitates Gender Empowerment in Global Supply Chains. *Gender, Work, and Organization* 29: 188–204. https://doi.org/https://doi.org/10.1111/gwao.12740.

Rahut, D. B., and M. Micevska Scharf. 2012. Livelihood Diversification Strategies in the Himalayas. *Australian Journal of Agricultural and Resource Economics* 56: 558–582.

Sen, A. 1992. *Inequality Reexamined.* Oxford: Oxford University Press.

Sugden, R. 1993. Welfare, Resources, and Capabilities: A Review of Inequality Reexamined by Amartya Sen. *Journal of Economic Literature* 31: 1947–1962.

United Nations (UN) ESCAP. 2017. *Fostering Women's Entrepreneurship in ASEAN: Transforming Prospects, Transforming Societies* (ST/ESCAP/2784). https://www.unescap.org/sites/default/files/ESCAP-FWE-ASEAN-full_0.pdf.

_____. 2020. Policy Guidelines for Supporting Women-Owned Micro, Small and Medium Enterprises (WMSMEs) Affected by the COVID-19 Pandemic in the Kingdom of Cambodia. https://hdl.handle.net/20.500.12870/807.

UNIDO and UNWOMEN. 2021. *Policy Assessment for the Economic Empowerment of Women in Green Industry Country Report: Cambodia.* Vienna.

Van der Vaeren, C. 2017. Getting Women Working. *The Phnom Penh Post.* 8 March. https://www.phnompenhpost.com/opinion/getting-women-working.

Vinh, D. 2021. Counting the Cost of COVID-19 to Cambodia's Informal Workers. *UNDP Cambodia.* 14 July. https://www.kh.undp.org/content/cambodia/en/home/blog/2021/counting-the-cost-of-covid-to-cambodias-informal-workers.html .

World Bank. 2022. Overview: The World Bank in Cambodia. 29 March. https://www.worldbank.org/en/country/cambodia/overview.

8

Informal Micro, Small, and Medium-Sized Enterprises and Digitalization: Challenges and Policy Actions in Indonesia

Shigehiro Shinozaki

Abstract

Most micro, small, and medium-sized enterprises (MSMEs) operate informally. While the informal parts of various sectors of the economy are assumed to contribute less to overall economic development, MSMEs are often a driving force behind national economic growth. Thus, formalizing informal MSMEs is critical to boosting national productivity, creating quality jobs, and promoting inclusive growth. This chapter examines the impact of the coronavirus disease (COVID-19) pandemic on informal MSMEs in Indonesia, using linear probability regression and descriptive analysis based on data obtained through year-long surveys conducted from March 2020 to May 2021. It also assesses the extent of the digital transformation and challenges brought on by the pandemic and offers policy implications based on the inferences. The estimates found two streams of business clusters among informal MSMEs—contracting firm groups that suffered through the pandemic and those that benefited. The COVID-19 crisis and mobility restrictions led many informal MSMEs to accelerate digitalization. But digitally operated firms could not always operate successfully during the pandemic, splitting businesses into those who suffered or benefited from the pandemic.

Keywords: COVID-19, informality, shadow economy, MSMEs, digitalization, SME development, access to finance, SME policy, Indonesia

1. Introduction

In developing Asia, the majority of micro, small, and medium-sized enterprises (MSMEs) operate informally, and many of them are in domestic trade or low-technology services. Informality here implies that these firms are not registered with government authorities. This is true for Indonesia, where traditional wholesale and retail trade dominate (63.5% of nonagriculture MSMEs in 2016).[1] Most MSMEs are unregistered family-run businesses or sole proprietorships. According to the International Finance Corporation (IFC 2013), unregistered informal firms are estimated to make up 77% of all MSMEs in developing economies. Asia and the Pacific host the most worldwide, with an estimated 153 million informal MSMEs in East Asia and the Pacific and 69 million in South Asia (using World Bank regional classifications). A critical challenge to achieve inclusive growth is to formalize (register) these informal firms and noncontract-based employees. Several studies show large numbers of informal firms coincide with lower economic development (Loayza and Rigolini 2006; ILO 2011; IFC 2013). A well-designed national policy framework to formalize informal MSMEs is needed to boost productivity and create quality jobs efficiently, where provincial governments play a critical role in promoting the formalization of MSMEs, given their spread nationwide.

The COVID-19 pandemic has significantly altered people's lives and livelihoods nationally, regionally, and globally. Lockdowns and associated quarantine measures—such as travel bans, temporary business closures, and social distancing—continue to seriously affect MSMEs, including informal MSMEs. Private businesses have cut back production and service delivery. An ADB study, which included Indonesia, found MSME sales and revenue dropped sharply relatively soon after the pandemic was announced in March 2020 (ADB 2020). Many MSMEs laid off employees to survive and faced a lack of working capital at the early stage of the pandemic. For many, it became difficult to continue operations.

In Southeast Asia, economic growth declined from 4.5% in 2019 to 3.2% in 2020. After the first year of the pandemic, private businesses began reopening as consumption and export markets recovered, with the

---

[1]   Data refer to Economic Census 2016.

region recovering a 2.9% in 2021 (ADB 2022). In Indonesia, the growth projection was more robust for 2021, a 3.7% rebound after a 2.1% decline in 2020. National policies focused more on economic recovery rather than strict lockdowns.[2] However, new COVID-19 variants, from the Delta to the Omicron, continue to impact economic growth. The longer it takes to contain the spread of COVID-19 the more it increases the risk of business failure and bankruptcy, especially for informal MSMEs that cannot access formal financial services or government support.

Given the drop in personal contact because of the pandemic, digitalization becomes critical for businesses, including informal MSMEs, to survive the new or next normal. It may also help them decide to formalize operations, which can offer many benefits. These include access to e-commerce and administering their business digitally. It can give informal MSMEs better access to the information they need, strengthen their networks, offer new market opportunities globally, reduce logistics and administration costs, widen funding opportunities such as peer-to-peer lending, and allow for greater business innovation (OECD 2021). Yet, despite these potential advantages, the shift toward digital transformation for MSMEs was not well promoted during the pre-COVID-19 period—as their traditional business models required physical and personal contact. However, the pandemic became an incentive for many small firms to go digital due to mobility restrictions. A recent global study by the Organisation for Economic Co-operation and Development (OECD 2021) finds that up to 70% of small firms have increased use of digital technology since the pandemic.

There are several barriers that hold informal MSMEs back from formalizing or registering their business. Some are unique to MSMEs, others are cultural. They include tax compliance, high reliance on informal finance, a lack of incentives or skills needed to expand business, and a tradition of not preferring to disclose one's business. Solid data analysis using granular firm-level data is critical to understand informal MSMEs, their challenges, and latent opportunities for growing their operations. It would certainly help in designing a feasible policy framework on how to better formalize and digitalize MSMEs.

---

[2]   The Government of Indonesia does not use the wording "lockdown" in its quarantine measures. The government imposed a large-scale social restriction "Pembatasan Sosial Berskala Besar" (PSBB) in April–May 2020 and a second PSBB in September–November 2020, which included temporary business closures and mobility restrictions. Due to the surging Delta coronavirus variant, the government again imposed a partial mobility restriction Pemberlakuan Pembatasan Kegiatan Masyarakat (PPKM—Emergency Community Activity Restrictions) in July–August 2021. The second wave of the pandemic has been contained since September 2021, with limited impact on the economy.

This chapter examines the impact of COVID-19 on informal MSMEs (sole proprietorships and family-run informal businesses, focusing on micro and small firms within MSMEs), using linear probability regression and descriptive analysis based on weighted data obtained from year-long ADB MSME surveys from March 2020 to May 2021 in Indonesia. It assesses the extent of their digital transformation and challenges during the pandemic and offers policy implications on how to formalize and digitalize MSMEs during the pandemic recovery. Section 2 reviews the literature analyzing the mechanics and size of informal economies and highlights the issues that keep businesses informal. Section 3 summarizes national policy responses to support MSMEs affected by COVID-19 in selected Asian economies, including support for the informal sector. Sections 4 and 5 discuss the study's methodology, data, and regression model. Sections 6 and 7 discuss the profiles of surveyed MSMEs and the pandemic's impact, a year into the pandemic, on informal MSMEs in select dimensions—revenues and financial conditions, including examples of digitally operated firms, followed by associated policy implications. Section 8 concludes the chapter by summarizing the chapter's purpose, key findings, and suggestions.

2. The Nature and Contours of Informal Economies

Although there is no standardized definition of the informal or shadow economy, several studies tried to define it by classifying types of underground activities. Schneider (2012) summarized broad definitions of shadow economies discussed in the literature: (i) illegal activities with monetary transactions (such as trade in stolen goods or drugs, among others) and nonmonetary transactions (such as smuggling)—in essence, activities deemed criminal; and (ii) legal activities evading or avoiding taxes (through unreported income from self-employment, wages, salaries, or assets from work, employee discounts, and fringe benefits, among others).[3] As this study centers on formalizing informal MSMEs to promote inclusive growth, the term excludes activities deemed criminal in this discussion. The shadow economy—including informal MSMEs— is thus defined here as "all market-based legal production of goods and services that are deliberately concealed from public authorities" to avoid payment of income, social security contributions, and compliance with legal labor market standards and certain administrative obligations (Schneider 2012: 6).

---

[3]   See Lippert and Walker (1997) on the structure of underground economic activities.

An International Finance Corporation (IFC) report (2013) summarizes the broader definitions of informality in three ways: (i) a dualist paradigm arguing that the informal sector is the residual component of an economy and one reflecting the inability of the formal economy to provide enough jobs; (ii) a structural paradigm arguing that the informal sector is interdependent with or part of the formal sector (providing cheap labor, inputs, and products to formal firms); and (iii) a legalist paradigm arguing that informal businesses operate to evade the exorbitant costs of complying with regulations.[4] "Informality" comprises firms that remain "unregistered with the [business] registration office, municipality, or tax authority, or owners and employees of microenterprises that employed few paid workers" (ILO 2012 cited in IFC 2013: 22). Informal employment is "employment without a contract, unregistered with the relevant authority such as the social security agency or Ministry of Labor, and employment not entitled to receive social security benefits" (ILO 2012 cited in IFC 2013: 22). This study uses these definitions of informal firms and employment to identify informal MSMEs from ADB survey data.

As shadow economic activity is unobserved, the estimation here broadly uses two techniques: (i) structural equation modeling to estimate a latent variable, or a multiple indicator multiple cause (MIMIC) model, using identifiable illicit activities as explanatory variables (such as the tax burden and regulation intensity) (Schneider, Buehn, and Montenegro 2010); and (ii) surveys using structured interviews (Feld and Larsen 2005, 2008, and 2009). Schneider (2009) summarized the literature estimating the main factors behind the growth of a shadow economy and found three major determinants: (i) an increase in taxes and social security contributions (a 35%–38% impact, based on average values of 12 studies); (ii) a tax or moral psychological effect (22%–25%); and (iii) quality of public institutions such as the level of corruption (10%–12%).

Figure 1 recomposes data from Schneider's research (2012) extracting data on Asia and Pacific countries based on five ADB subregions. It shows that the size of informal economies differs by country but is sizable. For 1999–2007, the highest informal share of a country's GDP was in Central and West Asia (averaging 46.7%), followed by the Pacific (34.2%), Southeast Asia (33.0%), South Asia (32.7%), and East Asia (15.2%). Among 10 Southeast Asian countries, Indonesia had a relatively small shadow economy at 18.9% of GDP on average. Although the data is old, 36.7 million Indonesian people were likely to be engaged in shadow economic activities in 1998, equivalent to 37.4% of

---

4   See Chen (2007) on the legalist paradigm.

the official labor force and 18.0% of the total population (Schneider and Enste 2002).

Figure 1: Size of the Shadow Economies in ADB Developing Member Countries (% of country's GDP, average in 1999–2007)

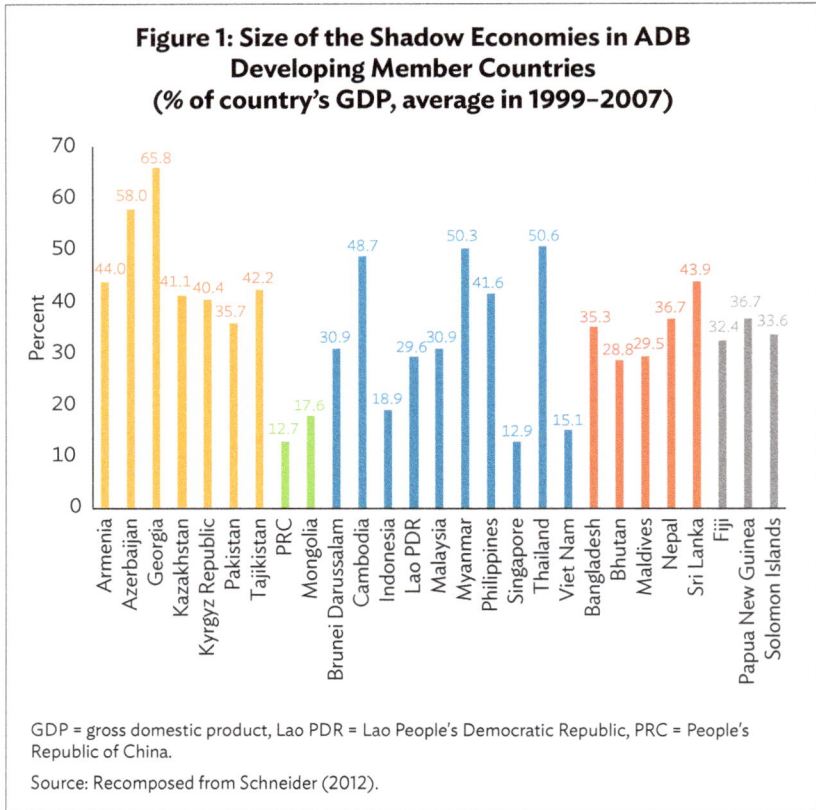

GDP = gross domestic product, Lao PDR = Lao People's Democratic Republic, PRC = People's Republic of China.

Source: Recomposed from Schneider (2012).

Informality brings about several disadvantages to MSMEs. Muhammad (2021) highlighted that an informal business has low profits and productivity, limited credit access, unofficial employment contracts, and no or little social security of workers.[5] By being formal, MSMEs are legally protected and will have social safety nets and more access to formal financial services and higher profits, while associated tax revenue

---

[5]   Muhammad (2021) referred to the discussion raised by Rand and Torm (2012).

increases.[6] Muhammad (2021) also argued why informal MSMEs stay at informal status, that is, because they believe that formalization would entail excessive regulations and complex administrative procedures, and is time-consuming and costly. The Government of Indonesia enacted Law No. 11 of 2020 on Job Creation to accelerate formalization of MSMEs, create more jobs, and escape from the middle-income trap. The law removes and simplifies business procedures (licensing). To successfully implement this law, however, effectively delivering information to informal MSMEs is needed, such as disseminating the benefits of formalization and demonstrating success cases of formalized MSMEs so more MSMEs can follow (Muhammad 2021).

3. Policy Responses to the COVID-19 Pandemic

From the start of the pandemic in 2020, Asian countries rapidly moved to contain the spread of COVID-19.[7] Each acted quickly to respond to the health-care emergency. They also adopted a wide range of policies designed to support households and businesses. These included debt financing, tax relief, and measures to help businesses retain their workers. Some came through economic stimulus packages with substantial government spending. Others did not. Informal sectors and/ or self-employed workers were also covered through cash assistance, tax holidays or extensions, and subsidies for vocational training. These various measures have continued for more than a year, either nonstop or on an ad hoc basis to groups both affected and unaffected by the pandemic—including private businesses, particularly MSMEs.

Debt financing is the most widely used policy instrument supporting MSMEs. At the time the pandemic started in 2020, a lack of working capital was clearly the most critical factor affecting private sector operations—due to a drop in forecast sales revenues caused by mobility restrictions. Central banks responded relatively soon by providing (i) liquidity support for financial institutions (via capital injections,

---

[6]   Boly (2020) discusses tax issues on small and medium-sized enterprises.

[7]   This section summarizes national responses to the pandemic in the Association of Southeast Asian Nations (ASEAN) plus Japan, the Republic of Korea, and the People's Republic of China, referring to various COVID-19 policy trackers developed by ADB, the International Monetary Fund (IMF), and the World Bank. Information is drawn from ADB. COVID-19 Policy Database. https://covid19policy.adb.org/; International Monetary Fund. Policy Responses to COVID-19. Policy Tracker. https://www.imf.org/en/Topics/imf-and-covid19/Policy-Responses-to-COVID-19; and World Bank. Map of SME-Support Measures in Response to COVID-19. https://www.worldbank.org/en/data/interactive/2020/04/14/map-of-sme-support-measures-in-response-to-covid-19 (accessed 30 November 2021).

reduced bank reserve requirements, and liquidity financing to banks, among others); (ii) debt restructuring such as debt moratoria, loan repayments deferrals, and eased regulatory compliance; and (iii) new lending to MSMEs (for example, refinancing facilities or special funding programs at reduced lending rates and/or credit guarantees).

Tax relief remains a key policy for providing economic stimulus in several countries. Corporate income tax reductions or exemptions and deferred payments are the main support benefiting MSMEs. Indonesia gradually reduced its corporate income tax to 22% in 2020 and 2021 and lowered it further to 20% in 2022—mainly targeting manufacturing. Other tax measures and reduced payments to government include (i) reduced or exempted social security contributions for affected MSMEs and industries; (ii) reduced or exempted value-added tax for businesses; and (iii) various tax holidays and/or tax breaks for businesses and specific sectors, especially small business owners and those that are self-employed. Indonesia temporarily suspended tax payments (for 6 months) for hotels and restaurants in major tourist destinations like Bali, where local government losses in tax revenues were compensated for by the central government.

Many Asian countries offered various subsidy schemes for employers to pay workers along with cash transfers for displaced workers in qualified MSMEs and priority sectors. Indonesia made cash handouts to street vendors, stalls, small shop owners, and informal sector workers (unemployment benefits). Other employment-related measures include revised terms of employment aligned to the new working environment—such as wage cuts and unpaid leave, expedited overtime work for COVID-19-related businesses, and vocational training subsidies for the self-employed and laid-off workers.

In several Asian countries, including Indonesia, businesses could avail of discounted or waived utility payments, rental and/or leasing fees, and government fees and charges. Other measures include deferred import tax payments for MSMEs that rely on imported goods for production, support for agricultural MSMEs selling products through e-commerce platforms, and support for digitalizing MSMEs.

All of this involved massive government spending. In Indonesia, as of 15 November 2021, total support packages implemented amounted to $115.3 billion, or 11.4% of 2020 GDP (ADB COVID-19 Policy Database). The government launched several economic stimulus packages in 2020: (i) economic stimulus focusing on tourism in February; (ii) fiscal stimulus for tax relief in March; and (iii) the National Economic Recovery (PEN) program, covering financial (credit guarantees) and nonfinancial (corporate income tax exemptions) for MSMEs. While there is uncertainty over how long it will take to contain COVID-19—

given existing and potential new variant outbreaks, there are increasing risks of further bloating national budgets and deteriorating bank balance sheets over the long term. This suggests the need for ways to better control budget expenditures with support to targeted groups. One important aspect is identifying the most effective means to encourage informal MSMEs and informal workers to formalize (or register) in order to ensure a smooth and stable economic recovery.

4. Data and Methodology

This chapter examines the COVID-19 effects on informal MSMEs using the data captured by a series of four MSME surveys in Indonesia, covering March–April 2020, August–September 2020, March–April 2021, and May 2021.[8]

Using the broad definitions of informal firms and employment discussed in Section 2, this study defines informal MSMEs as all micro and small enterprises (i) defined by Badan Pusat Statistik (BPS), Indonesia's central statistics office—micro firms have 1-4 employees, while small firms have 5-19 employees;[9] (ii) that deal with market-based legal production of goods and services as sole proprietorships and/or family-run businesses; and/or (iii) that are not registered with the business registration office, municipality, province, or tax authority. Informal employment is defined as those who work for informal MSMEs. From the survey data, micro and small enterprises that declared their company type as "sole proprietorship" or "others (family-run business)" are categorized as informal firms ("informal micro and small firms"), while respondents that declared "corporation or a partnership" or "cooperative or foundation" are considered formal firms.[10] This chapter focuses on informal micro and small firms as the target group for analysis.

---

[8]   The surveys were conducted on 17 April–22 May 2020 (covering March–April 2020), 17 August–30 September 2020 (covering August–September 2020), 27 March–30 April 2021 (covering March–April 2021), and 5–31 May 2021 (covering May 2021).

[9]   BPS defines a medium-sized enterprise as firms with 20 to 99 employees. Firms with more than 100 employees are classified as large enterprises. Indonesia has a national MSME definition—a productive entity owned by an individual or individual business unit with maximum net assets, excluding land and buildings, of Rp10 billion, or with maximum annual sales of Rp50 billion (Law No. 20/2008 on Micro, Small, and Medium-Sized Enterprises).

[10] The survey did not identify whether firms were "registered" or "unregistered." However, a local survey partner that conducted field interviews indicated that sole proprietorships can be regarded as unregistered informal firms.

The four surveys used a standardized questionnaire designed to assess the impact of COVID-19 on MSMEs. There were four components: (i) a company profile that identifies a company's primary business, location, operating period, employment, wage per employee, total assets, internet penetration/e-commerce, and exposure to global business; (ii) business conditions during the pandemic, including changes in the business environment, sales revenue, employment, wage payments, and fiscal and funding conditions; (iii) the business concerns MSMEs faced during the pandemic and actions they would take in case the pandemic would be prolonged; and (iv) policy interventions that MSMEs would like to receive from government to maintain or restart their business.

The surveys were conducted using two approaches: (i) online surveys through survey partners, including the Indonesian Chamber of Commerce and Industry (KADIN) and the Ministry of Finance, along with ADB's Facebook page; and (ii) field surveys conducted by a local survey firm, using trained interviewers. Due to the urgency of capturing MSME conditions to support policy design for MSMEs amid the pandemic, the first rapid survey chose an online survey approach through ADB's Facebook page. The same approach was used for the second 2020 survey. For the third and fourth surveys in 2021, the approach was modified to combine online and field surveys to increase the response ratio. The field surveys were conducted in the four main provinces of DKI Jakarta, West Java, East Java, and North Sumatra, given the high concentration of MSMEs in these areas. Thus, there were largely different groups of respondents in the four surveys. Nonetheless, the study also allows looking at the change in respondents within the same group of MSMEs a year into the pandemic.[11]

As the surveys used an online approach along with networks of survey partners, samples were not selected randomly and did not follow the existing national statistics framework. In particular, the online survey has the problem of self-selection and non-response bias.[12] To minimize this bias, a weighting adjustment had been frequently

---

[11]　For field surveys, a local survey firm tried interviewing all respondents of the first and second surveys; however, due to surging COVID-19 infections in the country, many previous respondents were unable to answer survey questions as many had already closed their businesses, were COVID-19 positive, or had already passed away. As a result, there were only 1.2% repeating respondents of those in the third survey. The fourth survey tracked the same respondents as the third survey, where dates of individual interviews were scheduled 1 month after the previous interview. The gap in the number of respondents between the third and fourth surveys was mainly due to the Lebaran Holiday (official Islamic holiday), which is 12–14 May 2021.

[12]　This happens when respondents have a choice of filling in or not filling in survey questions, which often occurs during online surveys.

used as a correction technique.[13] The study used auxiliary variables measured in both surveys and the existing sampling frame. Survey data were weighted using the combination of firm size, business sector, and firm location data captured by both MSME surveys and the BPS 2016 Economic Census. For firm size, MSME surveys had data on micro, small, medium-sized, and large firms, respectively, while BPS census data had only two broad categories—(i) micro and small firms, and (ii) medium-sized and large firms; the weighted data for analysis used these two classifications. For the business sector, the MSME surveys also had complete responses from agriculture, while agriculture was not included in the industrial classification of BPS census data on MSMEs; the weighted data for analysis are unable to capture agricultural MSMEs.

The surveys received 528 completed responses from firms across Indonesia in the March–April 2020 survey, 129 in the August–September 2020 survey, 2,515 in the March–April 2021 survey, and 2,207 in the May 2021 survey. To understand the extent of bias, the distribution of the unweighted survey samples was compared with an existing framework, the BPS 2016 Economic Census.[14] If the unweighted and weighted results are comparable, then self-selection and non-response bias may not be serious in the survey data. For more details on the differences between ADB and BPS surveys, see Appendix 1.

---

[13]   It should be noted that the weighting adjustment may not eliminate all the biases in the estimated parameters, but it helps minimize to some extent self-selection and non-response bias.

[14]   See Shinozaki (2022) for a detailed comparison between MSME surveys and national statistics distribution.

5. Linear Probability Model

A linear probability model (LPM) was designed to estimate the COVID-19 impact on MSMEs during the first year of the pandemic.[15] It focuses on four areas: (i) monthly revenue, (ii) employment conditions, (iii) wage payments, and (iv) financial conditions (Table 1). Based on Shinozaki and Rao (2021), the study considered that the factors affecting MSME operations and management during the pandemic include (i) the industrial sector MSMEs belong to, (ii) business location, (iii) operating period, (iv) business informality, (v) digital operations (e-commerce or use of the internet for business), (vi) business ownership (gender), (vii) global business exposure, and (viii) firm size (employment grouping). These are the independent variables for estimates. In this study, the analysis focuses on variables on informality and digital operations. The survey data were weighted in accordance with the BPS 2016 Economic Census.

$$Y_i = \alpha + \beta\,Ind_i + \gamma\,Reg_i + \delta\,Ops_i + \zeta\,Inf_i + \varphi\,Dig_i + \psi\,Wom_i + \eta\,GVC_i \\ + \tau\,MSME_i + \varepsilon \tag{1}$$

In this model, Y includes four areas with six dimensions (models) that measure the level of a firm's resilience to the pandemic and associated government measures (Table 1). Y_i in each model is a separate binary dependent variable for each observed firm i; Ind_i is the vector of categories for industry classification with "water supply (considered relatively stable sector regardless of the pandemic)" as base; Reg_i is the vector of categories for business location with "DKI Jakarta" as base; Ops_i is the vector of categories for years of operation with "0–5 years" as base; Inf_i is a binary variable that takes the value 1 if the establishment is a "sole proprietorship" or "others (family-run business)" and zero otherwise; Dig_i is a binary variable that takes the value 1 if the

---

[15]   There is an argument on the choice of econometric modeling in the presence of a binary dependent variable. It generally compares two approaches: (i) the linear probability model (LPM), and (ii) probit and logistic models. The LPM allows the fitting of data using a simple linear regression following the least squares approach. By contrast, probit and logistic regressions are drawn from the standard normal cumulative distribution function or the cumulative distribution function drawn from a logistic random variable. There are several pros and cons for both. Considering such pros and cons, this study chose the LPM approach. The main reasons are that (i) probit and logistic models rely on several strong assumptions with respect to error terms, which may not always hold; (ii) probit and logistic models are difficult to interpret and issues arise when justifying the results; and (iii) the LPM is convenient and easier to interpret, computationally less intensive, and reveals similar marginal effects to its nonlinear counterparts.

establishment is engaged in online selling (e-commerce) or uses the internet for business and zero otherwise; Wom_i is a binary variable that takes the value 1 if the owner of the establishment is a "woman" and zero if the owner is a "man"; GVC_i is a binary variable that takes the value 1 if the establishment is involved in a global supply chain or export/import business and zero otherwise; $MSME_i$ is a binary variable that takes the value 1 if the establishment is a "micro and small enterprise" and zero if the establishment is a "medium-sized and large enterprise"; and ε is a residual.

Table 1: Model Specification

Area (4)	Dimension (6)	Definition
1. Monthly revenue	Revenue 1	Firm's income/revenue condition 1. Totally no income/ revenue or none at the time of the survey.
	Revenue 2	Firm's income/revenue condition 2. An income/ revenue decrease as compared to the previous month or not.
2. Employment	Employment	Firm's employment condition assessed by a decrease or increase in employees (including no change) from the previous month or not.
3. Wage payments	Wage 1	Firm's wage/salary payment condition to employees 1. Totally no wage payments to employees or none at the time of the survey.
	Wage 2	Firm's wage/salary payment condition to employees 2. A decrease in the total wage payments from the previous month or not.
4. Financial condition	Finance	Firm's financial condition assessed as already having no cash/savings or running out of cash/funds in 3 months at the time of the survey.

Source: Author.

6. Profile of Surveyed MSMEs

In the March–April 2020 survey, 96.4% of the respondents (509 firms) owned micro and small enterprises, 98.5% (127 firms) in the August–September 2020 survey, 97.9% (2,461 firms) in the March–April 2021 survey, and 98.2% (2,167 firms) in the May 2021 survey. The rest were from medium-sized and large enterprises for all surveys. Readers should carefully interpret the medium-sized and large enterprise statistics for the August–September 2020 survey, given the small sample size.

There were several common features of firms surveyed at all four points of time (see Appendix 2). Most surveyed firms were domestically operating micro and small enterprises; and many of them were engaged in services—wholesale and retail trade, accommodation, and food services—as informal sole proprietorships or family-run businesses, many of which are in Java, especially West and East Java. Around half or more of those surveyed were young enterprises with 0–5 years of operations. Women-led firms accounted for less than half of the total surveyed. Monthly wages were low at around $200 per employee. The major difference across all surveys was the level of digital use in operations: firms surveyed in 2020 had relatively high digital use (around 60% or more of surveyed firms), while those in 2021 had low digital use in commerce (25% or less).

7. Findings from Descriptive Statistics and Econometric Analyses

The study provides a descriptive analysis based on the survey findings and uses the LPM to estimate the impact of the COVID-19 pandemic on MSME operations and fiscal conditions. It weighted the survey data based on the BPS 2016 Economic Census by firm size, sector, and location.

At the time the pandemic was formally proclaimed in March 2020, 49.5% of informal micro and small enterprises were forced to close their businesses relatively soon afterward. The share was higher than that of formal micro and small enterprises (44.9%) (Figures 2A and 2B). Those continuing operations accounted for 34.5%, but they faced a drop in domestic demand—the share was lower than that of formal micro and small enterprises (71.6%). There was a group that reported a better business environment than before the outbreak—typically those in essential goods or services and health care for households. But these were a small fraction (8.4%). One year into the pandemic, those reporting temporary business closures decreased to 10.7% of informal micro and small enterprises (the share of formal micro and small enterprises also sharply decreased to 7.6%). However, firms that had to contend with the drop in domestic demand increased to 64.7% of informal micro and small enterprises (the share of formal micro and small enterprises also stayed high at 64.4%). By contrast, informal micro and small enterprises that reported a better business environment grew to 26.4% (formal micro and small enterprises at 22.1%), suggesting the pandemic created two streams of business clusters: those that were disrupted and those that benefited from the pandemic.

Service-related informal firms followed the same trend as informal micro and small enterprises, as most were in services (Figure 2C). For informal manufacturing firms—typically those producing and selling goods (including food products) themselves—the share of those reporting a continuous drop in domestic demand increased from 54.0% in the first survey to 87.4% in the fourth. However, those reporting temporary business closures decreased from 37.5% in the first survey to 5.4% in the fourth (Figure 2D).

Overall, the business environment for informal micro and small enterprises (and services-related informal firms) likely improved, but many continued to face poor domestic demand 1 year into the pandemic, while some expanded their business. However, it should be noted that there were only a small portion of respondents participating across surveys (1.2% of those in the third survey); many informal micro and small enterprises may have closed.

The LPM estimates, based on the weighted data, provide a detailed picture of the impact of the COVID-19 pandemic on MSMEs.[16] Formula (1) was carried out in four areas (revenue, employment, wages, and finance) with six dimensions that affect a firm's resilience to the pandemic and associated government measures. Among those four areas, this chapter focuses on revenue and finance for analysis, addressing the impacts by business sector and location and on informal and digitally operated firms at four data points.

---

[16]   See Appendix 3 for the extract of regression outputs and Shinozaki (2022) for details.

Figure 2: Business Environment during the Pandemic

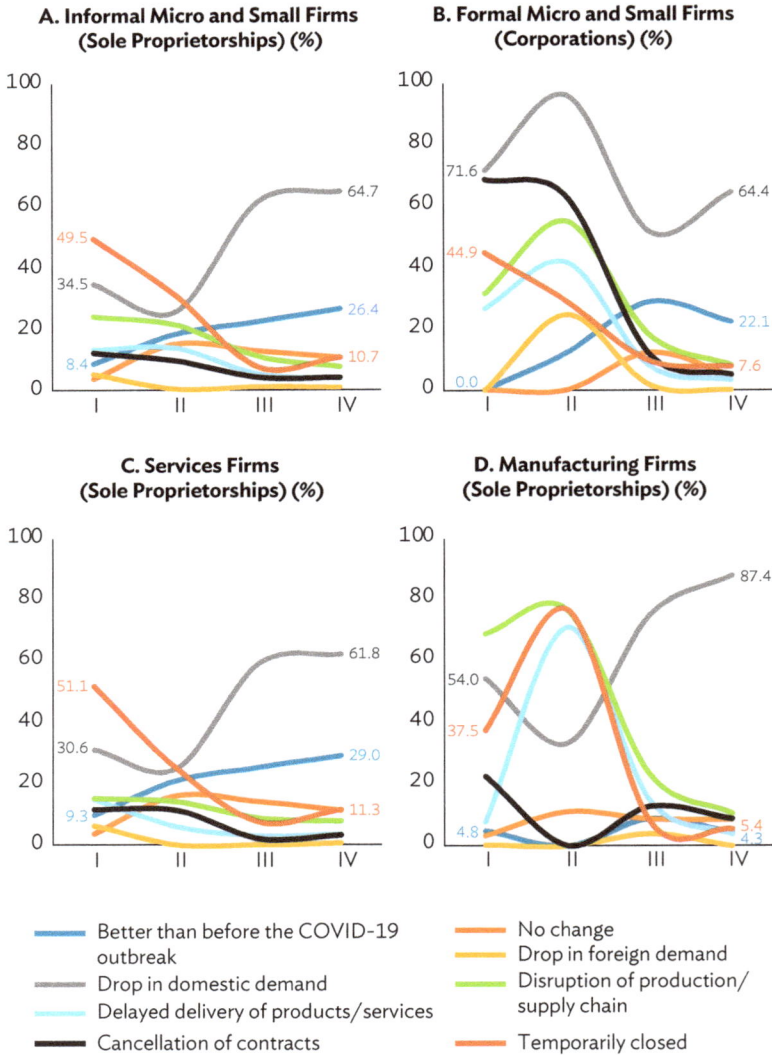

A. Informal Micro and Small Firms (Sole Proprietorships) (%)

B. Formal Micro and Small Firms (Corporations) (%)

C. Services Firms (Sole Proprietorships) (%)

D. Manufacturing Firms (Sole Proprietorships) (%)

Legend:
- Better than before the COVID-19 outbreak
- Drop in domestic demand
- Delayed delivery of products/services
- Cancellation of contracts
- No change
- Drop in foreign demand
- Disruption of production/supply chain
- Temporarily closed

I = March–April 2020; II = August–September 2020; III = March–April 2021; IV = May 2021.

Note: There are a total of 528 valid samples in Indonesia for March–April 2020, 129 for August–September 2020, 2,515 for March–April 2021, and 2,207 for May 2021.

Source: Calculation based on weighted data from MSME surveys in Indonesia for March–April 2020, August–September 2020, March–April 2021, and May 2021.

7.1 Impact on MSME Revenue

Impact by Sector

At the time of the initial outbreak in 2020, the regression result indicated that construction, administrative and support services, education, and arts/entertainment/recreation were more likely to have no revenue in April 2020 than water supply (as base, given its relatively stable operations) due to temporary business and school closures.[17] In April–May 2020, the government imposed "large-scale social restrictions" called Pembatasan Sosial Berskala Besar (PSBB), which required temporary business and school closures and restricted people's mobility and religious/social activities. It makes sense that the PSBB contributed to the zero-revenue condition of the industrial sectors mentioned above.

For firms that operated continuously after the 2020 outbreak, the estimates indicated that information and communication services were less likely to see decreased revenues in April 2020 than water supply.[18] The information and communication services were exempted from the PSBB as an essential service. The regression result was consistent with the business environment under social restrictions.

In August–September 2020, many industries—including manufacturing, construction, wholesale and retail trade, and accommodation and food services—were less likely to report no revenue than water supply, although estimates were not statistically significant. After the first PSBB (which ended May 2020), the economy was shifting into recovery. But due to surging COVID-19 infections later in the year, the government imposed the PSBB again (PSBB II) from September to November 2020.

In March–April 2021, "financial and insurance activities" and "human health and social work activities" were less likely to report no revenue than water supply.[19] As these industries are essential services, the estimates were consistent with household needs. Meanwhile,

---

[17]   In comparison with water supply-related firms, those in a no-revenue condition was 66.4 percentage points higher in construction (with .05 significance level), 90.4 percentage points higher in administrative and support services (with .01 significance level), 75.5 percentage points higher in education (with 0.1 significance level), and 96.4 percentage points higher in arts/entertainment/ recreation (with .01 significance level).

[18]   Firms' decreased revenue in information and communication services was 41.9 percentage points lower than water supply (with 0.1 significance level).

[19]   No-revenue in financial services and health/social services was 11.7 and 10.9 percentage points lower than water supply, with 0.1 and .05 significance levels, respectively.

revenue worsened in construction and transport. They were more likely to face decreased revenue even a year after the 2020 outbreak.[20]

In May 2021, just a month after the previous survey, the business environment in each industrial sector appeared sensitive to changing levels of COVID-19 cases. Zero revenue firms were more likely to increase in "wholesale and retail trade" and "other service activities" (including tourism).[21] Professional and technical business activities were also affected.[22] In Indonesia, the surging Delta COVID-19 variant was identified in 2021, with a second wave in mid-June 2021. The estimates indicated that small distributive trade and services were already affected a month before the second wave. Meanwhile, supported by the National Economic Recovery (PEN) program launched in May 2021, the revenue condition likely improved in construction.[23]

Impact by Region

The LPM estimates indicated that, from the beginning itself, many firms based in provinces were more negatively affected by the pandemic than the Jakarta-based firms. At the time the first wave was identified in 2020, compared with Jakarta-based firms (as base), firms in outlying regions such as Gorontalo, West Nusa Tenggara, West Papua, and West Sulawesi were more likely to report zero revenue in April 2020 due to business closures.[24] Many more firms in provinces across the archipelago were also identified with decreased revenue. DI Yogyakarta, Gorontalo, West Java, West Kalimantan, South Kalimantan, Central Kalimantan, Kepulauan Riau, Lampung, West Nusa Tenggara, West Papua, West Sulawesi, South Sulawesi, and Central Sulawesi were all more likely to see firms with decreased revenue than Jakarta-based firms in April 2020.[25] Meanwhile, Bengkulu, Papua, and Southeast Sulawesi were

---

[20]   Firms' decreased revenue in construction and transport was 35.3 and 41.2 percentage points higher than water supply, respectively.

[21]   Firms' no-revenue was 3.6 percentage points in trade (with .01 significance level) and 8.9 percentage points in other services (with 0.1 significance level) higher than water supply.

[22]   Firms' decreased revenue in professional services was 38.8 percentage points higher than water supply (with .05 significance level).

[23]   The pandemic's impact on firms with decreased revenue in construction was 35.6 percentage points lower than water supply (with 0.1 significance level).

[24]   49–62 percentage points higher with .01 significance level, except West Papua (0.1 significance level).

[25]   13–26 percentage points higher with .01, .05, or 0.1 significance levels.

less likely to report zero revenue than Jakarta-based firms.[26] But firms in these provinces were more likely to face decreased revenue than Jakarta-based firms, although figures were not statistically significant.

In August–September 2020, firms in South Sulawesi were more likely to see zero revenue than Jakarta-based firms.[27] Estimates in other provinces were not statistically significant.

In March–April 2021, revenues worsened in many provinces. Firms in Bali, West Java, Central Java, East Java, West Kalimantan, and West Sumatra were more likely to report zero revenue than Jakarta-based firms due to business closures.[28] Worsened (decreased) revenue of firms was identified in most provinces.[29]

In May 2021, the revenue condition of firms continued to worsen in the provinces. Firms in Bali, DI Yogyakarta, East Java, Riau, and North Sulawesi were more likely to report zero revenue than Jakarta-based firms due to business closures.[30] The estimates found that many local firms were more seriously affected by the pandemic than Jakarta-based firms a year into the pandemic. Possible reasons why some regions fared much worse than others include rural MSMEs' lower coping ability to the pandemic impacts and less accessibility of government assistance programs.

Impact on Informal Firms

Informal firms were more likely to be affected by the pandemic than formal firms. In August–September 2020 when COVID-19 cases surged, firms' no-revenue condition was 57.5 percentage points higher in informal firms than formal ones with .01 significance level. In March–April 2021, when the economy had begun a recovery, firms with no revenue were 24.5 percentage points lower in informal firms than formal

---

[26]   46–47 percentage points lower with .01, .05, or 0.1 significance levels.

[27]   72.8 percentage points higher with .05 significance level.

[28]   3–94 percentage points higher with .01, .05, or 0.1 significance levels.

[29]   Firms in Aceh, Bali, Bengkulu, Jambi, Central Java, West Kalimantan, South Kalimantan, Lampung, West Nusa Tenggara, East Nusa Tenggara, Riau, South Sulawesi, Southeast Sulawesi, North Sulawesi, and West Sumatra were all more likely to see decreased revenue than those in Jakarta (13–36 percentage points higher with .01 significance level except South Kalimantan [0.1]).

[30]   3–94 percentage points higher with .01, .05, or 0.1 significance levels. Firms in Bali, DI Yogyakarta, South Kalimantan, West Nusa Tenggara, South Sulawesi, and North Sulawesi were more likely to report decreased revenue than Jakarta-based firms (20–51 percentage points higher with .01 significance level).

firms, with .01 significance level. In May 2021, during the Delta variant surge, firms with no revenue were again 5.8 percentage points higher in informal firms than formal ones, with .05 significance level.

Impact on Digitally Operated Firms

A digitally operated firm engages in selling products and services online (e-commerce) or uses the internet for daily business. The LPM results showed that, at the beginning of the pandemic in 2020, digitally operated firms were less likely to be affected.[31] Firms' limited revenue loss condition was likely to continue in digitally operated firms in August–September 2020 and March–April 2021, but this condition seemed to reverse in May 2021, although figures were not statistically significant. The descriptive analysis based on weighted survey data provides a more detailed picture.

Figure 3 shows the gap of response ratio of the survey in revenue between digitally operated firms (informal and formal micro and small enterprises and medium-sized and large enterprises that use e-commerce or the internet for daily business) and non-digitally operated firms (those that do not use e-commerce or the internet for business, and thus rely on physical-contact-based operations). The gap is calculated as the share of digitally operated firms minus that of non-digitally operated firms to their respective populations, where a positive value indicates a higher impact on digital firms (a higher percentage share) than non-digital firms, while a negative value indicates a lower impact on digital firms (a lower percentage share) than non-digital firms.

Similar to other firms, digitally operated micro and small enterprises (those using the internet for business) had their operations seriously damaged at the beginning of the pandemic, but the impact on revenue was relatively limited as compared to non-digital micro and small enterprises in April 2020 (–6.3 for informal micro and small enterprises with income drops of over 30%, and –15.9 for formal micro and small enterprises with no revenue). The share of those reporting monthly income increases (over 10%) was slightly higher than non-digital micro and small enterprises (+1.1 for informal and +2.0 for formal micro and small enterprises in April 2020) (Figure 3A). By May 2021, however, two different groups emerged for digitally operated micro and small enterprises using e-commerce. One was for nonprofitable firms and

---

[31]   Firms' decreased revenue condition was 5.9 percentage points lower than non-digitally operated firms in April 2020, with 0.1 significance level.

Figure 3: Revenue—Digitally Operated Enterprises

A. By Firm Size (March–April 2020)

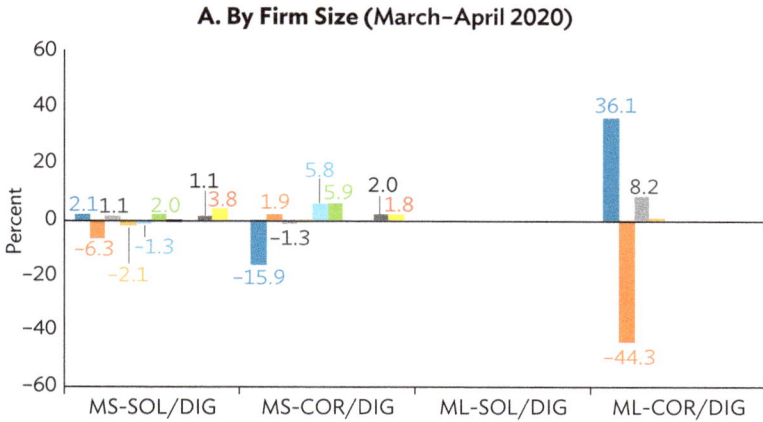

B. By Sector (March–April 2020)

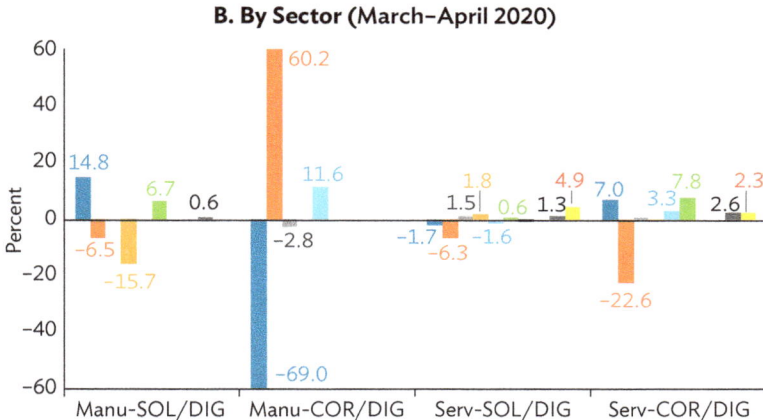

Legend:
- Zero (temporarily closed)
- More than 30% decrease
- 21%–30% decrease
- 11%–20% decrease
- 1%–10% decrease
- No change
- 1%–5% increase
- 6%–10% increase
- More than 10% increase
- Not applicable

COR = corporations, DIG = digitally operated firms, Manu = manufacturing, ML = medium-sized and large enterprises, MS = micro and small enterprises, Serv = services, SOL = sole proprietorships.

Note: A total of 528 valid samples in Indonesia for March–April 2020, 129 for August–September 2020, 2,515 for March–April 2021, and 2,207 for May 2021.

Source: Calculations based on weighted data from MSME surveys in Indonesia for March–April 2020, August–September 2020, March–April 2021, and May 2021.

continued on next page

Figure 3 continued

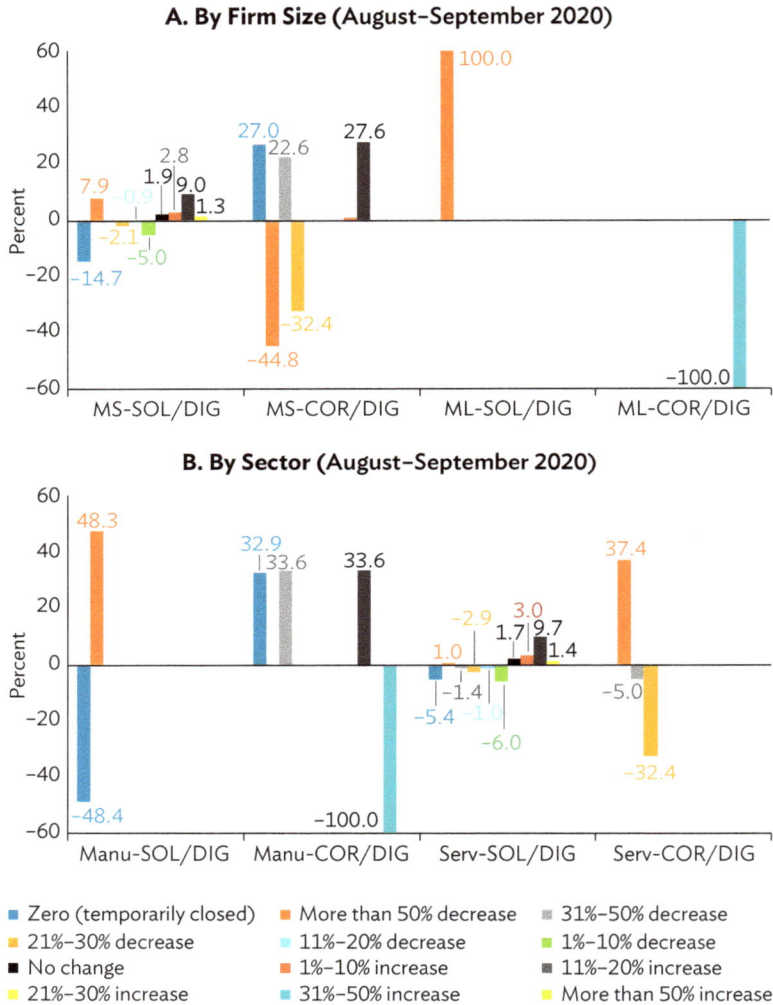

A. By Firm Size (August–September 2020)

B. By Sector (August–September 2020)

Legend:
- Zero (temporarily closed)
- More than 50% decrease
- 31%–50% decrease
- 21%–30% decrease
- 11%–20% decrease
- 1%–10% decrease
- No change
- 1%–10% increase
- 11%–20% increase
- 21%–30% increase
- 31%–50% increase
- More than 50% increase

COR = corporations, DIG = digitally operated firms, Manu = manufacturing, ML = medium-sized and large enterprises, MS = micro and small enterprises, Serv = services, SOL = sole proprietorships.

Note: A total of 528 valid samples in Indonesia for March–April 2020, 129 for August–September 2020, 2,515 for March–April 2021, and 2,207 for May 2021.

Source: Calculations based on weighted data from MSME surveys in Indonesia for March–April 2020, August–September 2020, March–April 2021, and May 2021.

continued on next page

Figure 3 continued

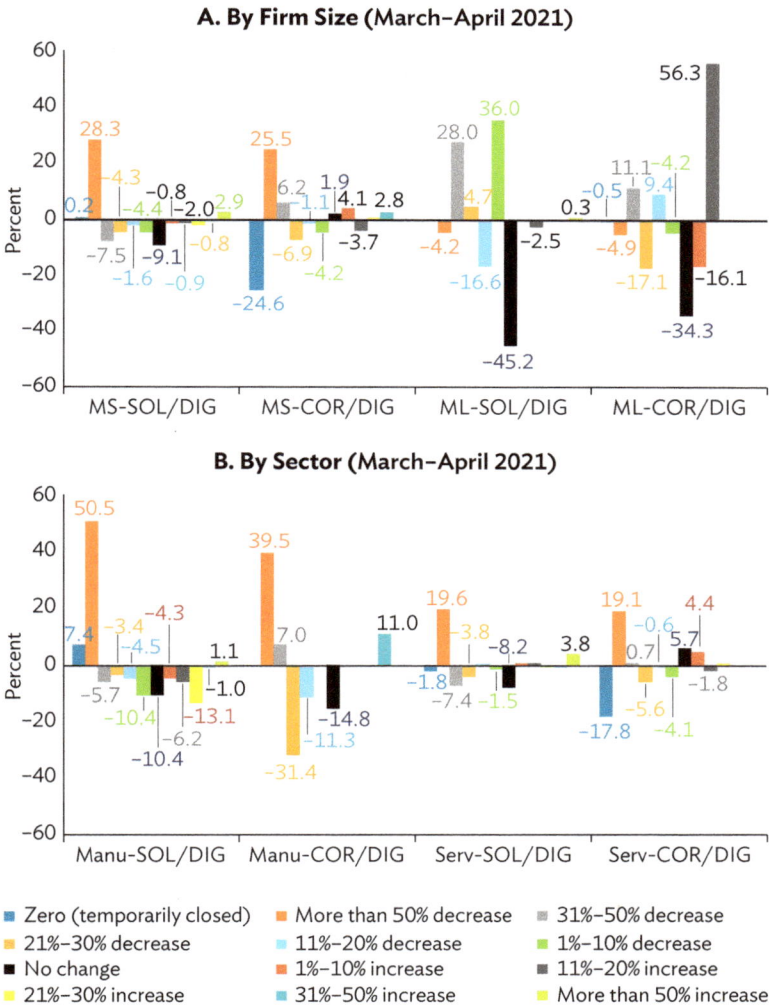

A. By Firm Size (March–April 2021)

B. By Sector (March–April 2021)

Legend:
- ■ Zero (temporarily closed)
- ■ More than 50% decrease
- ■ 31%–50% decrease
- ■ 21%–30% decrease
- ■ 11%–20% decrease
- ■ 1%–10% decrease
- ■ No change
- ■ 1%–10% increase
- ■ 11%–20% increase
- ■ 21%–30% increase
- ■ 31%–50% increase
- ■ More than 50% increase

COR = corporations, DIG = digitally operated firms, Manu = manufacturing, ML = medium-sized and large enterprises, MS = micro and small enterprises, Serv = services, SOL = sole proprietorships.

Note: A total of 528 valid samples in Indonesia for March–April 2020, 129 for August–September 2020, 2,515 for March–April 2021, and 2,207 for May 2021.

Source: Calculations based on weighted data from MSME surveys in Indonesia for March–April 2020, August–September 2020, March–April 2021, and May 2021.

continued on next page

Figure 3 continued

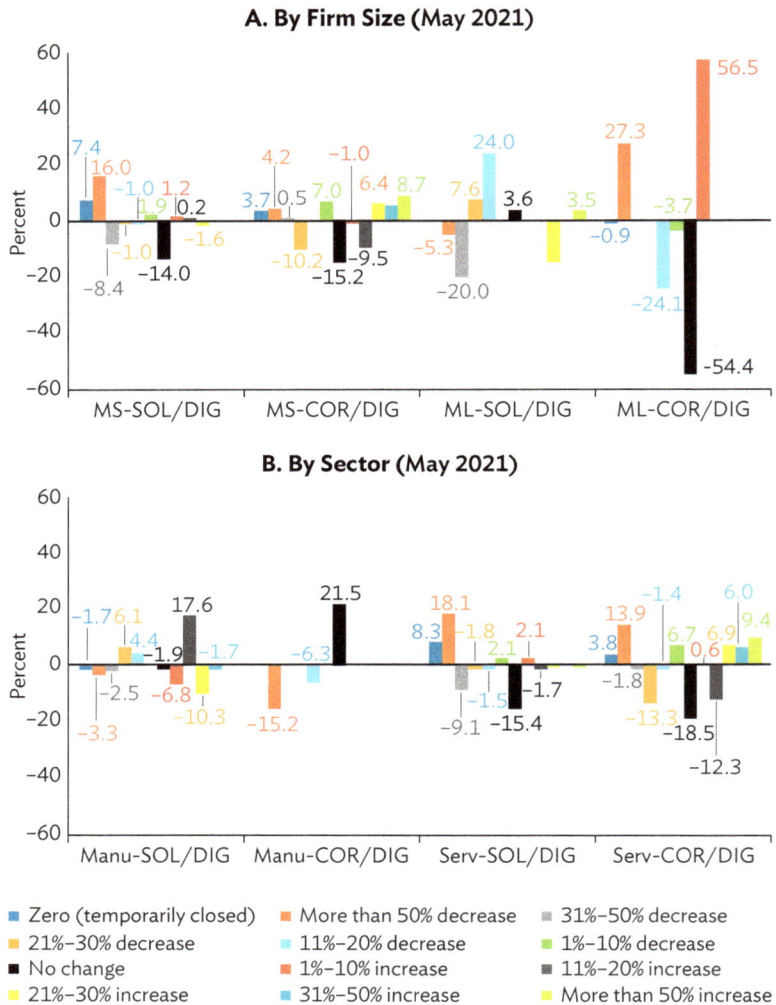

A. By Firm Size (May 2021)

B. By Sector (May 2021)

Legend:
- ■ Zero (temporarily closed)
- ■ More than 50% decrease
- ■ 31%–50% decrease
- ■ 21%–30% decrease
- ■ 11%–20% decrease
- ■ 1%–10% decrease
- ■ No change
- ■ 1%–10% increase
- ■ 11%–20% increase
- ■ 21%–30% increase
- ■ 31%–50% increase
- ■ More than 50% increase

COR = corporations, DIG = digitally operated firms, Manu = manufacturing, ML = medium-sized and large enterprises, MS = micro and small enterprises, Serv = services, SOL = sole proprietorships.

Note: A total of 528 valid samples in Indonesia for March–April 2020, 129 for August–September 2020, 2,515 for March–April 2021, and 2,207 for May 2021.

Source: Calculations based on weighted data from MSME surveys in Indonesia for March–April 2020, August–September 2020, March–April 2021, and May 2021.

the other for profitable firms.[32] For digitally operated medium-sized and large enterprises, high revenue was likely in formal firms between March and May 2021.[33]

For digitally operated firms in services (Figure 3B), the impact on revenue was also relatively limited compared with non-digital services in April 2020 (–8.0 for informal firms with no revenue or an over 30% decrease in income, and –22.6 for formal firms with an over 30% decrease). Meanwhile, the share of those reporting increased monthly income (over 10%) was slightly higher than non-digital firms in services (+1.3 for informal and +2.6 for formal firms in April 2020). Similar to digitally operated micro and small enterprises, however, both highly nonprofitable and profitable services firms emerged in May 2021, creating two types of business clusters.[34]

For digitally operated manufacturing firms, the impact on revenue continued to be severe at the end of April 2021.[35] But it likely improved in informal manufacturing firms operating digitally, with an increased share of those with high revenue in May 2021.[36]

7.2 Financial Conditions

Working Capital Condition

Mobility restrictions to contain the spread of COVID-19 at its onset immediately affected MSME business operations and their financial conditions. Working capital shortages were more serious in informal MSMEs as they normally cannot access formal financial services. As a

---

[32] For nonprofitable firms, +23.4 for informal and +7.9 for formal micro and small enterprises with no revenue, or more than 50% decrease in May 2021. For profitable firms, +1.4 for informal micro and small enterprises with up to a 20% increase and +20.6 for formal micro and small enterprises with a 21% increase or more in May 2021.

[33] +56.3 for formal medium-sized and large enterprises with an 11%–20% increase in March–April 2021 and +56.5 for formal medium-sized and large enterprises with up to a 10% increase in May 2021.

[34] For nonprofitable firms, +18.1 for informal and +13.9 for formal firms with more than 50% decrease in May 2021. For profitable firms, +2.1 for informal firms with up to a 10% increase and +22.9 for formal firms with increased income (of which +9.4 for those with increased income of over 50%) in May 2021.

[35] +57.9 for informal firms with no revenue or more than 50% decrease and +46.5 for formal firms with more than 30% decrease (of which +39.5 for those with a decrease of over 50%) in March–April 2021.

[36] +17.6 for informal firms with 11%–20% increase.

result, many were forced to close. Based on the weighted survey data, 55.8% of informal micro and small enterprises had neither cash nor savings, while 31.7% reported they would run out of cash or funds within a month of the survey (March–April 2020). Their financial condition was worse than formal micro and small enterprises.[37] It was similar in August–September 2020.[38] However, those reporting sufficient cash/ savings to maintain their business increased for both informal and formal micro and small enterprises in 2021, supported by the start of economic recovery. There was enough cash and savings to operate for 21.2% of informal micro and small enterprises and 24.6% for formal ones in March–April 2021. This increased to 24.1% for informal and 28.0% for formal micro and small enterprises in May 2021, while those out of cash fell to 26.1% of informal and 11.4% of formal micro and small enterprises, though the levels remained high.

Informal micro and small enterprises in services followed a similar trend as informal ones: 55.9% reported no cash with 32.2% to run out of cash in a month of the survey (March–April 2020). This was worse than formal firms in services. Similarly, in 2021, those with sufficient cash were in the informal services sector: 21.0% and 22.6% in March–April 2021 and May 2021, respectively; although improving, those out of cash remained high at 33.2% and 27.5% during the same period, respectively. Manufacturing firms followed the same trend as services.[39]

The LPM estimates for the most part did not show statistically significant results in industrial sectors in 2020. In 2021, with some economic recovery beginning, several industries were less likely to report they were in a "no or little cash" condition than water supply: 52.5 and 35.4 percentage points lower in financial services in March–April 2021 (with .01 significance level) and May 2021 (with 0.1 significance level); 80.5 lower in real estate (with .01 significance level) and 33.4 lower in education (with .05 significance level) in May 2021.

At the beginning of the 2020 outbreak, many provinces were less likely to report firms with no or little cash compared with Jakarta: Bali, Bengkulu, DI Yogyakarta, Central Java, East Java, Central Kalimantan, East Kalimantan, and West Sumatra (with .01, .05, or 0.1 significance

---

[37]   35.8% with no cash in hand and 39.2% to soon run out for informal micro and small enterprises.

[38]   64.6% with no cash and 15.0% to run out within 1–3 months for informal micro and small enterprises; while 17.5% with no cash, 24.7% to run out of cash in 1–3 months, and 57.3% to run out of cash in 3–6 months for formal micro and small enterprises.

[39]   55.6% out of cash for informal manufacturing firms in March–April 2020, dropping to 22.5% in March–April 2021 and 14.1% in May 2021. Those with enough cash increased to 22.2% in March–April 2021 and 38.3% in May 2021.

levels). In other words, the magnitude of those lacking cash would be higher in Jakarta. In 2021, financial conditions worsened in the provinces, though at different magnitudes. A lack of working capital was more pronounced in Bali, DI Yogyakarta, Jambi, Central Java, East Nusa Tenggara, South Sulawesi, Southeast Sulawesi, and West Sulawesi than in Jakarta during March–April 2021 (with .01 or .05 significance levels). This expanded with different combinations of provinces in May 2021.[40]

Informal firms were more likely to face working capital shortages than formal firms when the outbreak began in 2020 (March–April 2020): 13.1 percentage points higher (.05 significance level). In May 2021, this improved, with informal firms' cash shortages 14.9 percentage points lower than formal firms (0.1 significance level).

Digitally operated firms were less likely to be short on working capital than non-digitalized firms in March–April 2020 (12.9 percentage points lower, with .01 significance level).

Digital firms without cash were 4.6 percentage points fewer than non-digital firms, but the extent of firms that would run out in a month was 6.3 higher for informal micro and small enterprises in March–April 2020 (Figure 4A). Formal digital micro and small enterprises had a higher share of those with sufficient cash than informal ones. In August–September 2020, there were relatively few digital firms with no cash than non-digital informal micro and small enterprises, but those running out of cash in 6 months increased. During March to May 2021, those running out of cash improved but those already out of cash increased among informal micro and small enterprises, while the share of digital firms with enough cash was lower than non-digital informal firms. By contrast, among formal micro and small enterprises, digital firms with sufficient cash increased compared with non-digital firms (+26.3 higher in May 2021).

Informal firms in services followed a similar trend as informal micro and small enterprises (Figure 4B). Digital firms had a limited impact on working capital shortages at the beginning of the pandemic, but moving to 2021, those out of cash grew while those with enough cash were a smaller fraction than non-digital informal firms and digital formal firms in services. For informal manufacturing firms, the share of digital firms out of cash was higher than non-digital firms during March–April 2020; 1 year later, the condition of having no cash improved but those running out of cash in 3 months expanded. Digital services firms with sufficient cash were fewer than non-digital firms and formal digital firms in manufacturing.

---

[40]   Firms in West Nusa Tenggara and Riau were added. Firms in Banten, West Java, and East Java were less likely to report working capital shortages than those in Jakarta, with .01 or .05 significance level.

Figure 4: Financial Conditions—Digitally Operated Enterprises

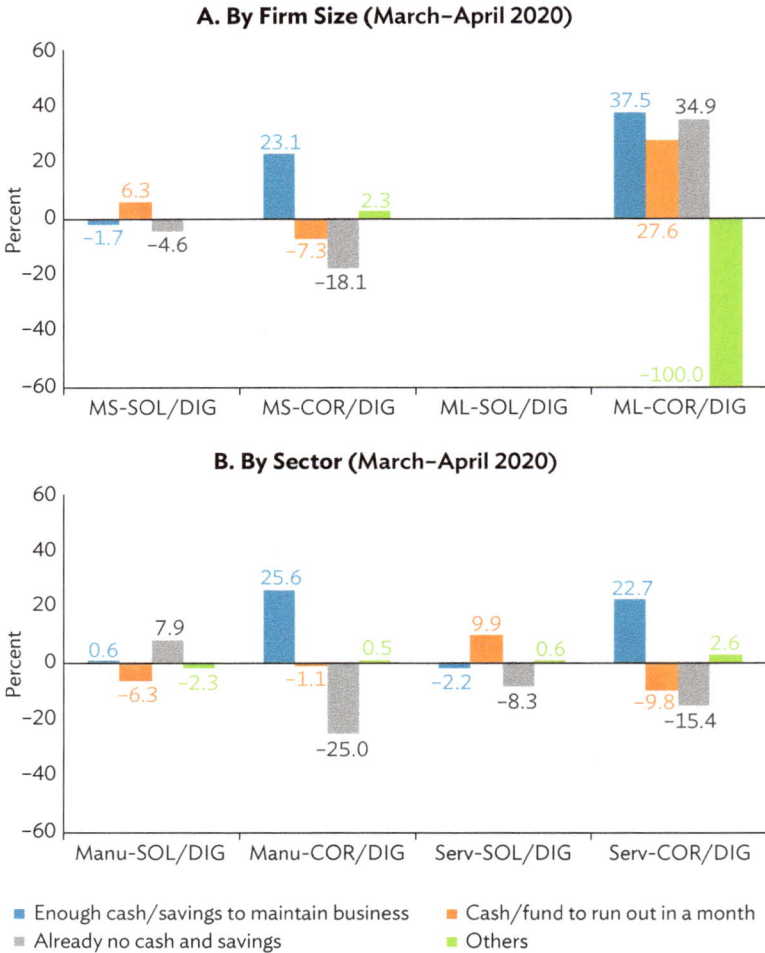

A. By Firm Size (March–April 2020)

B. By Sector (March–April 2020)

Legend:
- ■ Enough cash/savings to maintain business
- ■ Cash/fund to run out in a month
- ■ Already no cash and savings
- ■ Others

COR = corporations, DIG = digitally operated firms, Manu = manufacturing, ML = medium-sized and large enterprises, MS = micro and small enterprises, Serv = services, SOL = sole proprietorships.

Note: A total of 528 valid samples in Indonesia for March–April 2020, 129 for August–September 2020, 2,515 for March–April 2021, and 2,207 for May 2021.

Source: Calculations based on weighted data from MSME surveys in Indonesia for March–April 2020, August–September 2020, March–April 2021, and May 2021.

continued on next page

Figure 4 continued

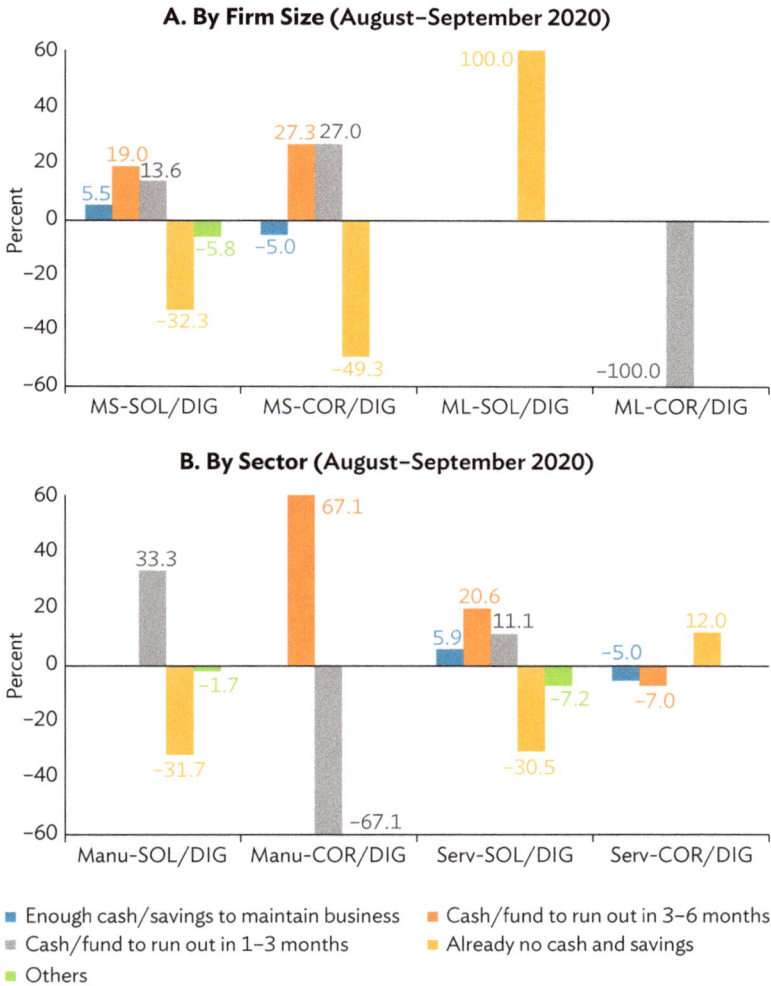

A. By Firm Size (August–September 2020)

B. By Sector (August–September 2020)

- ■ Enough cash/savings to maintain business
- ■ Cash/fund to run out in 1–3 months
- ■ Others
- ■ Cash/fund to run out in 3–6 months
- ■ Already no cash and savings

COR = corporations, DIG = digitally operated firms, Manu = manufacturing, ML = medium-sized and large enterprises, MS = micro and small enterprises, Serv = services, SOL = sole proprietorships.

Note: A total of 528 valid samples in Indonesia for March–April 2020, 129 for August–September 2020, 2,515 for March–April 2021, and 2,207 for May 2021.

Source: Calculations based on weighted data from MSME surveys in Indonesia for March–April 2020, August–September 2020, March–April 2021, and May 2021.

continued on next page

Figure 4 continued

A. By Firm Size (March–April 2021)

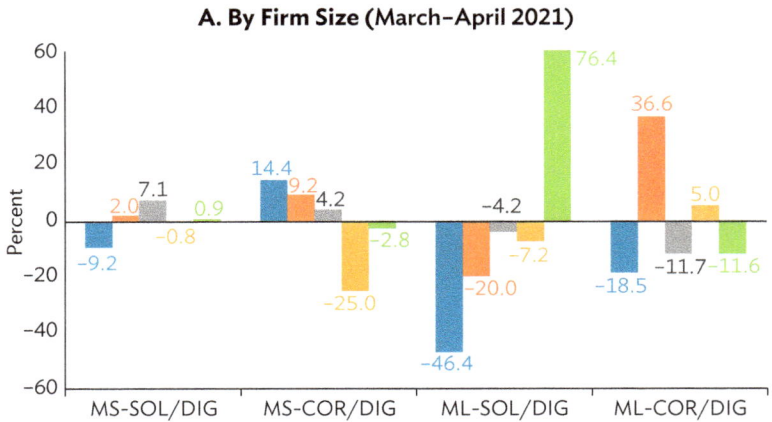

B. By Sector (March–April 2021)

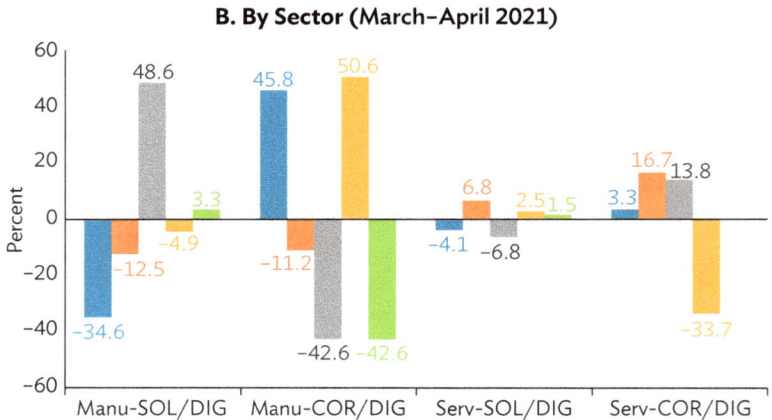

■ Enough cash/savings to maintain business   ■ Cash/fund to run out in 3–6 months
■ Cash/fund to run out in 1–3 months   ■ Already no cash and savings
■ Others

COR = corporations, DIG = digitally operated firms, Manu = manufacturing, ML = medium-sized and large enterprises, MS = micro and small enterprises, Serv = services, SOL = sole proprietorships.

Note: A total of 528 valid samples in Indonesia for March–April 2020, 129 for August–September 2020, 2,515 for March–April 2021, and 2,207 for May 2021.

Source: Calculations based on weighted data from MSME surveys in Indonesia for March–April 2020, August–September 2020, March–April 2021, and May 2021.

continued on next page

Figure 4 continued

A. By Firm Size (May 2021)

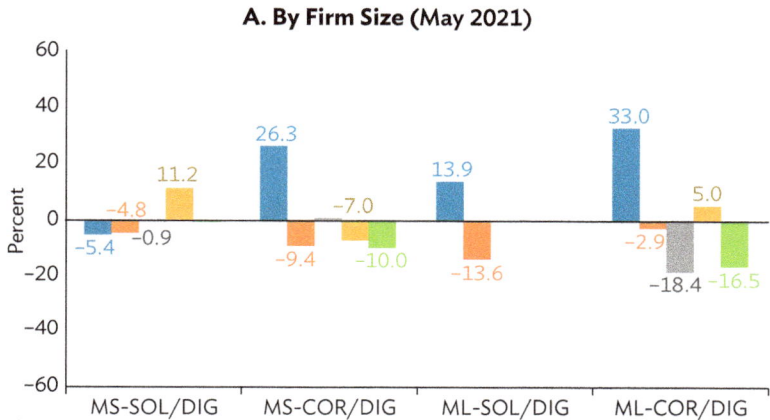

B. By Sector (May 2021)

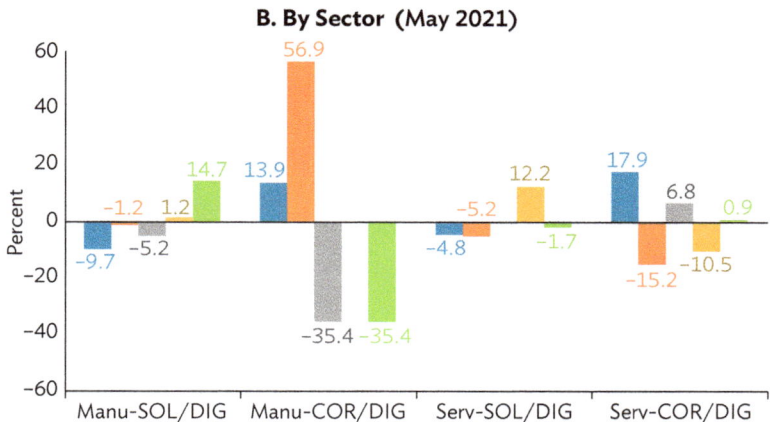

- ■ Enough cash/savings to maintain business
- ■ Cash/fund to run out in 3–6 months
- ▩ Cash/fund to run out in 1–3 months
- ■ Already no cash and savings
- ■ Others

COR = corporations, DIG = digitally operated firms, Manu = manufacturing, ML = medium-sized and large enterprises, MS = micro and small enterprises, Serv = services, SOL = sole proprietorships.

Note: A total of 528 valid samples in Indonesia for March–April 2020, 129 for August–September 2020, 2,515 for March–April 2021, and 2,207 for May 2021.

Source: Calculations based on weighted data from MSME surveys in Indonesia for March–April 2020, August–September 2020, March–April 2021, and May 2021.

Funding Condition

The pandemic along with social restrictions hit informal micro and small enterprises operations hard. In 2020, the majority already either had no cash or were on the brink of running out of cash. This improved in 2021 but working capital shortages remained high. There were more informal micro and small enterprises with sufficient cash, but less than formal micro and small enterprises. Those without cash were likely lower in digital firms than non-digital firms, but those running out of cash tended to increase in 2021. The question became how could informal firms manage operational costs and raise working capital to survive a prolonged pandemic?

Figure 5 illustrates the funding conditions of informal and formal firms during the pandemic thus far. Overall, firms mostly relied on their own funds and retained profits or borrowed from family, relatives, and friends. One year after the 2020 outbreak, they relied even more on their own funds, while they reduced borrowing from close relatives, as they availed of government financial support to businesses, which included informal sectors. At the same time, their access to bank credit increased moderately, again due to increased government lending assistance.

For informal micro and small enterprises, the share of those using their own funds increased from 29.4% in March–April 2020 to 75.4% in May 2021 (Figure 5A). Those borrowing from close relatives decreased from 32.2% to 21.0% over the same period. Those that successfully borrowed from banks increased from 2.3% to 15.6% during the same period, but only 8.6% of informal micro and small enterprises used government support to access bank credit (May 2021) through new lending facilities or credit guarantees. As formal micro and small enterprises were more likely to receive government support (12.1% as of May 2021), they could reduce informal borrowing more than informal firms (Figure 5B).

Informal services firms followed the same pattern as informal micro and small enterprises (Figure 5C). High reliance on using their own funds (99.2% as of May 2021) was more pronounced among informal manufacturing firms (Figure 5D).

Figure 5: Funding during the Pandemic

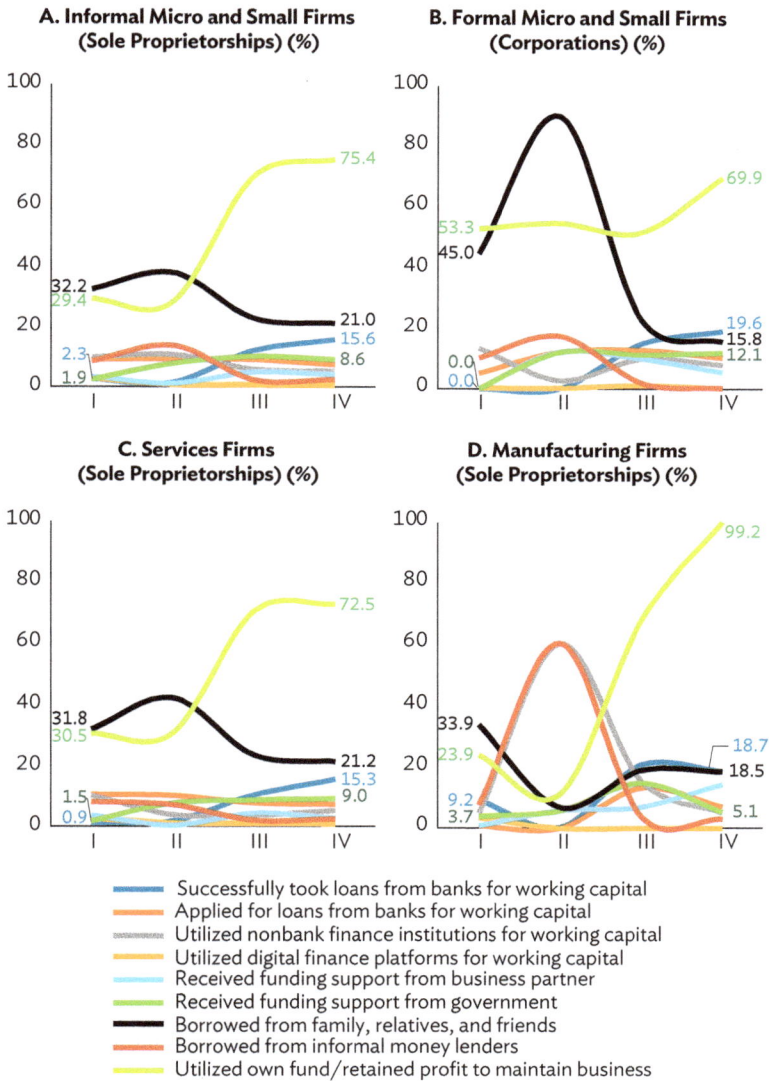

A. Informal Micro and Small Firms (Sole Proprietorships) (%)

B. Formal Micro and Small Firms (Corporations) (%)

C. Services Firms (Sole Proprietorships) (%)

D. Manufacturing Firms (Sole Proprietorships) (%)

Legend:
- Successfully took loans from banks for working capital
- Applied for loans from banks for working capital
- Utilized nonbank finance institutions for working capital
- Utilized digital finance platforms for working capital
- Received funding support from business partner
- Received funding support from government
- Borrowed from family, relatives, and friends
- Borrowed from informal money lenders
- Utilized own fund/retained profit to maintain business

I = March–April 2020; II = August–September 2020; III = March–April 2021; IV = May 2021.

Note: A total of 528 valid samples in Indonesia for March–April 2020, 129 for August–September 2020, 2,515 for March–April 2021, and 2,207 for May 2021.

Source: Calculations based on weighted data from MSME surveys in Indonesia for March–April 2020, August–September 2020, March–April 2021, and May 2021.

7.3   MSME Perceptions of the Pandemic Impact

Concerns Raised by Informal MSMEs

The surveys also monitored the main concerns of MSMEs and their expected problems should the pandemic continue. In March–April 2020, the top-ranked concern of informal micro and small enterprises was a lack of working capital (76.2% of informal micro and small enterprises), followed by a decline in domestic demand (36.8%), loan repayments (33.3%), supply chain disruptions (25.7%), tax payments (10.8%), and a decline in foreign demand (8.3%). One year after the outbreak, domestic demand became their top concern (65.4% in May 2021) with a lack of working capital second (56.7%). By May 2021, concern on supply disruptions, tax payments, and foreign demand fell to 16.9%, 4.3%, and 1.7%, respectively.

The length of the pandemic and frequent social restrictions created a serious concern over future demand for the products and services provided by informal micro and small enterprises. Government debt finance support eased concerns over working capital shortages and loan repayments by May 2021 to some extent. Relatively much less concern over taxes and foreign demand make sense as informal firms typically operate without paying taxes and operate domestically with little contact with global supply chains. As informal firms generally have their own supply networks to serve limited domestic markets, broad supply chain disruptions do not seem to be a major concern.

Formal micro and small enterprises had similar concerns as informal firms, but differed in magnitude. There was greater concern over "domestic demand decline" (72.4% in May 2021) and less on working capital shortages (43.6%) due to government financial assistance. But concerns on loan repayments (29.0%) increased. Concerns over supply disruptions and tax payments decreased. A small fraction (3.9% in May 2021) was a concern over a decline in foreign demand. Informal firms in services and manufacturing had similar concerns as informal micro and small enterprises—with a decline in domestic demand topping the list among informal manufacturers (78.4% in May 2021).

Actions Considered by Informal MSMEs

If the pandemic were to continue, half (50.3%) of all informal micro and small enterprises in the March–April 2020 survey reported wanting loan repayments to financial institutions delayed. This was followed by measures such as reducing employee wages (35.6%), deferring tax payments (23.4%), applying for bankruptcy (20.1%), laying people off (18.6%), and canceling contracts (12.1%). One year after the outbreak, all these fell to between 15% and 16% in the May 2021 survey—reducing wages moved to the top, followed by layoffs.

Formal micro and small enterprises also wanted financial institutions to delay loan repayments (68.3%), followed by deferred tax payments (53.2%), wage reductions (45.0%), layoffs (26.6%), and contract cancellations (13.3%). One year after the outbreak, as financial concerns eased due to government support, they considered further staff layoffs (44.1% in May 2021) as the top action followed by wage cuts (31.5%) as concerns continued over reduced domestic demand. Given the length of the pandemic, applying for bankruptcy gradually increased (7.9% in May 2021).

Informal firms in services agreed that delaying loan repayments was needed, although its share fell from 49.5% in March–April 2020 to 14.5% in May 2021. Wage cuts (13.9%) and layoffs (13.8%) were second and third, respectively, in the May 2021 survey. For informal manufacturing firms, wage cuts (32.4%) and layoffs (26.4%) were the top and second ranked coping actions reported in the May 2021 survey.

Policy Measures Desired by Informal MSMEs

The surveys also sought out the policy measures MSMEs wanted to see. In March–April 2020, subsidies to help businesses recover and cash transfers were the top policy measure desired (93.2%), followed by a comprehensive information platform on government assistance programs (86.7%) and assistance to pay salaries (85.2%). Assistance in paying wages, training and business literacy programs, and sector-specific support in areas such as tourism were more important to informal firms than to formal firms.[41]

Zero interest/collateral-free loan was the top financial measure informal firms wanted (96.7%), followed by special refinancing facilities with low interest (89.7%) and simplified loan procedures for faster bank approvals (89.7%). Zero interest/collateral-free loans, simplified loan procedures, and special credit guarantees were desired more by informal firms than by formal firms.[42] Access to new financing models or

---

[41]   The informal firm response ratio was 12.1, 17.6, and 13.4 percentage points higher than that of formal firms for wage assistance, training, and sector-specific support, respectively.

[42]   The informal firm response ratio was 10.8, 15.2, and 4.2 percentage points higher than that of formal firms for concessional loans, simplified loan procedures, and credit guarantees, respectively.

digital financial services was cited by 74.4% of informal firms, but their response ratio was 6.7 percentage points lower than that of formal firms.

One year into the pandemic, the policy measures informal firms sought changed slightly. During March–April 2021, subsidies for business recovery remained the top nonfinancial policy desired by informal firms (84.3%), but the second and third priorities changed to business development advisory services (83.0%) and support in skills upgrading of workers (81.1%). Only business development advice was higher for informal firms than for formal firms (0.7 percentage points higher than formal firms); all others were below the shares of formal firms. Zero interest/collateral-free loans remained the top financial measure for informal firms (75.4%), followed by faster bank loan approvals (67.2%) and special low interest refinancing facilities (65.6%). But all these measures were less likely to be desired by informal firms than by formal firms. "Facilitating access to new financing models (digital financial services)" was the lowest desired measure by informal firms (43.4%).

7.4 Policy Implications

Formalizing informal MSMEs and their employment is a critical step to promote MSME development, create a quality labor market, and accelerate inclusive growth. To this end, it is crucial that business owners are convinced they should look beyond maintaining the status quo—to shift from being stability-oriented to being more growth-oriented. Informal MSMEs typically serve low technology domestic markets with a limited customer base. The COVID-19 pandemic led to a new normal that allows owners of informal firms appreciate the advantages of formalizing their operations. Government restrictions on mobility and social distancing in response to the outbreak encouraged a shift from a personal contact-based business model to one that includes digitalizing operations—from simple use of the internet for daily business to selling goods and services online or e-commerce, which in becoming more visible is akin to a first step toward formalization. As revealed in the LPM results and survey findings, informal firms that went digital tried to rationalize their business operations and manage costs through staff and wage cuts. This likely made owners think about value creation for business growth. However, this likely does not yet represent most informal MSMEs (given the survey's limitations). A year into the pandemic, the survey results pointed to a distinction between two kinds of informal MSMEs—those who struggled with the pandemic and those who benefited (Figure 6). It is evident that digitally operated firms were among those who benefited, although they were not always successful.

A policy framework on formalizing informal MSMEs should be designed sensitively, focusing on firms' different coping abilities to the pandemic and providing incentives to informal business owners for growth under the new normal. Based on this study's findings, the following policy suggestions could help boost formalization and digitalization of MSMEs in Indonesia:

- **Provide timely information on government support programs for informal business.** Informal MSMEs had a difficult time accessing up-to-date information on government assistance programs. The March–April 2021 survey also found that the use of government assistance programs was limited among MSMEs primarily due to the fact that they did not know how to access available assistance.[43] Building a social-media-based comprehensive information platform on government assistance programs would be worth considering. It also provides effective information to informal MSMEs, such as benefits of formalization and digitalization of business, thereby helping achieve policy goals.

- **Elaborate targeted group assistance with necessary measures.** The LPM identified firms that suffered from the pandemic in terms of revenue, employment, and fiscal condition: (i) nonessential services including construction, administrative services, education, and entertainment; (ii) firms located in specific provinces outside the capital; (iii) young enterprises operating from 0 to 5 years; (iv) traditional distributive trade and services (including tourism); (v) women-led firms; (vi) internationalized firms; and (vii) digitally operated firms (nonprofitable firms having problems with operational and financial management). The assistance would target those more adversely affected with measures proportionate to each impact level.

- **Use a phased approach for assistance with well-scheduled budget allocations.** Given the uncertainty over controlling the pandemic, there is the increasing risk of bloating national budgets to continue government support programs over the

---

[43] The March–April 2021 survey in Indonesia assessed respondents' awareness of the following government programs: (i) subsidized loan program (*subsidi bunga*), (ii) credit restructuring fund (*penempatan dana*), (iii) credit guarantees (*penjaminan kredit* UMKM), (iv) income tax break facility (PPh final UMKM), (v) investment financing for cooperatives and MSMEs (*pembiayaan investasi* LPDP), and (vi) productive assistance for MSMEs (*bantuan presiden usaha* mikro). Only 5.4%–22.1% of MSME respondents (2,509) used these programs. For instance, 60.5% of the respondents answered that they did not know the application procedure for the income tax break facility.

long term. A phased approach for government assistance should be elaborated within a well-controlled budget framework.

- **Provide business development services, mentoring support, and skills development training for workers.** A drop in domestic demand is the top concern among informal MSMEs. Strengthening business competitiveness is critical for creating demand, to survive and grow during a post-pandemic recovery. Business development and advisory services, mentoring and business literacy programs, tax education/ incentives, and training to upgrade worker skills are critical. These could be delivered by government authorities, private business communities, and/or public–private cooperation. These also help create a base of quality jobs across the country.
- **Strengthen business registration services.** There remains a need to create, expand, or strengthen one-stop service windows for new business registration nationwide, addressing informal MSMEs, startups, and entrepreneurs.
- **Promote the digital transformation and increased use of technology in operations.** The digital transformation offers several benefits to informal MSMEs, startups, and entrepreneurships. It enhances access to business information, strengthens business networks, creates new business opportunities including access to global marketplaces and global supply chains, and reduces administrative costs. The rising mobile and internet penetration has contributed to developing the digital industry in Indonesia. In 2021, Indonesia's mobile-based ride-hailing firm Gojek and leading e-commerce firm Tokopedia merged to a new firm GoTo; it became the largest multiple digital service provider.[44] The Government of Indonesia supports e-commerce development for MSMEs (such as E-Smart IKM which aims to expand market access for small and medium-sized industries through e-commerce). The assistance would comprehensively include continuous guidance on e-commerce development, teleworking arrangements, technology transfer and adoption, and research and development for new business.
- **Expand the base of incubators and accelerators for entrepreneurship development.** Business incubator and accelerator programs can be developed under the business development and advisory services. These would support

---

[44]   See Daga and Potkin (2021).

strengthening business competitiveness and entrepreneurship development.

- **Diversify alternative financing options and provide growth capital for business.** Finance is critical for business development. Working capital shortages were a major concern for informal MSMEs to survive the pandemic. Supported by government financial assistance, access to bank credit has gradually improved for informal MSMEs. More diversified financing options should be developed to fulfill their unmet financing needs, including further development and dissemination of digital financial services (such as peer-to-peer lending and equity crowdfunding platforms) and a dedicated MSME equity market (an Acceleration Board under the Indonesia Stock Exchange).

- **Use more private sector resources for policy implementation.** As an informal MSME is a small business with only a few staff, it is important to attract private sector support to implement government policy goals on formalizing informal firms, for example, outsourcing financial and business administration of informal firms using advisory professionals such as certified public accountants. Through digitalizing informal MSMEs, the government can use their untapped growth potential for sustainable and resilient economic recovery; and private sector digital platforms can be strategic partners with the government. To effectively implement formalization and digitalization of MSMEs as part of post-pandemic policy actions, provincial governments should play a critical role in promoting these policy goals, given that MSMEs are spread nationwide and that rural MSMEs had experienced relatively higher impacts of COVID-19. Central government, local governments, and private sector should cooperate to this end.

Figure 6: COVID-19 Impact on Informal MSMEs—Evidence from Surveys and a Linear Probability Model

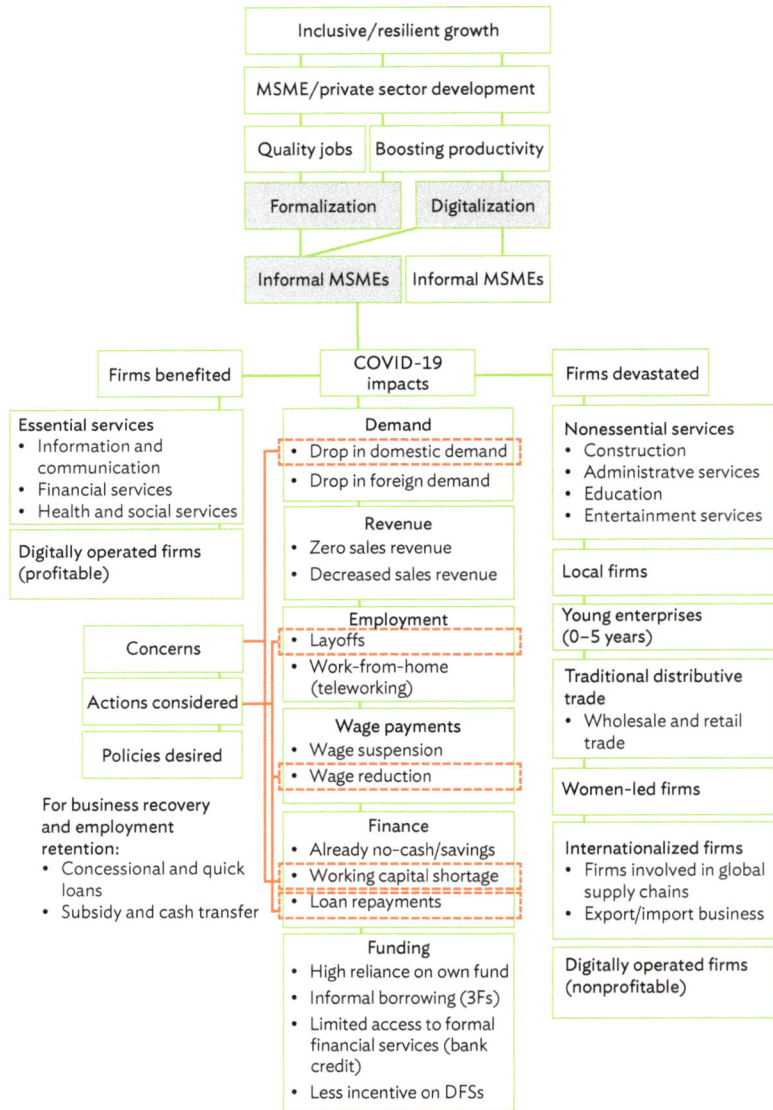

Inclusive/resilient growth

MSME/private sector development

Quality jobs | Boosting productivity

Formalization | Digitalization

Informal MSMEs | Informal MSMEs

COVID-19 impacts

Firms benefited

Firms devastated

Essential services
- Information and communication
- Financial services
- Health and social services

Digitally operated firms (profitable)

Concerns

Actions considered

Policies desired

For business recovery and employment retention:
- Concessional and quick loans
- Subsidy and cash transfer

Demand
- Drop in domestic demand
- Drop in foreign demand

Revenue
- Zero sales revenue
- Decreased sales revenue

Employment
- Layoffs
- Work-from-home (teleworking)

Wage payments
- Wage suspension
- Wage reduction

Finance
- Already no-cash/savings
- Working capital shortage
- Loan repayments

Funding
- High reliance on own fund
- Informal borrowing (3Fs)
- Limited access to formal financial services (bank credit)
- Less incentive on DFSs

Nonessential services
- Construction
- Administratve services
- Education
- Entertainment services

Local firms

Young enterprises (0–5 years)

Traditional distributive trade
- Wholesale and retail trade

Women-led firms

Internationalized firms
- Firms involved in global supply chains
- Export/import business

Digitally operated firms (nonprofitable)

3F = friend, family, fools; DFS = digital financial service; MSMEs = micro, small, and medium-sized enterprises.

Source: Author.

8. Conclusion

This chapter examined the impact of the COVID-19 pandemic on informal MSMEs (sole proprietorships and family-run informal businesses), focusing on micro and small firms in Indonesia. Linear probability regression and descriptive analysis were conducted using evidence obtained through year-long surveys from March 2020 through May 2021. It also assessed the extent of the digital transformation and challenges brought on by the pandemic and provided policy implications on formalizing and digitalizing MSMEs in the country. Due to the urgency of capturing the MSME conditions to support the country's policy design for MSMEs amid the pandemic, the rapid surveys used a hybrid approach that combined online and field surveys.

Informal MSMEs were hit the hardest, more seriously than formal MSMEs. Many businesses were forced to close, and domestic demand for their products and services dropped sharply. One year into the pandemic, the situation had improved but domestic demand had yet to recover. Meanwhile, two types of business clusters formed and grew: (i) the contracting firms hurt badly by the pandemic, and (ii) the groups of firms that benefited from the pandemic. This was most prominent among services firms.

The LPM estimates found that construction, administrative services, education, and entertainment services were the hardest hit initially in revenue, given the PSBB social restrictions. Information and communications, financial services, and health and social services experienced limited impact as they remained essential services. A year after the first outbreak, local firms in outlying regions felt the impact on revenue more than the Jakarta-based firms. As the pandemic wore on, the impact became more serious for young firms. Women-led firms also faced serious impacts on revenue, employment, and finance. Internationalized firms experienced a mixed impact in terms of revenue and employment, affected by social restrictions and balanced by global market openness. Private businesses began reopening as the economy started to recover in 2021. But small distributive trade and services—typically in informal sectors—reacted quickly to the surging Delta variant, 1 month before the second wave struck in mid-June 2021. They temporarily shut down or faced revenue losses again. Informal firms were more sensitive to the impact of the pandemic than formal firms. And business remained highly fragile given the uncertainty of COVID-19 infection rates.

The pandemic drove private businesses, including informal MSMEs, to go digital. Digitally operated informal firms—those using the internet for business or using e-commerce—experienced less impact in terms of their revenue than non-digital informal firms, creating a distinction between profitable and nonprofitable clusters, especially in services.

The pandemic and social restrictions also hurt the finances of informal MSMEs and created other divides. Working capital shortages were more serious than formal firms, and more evident among the Jakarta-based firms. As the pandemic continued, however, two groups emerged: those with sufficient cash or savings and those facing serious working capital shortages. These were closely associated with two business clusters—those who were severely hit by the pandemic and those who benefited by supplying essential goods or services. Young firms had more cash/savings problems than longer established firms. Digitally operated firms had less financial issues than non-digital firms. But even digitally operated informal MSMEs had to contend with volatile working capital conditions. Formal MSMEs with digital operations were more likely to have sufficient cash available.

Informal MSMEs relied heavily on their own funds and borrowings from close relatives at the start of the pandemic. One year later, such borrowing declined and access to formal financial services increased—largely due to available government financial assistance. However, MSMEs that could obtain credit from banks were few, so most relied more on internal funds to keep operating; many do not qualify for government financial assistance, and digital financial services was not an option for others.

The top concern of most informal MSMEs at the start of the pandemic was the lack of working capital. One year later, their top concern shifted to the decline in domestic demand, as the pandemic continued with emerging new variants, but working capital shortages remained the second most serious concern.

Informal MSMEs also indicated actions they considered should the pandemic get prolonged. At the time of the 2020 outbreak, they indicated negotiating with financial institutions to delay loan repayments. They were likely to take or expect bank credit assisted by the government. Wage cuts and layoffs became more prominent in May 2021, suggesting a shift from financial concerns to those involving employment.

The survey responses also indicated desired policy measures. Concessional and quick loans, along with subsidies and cash transfers for business recovery and worker retention, were the most desired. For more real-time assistance on available support programs, they wanted the government to set up a comprehensive information platform. In parallel, they wanted support for training and business literacy programs. As the pandemic continued, they increasingly looked to the government more for business development and skills upgrading support for workers, aside from continued working capital support.

Formalizing informal MSMEs is critical to boosting national productivity, creating quality jobs, and promoting inclusive growth. This requires a well-designed policy framework. The study suggests doing so by focusing on firms' different coping abilities to the pandemic, and similar potential crises, toward providing incentives for informal business owners to concentrate on growth under the new normal. Suggestions include strengthening business competitiveness and entrepreneurship development for firms to survive and grow during a recovery period, with an emphasis on digital transformation.

In Indonesia, the growth projection was for a robust 2021, a 3.7% rebound from a 2.1% contraction in 2020. However, future threats increase the uncertainty over economic growth and raise the risk of business failures and bankruptcies, especially for MSMEs that account for a large number of informal firms and employment. Formalizing informal MSMEs is now more critical to a policy agenda that aims to build a resilient economic recovery and sustainable, inclusive growth. This research, based on rapid surveys, illuminated several distinctions that emerged during the COVID-19 pandemic in terms of the firms' formality status, type of enterprise, digitalization, size, location, and other characteristics. Future research should look deeper to explain why such differences exist or arise, and how best to address them to make Indonesia's MSME sector more robust and resilient.

References

Asian Development Bank (ADB). 2020. *Asia Small and Medium-Sized Enterprise Monitor 2020*. Volume II: COVID-19 Impact on Micro, Small, and Medium-Sized Enterprises in Developing Asia. Manila.

_____. 2022. *Asian Development Outlook 2022*. Manila.

_____. ADB COVID-19 Policy Database. https://covid19policy.adb.org/ (accessed 30 November 2021).

Boly, A. 2020. The Effects of Formalization on Small and Medium-Sized Enterprise Tax Payments: Panel Evidence from Viet Nam. *Asian Development Review* 37(1): 140–158.

Chen, M. A. 2007. Rethinking the Informal Economy: Linkages with the Formal Economy and the Formal Regulatory Environment. DESA Working Paper No. 46. New York: UN Department of Economic and Social Affairs.

Daga, A., and F. Potkin. 2021. Indonesia's Gojek, Tokopedia to Create Biggest Local Tech Group. *Reuters*. 17 May. https://www.reuters.com/technology/ indonesias-gojek-tokopedia-merge-countrys-biggest-deal-2021-05-17/.

Feld, L. P., and C. Larsen. 2005. *Black Activities in Germany in 2001 and 2004: A Comparison Based on Survey Data*. Study No. 12. Copenhagen: The Rockwool Foundation Research Unit.

_____. 2008. "Black" Activities Low in Germany in 2006. *News from the Rockwool Foundation Research Unit*. March. 1–12.

_____. 2009. *Undeclared Work in Germany 2001–2007—Impact of Deterrence, Tax Policy, and Social Norms: An Analysis Based on Survey Data*. Berlin: Springer.

International Finance Corporation (IFC). 2013. *Closing the Credit Gap for Formal and Informal Micro, Small, and Medium Enterprises*. Washington, DC.

International Labour Organization (ILO). 2011. *Statistical Update on Employment in the Informal Economy*. ILO Department of Statistics. Unpublished note.

_____. 2012. *Measuring Informality: A Statistical Manual on the Informal Sector and Informal Employment*. Geneva.

International Monetary Fund (IMF). 2020. Policy Responses to COVID-19. Policy Tracker. https://www.imf.org/en/Topics/imf-and-covid19/Policy-Responses-to-COVID-19 (accessed 24 June 2020).

Loayza, N., and J. Rigolini. 2006. *Informality Trends and Cycles*. Policy Research Working Paper 4078. Washington, DC: World Bank.

Lippert, O., and M. Walker, eds. 1997. *The Understanding Economy: Global Evidences of its Size and Impact*. Vancouver: The Frazer Institute.

Muhammad, F. 2021. Enforcing Omnibus Law: Formalizing Micro, Small, and Medium Enterprises in Indonesia Using Behavioural Science. *Indonesian Law Journal* 14 (2). 95–118.

Organisation for Economic Co-operation and Development (OECD). 2021. *The Digital Transformation of SMEs*. Paris.

Rand, J., and N. Torm. 2012. The Benefits of Formalization: Evidence from Vietnamese Manufacturing SMEs. *World Development* 40 (5): 983–998.

Schneider, F. 2009. Size and Development of the Shadow Economy in Germany, Austria, and Other OECD Countries: Some Preliminary Findings. *Revue Economique* 60: 1079–1116.

_____. 2012. *The Shadow Economy and Work in the Shadow: What Do We (Not) Know?* IZA Discussion Paper No. 6423.

Schneider, F., A. Buehn, and M. C. Montenegro. 2010. New Estimates for the Shadow Economies All Over the World. *International Economic Journal* 24 (4): 443– 461.

Schneider, F., and D. Enste. 2002. *The Shadow Economy: Theoretical Approaches, Empirical Studies, and Political Implications*. Cambridge, United Kingdom: Cambridge University Press.

Shinozaki, S. 2022. *Informal Micro, Small, and Medium-Sized Enterprises and Digitalization: Evidence from Surveys in Indonesia*. ADBI Working Paper Series. No. 1310. Tokyo.

Shinozaki, S., and L. N. Rao. 2021. *COVID-19 Impact on Micro, Small, and Medium-Sized Enterprises under the Lockdown: Evidence from a Rapid Survey in the Philippines*. ADBI Working Paper Series. No. 1216. Tokyo.

World Bank. 2020. Map of SME-Support Measures in Response to COVID-19. 14 April. https://www.worldbank.org/en/data/interactive/2020/04/14/map-of-sme-support-measures-in-response-to-covid-19.

Appendix 1: Overrepresentation and Underrepresentation in the Survey Data

In comparison, micro and small firms were underrepresented by 1.6 percentage points for the first survey, 0.4 for the second, 0.8 for the third, and 0.4 for the fourth survey. Meanwhile, medium-sized and large firms were overrepresented by 1.6, 0.4, 0.8, and 0.4 percentage points, respectively. The difference between the surveys of the Asian Development Bank (ADB) and Badan Pusat Statistik (BPS) was limited.

The difference by sector share to total respondents between the ADB and BPS distribution was 4 percentage points or less (the majority had around 1% or less) for the first survey, except for manufacturing (9.7 percentage points below the BPS distribution). For the second survey, wholesale and retail trade was underrepresented by 23.1 percentage points, while "accommodation and food service activities" and "other services" were overrepresented by 14.2 and 12.0 percentage points, respectively. For the third and fourth surveys, the difference in each sector's share between the ADB and BPS distribution was 6 percentage points or less (the majority had around 1% or less), except for manufacturing (12.6 and 14.0 percentage points below the BPS distribution, respectively), accommodation and food service activities (14.9 and 12.7 percentage points above, respectively), and other services (10.6 and 10.7 percentage points above).

The difference by location between the ADB and BPS distribution was 5 percentage points or less (the majority had less than 1%) for the first survey. For the second survey, the difference was less than 5% (the majority had less than 1%), except for East Java (19.6 percentage points above the BPS distribution). For the third and fourth surveys, underrepresentation was identified in Central Java (14.2 and 14.5 percentage points, respectively), while overrepresentation was in West Java (16.8 and 20.4 percentage points) and North Sumatra (17.3 and 18.5 percentage points) due to addition of field surveys.

Appendix 2: Profile of Surveyed Micro, Small, and Medium-Sized Enterprises

During the first survey by sector, 79.9% of surveyed firms were in the services category, 10.8% in manufacturing, and 9.3% in agriculture. In the second survey, 79.8% were in services, 10.1% in manufacturing, and 10.1% in agriculture. In the third survey, 92.3% were in services, 4.2% in manufacturing, and 3.5% in agriculture. During the fourth survey, 95.0% were in services, followed by manufacturing (2.9%) and agriculture (2.1%). Wholesale and retail trade (43.6% in the first, 20.9% in the second, 38.6% in the third, and 43.5% in the fourth survey) and accommodation and food services (18.4%, 27.9%, 30.7%, and 28.9%, respectively) were the first- and second-largest sectors among the respondents in all the surveys. In terms of industrial classification—as the BPS 2016 Economic Census provides only nonagriculture sector data—the descriptive and regression analyses use two broad industry classifications: manufacturing and services (Table A1).

Table A1: Industry Classification

Industry Classification	BPS Industry Classification
Manufacture	Manufacturing Construction
Services	Mining and quarrying Electricity, gas, steam, and air conditioning supply Water supply; sewerage, waste management, and remediation activities Wholesale and retail trade; repair of motor vehicles and motorcycles Transport and storage Accommodation and food service activities Information and communication Financial and insurance activities Real estate activities Professional, scientific, and technical activities Administrative and support service activities Public administration and defense; compulsory social security Education Human health and social work activities Arts, entertainment, and recreation Other service activities

BPS = Badan Pusat Statistik (Central Statistics Office).
Note: Agriculture is excluded as it is not included in BPS statistics.
Source: Author.

By region, the top response rates were mostly from firms located in Java: West Java (15.3% in the first, 20.2% in the second, 34.0% in the third, and 37.8% in the fourth survey), East Java (13.6% in the first, 37.2% in the second, 21.0% in the third, and 22.6% in the fourth survey), Central Java (11.9% in the first and 10.9% in the second survey), and DKI Jakarta (11.7% in the third and 12.5% in the fourth survey). In the third and fourth surveys, North Sumatra accounted for 21.6% and 22.8% of surveyed firms, respectively.

Around half or more of those surveyed had been operating from between 0 and 5 years (mostly young startup microenterprises in services)—50.2% in the first survey, 60.5% in the second, 47.4% in the third, and 47.6% in the fourth survey. These were followed by those operating 6–10 years (29.0%, 24.0%, 24.7%, and 23.4%, respectively), 11–15 years (12.1%, 12.4%, 12.0%, and 11.9%), 16–30 years (6.8%, 2.3%, 12.6%, and 13.3%), and over 31 years (1.9%, 0.8%, 3.3%, and 3.9%).

By type of firm surveyed, the majority were sole proprietorships or family-run businesses, which are regarded as informal firms (88.4% in the second, 95.3% in the third, and 96.8% in the fourth survey), while the remaining were "corporation or partnership" or "cooperative or foundation" (11.6% in the second, 4.7% in the third, and 3.2% in the fourth survey), which are seen as formal firms. In the first survey, 79.4% of surveyed firms were microenterprises which have one to four employees or are typically family-run businesses. As there was no "type of firm" question in the first survey, this group can be regarded as informal firms, which is consistent with the definition set by ILO 2012 (see Section 2).

In terms of digital use, 71.4% of surveyed firms used the internet for daily business in the first survey, while 58.9% of surveyed firms were engaged in online selling or e-commerce in the second survey. By contrast, the firms engaged in e-commerce accounted for 28.2% in the third survey and 21.8% in the fourth survey. The level of digital use differs between firms in the first and second surveys (relatively high digital use) and the third and fourth surveys (low digital use).

By ownership, more than half of surveyed firms were led by a male (70.4% in the first, 52.7% in the second, 50.3% in the third, and 51.6% in the fourth survey). Firms led by a female accounted for 29.6% of surveyed firms in the first, 47.3% in the second, 49.7% in the third, and 48.4% in the fourth survey.

Most firms reported average monthly wages per worker of not more than Rp3.2 million ($200) (90.0% in the first, 92.3% in the second, 88.7% in the third, and 86.1% in the fourth survey).

As for a firm's internationalization, just a small portion of surveyed firms reported they were involved in a global supply chain or export/import business (5.7% in the first, 3.9% in the second, 1.7% in the third, and 1.3% in the fourth survey).

Appendix 3: Impact of the COVID-19 Pandemic on Micro, Small, and Medium-Sized Enterprises—Linear Probability Model

A. March–April 2020

Variables	(1) revenue 1	(2) revenue 2	(3) finance
Industry (base–water supply)			
Manufacturing	0.2584	–0.03508	–0.07843
	[0.3309]	[0.0772]	[0.1826]
Electricity, Gas, Steam, and Air Conditioning Supply	–0.06249	–0.1285	–0.1775
	[0.3782]	[0.1157]	[0.2136]
Construction	0.6640**	0.03577	0.006198
	[0.3368]	[0.0819]	[0.1921]
Wholesale and Retail Trade; Repair of Motor Vehicles and Motorcycles	0.2476	–0.1033	–0.1627
	[0.3203]	[0.0734]	[0.1801]
Transportation and Storage	0.5162	–0.003399	–0.0007579
	[0.3419]	[0.0635]	[0.1753]
Accommodation and Food Service Activities	0.4544	0.03049	–0.01188
	[0.3249]	[0.0769]	[0.1887]
Information and Communication	–0.009183	–0.4193*	0.1462
	[0.3500]	[0.2454]	[0.2316]
Financial and Insurance Activities	0.2358	–0.01003	–0.4653
	[0.3987]	[0.0794]	[0.3597]
Professional, Scientific, and Technical Activities	0.5076	–0.1207	–0.2996
	[0.3620]	[0.1082]	[0.2642]
Administrative and Support Service Activities	0.9044***	–0.07904	–0.03855
	[0.3283]	[0.1131]	[0.2071]
Education	0.7547*	0.1086	–0.4322
	[0.4198]	[0.1448]	[0.3259]
Human Health and Social Work Activities	0.5638	–0.2197	0.02938
	[0.3868]	[0.1977]	[0.2112]

continued on next page

Appendix 3 continued

Variables	(1) revenue 1	(2) revenue 2	(3) finance
Arts, Entertainment, and Recreation	0.9637***	−0.03576	−0.02548
	[0.3359]	[0.0758]	[0.1831]
Other Service Activities	0.1871	−0.08888	−0.08264
	[0.3368]	[0.0781]	[0.1841]
Location (base–DKI Jakarta)			
Aceh	−0.1258	0.02403	−0.1609
	[0.2585]	[0.1229]	[0.1202]
Bali	−0.1194	0.0116	−0.2633**
	[0.1757]	[0.1066]	[0.1246]
Banten	0.2042	0.0768	−0.07078
	[0.2018]	[0.1155]	[0.1021]
Bengkulu	−0.4657***	0.06765	−0.2152**
	[0.1542]	[0.0811]	[0.0950]
DI Yogyakarta	0.04249	0.1313*	−0.2967**
	[0.1902]	[0.0737]	[0.1339]
Gorontalo	0.6191***	0.1554*	−0.08985
	[0.1758]	[0.0875]	[0.0776]
Jambi	−0.2897	−0.276	−0.1328
	[0.2660]	[0.2987]	[0.0811]
Jawa Barat	0.1712	0.1261*	−0.06214
	[0.1710]	[0.0699]	[0.0741]
Jawa Tengah	0.01559	0.1203	−0.1400**
	[0.1803]	[0.0741]	[0.0707]
Jawa Timur	−0.1537	0.01588	−0.1317**
	[0.1585]	[0.0871]	[0.0662]
Kalimantan Barat	−0.156	0.1839***	0.02607
	[0.2149]	[0.0700]	[0.1592]
Kalimantan Selatan	0.03464	0.1901**	−0.02418
	[0.3205]	[0.0759]	[0.0731]
Kalimantan Tengah	−0.171	0.1260*	−0.09573*
	[0.3410]	[0.0756]	[0.0571]
Kalimantan Timur	−0.2539	0.1409	−0.6730***
	[0.1727]	[0.1057]	[0.2190]
Kep. Bangka Belitung	0.1748	0.02875	−0.6608

continued on next page

Appendix 3 continued

Variables	(1) revenue 1	(2) revenue 2	(3) finance
	[0.5054]	[0.1119]	[0.4674]
Kepulauan Riau	0.1669	0.2633**	0.07125
	[0.2713]	[0.1206]	[0.1326]
Lampung	0.1317	0.1822*	−0.0164
	[0.2788]	[0.0969]	[0.1007]
Nusa Tenggara Barat	0.5044***	0.1475*	0.09489
	[0.1920]	[0.0851]	[0.1400]
Nusa Tenggara Timur	−0.06771	0.1061	−0.1091
	[0.2024]	[0.1309]	[0.1713]
Papua	−0.4618*	0.07771	−0.1799
	[0.2630]	[0.0984]	[0.1128]
Papua Barat	0.4888*	0.1607**	0.1479
	[0.2625]	[0.0758]	[0.0981]
Riau	−0.3823	−0.4926**	−0.1118
	[0.2866]	[0.2404]	[0.1551]
Sulawesi Barat	0.5492***	0.2494***	0.08366
	[0.1595]	[0.0857]	[0.0932]
Sulawesi Selatan	0.01194	0.2269**	−0.2932
	[0.2442]	[0.0906]	[0.2475]
Sulawesi Tengah	0.179	0.2373***	0.01508
	[0.4046]	[0.0799]	[0.0702]
Sulawesi Tenggara	−0.4664**	0.09464	−0.06731
	[0.1808]	[0.0692]	[0.0762]
Sulawesi Utara	0.2711	0.02332	−0.14
	[0.2185]	[0.1380]	[0.1285]
Sumatera Barat	0.01633	0.08168	−0.1862*
	[0.2224]	[0.0847]	[0.0953]
Sumatera Selatan	−0.2945	0.1053	−0.1153
	[0.2194]	[0.0763]	[0.1419]
Sumatera Utara	−0.07445	0.04999	−0.1885
	[0.1828]	[0.0986]	[0.1189]
Informality (base–business with more than 5 employees)			
Sole proprietorship[1]	−0.02021	0.03188	0.1308**
	[0.0876]	[0.0347]	[0.0591]

continued on next page

Appendix 3 continued

Variables	(1) revenue 1	(2) revenue 2	(3) finance
Digitalization (base–personal contact based business)			
Digitally operated firms[2]	−0.1174	−0.05861*	−0.1292***
	[0.0969]	[0.0301]	[0.0485]
Constant	0.2352	1.0631***	1.1067***
	[0.4048]	[0.1166]	[0.2554]
N	479	479	448
Pseudo R-square	0.2016	0.2826	0.2588

Note: Robust standard errors in brackets.

*** $p < 0.01$, ** $p < 0.05$, *$p < 0.10$.

[1] Includes family-run and/or business with up to four employees.

[2] Firms that use internet for daily business.

B. August–September 2020

Variables	(1) revenue 1	(2) revenue 2	(3) finance
Industry (base–water supply)			
Manufacturing	−0.01736	0.09664	−0.007344
	[0.4043]	[0.1016]	[0.0304]
Construction	−0.7182	0.3137	...
	[0.4315]	[0.2219]	...
Wholesale and Retail Trade; Repair of Motor Vehicles and Motorcycles	−0.5258	−0.06377	−0.07688
	[0.4054]	[0.0925]	[0.0560]
Transportation and Storage	0.4793	−0.01621	−0.08218
	[0.4103]	[0.1099]	[0.0566]
Accommodation and Food Service Activities	−0.4233	−0.02002	−0.1871
	[0.4058]	[0.1297]	[0.1237]
Information and Communication	0.2728	0.3113	−0.02793
	[0.4007]	[0.2174]	[0.0622]
Financial and Insurance Activities	0.1539	0.174	−1.5132***
	[0.5268]	[0.4035]	[0.2525]
Professional, Scientific, and Technical Activities	−0.6119	−0.06992	−0.4114*

continued on next page

Appendix 3 continued

Variables	(1) revenue 1	(2) revenue 2	(3) finance
	[0.4017]	[0.1633]	[0.2281]
Human Health and Social Work Activities	−0.2187	0.2095	−0.1494
	[0.5699]	[0.2253]	[0.0973]
Other Service Activities	−0.2436	−0.0809	−0.07218
	[0.4349]	[0.1422]	[0.0589]
Location (base–DKI Jakarta)			
Banten	−0.1195	−0.2712	0.00479
	[0.3508]	[0.3571]	[0.0622]
Bengkulu	−0.08593	−0.03396	0.2781
	[0.2642]	[0.1587]	[0.2236]
DI Yogyakarta	−0.0349	−0.2418	0.1597
	[0.3077]	[0.2387]	[0.1806]
Jambi	−0.2745	−0.08386	0.05381
	[0.2893]	[0.1203]	[0.0739]
Jawa Barat	−0.02342	0.05362	−0.01274
	[0.3241]	[0.0813]	[0.0650]
Jawa Tengah	0.203	−0.1856	−0.1232
	[0.3732]	[0.1323]	[0.1343]
Jawa Timur	0.1747	−0.02445	−0.08997
	[0.3272]	[0.0891]	[0.0754]
Kalimantan Barat	−0.3997	0.2139	0.008703
	[0.4966]	[0.3858]	[0.1406]
Kalimantan Selatan	−0.4542	−0.02298	−0.06111
	[0.3022]	[0.1293]	[0.0637]
Kalimantan Timur	0.217	0.2788	...
	[0.3768]	[0.2291]	...
Kep. Bangka Belitung	−0.5862	−0.09356	−0.1155
	[0.4921]	[0.1214]	[0.1113]
Kepulauan Riau	−0.1354	0.1203	−0.01629
	[0.3182]	[0.1182]	[0.0733]
Maluku Utara	−0.2899	−0.06701	−0.06976
	[0.3401]	[0.1470]	[0.0893]
Nusa Tenggara Timur	0.06778	0.1073	0.3165
	[0.3758]	[0.1758]	[0.2274]

continued on next page

Appendix 3 continued

Variables	(1) revenue 1	(2) revenue 2	(3) finance
Sulawesi Selatan	0.7283**	0.209	−0.1256
	[0.3572]	[0.1576]	[0.1267]
Sulawesi Tengah	0.5806	0.1234	−0.04424
	[0.3805]	[0.3749]	[0.1035]
Sulawesi Utara	−0.01455	−0.07559	−0.06325
	[0.2529]	[0.1153]	[0.0920]
Sumatera Selatan	0.1959	−0.2909	0,.009759
	[0.4239]	[0.3498]	[0.0623]
Sumatera Utara	1.0498***	0.09481	−0.03117
	[0.3643]	[0.1440]	[0.0927]
Informality (base–corporation/cooperative)			
Sole proprietorship	0.5752***	0.3607	−0.03151
	[0.1901]	[0.3491]	[0.0526]
Digitalization (base–personal contact based business)			
Digitally operated firms[1]	−0.2065	−0.08694	−0.0119
	[0.1307]	[0.1041]	[0.0242]
Constant	0.3803	0.03773	1.0013***
	[0.5895]	[0.3548]	[0.0881]
N	116	116	109
Pseudo R-square	0.5348	0.2971	0.1997

Note: Robust standard errors in brackets.

*** $p < 0.01$, ** $p < 0.05$, * $p < 0.10$.

[1] Firms engaged in online selling or e-commerce.

C. March–April 2021

Variables	(1) revenue 1	(2) revenue 2	(3) finance
Industry (base–water supply)			
Mining and Quarrying	−0.09356*	−0.5808***	0.3896***
	[0.0516]	[0.1132]	[0.1239]
Manufacturing	0.006639	0.1027	0.06954
	[0.0581]	[0.1221]	[0.1307]

continued on next page

Appendix 3 continued

Variables	(1) revenue 1	(2) revenue 2	(3) finance
Electricity, Gas, Steam, and Air Conditioning Supply	−0.01847	−0.01583	0.1225
	[0.0569]	[0.2538]	[0.2481]
Construction	−0.02456	0.3528**	−0.1678
	[0.0525]	[0.1612]	[0.2379]
Wholesale and Retail Trade; Repair of Motor Vehicles and Motorcycles	−0.01309	0.08733	0.08481
	[0.0483]	[0.1111]	[0.1204]
Transportation and Storage	0.02799	0.4118***	−0.003575
	[0.1028]	[0.1176]	[0.1933]
Accommodation and Food Service Activities	−0.006727	0.1066	0.1826
	[0.0494]	[0.1126]	[0.1209]
Information and Communication	−0.05231	−0.05448	0.0896
	[0.0520]	[0.1473]	[0.1553]
Financial and Insurance Activities	−0.1166*	0.09249	−0.5252***
	[0.0655]	[0.3125]	[0.1497]
Real Estate Activities	0.3044	0.2891	−0.1903
	[0.2401]	[0.1955]	[0.3409]
Professional, Scientific, and Technical Activities	−0.0801	0.1444	0.1083
	[0.0576]	[0.1498]	[0.1464]
Public Administration and Defense; Compulsory Social Security	−0.04356	0.1416	0.2707
	[0.0674]	[0.1236]	[0.1984]
Education	−0.06203	0.0676	−0.04889
	[0.0839]	[0.1560]	[0.1553]
Human Health and Social Work Activities	−0.1093**	0.08274	−0.03422
	[0.0556]	[0.1876]	[0.1928]
Other Service Activities	0.01786	0.08583	0.1019
	[0.0638]	[0.1163]	[0.1264]
Location (base–DKI Jakarta)			
Aceh	−0.01475	0.3014***	−0.6078***
	[0.0222]	[0.0418]	[0.1846]
Bali	0.3366*	0.3116***	0.1136**
	[0.1829]	[0.0464]	[0.0504]

continued on next page

Appendix 3 continued

Variables	(1) revenue 1	(2) revenue 2	(3) finance
Banten	0.002007	−0.3603***	−0.4169***
	[0.0187]	[0.0884]	[0.0944]
Bengkulu	0.01907	0.2938***	0.04811
	[0.0482]	[0.0448]	[0.0486]
DI Yogyakarta	0.3781	−0.0603	0.09727**
	[0.2434]	[0.2693]	[0.0383]
Jambi	−0.01281	0.3153***	0.1581***
	[0.0362]	[0.0389]	[0.0434]
Jawa Barat	0.03369**	−0.02722	−0.1796***
	[0.0167]	[0.0371]	[0.0409]
Jawa Tengah	0.1550**	0.2525***	0.1034**
	[0.0767]	[0.0567]	[0.0411]
Jawa Timur	0.02920*	−0.09759**	−0.2399***
	[0.0163]	[0.0416]	[0.0450]
Kalimantan Barat	0.9346***	0.2529***	0.02625
	[0.0608]	[0.0707]	[0.0658]
Kalimantan Selatan	0.1047	0.1386*	−0.08299
	[0.0757]	[0.0816]	[0.0891]
Kalimantan Tengah	−0.1447	−0.5382***	−0.3125
	[0.1071]	[0.1659]	[0.2620]
Kalimantan Utara	0.0381	0.03751	−0.1125
	[0.0339]	[0.1497]	[0.1488]
Lampung	−0.02763	0.3103***	−0.0003647
	[0.0239]	[0.0373]	[0.0389]
Nusa Tenggara Barat	0.2176	0.2887***	−0.04908
	[0.1686]	[0.0476]	[0.1224]
Nusa Tenggara Timur	0.1308	0.3607***	0.2852**
	[0.0829]	[0.1218]	[0.1115]
Riau	−0.01594	0.2941***	−0.01621
	[0.0581]	[0.0443]	[0.1038]
Sulawesi Selatan	0.0363	0.3101***	0.1185**
	[0.0555]	[0.0378]	[0.0521]
Sulawesi Tenggara	1.0057***	0.2976***	0.1612**
	[0.0580]	[0.0703]	[0.0647]

continued on next page

Appendix 3 continued

Variables	(1) revenue 1	(2) revenue 2	(3) finance
Sulawesi Utara	0.03925	0.2784***	−0.1037
	[0.0383]	[0.0496]	[0.1639]
Sumatera Barat	0.04845*	0.3442***	0.1705***
	[0.0284]	[0.0484]	[0.0514]
Sumatera Utara	−0.007558	−0.04786	−0.06201
	[0.0157]	[0.0514]	[0.0446]
Informality (base–corporation/cooperative)			
Sole proprietorship	−0.2445***	0.01404	0.00581
	[0.0853]	[0.0535]	[0.0544]
Digitalization (base–personal contact based business)			
Digitally operated firms[1]	−0.03825	0.002242	0.0122
	[0.0387]	[0.0371]	[0.0283]
Constant	0.2253**	0.5453***	0.4466***
	[0.0899]	[0.1562]	[0.1561]
N	2,428	2,428	2,290
Pseudo R-square	0.2504	0.1967	0.2113

Note: Robust standard errors in brackets.

*** $p < 0.01$, ** $p < 0.05$, *$p < 0.10$.

[1] Firms engaged in online selling or e-commerce.

D. May 2021

Variables	(1) revenue 1	(2) revenue 2	(3) finance
Industry (base–water supply)			
Mining and Quarrying	0.00822	−0.2143	0.1115
	[0.0152]	[0.2793]	[0.1278]
Manufacturing	0.009071	0.009912	−0.1159
	[0.0239]	[0.1644]	[0.1251]
Electricity, Gas, Steam, and Air Conditioning Supply	−0.0164	−0.03359	−0.2916
	[0.0207]	[0.2318]	[0.2462]

continued on next page

Appendix 3 continued

Variables	(1) revenue 1	(2) revenue 2	(3) finance
Construction	−0.01581	−0.3563*	−0.2462
	[0.0247]	[0.1990]	[0.2344]
Wholesale and Retail Trade; Repair of Motor Vehicles and Motorcycles	0.03586***	−0.02004	−0.1179
	[0.0137]	[0.1482]	[0.1074]
Transportation and Storage	0.07395	0.02021	−0.1614
	[0.1019]	[0.2357]	[0.2343]
Accommodation and Food Service Activities	0.03432	0.09235	−0.07901
	[0.0316]	[0.1504]	[0.1091]
Information and Communication	−0.01925	−0.09711	−0.08479
	[0.0187]	[0.1878]	[0.1458]
Financial and Insurance Activities	0.02019	−0.2051	−0.3537*
	[0.0236]	[0.2730]	[0.2109]
Real Estate Activities	−0.06178	−0.02228	−0.8054***
	[0.0413]	[0.4200]	[0.1115]
Professional, Scientific, and Technical Activities	0.1155	0.3879**	−0.1366
	[0.1391]	[0.1764]	[0.1579]
Education	0.07724	0.1152	−0.3339**
	[0.0492]	[0.1871]	[0.1605]
Human Health and Social Work Activities	−0.02532	0.1049	−0.2779
	[0.0338]	[0.1990]	[0.1958]
Other Service Activities	0.08903*	−0.05613	−0.1497
	[0.0466]	[0.1580]	[0.1177]
Location (base–DKI Jakarta)			
Aceh	−0.1055	0.003246	0.1134
	[0.1418]	[0.1095]	[0.1276]
Bali	0.6627**	0.4016***	0.2103***
	[0.2714]	[0.0662]	[0.0482]
Banten	−0.02511*	−0.5635***	−0.4439***
	[0.0137]	[0.0458]	[0.0930]
DI Yogyakarta	0.3564*	0.3473***	−0.07187
	[0.2066]	[0.0489]	[0.1937]
Jawa Barat	0.02386	−0.1054**	−0.09855**

continued on next page

Appendix 3 continued

Variables	(1) revenue 1	(2) revenue 2	(3) finance
	[0.0202]	[0.0471]	[0.0440]
Jawa Tengah	0.05916	−0.02369	0.1141**
	[0.0598]	[0.1246]	[0.0527]
Jawa Timur	0.03174**	−0.3282***	−0.2117***
	[0.0151]	[0.0485]	[0.0479]
Kalimantan Selatan	−0.06036**	0.2049***	0.08123
	[0.0302]	[0.0687]	[0.0516]
Nusa Tenggara Barat	0.0665	0.5122***	0.3014***
	[0.0773]	[0.0597]	[0.0724]
Riau	0.7686***	0.02183	0.4947***
	[0.1538]	[0.1272]	[0.1580]
Sulawesi Selatan	−0.05528	0.3973***	0.2094***
	[0.0375]	[0.0861]	[0.0485]
Sulawesi Utara	0.0396***	0.2049***	0.08123
	[0.0302]	[0.0687]	[0.0516]
Sumatera Utara	−0.006849	−0.06888	0.0577
	[0.0145]	[0.0652]	[0.0464]
Informality (base–corporation/cooperative)			
Sole proprietorship	0.05821**	0.06302	−0.1492*
	[0.0277]	[0.0880]	[0.0778]
Digitalization (base–personal contact based business)			
Digitally operated firms[1]	0.03603	0.09382	−0.02533
	[0.0458]	[0.0667]	[0.0352]
Constant	−0.04159	0.7019***	0.5690***
	[0.0427]	[0.1965]	[0.1551]
N	2,160	2,160	2,039
Pseudo R-square	0.2278	0.2587	0.2021

Note: Robust standard errors in brackets.

*** p<0.01, ** p<0.05, *p<0.10.

[1] Firms engaged in online selling or e-commerce.

Source: Author's calculation based on weighted data from MSME surveys in Indonesia on March–April 2020, August–September 2020, March–April 2021, and May 2021.

9

Fintech, Government Aid, and Informal Household Businesses in ASEAN Economies during the Pandemic

Peter J. Morgan, Kunhyui Kim, and Long Q. Trinh

Abstract

This chapter examines the relationship between the use of financial technology (fintech) services, the provision of government aid, and firm performance, as measured by continuation of business and changes in revenue during early stages of the coronavirus disease (COVID-19) pandemic (until the end of 2020), using newly collected data by the Asian Development Bank Institute. The study finds that the use of fintech is positively associated with the firms' continuation in business and lower likelihood of suffering revenue declines during the pandemic. This may be because fintech makes it easier to broaden the customer base, receive and make payments, and obtain financing. Also, small informal firms are just as likely to benefit from using fintech services as larger firms. The study also finds that government aid was widely distributed to small firms and that, compared with their pre-pandemic incomes, the aid was comparatively large. However, no positive relationship was found between aid and business continuity or increase in sales. The evidence, however, finds government aid for small informal firms to be useful and calls for increasing support for fintech adoption.

Keywords: fintech, COVID-19 pandemic, SMEs, informal firms, firm performance

1. Introduction

The significant negative effects of the COVID-19 pandemic on micro-, small-, and medium-sized enterprises (MSMEs) have been well documented. This reflects the combined impacts of government measures such as lockdowns, limits on operating hours and transport, and disruptions to supply chains, as well as the greater unwillingness of persons to venture out because of fear of infection. On the other hand, many governments implemented major fiscal stimulus packages to provide financial and nonfinancial aid to firms and households. Another major feature of the pandemic has been an accelerated shift toward the use of financial technology (fintech) services, reflecting factors such as the greater attractiveness of online shopping, difficulties of traveling, and greater reluctance to engage in face-to-face transactions. Adoption of fintech may especially benefit informal and small firms. Investment costs are relatively low, and adopting fintech can improve firms' access to finance to ease their financial constraints. Using fintech can also facilitate advertising and payment processes for customers, thereby expanding the customer base. Firms may then offer their goods and services through e-commerce platforms and reach distant customers.

However, there has been less research focus on informal firms, due to the greater difficulty of obtaining data and difficulties in defining informal firms. Using a unique dataset of household businesses in seven ASEAN countries—Cambodia, Indonesia, the Lao People's Democratic Republic (Lao PDR), Malaysia, the Philippines, Thailand, and Viet Nam, this chapter investigates four related questions: (i) the impact of the pandemic on informal firms in urban areas; (ii) the ability of informal firms to access government aid; (iii) the impact of government aid on informal firms' continuity and business performance; and (iv) the impact of the use of fintech on informal firms' continuity and business performance. The chapter examines how government aid and the adoption or increased use of fintech services affected the business performance of informal firms in seven ASEAN economies during the pandemic. The survey data used for this study was collected by the Asian Development Bank Institute (ADBI). Focusing on the performance of informal firms in urban areas, the study finds that the use of fintech was associated with the continued operation of informal firms and with the increases in their revenue.[1]

---

[1]   Section 3 of this chapter explains the definition of informality as used in the study.

This chapter comprises five sections, including the introduction section. Section 2 provides a literature review. Section 3 describes the data, some stylized facts of the performance of informal firms during the pandemic, including the adoption of fintech services, and the empirical approach. Section 4 presents the empirical results from the analysis. Last, Section 5 provides concluding remarks and policy implications.

2. Literature Review
2.1 Firm Operation during Economic Crises: Overview

Many studies now have examined the effects of the COVID-19 pandemic on firm activities (Inoue and Todo 2020; Sun et al. 2021; Apedo-Amah et al. 2020; Hu and Zhang 2021; Dai et al. 2021; Sonobe et al. 2021; Adian et al. 2020). There are several ways in which the pandemic affected the firms, including supply shocks, demand shocks, uncertainty, and credit crunches (Apedo-Amah et al. 2020; Adian et al. 2020). Depending on the nature of a crisis, the effects and their transmission could differ. For example, during global financial crises, the major channel that is affected tends to be access to finance. However, the most prominent feature of the COVID-19 pandemic, which is different from previous crises, is that firms have experienced multiple challenges at once (Adian et al. 2020). Measures such as stay-home orders and lockdown policies reduced the supply of labor, and thus disrupted the supply chains. Brinca, Duarte, and Faria-e-Castro (2020) used structural econometric methods to decompose changes in working hours into supply and demand shock contributions to find that the supply shock contribution outweighs the demand shock contribution. Candia, Coibion, and Gorodnichenko (2020) suggest that, for some firms (and most households), the pandemic is a supply shock.

Firms are also affected by declining demand, stemming from several causes: declines in income, increases in precautionary savings, and increases in unplanned expenditures. Morgan, Trinh, and Kim (2022) showed that, in seven ASEAN countries, more than 70% of households experienced income declines in the early phase of the pandemic, and, compared with the first half of 2020, 45% did so in the second half of the year. Many business owners and managers of both large and small firms reported that negative demand shocks were their most pressing concern in the early phase of the pandemic (Hassan et al. 2020; Bartik et al. 2020). Meyer, Prescott, and Sheng (2022) further find that firms are overwhelmingly worried about the decline in demand. Bartik et al.

(2020) report that the main reason behind small US firms' temporary closure is demand shocks rather than supply shocks.

The pandemic has also increased economic uncertainty. Various economic theories indicate that uncertainty has negative effects on economic activities. Firms, especially small and informal ones, may delay their investment and face more financial constraints. Financial markets are generally understood to face asymmetric information and incentives, causing a wedge between the costs of internal funds and external funds (Jensen and Merkling 1976; Stiglitz and Weiss 1981). These problems are especially acute in developing countries. Due to the underdevelopment of the financial markets, firms in these economies tend to depend less on formal financial institutions for credit, and more on alternative sources of finance such as friends, relatives, informal moneylenders, and trade credit. The costs of these different sources of capital vary, depending on the asymmetric information cost of using each source of finance. Therefore, different sources of finance may cause firms to have different investment strategies. Moreover, the financing structure may affect the growth of firms (Ayyagari, Demirgüç-Kunt, and Maksimovic 2010; Allen, Gu, and Kowalewski 2012; Du and Girma 2012), and ultimately their investments (Trinh, Morgan, and Sonobe 2020).

2.2 Informal Firms during the Pandemic

There are various definitions of informality. According to the ILO Recommendation No. 204, the "informal economy" refers to all economic activities by workers and economic units that are—in law or in practice—not covered or insufficiently covered by formal arrangements (ILO 2015). Informal firms could be distinguished by various dimensions including institutions, business operation, and contribution of employers to social security, size of economic units, and location of workplaces (OECD and ILO 2019). Firms are considered as formal firms if they are registered under national legislation. This includes registration with social security, sales, or income tax authorities. Bookkeeping practices also distinguish formal from informal firms. Other criteria may include contributions to social security or declared labor or enterprise income to national authorities. However, as OECD and ILO (2019) note, the definitions of informal and formal firms vary significantly from country to country. In general, however, informal firms tend to be small in their size, revenue, and scale of operations.

Different firms may respond to economic downturns differently, depending on their characteristics such as size, formality, and ability to access credit during crises (Campello, Graham, and Harvey 2010;

Hallward-Driemeier and Rijkers 2013). There are several arguments for why this happens. Informal firms are more likely to be risk averse (Harhoff, Stahl, and Woywode 1998) and to be born "out of necessity" (Poschke 2013; Vivarelli 2013). Informal firms tend to share characteristics of small and young firms, such as facing a variety of constraints that make it harder for them to thrive and grow (Farazi 2014). They are also more likely to be credit-constrained—lacking access to formal credit, and depending more on informal sources of finance.

The small size of informal firms may be advantageous or disadvantageous during the pandemic. On one hand, informal firms may be more sensitive to swings in the economy and, thus, economic downturns hit them harder than larger firms (Gertler and Gilchrist 1994; Fort et al. 2013). This is because these firms have scant market power and limited margins of flexibility (Bugamelli, Cristadoro, and Zevi 2010). On the other hand, smaller enterprises may more easily adapt to economic downturns because they are more flexible and have fewer sunk costs (Narjoko and Hill 2007), are better at exploiting market niches (Hodorogel 2009), concentrate on activities characterized by economies of agglomeration rather than of scale (Berry, Rodriguez, and Sandee 2001), and are less reliant on formal credit (Ter Wengel and Rodriguez 2006).

Many studies find that informal firms have been more affected by the COVID-19 pandemic than formal and larger firms. Meyer, Prescott, and Sheng (2022) argue that, during the early phases of the pandemic, the major channel through which it affected firms' operations was demand shocks rather than supply shocks, mostly attributed to containment measures imposed by governments worldwide. Informal firms are more likely than formal firms to operate in non-pharmaceutical sectors, such as retail or transportation, which are more vulnerable to the disruptions caused by these measures (Fairlie and Fossen 2021). Evidence from 51 countries shows that small firms are more likely to experience a fall in sales than larger firms (Adian et al. 2020). Small firms are also less likely to report increases in sales than larger firms, and, likewise, Chinese small firms, for instance, are also more likely to face weak market demand (Sun et al. 2021).

2.3 Fintech and Informal Firms

In response to the pandemic, many firms have digitalized parts of their operations (Apedo-Amah et al. 2020; Sonobe et al. 2021). Digitalization can enable the creation of social businesses, support social customer relationship management systems, and open new and low-cost communication channels (Laudon and Laudon 2019; Turkina 2018; Aceto, Persico, and Pescapé 2019). Similarly, digitalization can help micro, small, and medium-sized enterprises (MSMEs) to develop and manage remote business operations and activities (Akpan 2010; Laudon and Laudon 2019; Akpan, Soopramanien, and Kwak 2021; Smith et al. 2020). This positive aspect of digitalization is especially important during crises such as the pandemic when mobility and social interaction are restricted.

Apedo-Amah et al. (2020) found that around 50% of the firms in their sample of 51 expanded their use of digital platforms during the pandemic period. Around 34% of firms increased or began the use of the internet, social media, and digital platforms; and 17% of firms invested in new equipment, software, or digital solutions (Apedo-Amah et al. 2020). Nonetheless, smaller firms are less likely than larger firms to adopt digital solutions, possibly due to the high cost involved and their low digital skills. Apedo-Amah et al. (2020) also find that the probabilities of using digital technologies, increasing their use, and investing in digital solutions all increase with firm size. Sun et al. (2021) find that the negative impacts of the pandemic are reduced for firms located in cities with high levels of digitalization.

Among digital solutions, fintech requires relatively low investment and adoption costs. Fintech services cost less than those of traditional banks and lessen information asymmetry for prospective borrowers (Vives 2017). This makes fintech potentially more inclusive and it provides additional opportunities for small and informal firms to overcome their financial constraints (Gao 2022). However, observers also caution against a one-size-fits-all approach to fintech policy making. There is a need to move beyond techno-centric paradigms, which view fintech instruments as easy technological fixes and lead to their dumping on emerging markets; instead, appropriate policy creation and adoption must carefully consider the intersection of multiple micro and macro factors (Boamah, Murshid, and Mozumder 2021).

2.4 Government Support and Firm Performance during the Pandemic

Many governments have used various policy measures to support firms during crises. Government aid was used to ease the financial constraints faced by firms during the pandemic as well as to mitigate the uncertainty perceived by firms (Cirera et al. 2021). Due to the pandemic's global scale, large-scale fiscal stimulus packages were implemented around the world.

While the literature shows positive effects of government aid in response to previous crises (De Mel, McKenzie, and Woodruff 2012; Bruhn 2020), evidence of the effectiveness of government aid during the pandemic is rather limited. Chen et al. (2020), Granja et al. (2020), and Chetty et al. (2020) found that government aid during the COVID-19 pandemic has been less effective in alleviating small enterprises' financial constraints or encouraging the reopening of small businesses. The same problem may be expected for informal firms since these firms experience even more difficulty in accessing credit. Using data from over 120,000 firms across 60 countries during April–September 2020, Cirera et al. (2021) find that firms without government support reported an expected drop in sales of 16%, while firms with government support expected a decline of 14%. The limited effectiveness of government aid, especially for small firms in general and informal firms in particular, possibly may be due to two reasons: (i) micro and small firms, many of which are informal, are about half as likely as large firms to access support; and (ii) firms receiving benefits were not necessarily those worst-hit, and hard-hit firms may not have received benefits (Cirera et al. 2021).

This chapter contributes to the literature in multiple ways. First, it enriches our understanding of the effects of the pandemic on the economy at a micro-firm level (e.g., Al-Awadhi et al. 2020; Baek, Mohanty, and Glambosky 2020; Sonobe et al. 2021; de Vito and Gómez 2020). Second, this chapter highlights the effects of digital transformation and adoption of fintech services on firm performance (Laudon and Laudon 2019; Turkina 2018). Focusing on the pandemic period, this study examines the role of digitalization as a coping strategy for firms to overcome external shocks. Last, this study explores the effects of government aid on firm performance.

3. Methodology and Data

3.1 General Approach

As stated earlier, this chapter investigates four interrelated questions regarding the impacts of the COVID-19 pandemic, government policies, and adoption of fintech services on the performance of informal firms in ASEAN economies: (i) the impact of the pandemic, (ii) the ability of informal firms to access government aid, (iii) the impact of government aid on informal firms' continuity and business performance, and (iv) the impact of the use of fintech on informal firms' continuity and business performance.

3.2 Data

The analysis uses a unique dataset derived from surveys of household firms in seven countries, namely Cambodia, Indonesia, the Lao PDR, Malaysia, the Philippines, Thailand, and Viet Nam.[2] The survey was designed by ADBI and implemented by survey companies in those countries. It was conducted in two rounds—the first from May through July 2020, and the second from the end of November through December 2020. Key characteristics of the survey are as follows:

- Due to COVID-19, it was a computer-assisted telephone survey;
- Stratified sampling was used, to be representative of the country as a whole, based on income, rural vs. urban, region, age of head of household, and gender of head of household;
- Approximately 1,000 households were surveyed in each country;
- The respondent was the head of the household or the person most knowledgeable of the household's finances;
- Administering each questionnaire took 12–15 minutes (about 17–19 minutes in some countries, partly due to screening questions);
- The questionnaire collected information on
  - household characteristics, including number of members, gender, number of employed members, number of members in school, age of head of household, education level, urban vs. rural residence, and income, including types of income;
  - fintech service usage information, both for the household and the household business (gathered in the second-round survey);
  - changes in income, employment, and working hours, compared with base periods of the end of June 2019 and June 2020, respectively; and
  - any financial difficulties experienced by the household, and coping measures used (e.g., reducing consumption, borrowing, delaying payments, or applying for government aid).

The study stratified each country sample according to income quartiles based on pre-pandemic income. Only households with at least one household business were selected, which resulted in a sample of 2,800 households (see Appendix for sample statistics).

---

[2]   The first wave of the survey was also carried out in Myanmar in 2020, but since 1 February 2021, it was not possible to carry out the second wave there. Therefore, the results for Myanmar are not included in this chapter.

Fintech usage by the household business was captured by two questions:

- As one of the coping strategies to deal with the pandemic, did the business start or increase using an internet/social media digital platform?
- Has your business ever used a digital platform to:
  a. raise capital/take loans
  b. pay your suppliers
  c. get payment from customers
  d. purchase or order goods for your business
  e. post or sell your products online
  f. other purposes (specify)

The first question captures changes in usage of digital platforms (including fintech) during the pandemic, although it does not distinguish those firms that started using fintech. In this chapter, this is referred to as "using digital platforms as a business adjustment." The second question provides more detail on the specific fintech services used, although it does not specify whether such use changed after the pandemic. This is referred to in the chapter as "using fintech services."

A key problem faced by the study was about defining informal firms. Informal firms play an important role in developing economies. However, the ADBI database had no information on whether a firm is formal (i.e., registered as a corporate entity) or informal (i.e., not registered as a corporate entity or without a tax identification code). Therefore, this study defines informal firms as households in the lowest three income quartiles (based on pre-pandemic income, excluding government transfers and remittances) that operated a business or worked in a household business. Only about half of the sample had data on pre-pandemic income; this yielded 1,394 households with household businesses, of which 979 were classified as informal firms based on the aforementioned definition. The study recognizes that any such definition is rather arbitrary, but, in the absence of specific information, it merits plausibility, since most informal firms are relatively small. Also, it allows the use of a uniform definition across countries. Finally, some sensitivity analyses using other definitions were also conducted (results available on request).

3.3 Stylized Facts: Household Businesses and Impacts of COVID-19

On average, 40% of households in the sample have a household business. The proportion of households having a business in the Lao PDR, Malaysia, the Philippines, Thailand, and Viet Nam ranges from 32% to 38%, while the share for Cambodian and Indonesian households in| the sample was 56% and 52%, respectively.

Figure 1 shows the breakdown by industry of the household businesses for urban households. Overall, the proportions of businesses are retail, 49.6%; personal services, 11.7%; agriculture (including farming and fishery), 6.8%; industry and manufacturing, 3.7%; construction, 2.8%; health and education, 1.2%; and others, 24.3%. Over half of the urban household businesses are retail services in the Lao PDR, the Philippines, Thailand, and Viet Nam. In Indonesia and Malaysia, the proportion of businesses without an identified sector is the highest, even larger than the retail sector. It is likely that many of those businesses are retail as well.

Figure 1: Distribution of Household Businesses by Sector for Urban Households (%)

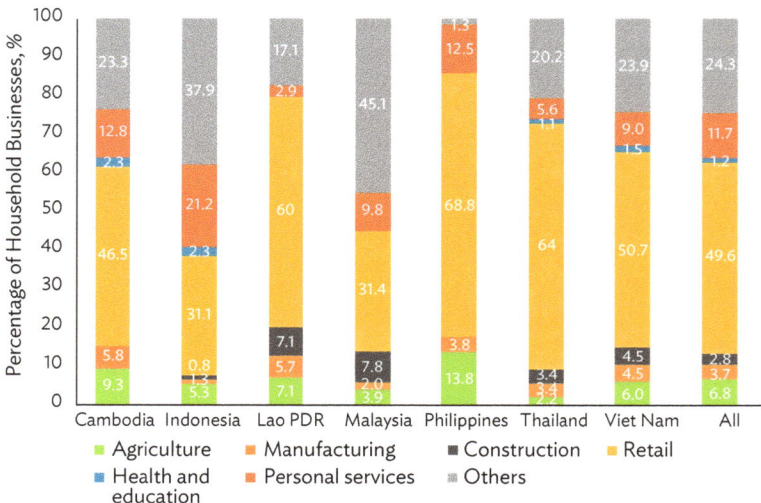

Lao PDR = Lao People's Democratic Republic.

Source: Authors' analysis from ADBI database.

COVID-19 and Household Business Performance

Despite the negative impact of the COVID-19 pandemic and non-pharmaceutical measures adopted in ASEAN countries, most of urban household businesses in the sample (over 80%) were still operating when the survey was conducted (Figure 2). Overall, only 8.8% of urban household informal businesses were temporarily closed and only 4.8% permanently closed, figures lower than corresponding shares for formal firms. The situations are quite similar across countries, except for relatively large shares of permanent closures in Thailand and relatively large shares of temporary closures in Malaysia and the Philippines. Moreover, no urban household businesses permanently closed in the Lao PDR and Viet Nam.

Figure 2: Impact of COVID-19 Pandemic on State of Business Operation of Urban Households (%)

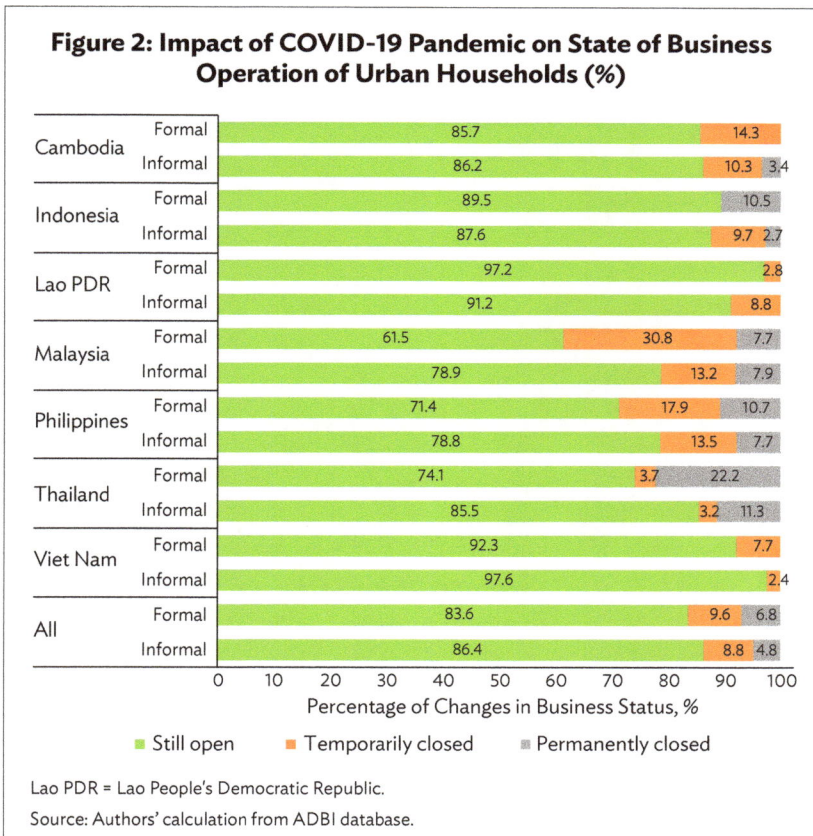

Country	Type	Still open	Temporarily closed	Permanently closed
Cambodia	Formal	85.7	14.3	
	Informal	86.2	10.3	3.4
Indonesia	Formal	89.5		10.5
	Informal	87.6	9.7	2.7
Lao PDR	Formal	97.2		2.8
	Informal	91.2		8.8
Malaysia	Formal	61.5	30.8	7.7
	Informal	78.9	13.2	7.9
Philippines	Formal	71.4	17.9	10.7
	Informal	78.8	13.5	7.7
Thailand	Formal	74.1	3.7	22.2
	Informal	85.5	3.2	11.3
Viet Nam	Formal	92.3		7.7
	Informal	97.6		2.4
All	Formal	83.6	9.6	6.8
	Informal	86.4	8.8	4.8

Percentage of Changes in Business Status, %

■ Still open   ■ Temporarily closed   ■ Permanently closed

Lao PDR = Lao People's Democratic Republic.

Source: Authors' calculation from ADBI database.

However, as presented in Figure 3, urban businesses were severely affected by the pandemic. Nearly 86% of urban informal firms saw a decline in revenue, while only 5.5% reported that their revenue was higher during the pandemic.[3] Overall, both formal and informal firms across all countries faced large decreases in revenue during the pandemic. A larger proportion of urban informal household businesses in the Lao PDR (14.7%), the Philippines (11.5%), and Viet Nam (19.5%) enjoyed higher revenues than in other countries. This could be because in 2020 the pandemic was relatively mild in the Lao PDR and Viet Nam.

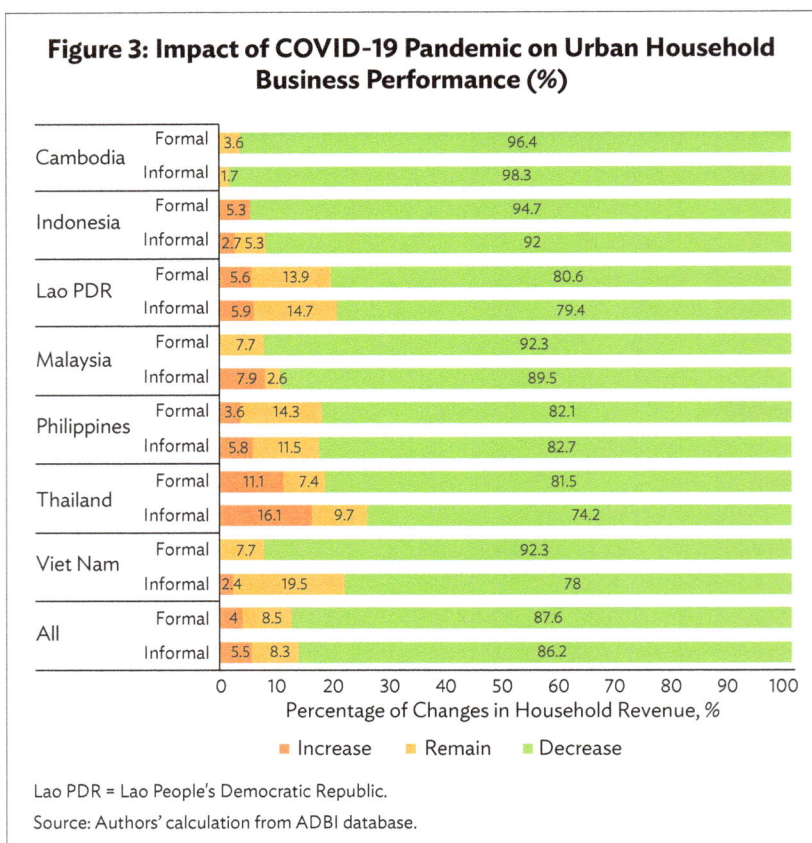

Figure 3: Impact of COVID-19 Pandemic on Urban Household Business Performance (%)

Lao PDR = Lao People's Democratic Republic.

Source: Authors' calculation from ADBI database.

---

[3]   Figures reflect household income, with household business as revenue.

Informal Firms, Fintech Adoption, and Firm Performance during the Pandemic

To survive through the pandemic, on average 31% of firms in the sample reported that they adjusted their business practices. The proportion of firms adjusting their business practices varied by country. More than 50% of Indonesian and Malaysian firms had done so. The figure was also high in Thailand (42%) and slightly lower in the Philippines (29%), but substantially lower in Cambodia, the Lao PDR, and Viet Nam. While the low figures in Viet Nam and the Lao PDR can be explained by the relatively low proportion of firms suffering a decline in income, the figure for Cambodia is hard to explain.

Figure 4 shows the percentage of firms that adopted or adjusted their usage of digital platforms. Overall, 17.6% of urban informal firms have used or adopted some digital platform during the pandemic versus only 6.2% of formal firms. Except for the Philippines, urban informal firms outdid formal firms in using digital platforms. Malaysian and Indonesian informal firms had the highest rates of digital platforms usage (39.5% and 30.1%, respectively). The fact that a large share of informal firms was able to increase their use of digital platforms during the pandemic suggests that the barriers to doing so, including investment costs, were moderate.

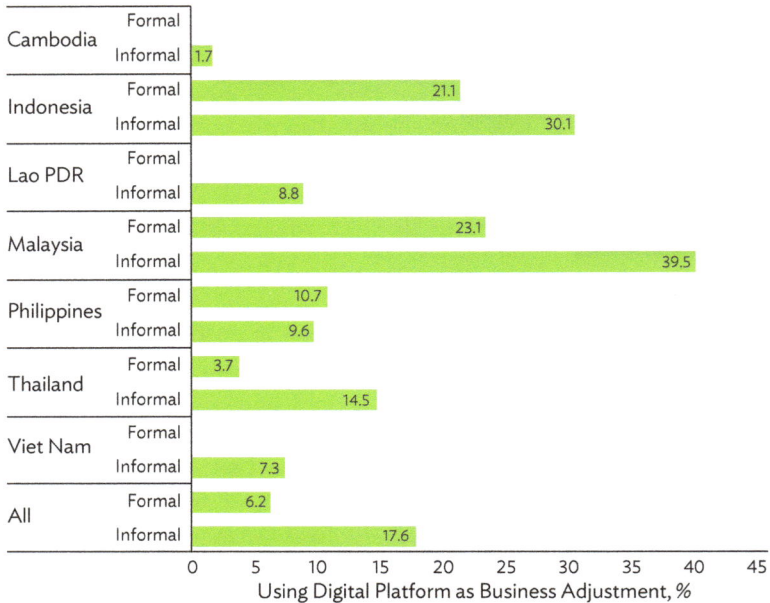

Figure 4: Share of Firms Using Digital Platforms as a Business Practice Adjustment (%)

Cambodia
- Formal
- Informal 1.7

Indonesia
- Formal 21.1
- Informal 30.1

Lao PDR
- Formal
- Informal 8.8

Malaysia
- Formal 23.1
- Informal 39.5

Philippines
- Formal 10.7
- Informal 9.6

Thailand
- Formal 3.7
- Informal 14.5

Viet Nam
- Formal
- Informal 7.3

All
- Formal 6.2
- Informal 17.6

Using Digital Platform as Business Adjustment, %

Lao PDR = Lao People's Democratic Republic.

Note: The share of firms is from among the urban household firms that adjusted businesses during the pandemic.

Source: Authors' calculation from ADBI database.

Use of Fintech Services during the Pandemic

Figure 5 shows the share of urban household businesses using fintech services in the sample. The results include firms that already used fintech services before the pandemic. Overall, approximately 35% of urban informal household businesses were using fintech versus 29% of formal firms. Both formal and informal Malaysian urban firms and formal Vietnamese urban firms had relatively high usage rates of fintech. In Indonesia, 38.9% of informal firms adopted fintech as well. However, only 13.8% of Cambodian informal firms and 21.2% of informal firms in the Philippines used fintech services. These results suggest that the size of the country (population) and per capita income (relative development) both positively affect the usage of fintech services by urban household firms. Also, similar to the results for digital platforms, the relatively high shares for informal firms suggest that barriers to adoption were not great.

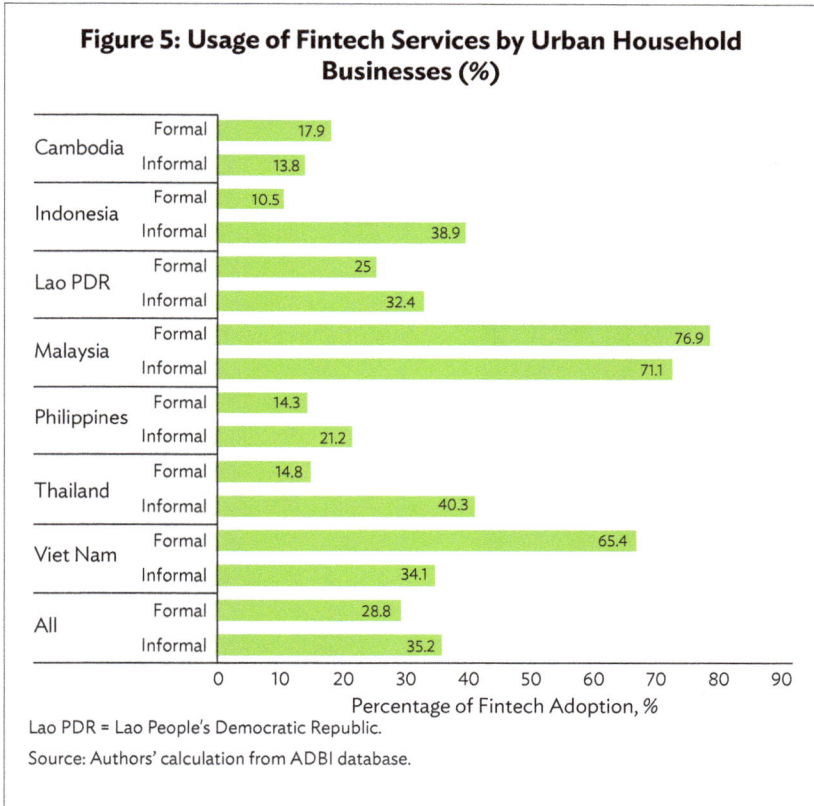

Figure 5: Usage of Fintech Services by Urban Household Businesses (%)

		Percentage
Cambodia	Formal	17.9
	Informal	13.8
Indonesia	Formal	10.5
	Informal	38.9
Lao PDR	Formal	25
	Informal	32.4
Malaysia	Formal	76.9
	Informal	71.1
Philippines	Formal	14.3
	Informal	21.2
Thailand	Formal	14.8
	Informal	40.3
Viet Nam	Formal	65.4
	Informal	34.1
All	Formal	28.8
	Informal	35.2

Percentage of Fintech Adoption, %

Lao PDR = Lao People's Democratic Republic.
Source: Authors' calculation from ADBI database.

Figure 6 shows the types of fintech services used by urban household businesses. The most commonly used service, regardless of formal or informal firms, is for getting payments from customers. Overall, 26.6% of informal firms used fintech services to get payments from customers and 13.8% of informal firms used fintech services to pay suppliers. Compared with formal firms, these shares were, respectively, higher for getting payments and lower for paying suppliers.

Figure 6: Types of Fintech Services Used by Urban Household Businesses

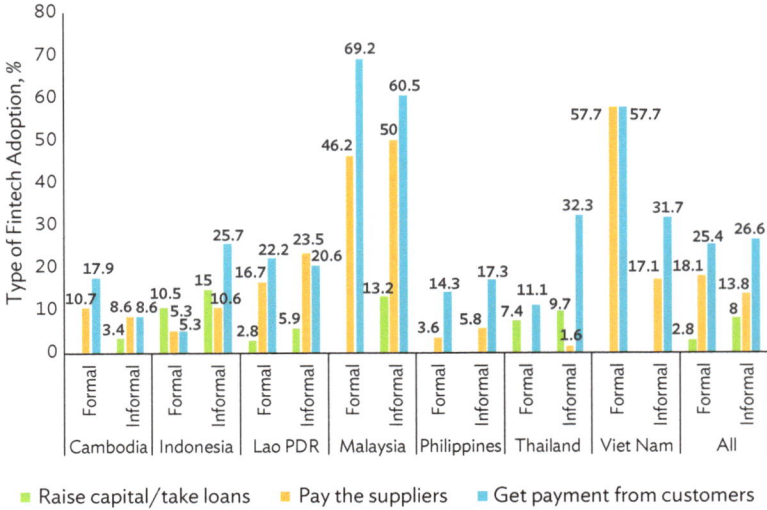

Lao PDR = Lao People's Democratic Republic.
Source: Authors' calculation from ADBI database.

The Role of Government Aid

This study also examined the relationship between government aid and urban households' business performance. Table 1 shows the share of urban households with businesses in each country that received government aid. Overall, 47.2% of informal firms and 36.7% of formal firms received government aid, indicating that a greater share of households operating informal firms received government aid than did those with formal firms. Only in the Philippines did a higher share of formal firms receive government aid. The shares of firms receiving aid were very high in Malaysia, the Philippines, and Thailand, and quite low in Cambodia and the Lao PDR—zero in the latter.

Table 1: Share of Urban Household Businesses Receiving Government Aid (%)

	Cambodia	Indonesia	Lao PDR	Malaysia	Philippines	Thailand	All
Informal firms	5.2	47.8	0	73.7	88.5	79	47.2
Formal firms	3.6	36.8	0	61.5	92.9	77.8	36.7

Lao PDR = Lao People's Democratic Republic.

Source: Authors' calculation from ADBI database.

Figure 7 shows the average ratio of government aid received to monthly pre-pandemic income. The amount of government aid was relatively high for households with informal firms in the Philippines and Thailand, and moderately high in Malaysia. However, the ratios in the other four countries were low enough to be negligible.

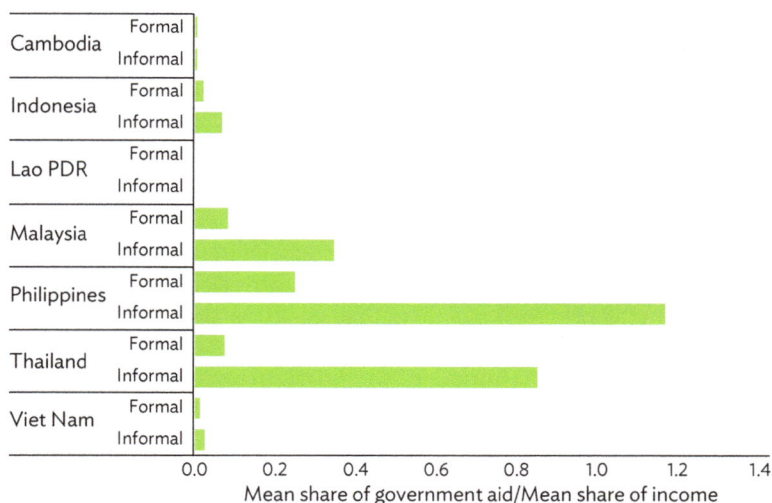

Figure 7: Ratio of Government Aid Received to Monthly Pre-Pandemic Income

Lao PDR = Lao People's Democratic Republic.

Source: Authors' calculation from ADBI database.

3.4 Estimation Methodology

This section explains the empirical methodology used in this research to examine the role of informal firms, fintech usage, and receipt of government aid on firm performance using the following equations:

$$Status_i = \alpha_0 + \alpha_1 Fintech_i + \alpha_2\ Informal_i + \alpha_3 Urban_i * Informal_i + \alpha_4 Urban_i * Fintech_i + \alpha_5 Urban_i + \alpha_6 Govaid_i + \alpha_7 Informal_i * Govaid_i + \alpha_8\ HH_i + FE_j + \delta \quad (1)$$

$$Revenue_i = \beta_0 + \beta_1 Fintech_i + \beta_2 Informal_i + \beta_3 Urban_i * Informal_i + \beta_4 Urban_i * Fintech_i + \beta_5 Urban_i + \beta_6 Govaid_i + \beta_7\ Informal_i * Govaid_i + \beta_8\ HH_i + FE_j + \gamma \quad (2)$$

where i indicates each household. $Status_i$ and $Revenue_i$ are the dependent variables of this research representing the performance of informal firms. $Status_i$ depicts the current status of the household business of households that operate a business or work in a household business: still open, temporarily closed, or permanently closed. $Revenue_i$ shows the changes in income of the household business or self-employed business: increase, remain, or decrease. Due to the nature of the dependent variables, the study used the ordered probit estimation method.

Fintech$_i$ represents the usage of digital fintech services in the following areas: raising capital and taking loans, paying suppliers, getting payments from customers, purchasing goods for the business, and selling products online. The variable takes the value of 1 if households used fintech in any of the above areas. The study also substituted fintech services used by informal firms (Informal*Fintech) as a robustness check to analyze the relationship between fintech services in informal firms and business performance. The high correlation (approximately 0.8) between fintech and Informal*Fintech is another reason why regressions were conducted separately to avoid possible heteroskedasticity. There may be questions about possible endogeneity and reverse causality, that is, firms that perform better are more likely to adopt fintech. However, the relatively low cost of entry and the significant uptake of digital platforms by informal firms during the pandemic, as shown earlier, suggest that reverse causality is less likely.

Informal$_i$ is a dummy variable that takes a value of 1 if the household is classified as having an informal business, or is owned by a household in the lowest three income quartiles that operated a business or worked in a household business; otherwise, it takes the value of zero.

Urban$_i$ indicates the area where households live. *Urban$_i$* takes the value of 1 when households are in urban areas, and zero otherwise. To distinguish the characteristics of urban households from rural households, the models also used interaction variables to indicate urban informal firms (*Urban$_i$* * *Informal$_i$*) and urban households that used fintech services (*Urban$_i$* * *Fintech$_i$*).

Govaid$_i$ captures receiving government aid. Two government aid variables were constructed: a dummy variable indicating whether households received any government aid, and the ratio of the amount of government aid received to monthly pre-pandemic income. Tables 3 and 5 in Section 4 show the empirical results using the dummy variable and Tables 4 and 6 show the results with the ratio of amount of government aid to pre-pandemic income. An interaction term between government aid and informal firms (*Informal$_i$* * *Govaid$_i$*) was also added.

HH$_i$ is a vector of control variables such as household characteristics. The vector includes gender of household head, age of household head, education of household head, the number of other income sources of the household, the household business sector, and adjustments to the pandemic made in the household business (coping strategies). The study further controlled for countries *j*. The δ and γ refer to the error terms. Summary statistics and the correlation table are shown in the Appendix.

4. Empirical Results

Tables 2 and 3 show the ordered probit results on the determinants of business status change using equation (1) in Section 3.4.[4] Columns (1) to (3) show the results for Fintech and columns (4) to (6) show the results for Informal*Fintech. The coefficients indicate the average marginal effects for each value: continued operation, temporary closure, or permanent closure of household business. "Fintech" indicates whether informal firms adopted fintech in their business. Fintech consistently contributes positively to the continuation of household business by 5.8% and 5.7%, respectively, for Tables 2 and 3.[5] Also, temporary closure and permanent closure are reduced when household businesses used fintech services. Although the magnitude is slightly smaller, fintech services used by informal firms (Informal*Fintech) show similar results

---

[4]   Coefficients for the constants are dropped as the tables show average marginal effects.

[5]   Note that coefficients here indicate additional 5.8% and 5.9% relative to those who did not adopt fintech in their business, and the coefficients are similar across the results tables.

to fintech services (Fintech). This suggests that using fintech services is a positive factor for continued operation of business.

Both informal firms (Informal) and informal firms in urban areas (Urban*Informal) are statistically insignificant in the model.

"Government aid" in Table 3 is a dummy variable indicating whether the household received any government aid or not. "Ratio of government aid" in Table 4 refers to the ratio of the amount of government aid received to pre-pandemic income. Informal*Aid and Informal*Aid (Ratio) indicate government aid received by informal firms. Both models (Tables 3 and 4) show statistically insignificant results on business status change, including government aid received by informal firms.

Among the control variables, gender of household head and the number of other income sources significantly affected change in business status. Household businesses with a male head survived better than household businesses with a female head. Household businesses with one or two additional income sources, such as a self-business, government transfers, and remittances, were more likely to remain in business. This implies that having one or two additional income sources provided households significant financial support during the pandemic, but more than two income sources did not have an incremental effect.

Table 2: Marginal Effects on the Determinants of Business Status Change (Government aid dummy variable)

Variables	(1) Continue	(2) Temp. closed	(3) Perm. closed	(4) Continue	(5) Temp. closed	(6) Perm. closed
Fintech	0.058**	−0.031**	−0.026*			
	(0.029)	(0.015)	(0.014)			
Informal*Fintech				0.053*	−0.029*	−0.024*
				(0.030)	(0.016)	(0.014)
Informal	0.000	−0.000	−0.000	−0.013	0.007	0.006
	(0.030)	(0.016)	(0.014)	(0.030)	(0.016)	(0.014)
Urban*Informal	0.019	−0.010	−0.009	0.018	−0.010	−0.008
	(0.040)	(0.021)	(0.018)	(0.039)	(0.021)	(0.018)
Urban*Fintech	0.024	−0.013	−0.011	0.042	−0.023	−0.019
	(0.042)	(0.023)	(0.019)	(0.038)	(0.021)	(0.017)
Urban	−0.018	0.010	0.008	−0.023	0.012	0.010
	(0.034)	(0.018)	(0.016)	(0.034)	(0.018)	(0.016)
Government aid	−0.003	0.002	0.001	−0.006	0.003	0.003
	(0.039)	(0.021)	(0.018)	(0.039)	(0.021)	(0.018)
Informal*Aid	0.006	−0.003	−0.003	0.009	−0.005	−0.004
	(0.040)	(0.021)	(0.018)	(0.040)	(0.021)	(0.018)
Male household head	0.032*	−0.017*	−0.015*	0.033*	−0.018*	−0.015*
	(0.019)	(0.011)	(0.009)	(0.019)	(0.011)	(0.009)
Other income sources (<=2)	0.406**	−0.134***	−0.272	0.394**	−0.133***	−0.262
	(0.191)	(0.023)	(0.172)	(0.193)	(0.026)	(0.171)
Other income sources (>2)	0.285	−0.075***	−0.210	0.278	−0.076**	−0.202
	(0.197)	(0.028)	(0.174)	(0.198)	(0.030)	(0.173)
Country fixed effects	Yes	Yes	Yes	Yes	Yes	Yes
Observations	1,394	1,394	1,394	1,394	1,394	1,394

Note: Results for other nonsignificant control variables are not shown.

Standard errors in parentheses. *** p<0.01, ** p<0.05, * p<0.1.

Source: Authors' estimation.

Table 3: Marginal Effects on the Determinants of Business Status Change (Ratio of government aid to pre-pandemic income)

Variables	(1) Continue	(2) Temp. closed	(3) Perm. closed	(4) Continue	(5) Temp. closed	(6) Perm. closed
Fintech	0.057*	−0.031**	−0.026*			
	(0.029)	(0.015)	(0.014)			
Informal*Fintech				0.052*	−0.028*	−0.024*
				(0.030)	(0.016)	(0.014)
Informal	0.006	−0.003	−0.003	−0.006	0.003	0.003
	(0.026)	(0.014)	(0.012)	(0.027)	(0.015)	(0.012)
Urban*Informal	0.018	−0.010	−0.008	0.018	−0.010	−0.008
	(0.039)	(0.021)	(0.018)	(0.039)	(0.021)	(0.018)
Urban*Fintech	0.025	−0.014	−0.012	0.043	−0.023	−0.020
	(0.042)	(0.023)	(0.019)	(0.038)	(0.021)	(0.017)
Urban	−0.019	0.010	0.009	−0.024	0.013	0.011
	(0.034)	(0.018)	(0.016)	(0.034)	(0.018)	(0.016)
Ratio of government aid	0.000	−0.000	−0.000	0.000	−0.000	−0.000
	(0.000)	(0.000)	(0.000)	(0.000)	(0.000)	(0.000)
Informal*Aid (Ratio)	−0.003	0.002	0.001	−0.003	0.002	0.001
	(0.004)	(0.002)	(0.002)	(0.004)	(0.002)	(0.002)
Male household head	0.032*	−0.017	−0.015*	0.032*	−0.018*	−0.015*
	(0.019)	(0.011)	(0.009)	(0.019)	(0.011)	(0.009)
Other income sources (<=2)	0.408**	−0.134***	−0.274	0.398**	−0.133***	−0.265
	(0.189)	(0.023)	(0.171)	(0.190)	(0.025)	(0.169)
Other income sources (>2)	0.288	−0.076***	−0.212	0.282	−0.077***	−0.206
	(0.194)	(0.027)	(0.173)	(0.195)	(0.029)	(0.171)
Country fixed effects	Yes	Yes	Yes	Yes	Yes	Yes
Observations	1,394	1,394	1,394	1,394	1,394	1,394

Note: Results for other nonsignificant control variables are not shown.

Standard errors in parentheses. *** p<0.01, ** p<0.05, * p<0.1.

Source: Authors' estimation.

Tables 4 and 5 present the results for change in business revenue using equation (2) in Section 3.4. Revenue of urban informal firms increased or remained unchanged during the pandemic, by more than 2.5% and more than 3.5%, respectively ($p<0.1$), compared with rural informal firms. This implies that, compared with rural firms, informal firms in urban areas suffered less from the pandemic.

Urban household businesses that used fintech services also suffered less from the pandemic, and this was also associated with increased revenue. Along with the results shown in Tables 2 and 3, this shows positive effects of use of fintech services on the performance of informal urban firms.

In Tables 4 and 5, coping strategies increased the probability of decreasing revenue by 3.7% or more. This suggests that other coping strategies were not effective in offsetting income declines or that the causality was reverse, that is, revenue declines led firms to adopt coping strategies. This could also confirm that adopting fintech services was more effective than other measures of coping strategies for the pandemic. Similar to the results in Tables 2 and 3, receiving government aid did not show statistically significant results on revenue changes of household business. This may reflect that the amounts of aid were not significant in four of the seven countries examined.

Table 4: Marginal Effects on the Determinants of Revenue Change (Government aid dummy variable)

Variables	(1) Increase	(2) No Change	(3) Decrease	(4) Increase	(5) Remain	(6) Decrease
Fintech	−0.010	−0.014	0.024			
	(0.012)	(0.016)	(0.028)			
Informal*Fintech				−0.008	−0.012	0.020
				(0.013)	(0.018)	(0.030)
Informal	−0.005	−0.008	0.013	−0.003	−0.004	0.007
	(0.012)	(0.017)	(0.028)	(0.012)	(0.017)	(0.029)
Urban*Informal	0.028*	0.040*	−0.068*	0.029*	0.041*	−0.070*
	(0.015)	(0.022)	(0.037)	(0.016)	(0.022)	(0.037)
Urban*Fintech	0.030*	0.042*	−0.071*	0.026*	0.037*	−0.063*
	(0.016)	(0.022)	(0.038)	(0.014)	(0.020)	(0.034)
Urban	−0.023*	−0.033*	0.056*	−0.023	−0.032	0.055
	(0.014)	(0.020)	(0.033)	(0.014)	(0.020)	(0.034)
Government aid	0.019	0.027	−0.046	0.020	0.028	−0.047
	(0.015)	(0.021)	(0.035)	(0.015)	(0.021)	(0.035)
Informal*Aid	−0.018	−0.025	0.043	−0.018	−0.026	0.044
	(0.016)	(0.022)	(0.037)	(0.016)	(0.022)	(0.037)
Male household head	0.002	0.003	−0.006	0.002	0.003	−0.005
	(0.008)	(0.011)	(0.018)	(0.008)	(0.011)	(0.019)
Other income sources (<=2)	−0.060	−0.064	0.124	−0.054	−0.059	0.113
	(0.066)	(0.055)	(0.120)	(0.060)	(0.053)	(0.113)
Other income sources (>2)	−0.056	−0.059	0.115	−0.051	−0.056	0.107
	(0.067)	(0.058)	(0.124)	(0.062)	(0.056)	(0.117)
Coping strategies	−0.015*	−0.022*	0.037*	−0.015*	−0.022*	0.037*
	(0.009)	(0.013)	(0.021)	(0.009)	(0.013)	(0.021)
Country fixed effects	Yes	Yes	Yes	Yes	Yes	Yes
Observations	1,394	1,394	1,394	1,394	1,394	1,394

Note: Results for other nonsignificant control variables are not shown.

Standard errors in parentheses. *** $p<0.01$, ** $p<0.05$, * $p<0.1$.

Source: Authors' estimation.

Table 5: Marginal Effects on the Determinants of Revenue Change (Ratio of government aid to pre-pandemic income)

Variables	(1) Increase	(2) No Change	(3) Decrease	(4) Increase	(5) Remain	(6) Decrease
Fintech	−0.011	−0.015	0.026			
	(0.012)	(0.016)	(0.028)			
Informal*Fintech				−0.009	−0.013	0.022
				(0.013)	(0.018)	(0.030)
Informal	−0.011	−0.016	0.028	−0.009	−0.013	0.022
	(0.010)	(0.014)	(0.024)	(0.010)	(0.014)	(0.025)
Urban*Informal	0.026*	0.037*	−0.063*	0.027*	0.038*	−0.065*
	(0.015)	(0.022)	(0.037)	(0.016)	(0.022)	(0.037)
Urban*Fintech	0.030*	0.043*	−0.073*	0.026*	0.037*	−0.063*
	(0.016)	(0.022)	(0.038)	(0.014)	(0.020)	(0.034)
Urban	−0.023	−0.032	0.054	−0.022	−0.031	0.053
	(0.014)	(0.020)	(0.033)	(0.014)	(0.020)	(0.034)
Ratio of government aid	−0.002	−0.002	0.004	−0.002	−0.002	0.004
	(0.002)	(0.003)	(0.004)	(0.002)	(0.003)	(0.004)
Informal*Aid (Ratio)	−0.000	−0.000	0.000	−0.000	−0.000	0.000
	(0.003)	(0.004)	(0.006)	(0.003)	(0.004)	(0.006)
Male household head	0.002	0.003	−0.004	0.002	0.002	−0.004
	(0.008)	(0.011)	(0.018)	(0.008)	(0.011)	(0.019)
Other income sources (<=2)	−0.074	−0.075	0.148	−0.068	−0.070	0.137
	(0.072)	(0.054)	(0.125)	(0.066)	(0.052)	(0.118)
Other income sources (>2)	−0.070	−0.070	0.140	−0.065	−0.067	0.132
	(0.073)	(0.057)	(0.130)	(0.068)	(0.055)	(0.122)
Coping strategies	−0.016*	−0.022*	0.038*	−0.016*	−0.023*	0.039*
	(0.009)	(0.013)	(0.021)	(0.009)	(0.013)	(0.021)
Country fixed effects	Yes	Yes	Yes	Yes	Yes	Yes
Observations	1,394	1,394	1,394	1,394	1,394	1,394

Note: Results for other nonsignificant control variables are not shown.

Standard errors in parentheses. *** p<0.01, ** p<0.05, * p<0.1.

Source: Authors' estimation.

5. Concluding Remarks

This chapter examined how the use of fintech and government aid impacted formal and informal firms in the pandemic. More specifically, using survey data collected by ADBI, the study investigated whether adoption of fintech services and the receipt of government aid affected the performance of household-operated firms in seven ASEAN countries. It also examined differences in the impacts on formal and informal firms. Businesses in the lower three quartiles of pre-pandemic household income were assumed to be informal firms.

Most significantly, this study finds that the use of fintech services was consistently positively associated with the continuation of both informal and formal household businesses. Use of fintech was associated with an increase in income of the urban informal household businesses. This suggests that firms' use of fintech supported their operations by making it easier for them to access customers, obtain financing, and receive payments. Given the circumstances of the pandemic, which made in-person contact difficult, this result is not surprising; but the evidence that this effect worked at least equally well for informal firms, too, is novel. Also, coping strategies other than fintech use did not show similar positive correlation with firm performance. When evaluating the effect of fintech use, the threat of endogeneity cannot be ruled out; yet, the low cost to access fintech services and their widespread use by informal firms reduces its possibility.

The observed strong effect of fintech services on firm performance partly reflects the peculiar circumstances of the pandemic crisis—restricted physical movement due to government measures as well as individual choice to limit person-to-person contact. What is clear is that the pandemic has accelerated the adoption of fintech services. Nonetheless, the more general benefits of expanding the potential customer base and having greater access to finance suggest that policies to promote the adoption of fintech would be beneficial during periods of both crisis and normalcy. Moreover, the study also found that small informal firms are just as capable of adopting fintech services as larger firms. There is, therefore, a strong case to be made for policies—for promoting subsidies and enabling regulatory convenience—that will encourage even small, informal firms to adopt fintech services. To that end, governments, by themselves, and by incentivizing market actors and collaborating with civil society actors, should also promote financial education and digital economy training for small firms.

Delivery of government aid was not found to be associated with improved firm performance, either in terms of continued operation or increase in sales; nor was there any significant difference between its impacts on formal and informal firms. This may be a result of reverse causality, meaning, firms that were worse off were more likely to apply for government aid. Also, the aid amount was very small in four of the seven countries. An encouraging finding is that, in all but one country, the share of informal firms receiving government aid was larger than that of formal firms. This suggests that the delivery of aid to smaller firms was largely efficient. Also, the ratio of government aid to pre-pandemic income tended to be several times larger for informal firms than for formal firms, which suggests that informal firms found aid to be significantly more beneficial. This calls for expanding government aid to small, informal firms in times of crisis, even though this study did not find that it significantly aided firm performance.

Finally, although it was beyond the scope of discussion in this chapter, it is important to note that barriers and challenges to fintech adoption and scaling-up vary by context across countries and cities (Boamah, Murshid, and Mozumder 2021). Hence, the policy moves suggested above should follow careful assessments of multiple development- and governance-related factors.

References

Aceto, G., V. Persico, and A. Pescapé. 2019. A Survey on Information and Communication Technologies for Industry 4.0: State-of-the-Art, Taxonomies, Perspectives, and Challenges. *IEEE Communications Surveys & Tutorials* 21 (4): 3467–3501.

Adian, I. et al. 2020. *Small and Medium Enterprises in the Pandemic: Impact, Responses and the Role of Development Finance.* Washington, DC: World Bank.

Akpan, I. J. 2010. Virtual Reality, 3D Visualization and Simulation in Decision Support. *Strategic Advantage of Computing Information Systems in Enterprise Management.* Athens: ATINER. pp. 13–44.

Akpan, I. J., D. Soopramanien, and D. Kwak. 2021. Cutting-Edge Technologies for Small Business and Innovation in the Era of COVID-19 Global Health Pandemic. *Journal of Small Business & Entrepreneurship* 33(6): 607–617.

Al-Awadhi, A. M. et al. 2020. Death and Contagious Infectious Diseases: Impact of the COVID-19 Virus on Stock Market Returns. *Journal of Behavioral and Experimental Finance* 27: 100326.

Allen, F., X. Gu, and O. Kowalewski. 2012. Financial Crisis, Structure and Reform. *Journal of Banking & Finance* 36 (11): 2960–2973.

Apedo-Amah, M. C. et al. 2020. *Unmasking the Impact of COVID-19 on Businesses: Firm Level Evidence from Across the World.* Policy Research Working Paper 9434. Washington, DC: World Bank.

Ayyagari, M., A. Demirgüç-Kunt, and V. Maksimovic. 2010. Formal versus Informal Finance: Evidence from China. *The Review of Financial Studies* 23 (8): 3048–3097.

Baek, S., S.K. Mohanty, and M. Glambosky. 2020. COVID-19 and Stock Market Volatility: An Industry Level Analysis. *Finance Research Letters* 37: 101748.

Bartik, A W. et al. 2020. The Impact of COVID-19 on Small Business Outcomes and Expectations. *Proceedings of the National Academy of Sciences* 117 (30): 17656–17666.

Berry, A., E. Rodriguez, and H. Sandee. 2001. Small and Medium Enterprise Dynamics in Indonesia. *Bulletin of Indonesian Economic Studies* 37 (3): 363–384.

Boamah E. F., E., N. S. Murshid, and M. G. N. Mozumder. 2021. A Network Understanding of FinTech (in) Capabilities in the Global South. *Applied Geography* 135 (October): 102538. https://doi.org/10.1016/j.apgeog.2021.102538.

Bugamelli, M., R. Cristadoro, and G. Zevi. 2010. International Crisis and the Italian Productive System: An Analysis of Firm-Level Data. *Giornale degli Economisti e Annali di Economia.* pp. 155–188.

Brinca, P., J. B. Duarte, and M. Faria-e-Castro. 2020. Measuring Labor Supply and Demand Shocks during COVID-19. *European Economic Review* 139: 103901.

Bruhn, M. 2020. Can Wage Subsidies Boost Employment in the Wake of an Economic Crisis? Evidence from Mexico. *The Journal of Development Studies* 56 (8): 1558–1577.

Campello, M., J. R. Graham, and C. R. Harvey. 2010. The Real Effects of Financial Constraints: Evidence from a Financial Crisis. *Journal of Financial Economics* 97: 470–487.

Candia, B., O. Coibion, and Y. Gorodnichenko. 2020. *Communication and the Beliefs of Economic Agents*. National Bureau of Economic Research Working Paper 27800. Cambridge, Massachusetts.

Chen, J. et al. 2020. Riding Out the COVID-19 Storm: How Government Policies Affect SMEs in China. SSRN 3660232.

Chetty, R. et al. 2020. *How Did COVID-19 and Stabilization Policies Affect Spending and Employment? A New Real-Time Economic Tracker based on Private Sector Data*. National Bureau of Economic Research Working Paper 27431. Cambridge, Massachusetts.

Cirera, X. et al. 2021. Policies to Support Businesses through the COVID-19 Shock: A Firm Level Perspective. *The World Bank Research Observer* 36 (1): 41–66.

Dai, R. et al. 2021. The Impact of COVID-19 on Small and Medium-Sized Enterprises (SMEs): Evidence from Two-Wave Phone Surveys in China. *China Economic Review* 67: 101607.

De Mel, S., D. McKenzie, and C. Woodruff. 2012. Enterprise Recovery Following Natural Disasters. *The Economic Journal* 122 (559): 64–91.

De Vito, A., and J. P. Gomez. 2020. Estimating the COVID-19 Cash Crunch: Global Evidence and Policy. *Journal of Accounting and Public Policy* 39 (2): 106741.

Du, J., and S. Girma. 2012. Firm Size, Source of Finance, and Growth-Evidence from China. *International Journal of the Economics of Business* 19 (3): 397–419.

Fairlie, R., and F. M. Fossen. 2021. The Early Impacts of the COVID-19 Pandemic on Business Sales. *Small Business Economics*: 1–12.

Farazi, S. 2014. Informal Firms and Financial Inclusion: Status and Determinants. *Journal of International Commerce, Economics and Policy* 5 (3): 1440011.

Fort, T. C. et al. 2013. How Firms Respond to Business Cycles: The Role of Firm Age and Firm Size. *IMF Economic Review* 61 (3): 520–559.

Gao, J. 2022. Has COVID-19 Hindered Small Business Activities? The Role of Fintech. *Economic Analysis and Policy*.

Gertler, M., and S. Gilchrist. 1994. Monetary Policy, Business Cycles, and the Behavior of Small Manufacturing Firms. *The Quarterly Journal of Economics* 109 (2): 309–340.

Granja, J. et al. 2020. *Did the Paycheck Protection Program Hit the Target?* National Bureau of Economic Research Working Paper 27095. Cambridge, Massachusetts.

Hallward-Driemeier, M., and B. Rijkers. 2013. Do Crises Catalyze Creative Destruction? Firm-Level Evidence from Indonesia. *Review of Economics and Statistics* 95 (1): 1788–1810.

Harhoff, D., K. Stahl, and M. Woywode. 1998. Legal Form, Growth and Exit of West German Firms: Empirical Results for Manufacturing, Construction, Trade, and Service Industries. *Journal of Industrial Economics* 46 (4): 453–488.

Hassan, T. A. et al. 2020. *Firm-Level Exposure to Epidemic Diseases: Covid-19, SARS, and H1N1.* National Bureau of Economic Research Working Paper 26971. Cambridge, Massachusetts.

Hodorogel, R. G. 2009. The Economic Crisis and its Effects on SMEs. *Theoretical & Applied Economics* 16 (5).

Hu, S., and Y. Zhang. 2021. COVID-19 Pandemic and Firm Performance: Cross-Country Evidence. *International Review of Economics & Finance* 74: 365–372.

Inoue, H., and Y. Todo. 2020. The Propagation of Economic Impacts Through Supply Chains: The Case of a Mega-City Lockdown to Prevent the Spread of COVID-19. *PloS one* 15 (9): e0239251.

International Labour Organization (ILO). 2015. Recommendation No. 204 Concerning the Transition from the Informal to the Formal Economy. https://www.ilo.org/ilc/ILCSessions/previous-sessions/104/texts-adopted/WCMS_377774/lang--en/index.htm.

Jensen, M. C., and W. H. Merkling. 1976. Theory of the Firm: Managerial Behavior, Agency Costs and Ownership Structure. *Journal of Financial Economics* 3 (4).

Laudon, K. C., and J. P. Laudon. 2019. *Management Information Systems: Managing the Digital Firm.* UK: Pearson Education Limited.

Meyer, B. H., B. Prescott, and X. S. Sheng. 2022. The Impact of the COVID-19 Pandemic on Business Expectations. *International Journal of Forecasting* 38 (2): 529–544.

Morgan, P., Q. L. Trinh, and K. H. Kim. 2022. Impacts of COVID-19 on Households in ASEAN Countries and their Implications for Human Capital Development: Medium-Run Impacts and the Role of Government Support. ADBI Working Paper Series No. 1312. Tokyo, Japan: Asian Development Bank Institute.

Narjoko, D., and H. Hill. 2007. Winners and Losers during a Deep Economic Crisis: Firm–level Evidence from Indonesian Manufacturing. *Asian Economic Journal* 21 (4): 343–368.

Organisation for Economic Co-operation and Development (OECD) and International Labour Organization (ILO). 2019. *Tackling Vulnerability in the Informal Economy.*

Poschke, M. 2013. Who Becomes an Entrepreneur? Labor Market Prospects and Occupational Choice. *Journal of Economic Dynamics and Control* 37 (3): 693–710.

Smith, A. C. et al. 2020. Telehealth for Global Emergencies: Implications for Coronavirus Disease 2019 (COVID-19). *Journal of Telemedicine and Telecare* 26 (5): 309–313.

Sonobe, T. et al. 2021. *The Impacts of the Covid-19 Pandemic on Micro, Small, and Medium Enterprises in Asia and their Digitalization Responses.* ADBI Working Paper 1241. Tokyo: Asian Development Bank Institute.

Stiglitz, J. E., and A. Weiss. 1981. Credit Rationing in Markets with Imperfect Information. *American Economic Review* (71): 93–410.

Sun, Y. et al. 2021. The Impact of COVID-19 on SMEs in China: Textual Analysis and Empirical Evidence. *Finance Research Letters.* p. 102211.

Ter Wengel, J., and E. Rodriguez. 2006. SME Export Performance in Indonesia After the Crisis. *Small Business Economics* 26 (1): 25–37.

Trinh, Q. L., P. J. Morgan, and T. Sonobe. 2020. Investment Behavior of MSMEs during the Downturn Periods: Empirical Evidence from Vietnam. *Emerging Markets Review* 45: 100739.

Turkina, E. 2018. The Importance of Networking to Entrepreneurship: Montreal's Artificial Intelligence Cluster and Its Born-Global Firm Element AI. *Journal of Small Business & Entrepreneurship* 30 (1): 1–18.

Vivarelli, M. 2013. Is Entrepreneurship Necessarily Good? Microeconomic Evidence from Developed and Developing Countries. *Industrial and Corporate Change* 22 (6): 1453–1495.

Vives, X. 2017. The Impact of FinTech on Banking. *European Economy* (2): 97–105.

World Health Organization. Coronavirus Disease (COVID-19) Pandemic. https://www.who.int/emergencies/diseases/novel-coronavirus-2019 (accessed 2 November 2021).

Appendix: Summary Statistics

Variables	N	Mean	SD	Min	Max
Business status	1,394	1.194	0.508	1	3
Business revenue	1,394	2.831	0.470	1	3
Informal	1,394	0.702	0.457	0	1
Urban*Informal	1,394	0.286	0.452	0	1
Fintech	1,394	0.276	0.447	0	1
Informal*Fintech	1,394	0.195	0.396	0	1
Urban*Fintech	1,394	0.137	0.344	0	1
Urban	1,394	0.412	0.492	0	1
Government aid	1,394	0.397	0.490	0	1
Informal*Aid	1,394	0.298	0.457	0	1
Ratio of government aid	1,394	5.181	87.62	0	3,000
Informal*Aid (Ratio)	1,394	0.404	1.911	0	51.02
Male household head	1,394	0.694	0.461	0	1
Household head age group	1,394	1.794	0.653	1	3
Household head education	1,394	1.836	0.803	1	3
Other income sources	1,394	2.075	0.280	1	3
Business sector	1,394	4.514	1.799	1	7
Coping strategies	1,394	0.256	0.437	0	1

N = sample size, SD = standard deviation.

Source: Authors' calculation.

10

Post-Pandemic Employment Recovery: Case Study of Tricycle Drivers in Metro Manila

Takashi Yamano, Yasuyuki Sawada, Shigehiro Shinozaki, Hyuncheol Bryant Kim, Syngjoo Choi, and Siho Park*

Abstract

To curb the spread of the coronavirus disease (COVID-19), governments have imposed lockdowns and movement restrictions, which has directly reduced transport workers' earnings dependent on rider fees. To assess the impacts of the pandemic on tricycle drivers in the Philippines, this chapter uses panel data of 1,660 drivers interviewed in 2019 and 2021. Only 19% of them worked under the enhanced community quarantine period in March–May 2020. In the following months, their operation rate increased to 66% during the general quarantine period in June 2020–March 2021 and to 90% by December 2021. The vaccination rate among drivers increased from 10% in May 2021 to 87% in December 2021. Although their work has resumed, their monthly earnings in late 2020 remained about half of 2019. After 2 years of pandemic, it is unclear whether the demand for public transport services will return to pre-pandemic levels. Governments need to provide clear regulations regarding tricycle services and help drivers adapt to post-pandemic conditions.

*   The authors are grateful to Ruth Francisco for her research assistance, the editorial team for their excellent support, and the Global Mobility Service, Inc. for their support on the surveys The study was partially financed by the Republic of Korea e-Asia and Knowledge Partnership Fund..

Keywords: urban transportation, public utility vehicles, tricycle services, COVID-19 pandemic, COVID-19 vaccines

1. Introduction

Since the World Health Organization (WHO) officially declared the coronavirus disease (COVID-19) a pandemic in March 2020 (WHO 2020), countries around the globe have gone through several cycles of varying restrictions on public movement and interaction (Tirachini and Cats 2020). The public transportation sector in many countries experienced severe restrictions (Shortall, Moutera, and Van Weeb 2021). In the Philippines, all public transportation services were suspended at the beginning of the pandemic (Government of the Philippines 2020a). Subsequent community quarantine policies gradually relaxed restrictions on public transportation, while imposing safety conditions to reduce the risk of transmission of COVID-19.

Due to the limited availability of mass transit services, road-based public utility vehicles (PUVs) are the primary transportation system in the Philippines (Chuenyindee et al. 2022). Among them, informal paratransit services provide on-demand and flexible transport options to passengers at low cost, but they also contribute to traffic congestion, and air and noise pollution (Cervero and Golub 2007; Phun and Yai 2016). Tricycles (auto-rickshaws) are among the most popular paratransit services in Metro Manila (JICA 2015). Compared with other modes, they provide cheap and convenient service, offering numerous routes and connections. The tricycle service constitutes the border between the formal and informal sectors. Tricycle drivers belong to Tricycle Operators and Drivers' Associations (TODAs), which are registered with and supervised by municipal governments. However, the tricycle drivers' incomes and financial conditions are closer to workers in the informal sector (ADB 2020b). Although there are studies that have measured the impacts of the lockdowns and movement restrictions on mobility, little is known about the magnitude of the financial hardships on the paratransit workers, and how they resumed work under changed circumstances.

This chapter uses panel data from tricycle drivers surveyed in both 2019 and 2021. In November–December 2019, 2,487 tricycle drivers were randomly selected from TODAs in Metropolitan Manila to be surveyed. The survey collected their demographic, financial, and employment information. The main findings of the 2019 survey have been summarized in an ADB report (ADB 2020a). Two years later, a follow-up telephone survey was conducted, with 1,660 respondents from the 2019 sample. The 2021 survey asked about drivers' working hours and conditions during different community quarantine periods, their COVID-19 vaccination status, and their financial behavior.

The analysis shows that only 19% of the drivers worked during the enhanced community quarantine period of March–May 2020, and the proportion increased to 66% during the general quarantine period in June 2020–March 2021, and to 90% by December 2021. Meanwhile, the vaccination rate increased from 10% in May 2021 to 87% in December 2021. However, the drivers' working hours and earnings remained much lower than that of 2019. Even though the economy and transport services appear to be returning to normalcy, it may take more time before the demand due to ridership returns to pre-pandemic levels.

2. Literature Review

To curb the spread of COVID-19, governments have imposed lockdowns and movement restrictions (Tirachini and Cats 2020; Shortall, Moutera, and Van Weeb 2021). The implications of the imposed movement restrictions can be of three types: avoidance of travel, shift in transport mode, and improvement of quality (Shortall, Moutera, and Van Weeb 2021). The first constituted measures that have reduced the use of public and shared transport. These measures included (i) not allowing nonessential services and large gatherings; (ii) requesting work-from-home where possible; (iii) domestic travel restrictions; and (iv) international travel restrictions. By the end of March 2020, more than 100 countries had implemented some combinations of these measures (Parady, Taniguchi, and Takami 2020). The second type promoted greater use of alternative means of transportation, such as private vehicles, motorcycles, and bicycles. Finally, the third type required or encouraged improved safety measures in public transportation systems, such as (i) additional space and social distancing, (ii) enhanced hygiene and health measures, and (iii) better capacity management for public transport.

The declines in mobility due to lockdowns and movement restrictions, measured by using big data, show significant declines in mobility in developed countries. Based on mobile phone location data from the United States, Lee et al. (2020) found that between January and April 2020 stay-at-home mandates were effective. A similar picture has emerged from studies of European cities and countries. Pullano et al. (2020) assessed the impact of a nationwide lockdown in France, using origin–destination flows captured by mobile phone data, and found that mobility fell by 65%, with the largest decline in regions with large, economically active populations with a high burden of COVID-19 cases.

In the Philippines, Hasselwander et al. (2021) analyzed aggregated cell phone and GPS data from Google and Apple to provide a comprehensive representation of mobility behavior before and during the lockdown. While significant decreases were observed for all transport modes, public transportation experienced the largest drop of 74.5%. In addition, Jiang, Laranjo, and Thomas (2022) analyzed cellphone-based origin–destination flows made available by a major telecommunication company. They found that the effect of lockdowns was strongest in cities where a high share of the workforce was employed in work-from-home friendly sectors or medium-sized and large enterprises.

Despite a growing number of studies on the impacts of COVID-19 and restrictions on mobility, few have examined the impact of such restrictions on workers in semiformal or informal public transport services. Unlike public workers with fixed salaries, tricycle drivers depend on their earnings from riders. Thus, the lockdowns and movement restrictions directly reduced their income. It is important to empirically assess the impacts on their work and financial situation, which impact their well-being.

3. Tricycle Services and the COVID-19 Pandemic in the Philippines

Many Asian developing countries have limited budgets to support environment friendly and efficient mass transportation systems such as mass rapid transit (MRT), light rail transit (LRT), or bus rapid transit (BRT). Paratransit services provide indispensable services in developing countries where mass transit systems are inadequate (Cervero and Golub 2007). Although paratransit can be defined in many ways, it is best described as an informal public transport mode that has developed to fill the service void left by inadequate private vehicles and/or conventional mass transit systems in cities where official authorization is not required or enforced for providing transport services (Cervero and Golub 2007). Examples of paratransit services in Southeast Asia include motodops and remorks in Cambodia, angkot and Bajaj in Indonesia, and jeepneys and tricycles in the Philippines (Phun and Yai 2016). Although paratransit vehicles are often in poor condition and drivers are largely unregulated, they offer a vital service in the form of personalized transport and feeder services to mass transit systems (Joewono and Kubota 2007). Governments in Asia and the Pacific, including in the Philippines, recognize the importance of paratransit services and have been struggling to integrate them with formal public transport systems.

According to the Philippines' Land Transportation Office, the number of registered motorcycles in the country was 8.0 million in 2019, which declined to 7.3 million in 2020. It is unclear whether the decline was mostly due to the COVID-19 pandemic, but the number increased again to 8.1 million in 2021. Of the 8.1 million registered motorcycles in 2021, about 1.5 million were tricycles. These vehicles, more commonly found in urban areas, are motorcycles with an attached sidecar (passenger cabin) connected to a third wheel. They can accommodate four to eight passengers, depending on the cabin size and are often used on narrower roads. Most of the tricycles are registered in Region III (269,906), Region IV (286,741), Region I (188,694), and the National Capital Region (142,577), all of which are parts of the main island of Luzon. Although it is unclear how many of the 1.5 million registered tricycles are used for commercial transport services, these numbers provide an upper limit of the number of commercial tricycle services. Commercial tricycle drivers are required to be in TODAs licensed by municipal offices.

As discussed above, the pandemic has prompted countries to undertake various policy responses to limit its spread. In the Philippines, the government quickly imposed an enhanced community quarantine (ECQ) in the National Capital Region (NCR) and other high-risk regions from 15 March 2020 to stop or slow the spread of COVID-19 and ease its impact (Government of the Philippines 2020a). The ECQ policy entailed stay-at-home orders and the suspension of public transport services, including tricycles, except for some essential utility services for medical and other essential frontliners. It also restricted entry to and exit from NCR with less stringent lockdown measures. These measures limited the physical mobility of people belonging to communities within NCR. The government also imposed temporary closures of schools and businesses. The first ECQ period ended on 15 May 2020 and was immediately followed by a less stringent lockdown policy (modified ECQ), which also served as a transition period toward a general community quarantine (GCC) that allowed greater mobility from 1 June 2020 (Government of the Philippines 2020b).

From 1 June 2020 to 3 August 2020, the movement of persons was allowed within NCR, along with the resumption of public and private transport services (Table 1). Tricycles were allowed to operate, but the number of passengers per tricycle was restricted to one in most local government units in NCR, and no back riders were allowed. Buses and other large vehicles were allowed to ply at half capacity, and taxis were allowed just two passengers per row. Curfew hours that prevailed during ECQ (8 p.m.–5 a.m.) were shortened during the modified ECQ (10 p.m.–5 a.m.). To assess the service quality of PUVs, including tricycle services, in the Philippines during the COVID-19 pandemic, Chuenyindee et al. (2022) conducted an online survey of 564 individuals about PUV services. They found that COVID-19 protocols, tangibility, and assurance variables have significantly affected customer satisfaction.

Table 1: Passenger Limits in Public Utility Vehicles

Mode	Maximum Allowable Capacity (A)	Additional Restrictions (B)
Tricycles	Maximum of one passenger in sidecar	No passengers shall be seated beside or behind driver
Public utility buses, jeepneys, and shuttle services	50% of vehicle capacity (excluding driver and conductor)	Passengers seated one seat apart; no standing passengers
		For jeepneys and shuttles: only one passenger in driver's row (if no conductor)
UV Express, taxis, and TNVS	Maximum two passengers per row	Only one passenger allowed in the driver's row

TNVS = Transport Network Vehicle Service (e.g., Grab taxi).

Source: Department of Transportation. Land Transportation Office Memorandum Circular No. 2020-2185.

The national government has since made quarantine restriction adjustments based on the number of COVID-19 cases and capacity utilization of health-care facilities (Government of the Philippines 2020c). Beginning in October 2021, the government adopted a new community quarantine classification system with only two community quarantine classifications—ECQ and GCQ. It assigns alert levels 1 (lowest) to 5 (highest) in GCQ areas according to the COVID-19 risk levels assessed. Local governments then determine movement restrictions based on age and comorbidities.

4. Methodology and Data

For the analysis in this chapter, three quarantine periods are defined: (i) ECQ from 17 March 2020 to 31 May 2020, when the government imposed its first lockdown restriction; (ii) GCQ I from 1 June 2020 to 28 March 2021; and (iii) GCQ II for the period of the last 4 weeks before the survey was conducted in November and December 2021. Data used in this report come from panel surveys conducted in 2019 and 2021 with tricycle drivers in Metropolitan Manila. The 2019 survey results have been summarized in an ADB report (ADB 2020a). In November and December 2019, a survey was conducted with two groups of tricycle drivers. One was a group of randomly sampled drivers from Manila and Quezon City. All tricycle drivers belong to TODAs; among the TODAs that gave consent to let the drivers participate in the survey, approximately 8 to 10 drivers per TODA were randomly sampled.

The second group is composed of tricycle drivers from Metropolitan Manila who had received financial technology loans from Global Mobility Service Inc. (GMS), a Japanese finance and technology (fintech) company focused on urban mobility providers for enabling sustainable development and social change.[1] They used the loans to buy tricycles and are now repaying GMS. This study calls the first group of drivers as the "conventional" (non-fintech) drivers, and refers to the second group as "fintech" drivers. Table 2 shows the distribution across different cities of the 2,487 drivers surveyed.

The survey included questions about various characteristics of the tricycle drivers. Basic demographic information was collected through a set of standard questions on drivers and their household members. Their socioeconomic status was also measured through questions about income, household assets, and work behavior.

Two years after the first survey, a phone survey was conducted seeking to reach all 2,487 tricycle drivers by using the contact information provided in the 2019 survey. The phone survey was able to reach 1,660 drivers, a response rate of 67%. After 2 years, some attrition was expected. Reasons for attrition included incorrect or changed phone numbers, nonresponse, and refusal to be interviewed (Table 2). An important consideration is whether the attrition caused a selection bias in the sample.

---

[1]   See Global Mobility Service, Inc. https://www.global-mobility-service.com/en/index.html.

Table 2: Geographic Distribution of Drivers Surveyed

District	In 2019 [count] (A)	Both in 2019 and 2021 [count (% of A)] (B)
Capital Manila	1,559	985 (63.2)
Quezon City	848	635 (75.4)
Others	80	40 (46.5)
Total	2,487	1,660 (66.7)

Notes: Others include Caloocan, Malabon, Makati, Mandaluyong, Muntinlupa, Navotas, Pasay, Pasig, and Pateros.

Source: Authors.

To examine attrition among the respondents, driver characteristics were compared with the demographic characteristics of the 2019 survey. Their ages ranged from 18 to 79 years, with a mean age of 43. Many drivers were married and lived on average with three to four family members.[2] Their mean level of education was 9.6 years.[3] Table 2 compares the characteristics between drivers who were surveyed in both 2019 and 2021, and those who were not included in 2021.

The results indicate that, compared with those not included in the 2021 sample, drivers who responded to both the surveys are more likely to be married and have a smartphone. This finding makes sense, because married drivers are more likely to be settled in one place and maintain the same phone number. As smartphones are becoming popular, those who have old mobile phones are likely to switch to smartphones and may also change their phone numbers in the process. The results in Table 3 raise concerns about attrition bias in the analysis of the 2021 survey, since the 2021 driver samples are somewhat different from the 2019 drivers who were randomly selected. The attrition may be controlled in the analysis by using exogenous factors that could have caused it. However, such exogenous factors are not available for this analysis. Thus, this study

---

[2]   A household is defined as a social unit consisting of a person living alone or a group of people living together in the same housing unit for more than 3 months, within the past 12 months, and sharing in the preparation and consumption of food. See Philippine Statistics Authority. Census of Population and Housing. Technical Notes. https://psa.gov.ph/population-and-housing/technical-notes.

[3]   This pertains to the education system before it was changed to a K-12 program, which requires 12 years of education before entering college.

was unable to control for attrition in the analysis, but concerns about potential attrition biases are noted when interpreting the results.

5. Results

5.1 Employment during Quarantine Periods, 2020–2021

In the 2021 survey, the respondents were asked about their employment status throughout the pandemic and community quarantines. This study has identified three periods, as discussed in Section 4. Under the three periods, some of the respondents worked as tricycle drivers or took different occupations. During ECQ, only about 18.6% of the respondents worked (Figure 1). The proportion of those who worked increased to almost 66% during GCQ I and nearly 90% in GCQ II.

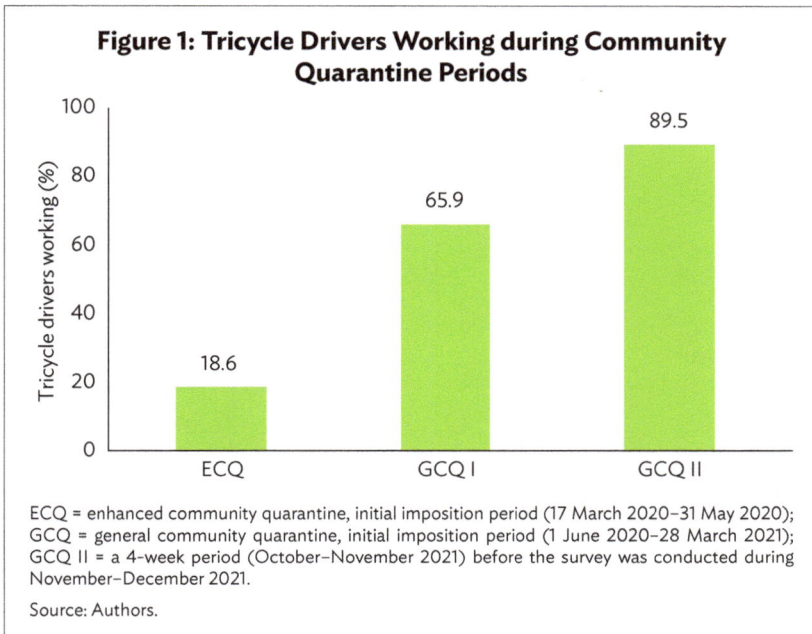

Figure 1: Tricycle Drivers Working during Community Quarantine Periods

ECQ = enhanced community quarantine, initial imposition period (17 March 2020–31 May 2020); GCQ = general community quarantine, initial imposition period (1 June 2020–28 March 2021); GCQ II = a 4-week period (October–November 2021) before the survey was conducted during November–December 2021.

Source: Authors.

During these episodes of community quarantine, tricycle drivers faced various restrictions. The first ECQ imposed strict restrictions that prohibited them from operating; thus, some of the respondents chose alternative occupations (Table 3). At the time of ECQ, 308 respondents worked, about 71% of them as drivers. However, the other 29% chose alternative occupations, including becoming delivery workers (6.5%), construction workers (1.3%), vendors and shop owners (1.6%), daily-wage workers (1.6%), and doing other jobs (17%).

During GCQ I, about 90% of those who went back to work worked as drivers of any vehicle (most likely, tricycles), and the rest took up different occupations. By the time of the survey in December 2021, which was the phase of GCQ II, about 90% of the respondents had resumed work as drivers. Among the alternative occupations, delivery work remained the most popular alternative. The absolute number of respondents who took up delivery work increased from 20 during ECQ to 52 during GCQ II, although the proportion of those working in delivery fell from 6.5% during ECQ to 3.5% during both GCQ I and GCQ II. The results in Table 3 suggest that the drivers struggled to find jobs throughout the pandemic, during the periods of community quarantine.

Table 3: Occupations during the Pandemic and Community Quarantine Periods, 2020–2021

Main Occupation	ECQ (Mar–May 2020)		GCQ I (Jun 2020–Mar 2021)		GCQ II (Nov–Dec 2021)	
	(A)	(B)	(C)	(D)	(E)	(F)
	Count	%	Count	%	Count	%
Driver of any vehicle	219	71.1	986	90.1	1,314	88.5
Delivery worker[a]	20	6.5	38	3.5	52	3.5
Construction worker	4	1.3	13	1.2	24	1.6
Street vendor/shop	5	1.6	10	0.9	18	1.2
Daily laborer	5	1.6	5	0.5	11	0.7
Technician	2	0.7	4	0.4	8	0.5
Others	53	17.2	38	3.3	58	3.5
Total who worked	308	100	1,094	100	1,485	100

ECQ = enhanced community quarantine, initial imposition period (17 March 2020–31 May 2020); GCQ I = general community quarantine, initial imposition period (1 June 2020–28 March 2021); GCQ II = 4-week period before the interviews with the respondents (October–November 2021).

[a] For example, Grab Food and Food Panda.

Source: Authors.

5.2 Incidence of COVID-19 and Vaccination Status

In the 2021 survey, the respondents were asked whether they had tested positive for COVID-19, and about their vaccination status (Table 4). Since the beginning of the pandemic in 2020, 36% of the drivers said they had been tested for COVID-19 at least once. Although only 3% reported having tested positive for COVID-19, 11% said they had experienced symptoms associated with COVID-19, such as fever with a dry cough, shortness of breath, and loss of taste or smell. About 7% had at least one family member who had tested positive for COVID-19, and 13% had at least one coworker who had tested positive.

Table 4: COVID-19 Experience among Tricycle Drivers

	Mean	Std. Dev.
Tested for COVID-19	0.36	0.48
Confirmed positive for COVID-19	0.03	0.16
Experienced any COVID-19 symptoms	0.11	0.31
Have family members been confirmed positive for COVID-19?	0.07	0.26
Has a coworker been confirmed positive for COVID-19?	0.13	0.34

Notes: COVID-19 symptoms include fever with a dry cough, shortness of breath, and loss of taste and/or smell.

Source: Authors.

Next, the drivers were asked about their COVID-19 vaccine status (Figure 2). Before the survey in December 2021, about 87% of the drivers said they had been vaccinated.[4] Vaccination started in the Philippines in February 2021, and about 9% of the respondents had received at least one dose of the vaccine before the end of May 2021. The proportion quickly increased during June–August 2021.

---

[4]   Vaccines available included Sinovac and Sinopharm (57%), Pfizer and Moderna (28%), Astra Zeneca (9%), and others.

Figure 2: Vaccination Rates Among Tricycle Drivers in 2021

Notes: The curve represents cumulative vaccinations until any given point during the year. The bars represent vaccinations for each month.

Source: Authors.

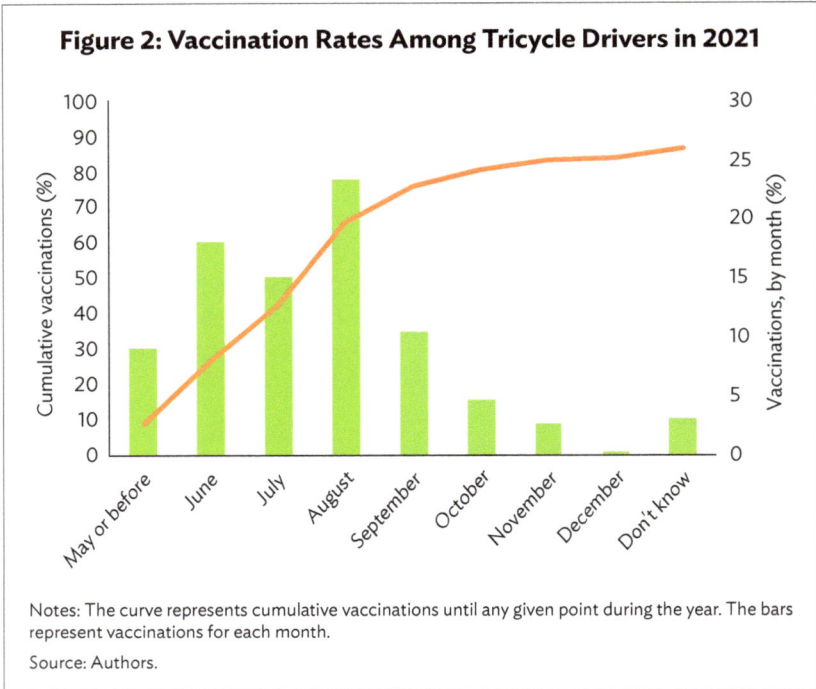

Among 218 unvaccinated respondents, 45% were willing to receive a COVID-19 vaccine, 29% were unwilling, and 26% were unsure (Table 5). Among those who were willing, about 8% cited not having the time as a main reason for not receiving vaccines. Other reasons include "doctors did not recommend" (about 7%) and "others" (almost 30%). Among those who were unwilling to be vaccinated, over 9% cited being afraid of adverse side effects as a main reason. A little over a quarter were unsure about receiving vaccines.

**Table 5: Willingness to Receive COVID-19 Vaccine
by Unvaccinated Drivers (n=218)**

Reason for not receiving vaccine, by willingness type	%
Willing to receive COVID-19 vaccine	**44.5**
I do not have time for vaccination	7.8
My doctor did not recommend it	7.3
Other	29.4
Unwilling to receive	**29.4**
I am afraid of adverse side effects	9.2
Others	20.2
Unsure	**26.1**
Total unvaccinated (n=218)	100

Source: Authors.

5.3 Working Hours, Income, and Loans in Late 2021

Even after the drivers resumed work, they did not work as much as they did in 2019 and earned less than before. The study finds that tricycle drivers worked, on average, 9.3 hours a day for 5.7 days a week in 2021, while they worked 11 hours a day for 6.3 days a week in 2019 (Table 6). From 2019 to 2021, the mean hours worked per week declined by over 26 hours, from about 70 to 54. Partly because of the reduced hours of work, the drivers' average monthly income declined by half, from ₱15,949 in 2019 to ₱7,716 in 2021.[5] Their spouses' monthly income also declined from ₱3,746 to ₱1,795 over the same period. The combined household income from both spouses, and other additional income, fell by over half, from ₱26,212 to ₱10,647. Finally, the survey asked about tricycle drivers' financial conditions in 2021. About 31% of them are paying back loans taken to pay for their vehicle. During the pandemic, about 80% of those who had loans missed at least one repayment installment.

---

[5]   The income figures in this chapter are in nominal values. In real terms, the 2021 income values would be smaller than the nominal figures.

A simple regression analysis helped identify the factors that affected the tricycle drivers' monthly earnings in 2019 and 2021 (Table 7). Another model was run with the dependent variable as a simple difference of earnings between 2021 and 2019. To enable comparison, the estimation models used data about the same 1,660 drivers who were included in both surveys. The 2019 regression results are consistent with the research's expectations. Age has a strong negative coefficient, which suggests that, for each extra year that a driver is older by, the monthly income declines by ₱55. However, because the average monthly earning of the drivers was ₱15,949, this amounts to only a 0.3% decline. A married and educated driver earned significantly more than others. The average monthly earnings of drivers in Quezon City were lower than those of their counterparts in Manila, while in other areas drivers earned more.

Table 6: Average Hours Worked and Average Income Earned by Tricycle Drivers

	2019	GCQ II (Oct–Dec 2021)	Difference
	(A)	(B)	(B) – (A)
Worked (%)	100	89.5	−10.5***
Working hours/day (hours)	11.2[a]	9.3 a	−1.9***
Working days/week (days)	6.3[a]	5.7 a	−0.5***
Working hours/week (hours)	70.3[a]	53.6 a	−16.7***
Monthly income (₱)			
Driver	15,949	7,716	−8,234***
Spouse	3,746	1,795	−1,952***
Household	26,212	10,647	−15,565***
Financial status			
Have loans (%)	NA	30.6	
Problems with repayment (%)	NA	78.0	
Number of respondents	1,660	1,660	

GCQ = general community quarantine, NA = not applicable.

[a] Represents the 1,485 respondents who worked in GCQ II 2021.
*** Significant at the 1% level (p<0.01).

Source: Authors.

Compared with the 2019 model, fewer variables proved significant in the 2021 model. Age has a larger and more statistically significant coefficient in the 2021 model, suggesting that the monthly income declines by ₱95 with each year added to a driver's age. Average monthly earnings in 2021 dropped to ₱7,716, a 1.2% decline, which was four times larger than that of 2019. In Quezon City, the mean monthly earning is about ₱1,065 lower than in Manila. Besides the age (of the driver) and the city dummy (for Quezon City), other variables are not significant, possibly suggesting more disruptions in the labor market for drivers. Married and educated drivers did not earn more than others, as they did back in 2019. The drivers in areas other than Manila and Quezon City earned relatively more in 2019, but that difference shrunk in 2021 and ceased to be significant.

Table 7: Determinants of Drivers' Monthly Incomes in 2019 and 2021 (OLS)

	2019 Income	2021 Income	Difference in Incomes (2021–2019)
	(A)	(B)	(C)
Driver Characteristics			
Age (years)	−54.5***	−95.2***	−40.7**
	(3.08)	(7.35)	(2.01)
Married (yes)	1990.7***	333.3	−1657.3***
	(3.65)	(0.84)	(2.66)
Education (years)	213.8***	36.6	−177.1**
	(3.26)	(0.76)	(2.36)
Number of household members	106.2	92.0	−14.2
	(1.13)	(1.33)	(0.13)
Quezon City (dummy)	−1287.5***	−1064.9***	222.6
	(3.17)	(3.58)	(0.48)
Other areas	4101.4***	136.5	−3342.2***
	(3.21)	(0.15)	(2.71)
Year 2021 (dummy)	–	–	−3342.2***
			(2.71)
Constant	14,430.5	11,088.3	–
	(13.3)	(13.9)	
Adjusted R-squared	0.032	0.041	0.013
Total	1,658	1,658	1,658

Note: Numbers in parentheses are absolute z-scores based on robust standard errors.
** significant at the 5% level ($p < 0.05$); *** significant at the 1% level ($p < 0.01$).

Source: Authors.

The last model, which uses changes in the monthly earnings over time, confirms the inferences drawn from the first two models. Older drivers have seen their average earnings decline more than those of younger drivers. Married, educated, and drivers outside of Manila and Quezon City have experienced larger earning declines than other drivers.

6. Conclusion

In the Philippines, in response to the spread of the COVID-19 pandemic, the government imposed a series of community quarantine programs that suspended or limited business operations. To assess the impacts of the pandemic and community quarantine restrictions on small and medium-sized enterprises, and understand their recovery process, this study examined the welfare and working conditions of tricycle drivers. Among public transportation services, tricycle services in the Philippines exist at the border between the formal and informal sectors, and tricycle drivers are among the most vulnerable transportation workers because of their limited financial resources. By using panel data from surveys of 1,660 tricycle drivers in 2019 and 2021, this study examined how their employment and incomes were impacted during periods of quarantine.

The surveys found that only 19% of the respondents worked during the first quarantine period (ECQ) during March–May 2020. In the subsequent quarantine periods between June 2020 and May 2021 (GCQ I), about 66% of them worked, and the percentage of those working increased to 90% by the time of the survey in November–December 2021 (GCQ II). Regarding drivers' COVID-19 and vaccination statuses, the survey found that 36% of the respondents had taken at least one COVID-19 test, and 3% of the total respondents tested positive for COVID-19. The vaccination rate rose rapidly from 27% in June 2021 to 87% at the time of the November–December 2021 survey.

Although most drivers have returned to work and 87% of those surveyed reported being vaccinated, their earnings remain lower than what they earned pre-pandemic. The mean weekly working hours declined by almost a quarter, from 70 hours in 2019 to 54 hours in 2021. The drivers' average income fell by more than half, from ₱15,949 to ₱7,716. Because their spouses' incomes also fell, the average household income among tricycle drivers declined by 60%. In late 2021, almost one in three tricycle drivers was repaying loans borrowed to buy the vehicles, and over three-quarters of them reported having missed at least one repayment installment. Thus, although work has resumed for many, the financial hardship experienced by tricycle drivers due to the pandemic was likely to continue beyond 2021.

Lockdowns and movement restrictions to control COVID-19 sharply reduced the use of public transportation vehicles such as tricycles. Many commuters avoided shared public vehicles because of the fear of contracting COVID-19. Given the disruptions to the informal and semiformal public transportation sectors, and the impacts on and responses by their operators and drivers, it is unclear whether the demand for shared public transportation vehicles, notably the tricycles in the Philippines, will ever return to pre-pandemic levels. Some regular commuters, pre-pandemic, may have arranged to work from home on a continuing basis, and others have switched to commuting by private modes of transportation. It is important for local governments to issue clear guidelines that require appropriate safety measures in shared public vehicles to ease riders' misgivings and keep them safe. Such guidance will help tricycle drivers and other informal and semiformal public transport providers adapt to post-pandemic requirements more effectively and expeditiously.

References

Asian Development Bank (ADB). 2020a. *Asia Small and Medium-Sized Enterprise Monitor 2020: Volume I–Country and Regional Reviews*. Manila.

_____. 2020b. *Asia Small and Medium-Sized Enterprise Monitor 2020: Volume III Thematic Chapter—Fintech Loans to Tricycle Drivers in the Philippines*. Manila.

Cervero, R., and A. Golub. 2007. Informal Transport: A Global Perspective. *Transport Policy* 14 (6): 445–457. https://doi.org/10.1016/j.tranpol.2007.04.011.

Chuenyindee, T. et al. 2022. Public Utility Vehicle Service Quality and Customer Satisfaction in the Philippines during the COVID-19 Pandemic. *Utilities Policy* 75: 101336.

Government of the Philippines. 2020a. Executive Order No. 112, s. 2020. Manila.

_____. 2020b. COVID-19 Inter-Agency Task Force for the Management of Emerging Infectious Diseases (IATF-EID). Resolution 41. Manila.

_____. 2020c. *Guidelines on the Implementation of Alert Levels System for Covid-19 Response in Pilot Areas*. Manila.

Hasselwander, M. et al. 2021. Building Back Better: The COVID-19 Pandemic and Transport Policy Implications for a Developing Megacity. *Sustainable Cities and Society* 69.

Japan International Cooperation Agency (JICA). 2015. *The Project for Capacity Development on Transportation Planning and Database Management in the Republic of the Philippines*. MMUTIS Update and Enhancement Project (MUCEP), Technical Report. https://openjicareport.jica.go.jp/pdf/12247623.pdf.

Jiang, Y., J. R. Laranjo, and M. Thomas. 2022. *COVID-19 Lockdown Policy and Heterogeneous Responses of Urban Mobility: Evidence from the Philippines*. Manila: ADB.

Joewono, T., and H. Kubota. 2007. User Perception of Private Paratransit Operation in Indonesia. *Journal of Public Transportation* 10 (4): 99–118.

Lee, M. et al. 2020. Human Mobility Trends During the Early Stage of the COVID-19 Pandemic in the United States. *PLoS One* 15 (11): e0241468.

Parady, G., A. Taniguchi, and K. Takami. 2020. Analyzing Risk Perception and Social Influence Effects on Self-Restriction Behavior in Response to the COVID-19 Pandemic in Japan: First Results. *SSRN Electric Journal*. 1–31. doi: 10.2139/ssrn.3618769.

Phun, V. K., and T. Yai. 2016. State of the Art of Paratransit Literature in Asian Developing Countries. *Asian Transport Studies* 4 (1): 57–77.

Pullano, G., E. Valdano, N. Scarpa, S. Rubrichi, and V. Colizza. 2020. Population Mobility Reductions During COVID-19 Epidemic in France under Lockdown. *Lancet Digit Health* 2 (12): e638–e649.

Shortall R., N. Moutera, and B. Van Weeb. 2021. COVID-19 Passenger Transport Measures and Their Impacts. *Transport Reviews*. DOI: 10.1080/01441647.2021.1976307.

Tirachini, A., and O. Cats. 2020. COVID-19 and Public Transportation: Current Assessment, Prospects, and Research Needs. *Journal of Public Transportation* 22 (1): 1–21.

World Health Organization. 2020. Opening remarks by WHO Director-General Tedros Adhanom Ghebreyesus at a media briefing on COVID-19. 11 March. https://www.who.int/director-general/speeches/detail/who-director-general-s-opening-remarks-at-the-media-briefing-on-covid-19---11-march-2020.

11

Learning from Informality during COVID-19: Leveraging Informal Services for Improved Planning in Asian Cities

Ashok Das and Bambang Susantono

1. Urban Informality, COVID-19, and the Urban Services Divide

This book contributes toward the big and urgent need for urban policy makers, planners, institutions of urban planning and governance, researchers of urbanization and urban societies, and a range of urban stakeholders to acknowledge and appreciate informality, and strive to engage with the urban informal sector proactively and effectively. As elaborated in the introduction and other chapters of this book, academic research has long called for urban planning and governance to be inclusive of informality, yet planning practice has been slow and sporadic in responding. However, the global scale of the coronavirus disease (COVID-19) pandemic and its destructive local impacts, worldwide, have underscored the urgency to do so. Across the world, extensive media attention on the pandemic's ravaging has helped generate unprecedented awareness among the public and governments at all levels about the prevalence, pervasiveness, value, and vulnerability of the informal sector. It has also catalyzed large multilateral institutions such as the World Bank, the International Monetary Fund (IMF), ADB, the Organisation for Economic Co-operation and Development (OECD), the UN and its agencies, the World Economic Forum (WEF), and a host of other development institutions, think tanks, and civil society organizations (CSOs). These institutions are concentrating on both deepening and scaling up understanding of the informal sector, realizing the nuances of how informality exacerbates the complex phenomena of urban poverty and resilience, illuminating COVID-19's impacts on informality and vulnerability, and monitoring recovery responses from across and within countries.[1] Such efforts, cumulatively, should intensify support for enabling cities to leverage the potential of informal sector actors. Growing national, regional, and local concerns about the increasingly evident impacts of climate change have generated a global consensus to manage and steer urbanization and development more prudently to mitigate climate change and make cities and communities more resilient. Such consensus drives extant global agreements such as the Sustainable Development Goals (SDGs) and the New Urban Agenda (NUA) to steer development more sustainably, equitably, and inclusively.

The emergent policy awareness, agendas, and action to make cities more sustainable, equitable, and inclusive require transforming urban planning to accept and constructively engage with informality. They are reflective of the sophisticated, rich, and voluminous research evidence that has been accumulating since the last decade or two and exposing incongruence between contemporary planning approaches and urban informality (for example, see Birch, Chattaraj, and Wachter 2016; Dahiya and Das 2020; Mahendra et al. 2021; Roy and AlSayyad 2004; Rukmana 2020). Consequently, scholars have been challenging the prevalent notions of urbanization, informality, and development with new conceptualizations and refined debates on urbanization in the Global South (Bhan, Srinivas, and Watson 2018; Parnell and Robinson 2012; Robinson and Roy 2016; Roy 2005; Satterthwaite et al. 2020; Scott and Storper 2015).

A recently-concluded, expansive, and in-depth investigation, the *World Resources Report: Towards a More Equal City* project comprises a series of publications—research for which took several years in multiple countries in the Global South across different urban sectors. As the project's synthesis report states, over 1.2 billion people worldwide live in slums and over 2 billion work in the informal economy, which has been battered by the COVID-19 pandemic (Mahendra et al. 2021). The report presents findings that raise deep concern—the current pace and scale of urbanization are unprecedented, with most of it occurring in low- and middle-income countries; the economic benefits of urbanization are being waylaid by deepening social and spatial inequalities in cities, with

---

[1]   The IMF, for instance, now has a policy tracker that covers 197 countries and summarizes the key economic responses governments are taking to limit the human and economic impact of the COVID-19 pandemic, with focus on the informal sector. See International Monetary Fund. Policy Responses to COVID-19. https://www.imf. org/en/Topics/imf-and-covid19/Policy-Responses-to-COVID-19.

the pandemic having sharply exacerbated such disparities; the urban services gap between the privileged few and the rest is enormous; self-provision of basic services by the urban poor is exhausting and wasteful, and often hazardous and environmentally unsound; and growing informality means that most economic activity lacks government regulations and oversight. Such trends have serious implications for poverty, inequality, resilience, and climate change. The aforementioned project also recognized the futility of measuring poverty and inequality in terms of income alone, and the multidimensionality of poverty, which is manifested in quality of access to services; hence, it examines inequality in terms of the burdens faced in accessing core services.

2. The Contributions of This Book

The research insights presented in the chapters of this book investigate informal modes of providing or accessing core and supporting services in Asian cities. It encourages shifts toward transforming extant urban policies and planning practice. Several of the chapters in this book discuss the challenges associated with providing the most basic yet indispensable services such as water, sanitation, and improved shelter, as well as how community-based and community-led processes, with adequate support, and with capable intermediaries can help overcome hurdles that deny access. The need for a multidimensional approach to poverty alleviation is stressed in most chapters, as its importance for system resilience became apparent during the pandemic. Collectively, the findings emphasize the need for formal urban planning approaches and economic development policies to embrace the informal sector to unleash the development potential of large swathes of the population. They also reflect an emerging wisdom from years of research (Banks, Lombard, and Mitlin 2020) that stresses the need for abandoning disparate sectoral approaches and pursuing integrated, intersectoral approaches. In light of the lessons from the disruptions wrought by the COVID-19 pandemic, multiple chapters illustrate how technological innovations—from low-tech water and sanitation improvements to the platform economy and fintech services—should be harnessed toward enabling the desired transformation of the informal sector. The specific contributions of individual chapters are highlighted below.

Guided by a multidimensional poverty approach, Virinder Sharma and Joy Amor Bailey discuss in Chapter 2 how small-scale, local initiatives with active community engagement in the Philippines—projects supported by multilateral agencies and global nongovernment organizations (NGOs)—can deliver contextually appropriate solutions for poverty alleviation and climate resilience. Joris van Etten and Tiffany M. Tran, in Chapter 3, argue for and analyze multidimensional poverty alleviation approaches in Indonesia's next generation of slum upgrading initiatives, focusing on the built form, the natural environment, community organization, and social and human development. Because of the transaction costs involved, they reckon such initiatives as challenging to implement even in a country like Indonesia that has a long history of and rich experience with slum upgrading. Besides financial and technical inefficiencies, most importantly, they call for revamping institutional arrangements to allow local-level institutions achieve greater capacity and autonomy, and suggest ways to do so.

Priyam Das, Lakpa Sherpa, and Ashok Das in Chapter 4 illuminate further how being deprived of basic services, especially water and sanitation, and social protections suddenly plunged the urban poor in informal settlements in Nepal and elsewhere in South Asia into deep distress during the COVID-19 pandemic. By focusing on urban contexts with less robust planning institutions, they assert the urgent need to build local government capacities to execute improved land use planning and ensure citywide provision of services, inclusive of informal settlements, toward climate proofing cities and making them resilient to economic shocks and public health exigencies. This urgency cannot be overstated given the increasing intensity and frequency of extreme weather events, the impacts of which are exacerbated manifold by inadequate and improper planning that routinely causes urban flooding in many if not most cities in developing Asia. While calling for improved planning capacity and greater local government initiative, the authors also caution that local governments cannot accomplish these objectives alone. Citing successful examples, they conclude that cities must involve urban poor communities in planning and actively collaborate with local civil society and academic institutions in conceptualizing, designing, and implementing planning that builds resilience.

In a related vein, Chapter 6 by Penny Dutton, Isabel Blackett, Neeta Pokhrel, Lara Arjan, Christian Walder, and Ellen Pascua also concentrates on urban water and sanitation and draws our attention to emerging innovations in developing economies, which are yet largely unrecognized and have the potential to transform extant burdened and ineffective service delivery mechanisms. Rich data collected from multiple cases during the COVID-19 pandemic help to substantiate the authors' call for promoting facilities, such as sanitation hubs in informal settlements, and providing water and sanitation through intermediaries such as social enterprises and small and medium-sized enterprises (SMEs). Chapter 6 demonstrates the innovation, agility, and resilience of a diverse set of decentralized intermediaries and how they bridge formal services and informal settlements. The explication of how social enterprises and SMEs are now operating on the ground advances planning knowledge about how efforts by CSOs and private sector actors can be scaled up in providing water and sanitation services to the urban poor. Decentralized governance and service provision with community participation and civil society stewardship are key elements. Besides valuable insights into technological and digital innovations, the authors discuss how CSOs operating at scales from the global to the local can work together with local governments and informal sector communities. They also point to associated social and gender equity gains to be had and suggest why and how external development partners and formal financing institutions can support these initiatives for the desired transformation.

By discussing the case of Dhaka, Bangladesh, before and during the COVID-19 pandemic, Chapter 5 by John Taylor, Ashok Das, Janet Naco, and Saiful Momen explicates the intricacies and implications of food security, or lack thereof—a critical aspect of development that has long been ignored by planning scholarship and practice. The issue has rightfully gained much attention in recent years, and especially during the pandemic. The research endeavor discussed in this chapter represents collaboration among various institutions—a multilateral institution, local CSO federations, community-based organizations (CBOs), informal sector workers and residents, local government institutions, and local and foreign universities. The chapter illuminates how multiple deprivations and vulnerabilities affect food security, which, in turn, hinders multiple development indicators. It clarifies in detail that it is not just food quantity but also the quality of nutrition that determines one's food security status, something that policies and programs for food support usually ignore or underemphasize. Globally, larger scale supply chain issues hindering food access became evident, but persistent local-level barriers remain largely unnoticed. In Dhaka, quotidian access to sufficient and nutritious food is influenced by various economic and spatial factors and access to basic services. Routinely, and more so during economic crises, groups like women, children, and the elderly tend to be rendered disproportionately food insecure. The chapter provides nuanced evidence of how the urban poor coped during the COVID-19 pandemic, suggesting that coping mechanisms, such as urban agriculture, are initiatives that planning ought to scale up for food security, economic, health, environmental, and other resilience-building benefits. The authors find that emergency food response during the pandemic was swift and effective because of well-established decentralized governance that allows trust and communication to flourish between informal settlement CBOs and local government representatives. They also are optimistic that more collaborative and targeted planning for food security is quite feasible and scalable, given ample precedence of leveraging collaboration among the state, CSOs, universities, and communities in Bangladesh for various development objectives.

Collectively, the next four chapters of the book attempt to clarify some contours, structures, and dynamics of informal sector micro and small enterprises (MSEs) and employment in Asia; highlight select economic impacts on firms and workers and health-related impacts on workers; and explore the transformative potential of new digital technologies such as fintech services for informal sector businesses. They present sophisticated quantitative analyses using data from various sources: official government datasets, primary survey data from multiple countries, and panel data. These chapters' useful insights into the informal sector indicate a serious lacuna—the general paucity of data about the informal sector, let alone those that are comprehensive and granular. Also evident is that occasional primary survey data collection for individual research projects cannot capture informality's diversity and complexities, underscoring the need for organized and continued data collection at the city level.

Dil B. Rahut, Jeetendra Prakash Aryal, Panharoth Chhay, and Peter J. Morgan in Chapter 7 explore the extent and nature of women's participation in urban informal SMEs in Cambodia, where nearly 70% of all employment is estimated to be informal. Lacking specific information about the status of formality of businesses in the official national survey dataset used, the authors assume low operating cost as a reliably conservative proxy for informal SMEs. Although it is well acknowledged that women constitute a large part of the informal workforce, globally, investigations of this nature are instructive for clarifying gender-based differences in the informal labor market and facilitating apt policy interventions. Cambodian women garner a larger share of ownership and employment in informal MSEs, possibly due to multiple social burdens and structural constraints they endure. Women mostly engage in sectors with low barriers to entry, and less so in those that require higher human and financial capital and are more lucrative. Also, the greater informal employment of women in tourism and its ancillary sectors meant that women suffered more from COVID-19 restrictions. The authors, therefore, call for policies that will support and promote women's education, skills development, and access to credit, by involving those who understand the challenge well—among others, CSOs, multilateral agencies, and academics and other researchers.

In Chapter 9, using survey data from seven Southeast Asian countries generated by the Asian Development Bank Institute (ADBI), Peter J. Morgan, Kim Kunhyui, and Long Q. Trinh investigate the pandemic's impact on informal and formal businesses, whether the aid offered by the government to weather the pandemic was accessible and helpful for informal enterprises, and whether fintech services proved useful. They find that government aid was largely well-targeted and accessible, and, even when modest, it helped informal businesses stay afloat. In general, firms that used or pivoted to adopting fintech services found it easier to survive or even thrive due to the ease of accessing customers and overcoming restrictions on in-person interactions. The authors recommend increased and expedient government support for informal businesses, especially in times of crisis, and policies to support their adoption of fintech services. They also caution that such policies should be carefully designed and contextualized because development challenges, policy environments, and governance vary greatly across countries. They suggest incentivizing private sector and civil society actors to promote financial education and digital economy training for small entrepreneurs in the informal sector.

Shigehiro Shinozaki reports in Chapter 8 his analogous but more extensive investigation of micro and small enterprises in Indonesia to stress the importance of supporting informal firms and enabling their formalization for urban resilience. Analyzing data from multiple primary surveys conducted during the pandemic (involving ADB, government agencies, and private consultants), he finds that informal businesses were hit hard by working capital shortages at the beginning. Government aid provided welcome relief but came slowly, and to avoid shutting down, informal firms relied heavily on friends and family for financial support. Informal businesses suffered disproportionately more than formal ones due to pandemic restrictions, and young businesses and women-led enterprises struggled more. Over time, small firms providing local services recovered better than those reliant on larger supply chains. Also, it was clear that firms that utilized digital platforms and e-commerce suffered less revenue losses, prompting the author to suggest formalization of informal firms through their digital transformation—indeed, this has been a key aim of GOJEK, a pioneer of Indonesia's [digital] platform economy.[2] The chapter suggests areas that will benefit from policy-targeting.

---

[2]   Interview with a senior GOJEK official at the firm's headquarters in Jakarta, 10 July 2017.

In Chapter 10, Takashi Yamano, Yasuyuki Sawada, Shigehiro Shinozaki, Hyuncheol Bryant Kim, Syngjoo Choi, and Siho Park analyze panel data to clarify the economic and health impacts of the COVID-19 pandemic on a particular group of informal sector workers in the Philippines—the tricycle drivers. The authors find that loss of employment in this group was particularly high because of lockdowns and strict mobility restrictions. Even though most drivers have returned to work, ridership and earnings are much lower than pre-pandemic levels. Aside from factors that have altered modes of working during the pandemic, real and perceived health risks associated with public transportation options are likely to continue to suppress their ridership. Given the ubiquity of tricycles in the Philippines and their economic significance, the authors call for local government action to protect their interests by requiring reasonable health and safety requirements to quell the apprehensions of public transport users.

3. ADB, COVID-19, and the Informal Sector

Guided by a multitude of experiences from its own research and practice, both before and during the COVID-19 pandemic, ADB has espoused a firm commitment to promoting constructive engagement with the urban informal sector for enabling cities in Asia and the Pacific to become resilient. ADB believes that building the resilience of informal communities requires a shared understanding of collective vulnerability in urban areas in light of climate change and other economic and environmental threats, and jointly finding with different stakeholders scalable solutions. To achieve this, the voices of all stakeholders need to be heard at the table for decision-making and planning. In 2021, ADB held a knowledge sharing event in Manila to increase awareness about climate-related challenges faced by the urban poor in Asia and the Pacific. The event highlighted how the raging COVID-19 pandemic decreased the region's overall resilience against disasters and underscored how the urban poor serve as society's first and last bastions of defense against future global challenges. Partnering with various types of external organizations, the event also called for wide-ranging collaboration among all concerned groups to identify opportunities for scaling up pro-poor policies and investments in housing and community infrastructure. Only when those in the informal sector are provided voice and agency to engage in dialogue can we appreciate their understanding of resilience, and they will be able to negotiate development interventions that can be truly effective.

Initial lessons learned by ADB from the impacts of the COVID-19 pandemic clearly point to the need to forsake business-as-usual approaches if working with the informal sector is to be effective. Traditional methods of engagement need to be reconfigured. Even technically innovative project designs must be community-based, and approaches to capacity building and community participation need to be devised carefully—in ways that transform informal sector actors from mere spectators to codesigners of their future. For example, an ADB technical assistance (TA) in Makassar, Indonesia supported the revitalization of informal settlements and their environments using water-sensitive approaches. Completed in 2021, the RISE project introduced decentralized green infrastructure to biologically treat contaminated and polluted wastewater. The project demonstrated the effectiveness of water-sensitive approaches for flood risk reduction and urban environmental improvement. ADB espoused a community codesign approach to ensure that local stakeholders, particularly residents of the project sites, were engaged as decision makers and project owners throughout the design, implementation, and operations and maintenance phases. Sustained community participation built strong community ownership. Residents provided in-kind support and undertook simple civic works that expedited construction. The local government committed to support the operation and maintenance, as well as improve other urban services like streetlighting and solid waste management in the area. The TA successfully demonstrated that, with community participation, decentralized infrastructure for water and sanitation can be delivered at scale and customized to informal settlement settings.

Besides the themes and areas identified for public action and planning that can be transformative for the informal sector, there are several other areas of emphases for multilateral institutions such as ADB. A recent World Bank study offers a detailed road map for planners and policy makers to cope with the many challenges of urban informality in developing countries (Ohnsorge and Yu 2021). The study recommends comprehensive and integrated measures in different spheres and at various levels, such as improving macroeconomic policies, governance, and business climates; streamlining tax regulation and administration; increasing flexibility in labor markets; developing the financial services sector to create incentives for informal firms to invest in higher productivity activities and formalize; and ameliorating public services delivery. Such policies can also invigorate private sector activity to address informality. Attention also needs to be paid to how policy reforms can yield unintended consequences. For instance, unless accompanied by measures that increase labor market flexibility, trade liberalization policies that raise competition have also been known to expand informality. Furthermore, planning and governance reforms complemented by training programs, public awareness campaigns, and strong enforcement tend to reduce informality.

The avowed focus of ADB can help transform local governance and planning in Asia and the Pacific through programs and policy assistance that encourage local governments to work together with other local non-state actors. Collaborative efforts can help in actively incorporating the informal sector into planning and ensuring that all development efforts are sensitive to informality. There is no one-size-fits-all approach to being inclusive of informality. The litmus test for successful urban planning in any city will be how comprehensively it supports informal sector workers and residents, and how it enhances their overall resilience.

4. Toward Transformative Planning for the Informal Sector

In concluding this book, this section discusses some essential ideas in regard to implementing lessons from this book and other contemporary research. It also reflects on related critical issues that are beyond the scope of the individual chapters but have implications for the recommendations emanating from them. We hope these can spur the transformation of planning in cities of Asia and elsewhere in the Global South to being more inclusive of the informal sector. The findings, inferences, and recommendations that emerge from the chapters of this book align with the seven transformations deemed vital, by the recent summary report of the *World Resources Report: Towards a More Equal City* project, for making cities in the Global South more equal, sustainable, and prosperous for all. Mahendra et al. (2021) outline the transformations being sought: (i) prioritizing the vulnerable in infrastructure design and delivery; (ii) partnering with alternative service providers for exploring service provision models; (iii) improving local data through community engagement; (iv) recognizing and supporting informal workers; (v) increasing urban investment and targeting funds creatively; (vi) improving urban land management with transparency and integrated spatial planning; and (vii) improving urban governance and strengthening institutions by creating diverse coalitions with various urban stakeholders. This section delves a bit deeper into how such transformative planning can be realized. To that end, it posits the following: academic education that trains urban policy experts and planners needs reforming; local urban planning and governance needs to vigorously engage civil society and other non-state stakeholders; and multilateral institutions can play an instrumental role in catalyzing the above.

Most urban research across technical and social sciences disciplines tends to explicate very well the problems, challenges, and their causes. More nuanced research also demonstrates the complexity and intersectionality of contemporary urban issues, including informality. Good research products offer salient recommendations about "what" needs to be done to improve the status quo, and "why" that is essential or beneficial. Yet, despite voluminous research on urbanization, urban poverty, inequality, and informality, the realization of efforts on the ground seem to considerably lag behind knowledge production. This is likely because the business of governing, planning, developing, and managing the city is a highly complex affair. In cities of the developing economies where all resources are scarcer or weaker, the challenge is compounded manifold. For those who plan and manage the city, usually under trying conditions, understanding "what specific policy objectives are important and why" is important but not sufficient. They need to know more about actual moves by which such objectives can be attained. That is why research that seeks to inform and improve urban planning and management has to move beyond just the "what" and "why" foci to explaining the "how" of it. Urban planners and policy makers need to appreciate specific actions and processes that can lead to desirable goals by understanding the value of including unconventional actors, having flexible institutional arrangements, and deepening community participation (Das and Dahiya 2020).

4.1   Focus on Education for Improved Understanding, Planning, and Governing of Cities

This book clarifies intricate links that tie urban informality to urbanization and climate change. Informality is exacerbated by rapid urbanization and climate change, and the inability to ameliorate urban informality hinders efforts to create livable cities for all (Susantono and Guild 2021). A serious lack of professional and educational capacities in most developing countries is impeding progress toward SDG 11 (sustainable cities and communities), which seeks to make cities and human settlements inclusive, safe, resilient, and sustainable (Oborn and Walters 2020). Not achieving SDG 11 would profoundly compromise the UN 2030 Agenda for Sustainable Development and other global commitments to combat climate change, while further increasing inequality and vulnerability in cities. The first and urgent step for building capacity is to increase the number of planning schools in developing countries. For instance, in OECD countries (advanced economies), the average ratio of planning schools per million population is about 0.73, whereas in Nigeria, it is only about 0.18; the United Kingdom with a population of over 67 million[3] has 28 planning schools as compared to just 5 in Pakistan, whose population is over 220 million,[4] although the latter is urbanizing over three times faster (Oborn and Walters 2020). As Chapter 8 of this book pointed out, the entire country of Nepal has one planning school. Likewise, in the most populated, largest economies of South and Southeast Asia, let alone cities, there is no planning school yet in a third or more of the states/provinces (Setiawan 2018), which also tend to be less developed but briskly urbanizing regions.

While the supply of planning education has to increase, merely having more planning schools is not sufficient for the transformative planning desired. The relevance and efficacy of planning education also has to improve. To address the challenges of urban informality and urban resilience, planning education in and for the Global South needs to provide new emphases and modes of learning, and inculcate new sensitivities (Fan et al. 2022; Frank and Silver 2018). Planning education in developing Asia and the Pacific continues to train students in problem solving by heavily instilling positivist, scientific, and technocratic perspectives (Das and Dahiya 2020). Transforming planning practice for it to become inclusive, equitable, and humane, however, requires not just technical proficiency, but a deep appreciation of the nuanced intersectionality of the social, cultural, environmental, economic, and political dimensions of urban society. As was discussed in the introduction chapter of this book, the institutional frameworks and apparatuses of planning in most developing countries are still steeped in and reflect colonial planning legacies that propagate the formal-informal binary, thereby failing to engage with urban informality. If policy makers and urban professionals, especially planners, lack a cross-disciplinary and multidimensional awareness to operate from, planning's desired transformation of cities to being more inclusive, equitable, and resilient will remain elusive.

---

[3] See Government of the United Kingdom. Office for National Statistics. https://www.ons.gov.uk/peoplepopulationandcommunity/populationand migration/populationestimates.

[4] See World Bank Data. Population, Total – Pakistan. https://data.worldbank.org/ indicator/SP.POP.TOTL?locations=PK.

Most planning curricula in developing Asia, unfortunately, place negligible emphasis on the theories and discourses about equity, justice, inclusivity, and civil society, and, in general, lack broader social sciences wisdom (Das 2019). Most progressive planning literature is yet new and emergent, draws mostly from experiences in developed economies, and is published in the English language; to be widely impactful in developing economies, seminal works of this nature need to be translated into local languages and supplemented with research that evidences phenomena and experiences from local contexts (Das 2019; Wahab and Agbola 2017). Consequently, local government offices and planning institutions usually comprise public officials who are apathetic or loath to engaging with the informal sector and enhancing participation in planning processes; they may also be those who resist moves that seek to reform the conventional ways and means of planning. External aid programs promote community participation in planning activities, and most national and local planning guidelines now require participation, especially by marginalized and vulnerable groups; yet, attaining that in routine local planning is rarely satisfactory. For instance, in recent years, many countries have revamped their institutional arrangements for disaster risk reduction and resilience by creating new subnational institutions, but their comprehensive efficacy is yet limited or unproven (Das and Luthfi 2017).

With increasing and better urban research evidence, there is a growing consciousness among policy experts that resolving most urban challenges requires interdisciplinary understanding and approaches (Banks, Lombard, and Mitlin 2020), including technical and traditionally siloed areas such as transportation planning (Kim 2021). For instance, COVID-19 busted a long-held notion that density begets contagion because dense slums had much lower infection rates than less dense affluent areas, and it was realized that economic geography much more than physical geography determines a city's ability to respond and be resilient (Lall 2020). It is not just planning education that has to be infused with more interdisciplinary perspectives and informed by cross-disciplinary research, especially in regard to appreciating why and how issues of informality, inequality, and injustice pose serious challenges to cities. In fact, nowadays, most critical planning scholarship and the progressive planning curricula around the world reflect moves toward embracing the plurality of disciplinary perspectives and methods of inquiry.

However, planning scholars and practitioners are not the only professionals who influence urban policies and planning initiatives. Professionals trained in several social sciences and other disciplines—*inter alia*, management, economics, law, political science, geography, sociology, anthropology, gender studies, public health, and environmental studies—also work in and shape institutions of urban planning and governance. Likewise, research produced by economists and researchers in other disciplines, especially at national institutions and multilateral development agencies, significantly influences the creation and implementation of urban development policies and planning programs at the local level. Thus, it is vital that curricula in these other disciplines also impart optimal facility in interdisciplinary and multidisciplinary perspectives and encourage cross-disciplinary learning and mixed methods research. Those who research urbanization, urban poverty, and urban informality should know about the contemporary wisdom on informality from different disciplines, along with some basic knowledge of key planning principles and logics. A lot of good research will then be able to transform planning by going beyond the "what" and the "why" to also indicating the "how" for those who can effect change on the ground.

4.2 Engaging Civil Society and Universities in Local Planning

To effectively address the challenges of urban informality, most chapters in this book illuminate and/or recommend, for diverse ends, that local governments engage extensively with civil society organizations (CSOs), especially with local nongovernment organizations (NGOs) and community-based organizations (CBOs). Several chapters have also stressed the value of involving local universities in the planning process. Research indeed has long behooved local governments to engage with civil society for alleviating urban poverty and empowering squatters and slum dwellers (Mitlin and Satterthwaite 2004). Scholars have also articulated how engaging CSOs, universities, and other nonstate actors in urban environmental management (Daniere and Takahashi 2002), urban governance (Cheema 2013; Cheema and Popovski 2010), and disaster governance (Miller and Douglass 2016) benefits cities in Asia and the Pacific and advances the NUA and SDG 11 objectives (Dahiya and Das 2020; Roitman and Rukmana, forthcoming). The indispensability of involving diverse local stakeholders to make local planning more inclusive of the informal sector cannot be overstated.

The contribution of CSOs to providing services to the urban poor is noteworthy, with such services often surpassing formal provision in terms of quality (Banerjee and Duflo 2011). The informal origins of today's popular concept of coproduction in the Global South exemplify how poor urban communities working with CSOs have been able to secure significant improvements to their living environments when governments are either unwilling or unable to deliver land and services (Watson 2014). Formal coproduction involving the state, CSOs, and poor communities have been witnessed in various sectors, such as water and sanitation, health services, education, and microfinance; and much scaling-up has been demonstrated, such as in solid waste management and slum upgrading. To enable planning's constructive engagement with informality, civil society actors and universities can help with generating data on the informal sector through community mapping, institutionalizing community-based planning, and supporting community-led processes. Capable NGOs and CBOs have a deep understanding of local urban informality and are usually more trusted by urban poor communities than local government agencies.

One of the biggest challenges to addressing urban informality is nonexistent or highly insufficient data on informal settlements and informal enterprises and work, as indicated in the chapters of this book. To enable the creation and updating of data on the informal sector, local governments should support and partner with local NGOs and CBOs. Given the daunting scale of informality in developing cities and its shifting characteristics, local governments usually lack adequate resources, expertise, and experience to produce quality data on their own. Any data on the status of informality gathered through national decadal censuses or national surveys, if at all, are likely to be weak in capturing essential local nuances and infrequent enough to not be able to track informality's fluctuating nature. On the other hand, NGOs and CSOs in different parts of the world have refined techniques of collecting data about informal sector workers and informal settlements by working directly with urban poor communities (Archer, Luansang and Boonmahathanakorn 2012; Patel, Baptist, and d'Cruz 2012). Such coproduced data and community mapping have been instrumental in making the informal sector visible to policy makers, empowering the urban poor, and facilitating the effective provision of services. Besides many internationally prominent CSOs—such as several large NGOs in South Asia, the Asian Coalition for Housing Rights (ACHR) in multiple Asian countries,[5] Kota Kita in Indonesia,[6] Catalytic Communities in Brazil,[7] the Pamoja Trust in Kenya,[8] and the Slum Dwellers International

---

[5]   Asian Coalition for Housing Rights. http://www.achr.net/.

[6]   Kota Kita. A City for All. https://kotakita.org/.

[7]   CatComm. Catalytic Communities. https://catcomm.org/.

[8]   Pamoja Trust. https://pamojatrust.org/.

and its affiliates on multiple continents[9]—there are likely thousands of local NGOs in developing economies that are proficient in creating, using, and disseminating data. Among others, Kota Kita and Catalytic Communities have also been pioneers in adopting online and digital technologies for empowering urban poor communities by training them to use the same for mapping, making claims, and networking (Taylor and Lassa 2015; Williamson 2003).

With proper and sustained government support, the coproduction of data and mapping can be scaled up, institutionalized, and routinized, and more local CSOs can be trained and involved in the process. At the city level, decentralization and coproduction of data hold the potential to overcome the information gap about informality. Even sporadically, some cities have already successfully partnered with CSOs on various planning, upgrading, and governance initiatives. Thus, with political will and commitment, the coproduction of decentralized data on informality can be realized. It is also important to remember that bigger cities have a much greater concentration and diversity of CSOs. For local governments to be able to manage informality better, they must also support the growth of local civil society by incentivizing and involving CSOs.

Multiple chapters in this book have discussed the benefits of community-based and community-led projects with CSO support. Often, capable local NGOs in cities of the Global South are the only agents able to prepare informal sector communities and the urban poor in engaging meaningfully as partners in collaborative planning and development (Baruah 2004; Das 2018). Community-managed planning efforts without effective NGO intermediaries, either due to the context or by design, tend to be less impressive than desired (Antlöv, Brinkerhoff, and Rapp 2010; Das 2015; Grantham and Baruah 2017). Skilled and experienced NGOs can empower marginalized communities of the urban poor by mobilizing them, especially women; teaching organizational, management, and negotiation skills; and building leadership (d'Cruz and Mudimu 2013; Roy 2010). Of course, local level collaboration involving the state, poor communities, and CSOs is rarely without problems, such as partners succumbing to pressures and lures of patronage (de Wit and Berner 2009); however, it is reasonable to expect such problems to be eliminated as collaborative processes become more routine and familiar.

State-civil society collaboration that is desirable for transformative planning to address urban informality can be catalyzed by leveraging a largely underutilized resource available in most cities—local universities

---

[9]   SDI. Women Transforming the Slums of their Cities. https://sdinet.org/.

(Das and Dahiya 2020). The need for expanding planning schools and reforming planning education was discussed above. Less recognized is the fact that in cities that have had successful collaboration with civil society and communities, local universities have usually been partners and facilitators. Universities produce and circulate the most current wisdom on contemporary issues, and many university researchers are engaged in local research. This is particularly true for urban informality—a phenomenon given to widespread misconceptions and flawed assumptions both among the public and public officials.

Local and nonlocal scholars who conduct field research to study the informal sector usually have well-established connections to local CSOs and communities. Therefore, to enable progressive engagement with the informal sector, local governments can involve planning, architecture, and other relevant university departments and researchers in several ways: (i) train public officials to improve their understanding and appreciation of informality; (ii) guide CSOs and CBOs in collecting community data, conducting community-mapping, and managing community development initiatives; (iii) conduct research and evaluate programs on informality; and (iv) help to co-plan and codesign upgrading, services provision, and other community development initiatives. Extending such opportunities to local universities can help cities garner quality inputs at low cost. More importantly, such involvement of universities enables students of planning and related disciplines gain valuable exposure to the informal sector by getting involved in research and consulting projects. In the long run, this can yield a local cadre of planners and urban professionals adequately sensitized to the needs and challenges of informal settlements, informal workers, and informal service providers. Indeed, the creation of such a cadre of local government officials over decades of sustained city-university-community engagement significantly contributed to transforming planning and governance in Surabaya, Indonesia (Das and King 2019).

4.3 Engagement Possibilities for ADB and Other Multilateral Institutions

In addition to the extraordinary death toll from COVID-19, the pandemic also wreaked untold devastation on national and local economies. The lives and livelihoods of people in the urban informal sector have been harmed like never before. Amid this pall of gloom since March 2020, a potential silver lining is the call to action brought about by the revealing of the scale of urban informality and the extreme vulnerabilities associated with it. As mentioned earlier, it is very welcome that a host of multilateral agencies are focusing on and committing resources toward understanding, documenting, tracking, and supporting the informal sector. Besides multiple ADB initiatives discussed in different chapters, and several recent knowledge products, this book itself embodies ADB's growing commitment to transforming the exclusionary nature of urban planning and policies in developing economies to being more inclusive of urban informality.

All the desired inputs and actions discussed above for enabling planning that is inclusive of informality can benefit from the resources and reach of ADB and other multilateral institutions. Specifically, this chapter emphasizes expanding and reforming planning education for more progressive and effective practice outcomes; improving the quality of data on local informality —from creation to dissemination; enabling local CSOs and universities to concentrate on addressing informality in their own spheres of work; and collaborating with local government agencies. As was evident in the discussions in most chapters, resource constraints at the local level impede swift action and smooth progress in executing new approaches and innovations. The COVID-19 pandemic also proved that the scale of informality exceeds the capacity of the state to address by itself the various aspects of informality.

Multilateral agencies could be more actively engaged at the local level to build the capacity of state and nonstate institutions. For instance, they could strongly incentivize local governments to adopt more inclusive approaches to planning and implement programs that advance coproduction of services. The benefits of digitalization of informal services, the platform economy, and fintech services were stressed in multiple chapters of this book. The coproduction of urban services using new digital technologies is indeed a fast-growing phenomenon (Faldi, Ranzato, and Moretto 2022). ADB could work with local governments and universities in promoting digital innovations by both for-profit and nonprofit actors to serve the peculiar needs of local informal service providers.

The COVID-19 pandemic reemphasized the need for much more public investment in public goods and basic services, especially in informal settlements. Social protection to informal sector workers and small enterprises could be expanded; and public welfare provisions (such as food, health, and education) could be made portable so that internal migrants are less vulnerable to crises. Despite the ubiquity of mobile devices today, the harsh lockdowns due to COVID-19 brought into sharp relief the deep digital divide between the privileged and the urban poor. It was most starkly evident in how the lives of informal settlement dwellers were impacted—social distancing, remote work, and online education were infeasible due to economic, infrastructural, and space constraints. Arguably, children in informal settlements who were deprived of access to schools have suffered the harshest, most damaging, and longest lasting impacts. These consequences of the pandemic raise important questions about public goods and the role of the state in a post-pandemic world. Should Wi-Fi now be considered an essential public good? Should the state provide it for free in informal settlements, informal marketplaces, and schools and community facilities? Multilateral institutions should encourage city leaders to explore such possibilities and aggressively pursue desired ends. Both will likely benefit from engaging with nontraditional partners such as federations of CSOs, workers' unions, and university researchers.

For local governments to initiate transformative planning by engaging with the informal sector, ADB and similar institutions can play a pivotal role in overcoming what is arguably the biggest hurdle—the paucity of data. Multilateral institutions could fund the development of small research centers in local universities and the creation of data management and dissemination units in local governments, which can coproduce with civil society and community stakeholders high quality data, regularly and sustainably. This will also provide many students and others vital appreciation of the informal sector in one's own city or region. Incrementally enabling the production of and access to good data for all will prove beneficial in addressing urban informality in more ways than can be imagined at this moment. Data availability starkly distinguishes developed societies from developing ones, which is reflected in significant differences in the volume and quality of their knowledge production.

As we conclude writing this chapter, the world faces an increasingly uncertain future due to contagion, climate change, and conflict. Over the past two and a half years, one thing has emerged as certain—continuing to ignore the informal sector is imprudent. It is antithetical and perilous to the emergent consensus that cities need to be sustainable and resilient. We hope this book contributes toward a better understanding of urban informality in Asia and the Pacific and stimulates efforts by different stakeholders to alter harmful perceptions and treatment of the informal sector.

References

Antlöv, H., D. W. Brinkerhoff, and E. Rapp. 2010. Civil Society Capacity Building for Democratic Reform: Experience and Lessons from Indonesia. *VOLUNTAS: International Journal of Voluntary and Nonprofit Organizations* 21 (3): 417–439. https://doi.org/10.1007/s11266-010-9140-x.

Archer, D., C. Luansang, and S. Boonmahathanakorn. 2012. Facilitating Community Mapping and Planning for Citywide Upgrading: The Role of Community Architects. *Environment and Urbanization* 24 (1): 115–129. https://doi.org/10.1177/0956247812437132.

Banerjee, A. V., and E. Duflo. 2011. *Poor Economics: Rethinking Poverty & the Ways to End It*. London; Noida, India: Random House.

Banks, N., M. Lombard, and D. Mitlin. 2020. Urban Informality as a Site of Critical Analysis. *The Journal of Development Studies* 56 (2): 223–238. https://doi.org/10.1080/00220388.2019.1577384.

Baruah, B. 2004. Earning Their Keep and Keeping What They Earn: A Critique of Organizing Strategies for South Asian Women in the Informal Sector. *Gender, Work & Organization* 11 (6): 605–626. https://doi.org/10.1111/j.1468-0432.2004.00251.x.

Bhan, G., S. Srinivas, and V. Watson, eds. 2018. *The Routledge Companion to Planning in the Global South*. London: Routledge Companions; New York, NY: Routledge.

Birch, E. L., S. M. Wachter, and S. Chattaraj, eds. 2016. *Slums: How Informal Real Estate Markets Work*. The City in the Twenty-First Century. Philadelphia: Penn, University of Pennsylvania Press.

Cheema, G. S., ed. 2013. *Democratic Local Governance: Reforms and Innovations in Asia*. Shibuya-ku, Tokyo, Japan: United Nations University Press.

Cheema, G. S., and V. Popovski, eds. 2010. *Engaging Civil Society: Emerging Trends in Democratic Governance*. Trends and Innovations in Governance Series. Tokyo; New York: United Nations University.

Dahiya, B., and A. Das. 2020. New Urban Agenda in Asia-Pacific: Governance for Sustainable and Inclusive Cities. In *New Urban Agenda in Asia-Pacific: Governance for Sustainable and Inclusive Cities*, edited by B. Dahiya and A. Das, 3–36. Advances in 21st Century Human Settlements. Singapore: Springer.

Daniere, A., and L. M. Takahashi. 2002. *Rethinking Environmental Management in the Pacific Rim: Exploring Local Participation in Bangkok, Thailand*. Burlington, Vermont: Ashgate.

Das, A. 2015. Autonomous but Constrained: CBOs and Urban Upgrading in Indonesia. *Cities* 48 (November): 8–20. https://doi.org/10.1016/j.cities.2015.05.009.

———. 2018. Is Innovative Also Effective? A Critique of Pro-Poor Shelter in South-East Asia. *International Journal of Housing Policy* 18 (2): 233–265. https://doi.org/10.1080/14616718.2016.1248606.

———. 2019. For an Equitable Indonesian City: Reflections on Planning Practice and Education. *Ruang*. July.

Das, A., and B. Dahiya. 2020. Towards Inclusive Urban Governance and Planning: Emerging Trends and Future Trajectories. In *New Urban Agenda in Asia-Pacific*, edited by B. Dahiya and A. Das, 353–384. Advances in 21st Century Human Settlements. Singapore: Springer.

Das, A., and R. King. 2019. Surabaya: The Legacy of Participatory Upgrading of Informal Settlements. *Working Paper: Towards a More Equal City*. Washington, DC. https://www.wri.org/wri-citiesforall/publication/surabaya-legacy-participatory-upgrading-informal-settlements.

Das, A., and A. Luthfi. 2017. Disaster Risk Reduction in Post-Decentralisation Indonesia: Institutional Arrangements and Changes. In *Disaster Risk Reduction in Indonesia*, edited by R. Djalante, M. Garschagen, F. Thomalla, and R. Shaw, 85–125. Disaster Risk Reduction (Methods, Approaches and Practices). Cham, Switzerland: Springer International Publishing. https://doi.org/10.1007/978-3-319-54466-3_4.

d'Cruz, C., and P. Mudimu. 2013. Community Savings That Mobilize Federations, Build Women's Leadership and Support Slum Upgrading. *Environment and Urbanization* 25 (1): 31–45. https://doi.org/10.1177/0956247812471616.

de Wit, J., and E. Berner. 2009. Progressive Patronage? Municipalities, NGOs, CBOs and the Limits to Slum Dwellers' Empowerment. *Development and Change* 40 (5): 927–947. https://doi.org/10.1111/j.1467-7660.2009.01589.x.

Faldi, G., M. Ranzato, and L. Moretto. 2022. Urban Service Co-Production and Technology: Nine Key Issues. *International Journal of Urban Sustainable Development*, 1–16.

Fan, Y. et al. 2022. Improving Global Planning Education by Centering the Experience of International Students in U.S. and Canadian Planning Schools. *Journal of Planning Education and Research*. May (0739456X221093645). https://doi.org/10.1177/0739456X221093645.

Frank, A. I., and C. Silver, eds. 2018. Urban Planning Education: Beginnings, Global Movement and Future Prospects. *The Urban Book Series*. Cham: Springer International Publishing.

Grantham, K., and B. Baruah. 2017. Women's NGOs as Intermediaries in Development Cooperation: Findings from Research in Tanzania. *Development in Practice* 27 (7): 927–939. https://doi.org/10.1080/09614524.2017.1349734.

Kim, K. 2021. Impacts of COVID-19 on Transportation: Summary and Synthesis of Interdisciplinary Research. *Transportation Research Interdisciplinary Perspectives* 9 (March): 100305. https://doi.org/10.1016/j.trip.2021.100305.

Lall, S. 2020. Yes, Cities Will Survive COVID-19, But They Must Manage Their Economic Geography. *Sustainable Cities*. World Bank Blogs. 18 June. https://blogs.worldbank.org/sustainablecities/yes-cities-will-survive-covid-19-they-must-manage-their-economic-geography.

Mahendra, A., J. Du, A. Dasgupta, V. A. Beard, A. Kallergis, and K. Schalch. 2021. Seven Transformations for More Equitable and Sustainable Cities. *World Resources Report: Towards a More Equal City*. Washington, DC: World Resources Institute. https://doi.org/10.46830/wrirpt.19.00124.

Miller, M. A., and M. Douglass, eds. 2016. *Disaster Governance in Urbanising Asia*. Singapore: Springer.

Mitlin, D., and D. Satterthwaite, eds. 2004. *Empowering Squatter Citizen: Local Government, Civil Society, and Urban Poverty Reduction*. London; Sterling, Virginia: Earthscan.

Oborn, P., and J. Walters. 2020. *Planning for Climate Change and Rapid Urbanisation: Survey of the Built Environment Professions in the Commonwealth*. Survey. London: Commonwealth Association of Architects; Commonwealth Association of Planners; Commonwealth Association of Surveying and Land Economy; Commonwealth Engineers Council. http://commonwealthsustainablecities.org/survey/.

Ohnsorge, F., and S. Yu, eds. 2021. *The Long Shadow of Informality: Challenges and Policies*. Washington, DC: World Bank. https://www.worldbank.org/en/research/publication/informal-economy.

Parnell, S., and J. Robinson. 2012. (Re)Theorizing Cities from the Global South: Looking Beyond Neoliberalism. *Urban Geography* 33 (4): 593–617. https://doi.org/10.2747/0272-3638.33.4.593.

Patel, S., C. Baptist, and C. d'Cruz. 2012. Knowledge Is Power – Informal Communities Assert Their Right to the City Through SDI and Community-Led Enumerations. *Environment and Urbanization* 24 (1): 13–26. https://doi.org/10.1177/0956247812438366.

Robinson, J., and A. Roy. 2016. Debate on Global Urbanisms and the Nature of Urban Theory. *International Journal of Urban and Regional Research* 40 (1): 181–186. https://doi.org/10.1111/1468-2427.12272.

Roitman, S., and D. Rukmana, eds. Forthcoming. *Routledge Handbook of Urban Indonesia*. New York: Routledge.

Roy, A. 2005. Urban Informality: Towards an Epistemology of Planning. *Journal of the American Planning Association* 71 (2): 147–158.

_____. 2010. *Poverty Capital: Microfinance and the Making of Development*. New York: Routledge.

Roy, A., and N. AlSayyad, eds. 2004. *Urban Informality Transnational Perspectives from the Middle East, Latin America, and South Asia*. Lanham, Maryland: Lexington Books.

Rukmana, D., ed. 2020. *The Routledge Handbook of Planning Megacities in the Global South*. New York: Routledge.

Satterthwaite, D. et al. 2020. Building Resilience to Climate Change in Informal Settlements. *One Earth* 2 (2): 143–156. https://doi.org/10.1016/j.oneear.2020.02.002.

Scott, A. J., and M. Storper. 2015. The Nature of Cities: The Scope and Limits of Urban Theory. *International Journal of Urban and Regional Research* 39 (1): 1–15. https://doi.org/10.1111/1468-2427.12134.

Setiawan, B. 2018. The Roles of Planning Education in the Decentralization and Democratization Era: Lessons from Indonesia. In *Urban Planning Education: Beginnings, Global Movement and Future Prospects*, edited by A. I. Frank and C. Silver, 219–231. The Urban Book Series. Cham: Springer International Publishing. https://doi.org/10.1007/978-3-319-55967-4_15.

Susantono, B., and R. Guild, eds. 2021. *Creating Livable Asian Cities*. Manila: Asian Development Bank. https://www.adb.org/publications/creating-livable-asian-cities.

Taylor, J., and J. Lassa. 2015. How Can Climate Change Vulnerability Assessments Best Impact Policy and Planning? Lessons from Indonesia. 10743IIED. *Asian Cities Climate Resilience Working Paper Series*. London: IIED. http://pubs.iied.org/10743IIED.html.

Wahab, B., and B. Agbola. 2017. The Place of Informality and Illegality in Planning Education in Nigeria. *Planning Practice & Research* 32 (2): 212–225. https://doi.org/10.1080/02697459.2016.1198565.

Watson, V. 2014. Co-Production and Collaboration in Planning – The Difference. *Planning Theory & Practice* 15 (1): 62–76. https://doi.org/10.1080/14649357.2013.866266.

Williamson, T. 2003. Catalytic Communities in Rio: Virtual and Face-to-Face Communities in Developing Countries. *Journal of Urban Technology* 10 (3): 85–109. https://doi.org/10.1080/10630730320 00175426.